The Whole Story

Editors on Fiction

The Whole Story

Editors on Fiction

A Collection of Essays and Stories
Edited by Warren Slesinger

The Bench Press

Sponsored by the Richland-Lexington Cultural Council, this project is funded in part by the South Carolina Arts Commission which receives support from the National Endowment for the Arts.

The Bench Press
1355 Raintree Drive
Columbia, SC 29212

Printed in the United States of America

98 97 96 95 94 5 4 3 2 1

Grateful acknowledgments are hereby made to the editors of the magazines and the authors for permission to reprint these stories.

Library of Congress Cataloging-in-Publication Data

The whole story : editors on fiction : a collection of essays
 and stories / edited by Warren Slesinger. p. cm.
Includes index.
   ISBN 0-930769-12-0
   1. Editing. 2. Fiction–Technique.   I. Slesinger, Warren.
PN162.W48 1994
808'.06683–dc20   94-21549
                                                                CIP

*To editors far and wide
but especially to the editors
who chose these storeis
and set forth their thoughts
about them*

*and to the authors of these stories
for so, so much.*

Contents

Introduction

Literary magazines provide us with the primary cross-section of the fiction written in the United States at any given time and we depend on the editors to make the best selections from the submissions that they receive. Since their choices have a direct influence on our further reading, it is important for us to know how these choices are made.

The Whole Story is a collection of twenty-four essays, each of them specially commissioned, from editors who are associated with some of the nation's leading literary periodicals. These editors discuss their personal editorial methods, the general policies of their magazines and the overall state of reading and writing in the United States

Each of the editors selects for reprinting here a short story that originally appeared in his or her magazine—a story offered to the reader both for its merits and by means of illustrating a range of points about editorial decision-making including the relationship between the editor and the writer, questions raised in the reading process and the recognition of a truly outstanding story.

The Bench Press contacted twenty-five well-established writers for information about the literary magazines which they most respected and to which they most often submitted their own work. From their replies, we compiled a list that we compared with the lists of magazines consulted by the editors of the most recent editions of *The Best American Short Stories, Prize Stories: The O. Henry Awards, New Stories from the South: The Year's Best* and *The Pushcart Prize: The Best of the Small Presses* and expanded the list considerably. We telephoned and corresponded with the editors of fifty magazines that represented a wide range of interests and commitments and are happy with the extent of the response that this volume exhibits.

What this collection makes clear is that an editor does not try to promote a cause or defend a position but to discover new writing in order to share with others the experience of reading the best of it. The decision to publish depends on the depth, initiative and common sense of the editor. These are the essentials of good judgment. It was exercised in the selection of these stories and it is evident in each of these essays.

The Whole Story will appeal to students and teachers, other serious readers and writers, and the editors of literary and non-literary publications.

W.S.

The Whole Story

Editors on Fiction

A Story Needs Two Stories
Ronald Spatz

Musings about the nature of cold and warmth might be expected from a long-time editor of an Alaskan magazine. Yet be assured that few of the stories I've selected for the pages of *Alaska Quarterly Review (AQR)* over the years dwell on matters of temperature, although cold and warmth are certainly key to Cory Wade's "The Woman Who Slept With a Tortoise," the story I've selected for *AQR's* contribution to *The Whole Story: Editors on Fiction.*

Despite the fact that "The Woman Who Slept With a Tortoise" at first blush appears quite a bit different from most of *AQR's* fiction, it is nonetheless a good "representative story" to illustrate my editorial vision. But since it's not one of *AQR's* deeply felt traditional narratives or a fiction that expands the boundaries of narrative form, what kind of story is it?

Cory Wade's "The Woman Who Slept With a Tortoise" is a story indebted to the tale and the fable. It relies on the delicacies of detail and the subtleties of nuance to imbue its narrative with freshness and resonance. This is a lyric piece that sticks. It envelops you in indolence, in a most primal and sensual warmth. Ultimately, in its quiet and gentle way, it is an elegant seduction. However, if that were its sum total, "The Woman Who Slept With a Tortoise" would be a pleasurable, albeit limited, stylistic tour de force. And no matter how lovely the writing, a story about parallel desires of tortoise and woman to sun themselves, eat tropical fruit, and be warm—and to stay that way—would not have been enough to merit publication in *AQR*.

I agree with Grace Paley that a "story basically needs two stories. No matter whether it is long or short, it's just not interesting unless it has two stories. Not like a plot and a subplot—nothing like that; but two stories which address each other." (*AQR* Vol. 7, No. 3 & 4, 1989). Underlying its silky, appealing cocoon of warmth, "The Woman Who Slept With a Tortoise" is a story of a woman's isolation, her inability to love and live much beyond her autonomic nervous system. For her, warmth and imagination function as an anaesthetic. They insulate her and lull her into a comfortable but deadly self-deception and depression. Her attraction to the tortoise is that "he was always quiet" and "never reactive or moody . . . she had encountered those traits in humans and was not drawn to them." Her response to cold temperatures is no different—escape. She rejects the "cold, hard" facts of life and fantasizes a return to the womb-like safety of home—an idyllic, warm tropical paradise. The never-ending conflict inherent in the human condition is mirrored in the story's cyclical, reflective structure: the selfish, natural instinct to withdraw from pain versus the risks of living life to the fullest. Ms. Wade vividly depicts how natural and inexorable is the slide into the "warm" world of the senses absent of all adult responsibilities and struggle. It is in the interrelationship between the "two stories" that "The Woman Who Slept With a Tortoise" rises above an exercise in style and craft and becomes compelling. In this essential way, it is representative of the fiction I select for *AQR.*

Having written that, it sounds a bit like I'm saying that editing is a process of academic, literary analysis. It isn't—at least not for me. It is an intuitive process based, of course, on my literary values. A genuine interest and appreciation of both traditional and experimental fictional forms helps. But in the final analysis, it comes down to trusting your intuition. And to be an editor of any real consequence, over time, you have to stick to your intuition in the face of what's popular, politically correct, or critically praised at the moment. You need a little luck and a reservoir of courage, if you hope to have a chance, especially when editing a literary magazine, of actually adding something of lasting value to the universe of literary art. In other words, whether you're in the Alaskan tundra in the dead of winter, or in Phoenix, Arizona, in the peak of summer, an editor can't afford to get "cold feet" when going through a stack of manuscripts.

The Woman Who Slept With a Tortoise

Cory Wade

Neither of them tolerated cold very well, nor liked it much. She had been born on an island in Malaysia while the tortoise came from the equatorial tropics. They shared an affinity for warm air, long hours of sun, and ripe fruit. In summer, the good season, they ate nectarines all day, alternating at times with watermelon. They were both thirsty and drank large quantities of water. They liked early sun the best, both of them lying out on the grass every morning until the sun rose up directly overhead. Then they headed for the shade, either the covered patio or the orange tree. Neither of them ate much of the fruit that fell from the orange tree because it was too tart, too much like eating lemons. She had occasionally been able to manage a piece or two, but he had never expressed the slightest interest in it.

Sometimes, while they were both lying out on the lawn, smelling the dandelions and clover beneath them, she dreamed that she and the tortoise were somewhere very hot and green, perhaps an island, perhaps like the one she had been born on, where watermelons sprang up everywhere, as common as weeds, and nectarines hung thick and sweet from every tree.

They had a lot in common, her occasional willingness to swallow the juice of bitter oranges notwithstanding. She enjoyed being quiet and he was always quiet. He was never reactive or moody. She never was either, though she had encountered those traits in humans and was not drawn to them.

She had fallen in love with him the first moment she had seen him. He was without any question, beyond any doubt, the most beautiful tortoise imaginable. His face and neck and paws were all brightly spotted with orange and yellow, almost exactly the same shades as a nectarine. He was over a foot long with an oval, almost hourglass-shaped shell. He came from the Amazon Basin, where many of his kind built nests of leaves on the rain forest floor and lived almost entirely on wild plums.

Warm rain was quite welcome to him, as she discovered when she turned the sprinklers on during the first heat wave of summer. As he walked around in the damp grass, stopping to press his long neck into the little pools of water that formed at the base of the blades and drink, she walked next to him, pressing her toes into the green puddles wherever he stopped. But he didn't enjoy cold rain or a hard wind or the temperature dropping below 70. She was exactly the same way. Their sleeping together began in winter. It had been August, still the good season, when she first brought him home, and the gradual but inescapable onset of cold did not appeal to either of them. They got to know each other's habits in Autumn, a season she had never especially cared for. Apparently he didn't either, since there was less sun with every day and finally, sometime in October, the nectarines stopped. She went everywhere trying to find some but they were gone. This fact alone didn't make it any easier to give up the good season. There were a few rangy melons after that in November but nothing like what they had had before.

The loss of the nectarines was a terrible blow. Her whole life she had felt a strange ache each September, a peculiar erratic pain that never got any better or ever really went away, over having to give up the good season; and when fragrant indolent juicy fruit stopped, followed by hard industrious pragmatic apples, it was a clear sign that things were going to get worse.

The worst thing was, of course, the cold: the cold that sucked the life from everything lovely and fragile, that drove out the crickets, withered the sweet peas, beat down the honeysuckle, stiffened the tomatoes, shriveled the magnolias, pinched the rosebuds, froze the cocoons and frosted the finch's nest. The tortoise began to eat less, and so did she.

One especially cold night in January they both wanted to sit on the heat vent in the bedroom floor. She could sit there for only a little while before the skin on her legs began to turn pinkish and itch and she had to slide forward onto the carpet. But for a few moments there was nothing quite like the stream of hot air rushing up from the floor. The tortoise liked it just as much but because his skin was thicker he could sit on the vent longer before sliding off onto the carpet. When in January they wanted to sit there at the same time, they discovered that the vent wasn't long enough for both of them. So she picked him up and placed him lengthwise across the triangle of her folded legs.

Together they enjoyed the stream of warm air this way until, when her legs began to itch, she got up to turn the heat off and get into bed. From her pillow she watched him still sitting on the vent long after any heat had come through it, and she thought about how much he liked to be warm, possibly even more than she did. She had never met anyone who liked to be warm more than she did. So she wrapped him in a thick cotton bath towel and, instead of setting him on his mat on the floor, put him in bed with her. That was the way they began sleeping together.

She came to enjoy rolling over to the hard oval dome of his shell, faintly warm under the cotton towel. And she was always reassured by his slow regular breathing. If in the night she awoke feeling lonely or displaced or depressed she would turn toward the towel and listen to his long deep breaths.

After a time she began to worry about how the tortoise would feel if she ever met a wonderful man, a man so wonderful that she wanted to sleep with him. She wondered if the tortoise would feel lonely or displaced or depressed about being returned to the floor after sleeping in the bed for so long. But as time went on, she didn't meet a wonderful man—at least, not one so wonderful that she wanted to sleep with him instead of the tortoise. But there was always the possibility that she could meet such a man. The problem began to trouble her daily. She would wake up in the morning hearing the tortoise's slow steady breathing and begin to feel sad even before her eyes were open.

Then one morning she woke up and had the solution. It had come to her in the night as she listened to the tortoise's slow regular breaths. The answer was so simple she wondered why she hadn't seen it before. If she did meet a man, a wonderful man she liked enough to sleep with, all three of them could sleep together. Then the tortoise would never feel lonely or displaced or depressed. As for the man—the tortoise would never dream of interfering with her and the man; so why would the man think of interfering with her and the tortoise? He would want the tortoise to be contented as much as she did. Everything could stay just as it was. Nothing had to change. Soon the good season would return and she and the tortoise would eat nectarines again and lie in the early sun. The man would fit into their lives. Nestling deeper into her pillow for warmth, she looked at the tortoise sleeping in the rolled-up bath towel. His rhythmic breathing made her feel a little drowsy again, now that everything was solved. She began to think of summer.

Soon she was dreaming that she and the tortoise were somewhere very hot and green, perhaps an island, perhaps like the one she had been born on, where watermelons grew everywhere, as common as weeds, and nectarines hung thick and sweet from every tree.

Literary Energy
Robert S. Fogarty

With the publication by Algonquin Books of Emile Capouya's stunning collection of stories *In the Sparrow Hills* in 1992, my thirteen year contract with his work came full circle. Although I knew his name as the literary editor of *The Nation* in the 1970s and as an editor at Schocken Books, I first read him in 1981. He submitted the title story of the now published collection to us as an unknown fiction writer–so unknown, in fact, that when I scanned the slush pile one Saturday his name did not leap out. At that time in an effort to keep in contact with the submission pile before it was clarified by our readers, I was in the habit of reading every piece of slush that came in on a Saturday.

That lucky Saturday led me to a thirty-five page story and to the publication of three other stories over a ten year period. At that point in time (but no longer) we allowed students to read manuscripts and gave them a limited right of refusal. Because of its length and type I suspect our young in-house readers might not have passed it on but rejected it out of hand. However, I rescued it, read it that afternoon and knew we would take it but passed it on for other opinions–a reversal of our usual procedure where I am the final reader of work under construction.

After finishing it, one of our experienced in-house readers wrote: "Well, well, well I have just gingerly finished this (it is I who feels finished not to say exhausted to make sensible comment) and feel enriched, entertained and there, at the end, poignantly amused. How it wanders. What a labyrinth; what a Jamesian extravaganza! What patience our readers are going to have to stick it out . . . All in all, this is a moral tale, a philosophical piece." After we published it, it was anthologized in a collection (along with Raymond Carver's "Cathedral," a favorite of mine for highly personal reasons) edited by Gary Fisketjon and Jonathan Galassi, then praised by Anatole Broyard in the *The New York Times* who said it had "more pure literary energy than anything else in the book." Capouya continues to write, to edit and I continue to publish him. Along the way a Dutch publisher noticed him in the *Review* and wanted to make him available to European readers; then Louis D. Rubin Jr., Algonquin's founder, got wind of him and brought his collected stories out in a handsome volume.

During this time, Capouya started his own house—New Amsterdam Press—with his wife Keitha, but for a time I was his only editor. He wrote (it had to be on the side) and I read and with every story that appeared in the *Review* I knew that we were fulfilling the mission of the magazine—to encourage talent by printing the "best words in the best order." How he wrote in between his responsibilities of starting a new imprint, attending trade shows and reading other writers' work escapes me; yet, every year or two another Capouya story—always immaculately crafted—appeared at the *Review*. As a writer he is not easily pigeonholed into any of the current categories; he asks his readers to stay with each story and allows his characters to come forward as we go forward with them. If one needs to find him in a category look under Conrad or Kipling or Turgenev or Chekhov—all masters of the short form. Each story was simply set, familiar in tone and language, always hinting at something else, some mystery that was about to unfold, some other story that lay behind the surface tale forcing the reader to become a part of the story, to imagine with the characters.

With "In the Sparrow Hills" I recognized the real life characters such as Avrahm Yarmolinsky, the Russian literature scholar and husband of Babette Duetsch, who was already known to me through his translations and an obscure book about a Russian utopian, William Frey, who served as the prototype for a character in Tolstoy's *Resurrection.* And, of course, there was Delmore Schwartz who makes a cameo appearance in the story. Obviously a great deal more was lurking here than a literary *People* magazine piece or a Doctorow look alike. That was made apparent by Capouya's throwaway opening line: "This is not a story." If not a story then what? Obviously a story, but of what kind and about what: storytelling, remembrance, memory, history, personal odyssey? Or was it just a tale? Unlikely.

Stories (about 4000 a year) come to the *Review* from every imaginable source, in every imaginable length and format and in every imaginable voice. All get read at least once by a reader and nearly all are rejected. We publish what we like and what strikes us as both original and crafted. In addition to the three or four stories we run in every issue, we now do an annual all-fiction number that takes in a range of voices; in a recent number we began with James Purdy and ended with Lily Tuck. Our selection process is similar to the one used with "In the Sparrow Hills" and it is a deeply flawed one. Not all stories get the same attention, not all writers are read when readers are at their optimum alertness, not all wonderful stories get published. Fortunately there is a plethora of magazines and if we miss a magnificent story, then it will surely find a reader on some Saturday morning who knew after the first paragraph that the chase was on.

In April, 1994, the American Academy of Arts and Literature awarded the Sue Kaufman Award for the best work of new fiction to Emile Capouya for his collection *In the Sparrow Hills*.

In the Sparrow Hills
Emile Capouya

This is not a story. The people I mention here for purposes of corroboration are men of flesh and blood—or, as the Spaniards say, more tellingly, men of flesh and bone. Two of them are very much alive, and the third not long dead, all of them public figures in a small way, the only way in which literary men in our time are likely to be public figures if there is anything to them. I have no hesitation about mentioning their names. I haven't asked their permission, but the matter in regard to which I want them to back me with their testimony is a question of fact, quite impersonal. The one who is no longer alive can scarcely be my witness in any active sense, and yet he is for my purposes the most important of the three, since the business I have in mind falls directly within his professional specialty. I hope to be believed when I report what he said about it because I met him when I was very young, he was kind to me for something like thirty years, and I took the liberty of loving him. That is, I hope to be believed because it should be clear that I would not invoke his spirit falsely. Besides, we human beings live by trust. In this city, if you ask a passerby for directions the chances are very good that he will misdirect you. But I should judge that the chances of being purposely misdirected are just about zero. People are always in a hurry here. People are always confused. Only when they are abstracted does the look of confusion leave their faces—and then, when you awaken a stranger from his dream and put to him a puzzle in geography about a place where he himself finds his way without reflection, by habit, it is only to be expected that his hurried answer will not always meet an ideal standard of accuracy.

I was thinking about all that the other evening in the restaurant. Then the waitress brought the bill, I looked at it, I handed her a credit card, and I went back to thinking about the propriety of mentioning Avrahm Yarmolinsky in order to have the support of his name for what I mean to say. I was thinking that the mere suspicion that I might be citing him for interested motives after his death would in a sense slander him by associating him with those interested motives. And I was thinking that since my motives were reducible to one, to establish a point of literary history on his testimony and that of two other gentlemen, I didn't see why anyone would want to impugn my credit. It's as if I were to announce that I had broken my leg in early March of 1965, as in fact I did do, and people who knew me at the time know that I did, though they cannot be expected to recollect the month and the year. Now, if I were to make that statement, why should it awaken doubts, and reflect badly on the integrity of my witnesses? The waitress came back and said, "Sorry, sir, your card has been declined."

She is a brusque, rawboned young woman. Not many weeks ago I was in the restaurant, and her hoarse voice sounded suddenly from the kitchen: "When I heard the Pope was dead I just freaked out. I mean I just freaked out." There was no mistaking the excitement in her tone, but since I couldn't see her face I had no way of judging the quality of her excitement. What sounded like a note of jubilation was almost certainly something else. It was hard to imagine that her life was so empty of excitement that she welcomed the Pope's death because it relieved the tedium. I call the place a restaurant, but it's more gin mill than restaurant, much more gin mill. It's just down the block and in that sense convenient, but it's noisy at night, lots of action, and waitressing is hard work. No doubt there's plenty of tedium in it, but plenty of excitement too. It wouldn't be that. But her words told me nothing by themselves—the beauty of that language is that it doesn't give anything away—and I could not see her face. I remember that I felt more friendly to her because she had been stirred, in some way, by the death of that old man.

She had slapped the card upon the table, as a card-player slaps down a card in triumph or disgust, and had turned away about her other business before I had understood what she had said. Declined? The term was oddly decorous. Had I gone beyond my limit? It was possible. When cash is short you use the card to take up the slack, and then card on card. But I was sure that I had paid the last installment. Or even if I hadn't, the credit company would not yet have had time to publish my card number with those of other delinquents in the closely printed booklet. Did the restaurant have a direct line to the company, and had they telephoned? How strange. The likeliest thing was that someone had made a mistake. And I began to feel offended that a regular customer should be treated so offhandedly when there was a good chance that he was not at fault. Then I noticed that the bill, too, was back on the table. I took out a ten and two singles, put them on top of the bill, and set about finishing my beer.

The waitress sailed by and picked up the money, awkward but swift. As she did, I saw something out of place, and a moment later I knew what it was. I had seen two tens and a single rise from the table with the bill. But if I was right about that, then I had made a mistake earlier when I thought I had taken a ten and two singles from my wallet. I counted the money I had left. It seemed about ten dollars short. But I am not reliable when it comes to things of that kind. I finished my beer, thinking that if I had overpaid the waitress, she'd soon be back.

She didn't come. The man behind the bar saw me tilt my chair and look round for her. He asked if he could help me. I told him my credit card had been refused, I didn't know why, but in any case I had given the waitress cash, a ten and two singles, I had thought, and then I had had the impression that it was a single and two tens. He said she'd be back. After a moment she appeared. "The check was $10.09. I gave the bartender a ten and nine cents and kept the two singles for my tip. Here, this is what I have in my pocket." She showed me a roll of singles. "I don't have a ten on me." I said, "Oh, I'm sorry. That's fine, then." And I felt relieved. I got up and went out into the street. But while walking I saw two tens and a single rise from the table, and I remembered that I seemed to be ten dollars short. But why would she have done a thing like that? I wasn't drunk. I had had a bottle of beer with my dinner. It would have been foolish of her to do a thing like that deliberately. At worst she had made a mistake, just as I certainly had done. To suspect her would be unjust. Besides, it was simply too painful to suspect people. We live by trust.

Now, I want to offer Avrahm Yarmolinsky's testimony on one small point—and certainly not least because I feel honored to be able to mention his name as that of a friend. Of course, he was a great scholar, and everyone respects such attainments. But, on the other hand, only a scholar in Yarmolinsky's field could really appreciate him on that ground. For me, respect for his learning was partly a form of superstition, relying on evidence of things unseen, the vulgar kind of faith that has the effect of making certain people popular because they are popular. What really moved me was his character.

For many years he was head of the Slavic Languages Division of the New York Public Library, and he worked at the Forty-second Street building. Whenever I enter that mausoleum I feel entombed. But though he spoke gently and was naturally self-effacing, as befitted a senior servitor of that great mortuary of books, he showed how much spirit and passion could find lodgment in such a place. His figure was slight, so that he looked like a grown-up boy, and he had a diffidence that seemed adolescent. His silences seemed adolescent, but if they arose out of shyness I never felt that they were self-regarding. In his presence my own tormenting social awkwardness lost much of its burden of self regard. When I used to visit him and he would come forward to shake my hand—carrying his own hands in an odd way, knuckles to the fore—his Russian head that was shaped like a slender keystone, with the short, stiff hair brushed up *al Umberto,* would be slightly tilted and would be regarding me like a block of cordial granite. After our hands had met, his eyes would shift gratefully elsewhere, and the ceremony of greeting, made difficult by affection, would have been successfully accomplished.

He had very little small talk and no grand pronouncements. I have never known a man who inquired how you were with so clear an intention of listening to the answer. It used to make me feel as if I were talking to my father, and must be careful not to hurt him by giving too blunt an account of my life and prospects. On the other hand I felt obliged to tell him the truth, and I managed it by telling him generalities: I found my job difficult because publishing houses were likely to be ignorant or venal—things of that sort. I knew that if I were to give him instances or details I should soon grow passionate and afflict him with my professional *déboires.* That is what usually happened when I talked about those things with my own father, for he used to question me with an affectionate pertinacity born of his illusion that his son was a romantic who needed to be protected from the impulse to footless martyrdom. But he himself was the romantic idealist, as his brothers often told him, and not by way of praise. He had managed to live decently, honorably, in a world now quite vanished. I had earned my living in the new world by compounding with the enemy on every important point. My father imagined that I was baring my breast to all God's dangers, like the heroic Swiss who gathered the spears of six spearmen into his bosom to make a breach in the enemy rank through which his comrades might pass. So when my father, affectionately reproachful, and with mild irony for what he supposed was my moonstruck vision of the world of commerce, would press me for the story of my latest discomfiture, I would lose all self-control, and tell him the circumstances of the prehistory of the incident, and then its history, and at last I would impart to him my moral reflections upon it—sometimes an hour's business. At the end of it he would be shaking his head sadly, and I would feel that I had abused him, for he is candid as a child and the news of the world's small evils appalls him forever. On one of those occasions he said to me, "What I cannot understand is that you haven't sat down with your boss and explained those things to him. He would surely see that it must be in everyone's interest to abandon such a policy— if policy it can be called, since it is so clearly retrograde." And after that demonstration of his hopeless good faith and naiveté I felt especially tender to him. He was a spar from the wreck of that old world, adrift in the new, unconscious that when the skies change, men's hearts change with the skies.

Avrahm Yarmolinsky was innocent in the same way, but he never pressed me. He may have been too diffident to examine his own sons and prescribe for them. In any case our relations did not authorize anything of the kind. It was I who asked most of the questions, and these were generally of the impersonal sort. I would ask him about Russian and Soviet literature—like most Americans I have almost no acquaintance with the literatures of the other Slavs. I remember him saying, with a pained smile, something like, "The literature of the recent Soviet period is really quite poor. Pasternak, Solzhenitsyn—those immensely gifted writers are not at all characteristic. They have skipped over generations, going back for their inspiration to the great Russian masters of the nineteenth century. A novelist like Sholokhov is a vigorous writer—one of few—but he has nothing like the imagination of the great nineteenth-century writers, nothing like their psychological penetration, let alone their moral impetus and philosophic power." All this hesitantly, with a pained smile from first to last.

Yet I had seen him an energumen. When I was in my early twenties, it must have been shortly after the war, I was his guest at a dinner party. Among the other guests was an affable marl with a guitar—I gathered he was a neighbor—who sang very pleasantly, "The fox he run to his cozy den, there were his little ones, eight, nine, ten. . . ." And there was a young Czech woman, large-limbed and handsome, who took the guitar from him and sang something softly, her voice low and moving. There were two Poles, I think, and a Yugoslav. At times when no one sang, Yarmolinsky talked to his Slavic friends with startling volubility, turning from one to the other, and shifting from one tongue to another as if he were a mere mindless polyglot—but speaking in so emphatic a tone and with such evident high spirits that he seemed transformed by enthusiasm. It may be that while he wrote English very well, he did not really feel at home in the language, so that it was a relief to his spirit to talk with animated Slavs.

I never afterward saw him exhibit anything approaching abandon, but I had been pleased by that evidence of fire as a youngster is apt to be pleased, and liked him the more for it. It was the memory of having seen him exhilarated in that way that persuaded me to tell him, many years later, of a literary admiration of mine. I don't know why I am so disinclined to speak of such things ordinarily, but I am. Mostly, I am ashamed to speak of them. Among persons of a certain social class, as I have noticed, or at least in certain circles, enthusiasms of the kind are common coin. And I have worked in a trade—the book trade—in which grown men often say, "That's a manuscript that I'm really excited about." Perhaps it's because they say it often that my stomach turns. Perhaps it's because the expression, in a man's mouth, sounds faintly androgynous. But chiefly I think it is a kind of shrinking snobbery on my part that makes me take their professional excitement so seriously, since I know very well that they are not exposing their intimate feelings when they say things of the sort. Their emotion is aroused by the qualities that the manuscript in question offers under the aspect of a commodity. Everyone in the trade understands that very well. And in what sense would it be useful for people in a publishing house to be susceptible to the appeal of a manuscript that was destined to fall stone dead in the market? My snobbery isn't a response to the vulgarity of an enthusiasm domesticated for the purpose of selling books. It's that I shrink from avowing any literary enthusiasm at all, as if the subject were unfit for mention in mixed company. And the ebullient interest that the trade takes in books on which one can make a decent profit, for all its seeming innocence, its genuine innocence, glances too nearly at this foible of mine, simply because the object of the motion is something that has been written. I am far from being immune to the values expressed in the practice of publishing houses; if you were, you couldn't work in one. No, I share them fully. But I feel it isn't decent to proclaim those values because in the nature of things they are at least distantly related to the ones that arise from genuine works of literature. That is an odd scruple that I myself cannot account for—seeing that I have spent many years in the trade—and that I am not at all proud of. If I were to be honest I should have to say that my violent delicacy on this question is cousin to my abhorrence of the waitress's patchouli. For she moves in a nimbus of the scent. She leaves it on the edge of a dish, on the lip of a glass, on the silver. Sometimes I am assailed by the smell hours later if I pass my hand near to my face. When that happens I can't understand how it is that I never remember how much I dislike the smell of the waitress until I have actually crossed the threshold of that restaurant. And certainly I know that a hoarse voice and patchouli do not amount to moral obliquity. She is a young woman, doing the things that are socially available for her to do. At most her pungent musk represents a social error, and not even that, no doubt, among her friends, who must include people who are estimable by any reasonable standard and yet are in no way affronted by the use of strong perfumes. I cannot bear it, but I hope I am not such a fool as to make the practice my test for decency, honor, self-respect.

The fact is that there is an ugly streak in my character, a kind of repercussive violence that I am well aware of and should be happy to be without. When I was young it sometimes took dangerous forms. The war had been over for a couple of months when I sailed as A. B. on the *Waterbury Victory,* New York to Antwerp, in midwinter. I was the only A. B. on the ship who had a ticket—the others were acting A. B.'s and by law could go no higher than ten feet above the deck. The first day out, the mate had me go aloft to the mainmast truck to chip and paint my way down the mast. I eased into a bosun's chair, with a chipping hammer, a wire brush, and a pot of red lead secured to the chair's bridle, and a marlinspike on a ropeyarn lanyard over one shoulder and across my breast. It was blowing half a gale, and I was swayed aloft by my gantline, whose end had been taken to the winch. The bosun tended my line, and he ran me up steadily, but he couldn't do anything to keep the roll of the vessel from knocking me about. *The Waterbury Victory* was a famous roller. Later on during that passage, to see just how she rolled, I rigged a clinometer in the crew's mess, a hacksaw blade pivoted on a nail in the bulkhead, and the degrees of its swing shown on an arc drawn with a protractor. The certificate on the bridge said that the ship was rated for forty degrees. The men took the clinometer down at last because she would roll to forty-four and hang there a long time before rolling as far the other way. On this day she gave me a pounding. I reached the truck with bruised knees and skinned knuckles, in a temper that they would think to send a man aloft to do an anytime job when it was blowing fresh.

When I was nearly at the truck I balled up a fist and thrust it out to one side for the bosun to see. At once he slacked the line on the windlass drum and held me motionless. Then I made to marry the two parts of my gantline to hold me in place while he threw the line off the windlass. But I saw that the dangling paint pot would foul the long bight of line that I must overhaul with my free hand, in order to bring it up through the bridle and up and over my body to make the hitch that would support me aloft and allow me to descend at will, a few inches at a time. So I put out my fist again, looking down sidelong toward the winch and calling to the bosun to hold it. He nodded. It took me a few moments to shorten the tail on the pot and secure it to the other leg of the bridle. As I turned from doing that, the chair fell eight feet.

It would have fallen farther, but I had a hand on one part of the gantline, and I had married it to the other almost before I knew that I was falling. Now with both hands holding the lines together, I looked below me. The bosun was gone, and one of the ordinaries, a green boy, was at the winch. Or rather six feet away and with his back to it. I shouted at him, and he began to haul me up with a snap that broke my grasp on the gantline and burned my hands. I shouted again and he stopped. It took a long time to make him understand that he must throw the turns off the winch. One's strength goes quickly aloft. I was weak by the time I started to haul up the long bight of the gantline with my right hand. There were many pauses, when I took the strain by pressing the line against the chair's bridle with my thigh, and it was a painful business getting a long loop through the bridle, and my legs and then the whole rig through the loop, till the hitch was formed at the bridle's throat. Then I sat for a while, getting over my scare and waiting for the strength to come back to my arms. I was safe now, and under my own steam, and the thing to do would be to stand on the seat of the bosun's chair, one hand for the ship and one hand for myself, and start to chip away at that six foot of topmast that I could no longer reach while sitting. But after a while it was clear that I hadn't the strength to wriggle my knees up above the level of the seat and pull myself to a standing position. By now, too, I had passed a frapping line around the mast to keep me from surging as the ship rolled, for her course kept us nearly in the trough of the sea; I was afraid to cast off that line and try to stand up. So I began to work where I was. My arms were so nearly numb that I had to shift the hammer from hand to hand.

Then the bosun called me from below. He motioned furiously, telling me to go higher. I shook my head. I attacked the mast again. A little after that I heard him shout from much closer. He had run up the ladder, which went as high as the crosstrees, and some twenty-five feet below me he was bellowing in the wind. He was tall and powerfully made, black Irish with raging blue eyes. The wind was so high that it stirred the thick black mustache bowed over the mouth that was venting fury at my bad seamanship. It seemed to me that I could see down his throat. I had been shivering in my thin clothes, mostly from weakness, but in an instant that was over. Seizing the heavy marlinspike that hung from my shoulder, I broke the lanyard with a jerk. "Boats, you left a green kid to tend my gantline. I'll settle with you when we're both on deck. Now stand from under or I'll drop this spike point-first." The bosun was a thorough seaman. His expression showed that he was appalled, not by the threat but by the breach of discipline—I must be raving mad. Almost at once he lowered his head and began to descend the ladder. He must have been a bold man, too, because he never looked up to see what I might be at.

I painted my way down to the crosstrees when I was called for my wheel watch. The paint locker was housed in the mast tabernacle on deck, and I stowed my painting gear there and drew kerosene from a drum with a spigot on it to clean up a bit before going to the wheel. I was in a fever, but I did not see the bosun. On the bridge the man at the wheel told me the course and that she was carrying a little left rudder as she sheered away from the seas. I saw nothing in his expression, nor in the mate's. But I was in no condition to notice, and from the bridge the mate, at least, may have seen something amazing, a sailor aloft holding out a marlinspike over the bosun's head. When my watch was over, I saw the bosun in the mess, but we did not speak. The next day during my watch I went to the paint locker, and the bosun, his back to me, was mixing paint. He sang,

> How can it be, you fair young maiden,
> No man has taken you to wife?
> Are all the lads or blind or crazy?
> Or do you love your single life?

I stopped a few feet from him. He stirred paint and sang. After a while I moved forward again, and he turned and handed me the paint pot, saying, "There you are." And that was that. Except that I reflected for the first time that I had offered to kill a man because he had been somewhat overbearing. I thought, too, that my father, with his soldierly sense of duty, would feel consternation if he were to hear of it. But since then I have done other foolish things.

Now, I mean to make a small point of literary history, not compose a work of art. If I were telling a story, I would do it according to the rules. I would not ruminate on things widely separated, and I would not be the subject of my own reflections. The work would be a narrative, it would have a shape, it would be faithful to itself. But I am engaged in something of a very different order, in which I am forced to speak of myself, and these wandering reflections are a way I have found that will permit me to talk about something that must seem surprising. These scattered memories as they arise have the effect of inspiriting me to go on to the historical matter I have it at heart to deliver. They remind me that I have a life, a self, as real as other men's—something I lose sight of whenever I am called to say what is counter to received opinion, or is simply unexpected, and if only for that reason somewhat disobliging. Then I doubt my right to speak. The sensation is of an attack of moral dizziness. But I should like to be able to persuade the reader, not that presently he will learn something to his advantage, as the writers of mystery stories used to say, but that he will learn something unexpected. Each new thing, it seems to me, changes the shape of the world. So I trust that all this military music, artless in the worst sense, will not prove a mere imposition when I have come to saying what it has been given to me to say.

I told Avrahm Yarmolinsky about a story of Chekhov that I had read while I was in college. It was in a volume that had the look of penury about it, bound in a cheap gray cloth filled with an unpleasant sizing, and the reedy lettering stamped in a blue that must always have looked faded and pinched. But that Chekhov collection had been assigned in a course I was taking, and I was glad to have come upon the last copy in the library. I was at college soon after the war. Many of the men in my class had been in the service for a long time; it was a great luxury for them to be in a college and reading books. They were eager to read, so that the books reserved for particular courses were hard to find. I carried off my dispirited-looking prize with satisfaction, and the two moods attended me as I read the stories. All of them appeared to me to have been composed expressly to be gathered into a volume bound in shoddy gray cloth with watery stamping. Nevertheless, to my astonishment, they were desolating and exalting.

One of those stories has been with me ever since. A gentleman walks out into the country—was it on the outskirts of St. Petersburg or of Moscow? The latter, perhaps, for I think I remember mention of the Sparrow Hills. Winter is near. The day is somber. Wandering absently, the gentleman is only half aware of the signs of the dying year about him, but his musings have taken their tone from the brown landscape and the wintry light. Then he comes upon a shepherd. Greeting him, he remarks on the cheerless look that the day has taken on. And after a moment the shepherd makes him this answer: "Your honor, the world is running down. A few years ago in these parts you would start a hare from his form at every step. If you paused among the poplars, the grouse would startle you with the sudden noise of his wings—sometimes two, three, four in succession bursting from the copse, each one taking you by surprise. The geese have been flying south all this month, but they are few, and most go by in silence. All my life long I was used to hear them before they could be seen, calling with a sound like the barking of dogs far off, and the flocks were so great that the long double line stretched to the limit of sight. The ducks are few now, too, in this season when they should be many. And each year in spring the woodcock would call in the clearings at twilight, then fly into the air and circle high up, and plummet down with their wild whistle—times I have heard them three at once, calling and whistling in different places. None came this past spring. The ewes scarcely bear. The grass is thin. The health is gone out of the world.

"Men are sickly in body and spirit. For how could the increase fail and man's life be sound?"

And at these words the gentleman's heart contracts as if for a long time he has been suffering unaware and has just heard the name of his trouble. Or as if he has long been suppressing a painful intuition, and now his fellow has given it expression in terms that sweep away his resistance and leave him unmanned.

Something like that happened to me in New Orleans long ago, during the war. I was ashore, waiting for a ship, and so as not to be idle I had taken a job breaking freight for a trucking company. I worked at night, loading drums of lard, barrels of flour, cases and cartons of general merchandise for Shreveport or Lafayette or as far as Birmingham. It was interesting work. Sometimes the boss would give me directions, but mostly the strategy of loading was left to me, and I found it like ship stowage, though a good deal more simple since the tractor-trailer was not expected to roll and pitch with the seas. But still there was the job of getting the mass of goods out of the shed and into the trailer in the best order and with a minimum of double handling. It was tactically interesting, too. To break back a drum that weighed more than I did, slide the tongue of the hand-truck under it, draw it onto the hand-truck and start the load moving forward in the same instant in order to gain enough momentum on the narrow dock to be able to run it up the steel ramp into the body of the trailer—that took a little doing. And the heavy things had to be placed to best advantage, the casegoods and cartons had to be stacked in bulkheads so that they would not shift. The time went quickly between ten-thirty at night and four-thirty in the morning, and when I needed to straighten my back it was lawful to light a cigarette. Since it was summer, I would be going home in the first light. It was good work.

I was thinking of all that and feeling pleased as I knocked off one morning. I had just been paid. I had worked hard, but I had not been bored and I was not tired. I was looking forward to joining a ship in four days' time. I caught the streetcar. At the next stop a large blond man in white overalls boarded the car.

Though it was nearly empty, he took the seat beside me. He was in good spirits and he wanted to talk. He and his wife had come from Mississippi a few weeks ago so that he could take a job with a contractor who was building a government depot on the outskirts of the city. He said he did anything that had to do with framing—rough general carpentry for construction, as he summed it up. He added after a moment, "The money is good. And it's good work." That chimed in so well with my mood that

when he asked me what I did I began to describe the pleasures of breaking freight. He said thoughtfully, "Every trade is interesting when you
come to learn of it. Every trade." But I was anxious that he not think I was
a warehouse laborer. I told him I was a seaman, and I began to talk of my
art and mystery.

We had been sitting companionably in the rattling car, looking
straight ahead but glancing at each other occasionally—it was a pleasure to
look at his broad red open face, his fine mild eyes. But now he turned to
me in surprise and commiseration. "Oh, you poor young man. Then you
spend your life upon the sea. You have no woman to share your
thoughts—" He broke off as if the idea were too immense for speech, or as
if he felt that he had been indelicate in alluding to my friendless state. But
after a while he said, "There's pain in every life. Now, this job of mine is a
godsend for the money it pays. The crew are all decent fellows. But I have
to work nights, you see. If only I could work days, why, I'd be happy as a
bird." I asked him if there was no chance of changing to the day shift. He
shook his head. "Seems not. I've asked." I had put the question in sympathy, of course, and out of politeness, but also to give myself a breathing
space. I had to take account of a new idea that threatened to change the
aspect of the world. I can scarcely recall now the sense of privilege I used
to feel in bearing the discipline of the vessel, the order of the watches, the
monotonous, workful, violent life. I liked living out in the weather. Ships
satisfied whatever aesthetic instinct I had. I used to listen to the older
seamen with the attentiveness of a disciple, and in a short time I had
grown skillful in my calling. When I had been two years at sea, on board
the *Jacob Thompson* our Swede bosun asked to look at my knife because he
wanted to examine the pigtail of square sennit I had put to the handle so
that I could haul it out of its deep sheath without a struggle. "That's
delicate work. How long you been going to sea?" I hesitated to tell him
how little salt water I had sailed over. "I know. You don't want to say
you're just a water-rat like me. I made my first voyage as cabin boy when
I was five years old. We come to Bremerhaven and I try to walk home to
Sweden." I felt guilty at taking credit falsely, but I was delighted that the
bosun, who had shipped in sail, should mistake me for a veteran. And
since I was young, it was from the vantage point of my office, as the
Spaniards call it, that I saw all the world. I took for my own the lines of
my shipmate, Juan Soto Galan, the ones that end his poem on Helen of
Troy:

All talent is kin. What she cannot help,
The naked knife of her glance—
Leapt from the sheath to the hand, from the hand to the mark—

Is like the careless way I turn a splice,
Better than any rigger's loft ashore,
Or read the ship hull-down on the horizon
And tell my wondering mates her name and port.

I took those lines for my own, satisfied that the craft was manly, but now that carpenter, a fellow man and a substantial one, had suggested to me that it was not fully manlike, that it excluded something essential. The suggestion was painful and luminous. If after the war we had not sold most of our ships to the Greeks and the Norwegians, and registered what was left under flags of convenience, no doubt I should have been a seaman to this day. It's no easy thing to find good work, work that one is suited for. But when the carpenter spoke I understood that the life I had embraced was, in my own terms, no more than half a life.

That realization, unsettling as it was, concerned a relatively narrow train of conduct and custom. It knocked me off my pins for a time, but it was a long way short, in its unsettling effects, of the story in the Chekhov collection. That story, which I have compressed to the point of distorting everything but its import, though I could recite it at much greater length, and, I believe, very nearly in the words of the original—except that I will not introduce a work of art on a grander scale than is called for in an account whose proper business is with a modest item of literary history—that story, I have said, has been with me for many years. It made at once the same impression of painful enlightenment that the carpenter's words, his tone, the expression of his face, had made upon me, as if I had suddenly been enfranchised to suffer understandingly what I had hitherto borne unaware. But it was very much more powerful and lasting, a kind of astonishment of discovery possibly equal to the change occasioned by the shepherd's words in the soul of that wanderer in the Sparrow Hills. In both cases the prophet's ignorance as well as his knowledge vouched for his saying. But what the shepherd said struck me as more impersonal in its application and not to be eluded. Chekhov, out of the *trop plein* of his energies and passions, and out of the pessimism of a dying man—for he was dying of tuberculosis—had composed that threnody for his world. And that world was indeed ready for death. In a quarter-century it was dead. It is a universal assumption that the world we inherited from that time is a dead world. Naturally we ignore the fact. Life has always been hard, no doubt. But to live in a dead world calls for a ceaseless tautening of the imagination that has made us a race of hysterics. However, that is by the by.

I told Avrahm Yarmolinsky how I had come upon the Chekhov story in my college course years back. I made no reflections upon it. I was meaning to ask him if he knew of the collection in which I had found it, or any other that contained it, since I wanted to read it again. But at one point in my detailing of the incident I began to falter. Something in his manner had made me lose the clue of my thought. The current of sympathetic attention that flows from the listener to sustain the speaker had been suddenly interrupted. Yarmolinsky's grave face was stony. I felt that before I was aware of what it meant. But then experience told me what was about to happen, and I began at once to feel ashamed, like a man caught out. The first instance of it that I can recall consciously had happened some years before, when I was working for Jack Steinberg in the one-horse publishing firm that he later made into a notable house. He was about to entrust some copy-editing to me, and he asked me if I knew what to do with commas and periods when they occurred in the neighborhood of quotation marks. I answered bouncily with a homemade formula. Jack was a passionate man who habitually spoke gently. He was easy to work for—indeed, endlessly indulgent. And I used to feel rather reassured than not by the glint of iron under his affable habit. This time his expression changed abruptly. He said, "Here's *The Chicago Manual of Style*. Take it home, go through the whole thing, so you'll know that it covers everything. And the index is complete. Don't go near that manuscript till you have some idea of what the questions are and where you can find the answers." But I had known myself to be inexcusably at fault before he spoke, simply from the rigidity of his face. And only a few months ago in conversation with a friend, I said casually that I didn't think much of a science of clinical psychology that had changed the definitions of psychosis and neurosis twice in my lifetime. My friend is a physician, profound and droll, with a manic comicality of invention; in discussion a playful tiger. Now all drollery ceased together. His face set, he told me that those definitions had not changed, and he quoted the textbook formulae. What I had meant to say was that their meanings had changed, since they were being applied to clusters of symptoms that were in practice regarded in quite another way than they had been when the definitions were first adopted. One indication was the discovery—less than twenty years old— that neurosis is not the monopoly of the middle class, and psychosis not the specialty of coarse natures lower in the social scale. But I could say none of that, for my friend's face was implacable. I think of Marlow in *Lord Jim*, consulting the French naval officer about the moral bearings of Jim's case, and being much heartened by his ready understanding of the natural fear that had overcome the young man. And so Marlow finds the courage to ask, then, if he is not disposed to take a lenient view of Jim's conduct. And the Frenchman scrambles to his feet, as if eager to keep his garments from contamination by the possibility of leniency, and announces the judgment of his entire nation upon the matter: There is still the question of honor. And as for what may come when honor is forfeit, he can offer no opinion because he knows nothing about that. Implacable. Though I think he is in the right.

Yarmolinsky said quietly, mournfully, "There is no such story of Chekhov. Almost every scrap attributable to Chekhov that is of literary significance has been collected. That story is not in the corpus."

I understood that the judgment could not be appealed. Yarmolinsky had edited Chekhov, written about him. And I am unreliable about literary sources, my acquirements in such matters being a late growth. But that I should mistake the authorship of a story that corresponded to my buried premonitions of the meaning of my own life, that I should be wrong about the gray binding and faded blue lettering that I had borne for years like a weight upon the heart—had I ever been inside that library, did I attend that college?—these things seemed astounding. Learned men have erred. But then, it could not be Turgenev. I had read *A Sportsman's Notebook* over and over. And it was not Tolstoy or Gogol. And of the small number of Russian and Soviet writers with whom I was familiar, it was inconceivable to me that the author of that sketch might be anyone but Chekhov.

In the week that has gone by since my credit card was rejected in the restaurant, I have received the monthly statement of account. From that statement it is clear that if the company had allowed me to charge my restaurant bill of $10.09, there would still have been a balance in my favor of over thirteen dollars. I won't use that card again. I don't like to pay interest to capricious people. I've read that one of the credit card companies, I forget which, has issued fifty million cards. A number of that magnitude guarantees many chances for error, but it also makes discourtesy routine, and suspicion business as usual. How often I've tendered a card for some small purchase, and the clerk has reached under the counter to get the closely printed booklet, and run down the columns of figures to see if the man standing before him is to be regarded as a citizen or a pariah. I used sometimes to pretend ignorance. I would ask, "Are those the good ones or the bad ones?" Usually the clerk would seem a bit taken aback, even embarrassed. "The bad ones." "And have you found any yet?" I never spoke to a clerk who had. But some said that at other counters, elsewhere in the store, or at a branch in another borough, a bad one had turned up. I dropped the game after a while. Those were the terms on which the clerk earned his living. I had thought to educate him about his relations with his fellows, but that was presumptuous. If I had accomplished anything, it was to add a drop of bitterness to his cup.

But it's like trying to give your check for a purchase in a department store. In this city you must produce your driver's license or no soap. Once I had my passport with me, and I was curious to see if the spread eagle and the Great Seal of the United States of America, and the endorsement of the secretary of state, and my photograph—bearded, however—and my signature would turn the trick. No. I had to produce my driver's license. "Patience," my father says when I confront him with things of the kind. But I had a French friend once who used to exclaim on such occasions, *"Quelle époque!"* More pointed and more heartfelt. For our nerves are raw from the climate of affronts and suspicion that we have accustomed ourselves to endure. I go to some lengths myself not to add to the miasma rising from the marsh. Many years ago, a man named Hardesty, from Wilmington, Delaware, borrowed ten dollars from me in a Southern port. He didn't mention that he was shipping out next day. He had been cadet master of our class at the school in St. Petersburg, Florida, where we were to be dubbed (wonders of the war!) ensign, second lieutenant, or third mate if we passed the courses. On our very first evening at the school, while we were in formation in the street outside our barracks, Hardesty had awarded me ten demerits—thirteen meant expulsion. He said, textually, "That will cost you ten demerits." We had been laughing at a mild joke an officer had made; my laughter had gone on a hemidemisemiquaver too long. I said, "That will cost you more than that." And I stepped out of the rank to strike him. But the officer, a lieutenant named Sargent—a very decent man—said quietly, "Stop, mister." The honorific mister was an earnest of my prospective translation to third mate. "Go back to your formation."

In my three months at the school I never collected the last three demerits, so I was duly graduated as an officer in the merchant marine. Hardesty was too. (I believe he had no demerits whatsoever. How would he have come by any?) Four months after that, both of us happened to be in New Orleans, waiting to ship out. I came upon him in Bourbon Street. I think we had not spoken since the night he had awarded me ten demerits. He said, "I'm flat broke. Lend me ten till Saturday." Since I detested the man I could not refuse him the money. And he was gone next day. Recently I told the story to a friend of mine. I told him that by accident I had just learned that there were people of that name still living in Wilmington, that I was going to go there some day and get back my ten dollars with interest. My friend said, "Don't talk like that. Don't even think like that." Now, I am opposed to capital punishment. I can scarcely imagine a nastier custom than allowing public functionaries to assume our responsibility for condemning and murdering a human being. But I have nothing against private vengeance–though I would think it reasonable that my fellow citizens try to restrain me if they believe that I intend an act of violence.

But what was I to make of the announcement, on the part of a scholar in the field of Russian letters–specifically an editor and biographer of Chekhov–that the volume I had read as a class assignment, containing the story I have mentioned, was not by Chekhov at all? Of course, Yarmolinsky did not say precisely that. He simply denied that the story I had told him in summary had been written by Chekhov. Well, I made nothing of it. If the theory of the heliocentric organization of the solar system were overthrown tomorrow, I should be very much interested in the new ingenuities that science was substituting for the familiar ones. But of course one expects some such overthrow. And science does not de- mand of us a slack-jawed faith in its proposals, just a provisional accep- tance of the presumed state of the art, so that investigation may proceed. The Chekhov story is another matter. It happened to me. It is part of my life. I made nothing of Yarmolinsky's denial. And there is a further oddity in all this. Why hadn't Yarmolinsky told me the true authorship of the story? He knew Russian literature as the dog knows the coverts, as at one time, a pilot of the Hudson River, I knew the courses, buoys, lights, and landmarks from Ambrose Light to Albany. It is not credible that in my desultory reading I had happened upon a wonderful Russian author unknown to him. That seemed scarcely more likely than that some writer entirely foreign to Russia would set his sketch of the end of the world in the Sparrow Hills, and report it as a colloquy between a muzhik and a gentleman. I could make nothing of Yarmolinsky's denial.

The poet M. L. Rosenthal is steeped in Chekhov. Not, I imagine, because he takes him for Aeschylus or Shakespeare, but because there are strains in that music that touch his heart. I understand that very well. When I was young, it was Auden, not Yeats, who touched me most. Yeats was the bigger man, Auden the more clubbable–not that his throwaway manner is without a kind of diffident nobility:

> England to me is my own tongue,
> And what I did when I was young . .

In any case, Rosenthal is my friend, and some years after Yarmolinsky had set me that puzzle, he happened to speak of Chekhov's "Ward Six." There's no doubt about that one, at least. And then he mentioned the film that the Russians had made of Chekhov's "The Lady with the Dog." I had seen that. For a few moments two middle-aged men thought of Chekhov, his plays, his stories–and the plague that those stories have unleashed upon us because their atmosphere of things unresolved, of less than heroic pain, can be evoked readily enough by writers who have no genius. And one thing leads to another: I told him my Chekhov story. He said he had never read it. He was surprised. How could one miss a story like that? He would look for it.

But he never did unearth it. He said later that it sounded like something that Chekhov might have written, but apparently he hadn't. At least he himself could find no trace of it among the editions of Chekhov that he had looked through. He wondered if it might not be another writer.

Yes, but who? The problem is rendered more acute by the scantiness of my information about Russian authors. If I know of no more than a dozen, how can I possibly make a mistake? Reviewing them while counting on my fingers, it is clear that none of them except Chekhov could possibly be the author. Well, Gorky and Isaac Babel are remote possibilities. But Gorky did not take that view of life. To introduce the shepherd's monologue somewhere in a story–that would be possible for him. But to make it the high point of a sketch designed to express an intuition of cosmic failure is simply not Gorky. And Babel writes in saber strokes. The impractical-seeming parries that guard cheek and flank, the florid moulinets that are nevertheless the shortest route to an opening, the sudden attack with the point–these make a wild skirling music, an exuberant *Totentanz.* He would never let a peasant speak connectedly, collectedly, so long a speech, one that gave no occasion for explosive satisfaction in bitterness. Now, I am not even remotely a scholar, but in these matters I have a certain flair. I told my friend–the one who said I must not dream of spilling Hardesty's blood–that in these matters I had absolute pitch. He said, "In these matters no one has absolute pitch." Of course. But absolute pitch is relative; some people are tone-deaf. I have relative absolute pitch, and I will not abate my claim any further, because I have a duty to the truth. And it's a small enough talent that I claim. It would seem that I haven't a shred of imagination. And I can't even read Babel or Gorky or Chekhov in their own language. But the Chekhov story cannot have been written by either of the others. It might have been written by Turgenev, but I have read no other stories or sketches of his except those that figure in *A Sportsman's Notebook,* and it is not among them. How can I be mistaken when I have too little information to make any confusion of the kind remotely plausible?

Certainly ignorance can lead one into error sometimes, and sometimes into sin. But this is not that sort of occasion. I know because I have been led into both, and I can recognize them. Once, for example, when I was on the *Jean-Baptiste LeMoyne,* south of the Florida Keys, I made a serious mistake at the wheel. We had been steering southeast, and the mate told me to come right easy, meet her, and steady her on one-eight-nine. We were making a long plunge into the Caribbean. I carried out the order and reported, "Steady on the one-eight-nine, sir." He said, "Keep her so." He left the wheelhouse and went up the vertical ladder to the flying bridge. I heard him stride across the deck above my head. I assumed he meant to take an azimuth of the sun. Then he called down through the speaking tube, "What is your heading now?" I had looked up involuntarily when I first heard his voice, and I looked at the gyro compass again. "One-eight-nine, sir." He asked me the same question two more times in the next two minutes. The compass did not go a single click right or left—the sea was calm—and each time I answered confidently, "One-eight-nine." Then he ran across the deck above my head, tumbled down the ladder, and came into the wheelhouse on the run. He stared at the compass. He said, "Your heading is one-nine-four." I looked. That's what the compass said, and I had been certain that it had not moved. I had been reading one-nine-four as one-eight-nine, steering five degrees off course. He said, "You deliberately tried to fool me." My shame at having wandered from the course kept me from understanding the accusation. He said, "You tried to make a fool of me." When I could speak, I said, "I'd be a fool to try that. I made a mistake. You were taking an azimuth, weren't you? You had the gyro repeater right under your nose." That wasn't polite, but I was terribly rattled. He said, "You tried to make a fool of me. I won't forget that." To be unskillful was bad enough. To be taken for a cheat and a liar was nearly unbearable. There was nothing more I could say. I thought bitterly that I was the best sailor in the watch. It did not even occur to me that he may have thought so too, and could not account for my being off course during long minutes, cheerfully answering one-eight-nine the while, unless I had meant to mislead him. We were to load oil in Aruba for Valparaiso, but from Aruba we carried the oil back to Perth Amboy, so that the voyage was over in three more weeks. That was lucky. When I signed off the vessel, I said to him, "Mister mate, I misread the steering compass. There's no excuse for that. But I wasn't trying to fool you." He said, "I know what you were trying to do." And that was that. It has troubled me for thirty years, and not because it was the worst mistake I ever made. I've done worse things, all right. It's that the man thought I had lied about something I would never lie about. Since then lovers have said I lied about things one doesn't lie about, and the accusation has hurt less. Men and women are not to understand one another. But that ship's officer and I were members of the same craft. There was nothing to misunderstand. I have never forgiven him.

Here is an odd thing. That man could not be persuaded, years ago, because he had been disappointed in his expectations. A good helmsman stays on course, and if in heavy weather the ship's head is nearly ungovernable, he meets her on each swing to keep her as much as possible from ranging, and tries to average his course—as a young man I heard with a curious elation that "govern" was related to the Greek word for "rudder." And many years later I am obdurate about that man because he felt that I had broken the bond of faith that sustains us all. He was a good seaman, and he should have known my heart by his own. At one time a woman who had a tenderness for me nevertheless found that every action, every gesture of mine, was an offense. I asked her, "Why did you choose me, then?" Her answer undid me: "Everyone lives in a dream of love." The most painful lines in *Don Quixote* turn on the grim joke of our illusions. The don is at last persuaded that what he had taken for a castle and for noble courtesy were hired lodging and professional hospitality. He says, "This is an inn, then?" "And a right good one," the innkeeper returns with perfect satisfaction. The don says, "I have been sadly deluded all this while." The Spanish is more virile and more hopeless— *"Engañado he vivido hasta aqui."*

It must be for reasons like these that I feel an unlikely twinge of resentment at Avrahm Yarmolinsky for having denied my testimony, and at my friend Mack Rosenthal. It is as if they sought to dispel a kindly illusion. No doubt they could not consider what the result might be if they succeeded, since they were themselves testifying to their best knowledge. They were testifying to what they knew, and we owe one another just that.

Now, Rosenthal is a remarkable poet, and the measure of it is that he is, statistically speaking, insane; an essential part of his trade is to conciliate his generation, but he takes no interest in the job. Hamlet says of Osric, "He did comply with his dug before he sucked it." Yes, but Osric has got on, hasn't he, and at the end of the play he is hale and hearty, and in a position to commend his services to Fortinbras. Rosenthal has no such gift. Like every real poet he has had to invent a new language, but his language is unacceptable to the nation we have become. It is not hieratic, remote, like the language of Stevens. It is not a fit vehicle for sly, poisoned confession, like the language of so and so. He doesn't know how to talk tough, like the tribe of the terrified tough. The most noted of his fellow poets are a generation of Malvolios who have had greatness thrust upon 'em. He has no talent for that. A painful case.

He has courage that he would do well to keep out of his verse, courage of readiness and courage of compunction. I was lunching with him one day at his college. Holding our trays before us, we were in line to pay the man at the cash register. There was a foreigner ahead of us in line. He was confused, and the man at the register was insolent. I turned away, mentally, from the business. I'm a modern American. My motto is, Don't look at me—I just work here. I paid, and waited for my friend to join me. He said in a low tone to the man at the register, "I heard what passed between you and that man. He's a foreign visitor, a guest of the university, a guest of the country." The man at the register said something negligently exculpatory. Mack said, "That won't do. I'm going to see to it that you won't be impolite to a stranger again." I felt embarrassed for my friend. He seems to think he lives here, not on Mars or on television.

Another time we had lunch at the White Horse. As we entered we saw a big fellow sitting on a stool with his back to the bar, his elbows braced on it. He was heavy-bodied, with a sunburned face, and his nose looked as if someone had broken it for him not too long ago. He was drunk. He seemed to find us amusing. I excused myself to make a phone call and went past the end of the bar to the public phone. While I was dialing the number I heard Mack's voice. I glanced over that way, and things didn't look right. When the phone had rung five times I hung up. I steamed over to Mack and said, fatuously, "Do you know this man?" He said, "No, I don't. But he seems to think that he knows me." "I know you," the man said, and he laughed. I turned to him, but Rosenthal took my arm and said, "Let's go into the other room." We did, and we ordered our lunch and the house's infamous half-and-half. Suddenly Mack said, "My God, it's Delmore Schwartz. I didn't recognize him. He's gained a lot of weight, and he looks as if he's been in a fight. I have to apologize to him." With great difficulty I kept him from doing that; in Schwartz's condition it would have been a mistake. "That's terrible," Mack said. "I never recognized him. I'll have to find someone who knows where he's living now, and write to him." I had always thought of Delmore Schwartz as the man who had at the outset the essential gift that most of the poets who were his exact contemporaries never chose to demonstrate, the ability to make a great line. He made only a half-dozen of them, but they are perfectly diagnostic for poetry. One would be enough—"The scrimmage of appetite everywhere." That line is Dantesque. So I was thinking that on my meeting that extraordinary man I had tried to edge him into a brawl.

But what I had begun to say is that Rosenthal is magnanimous and not sentimental, and he can't seem to keep the first quality out of his poems, nor inject into them a saving dose of the other. In sum, he lacks a decent respect of the opinion of mankind. On his head be it.

As might be imagined, those traits make him an inconvenient friend. I get back at him as best I can. He admired, rightly, Horace Gregory's version of Catullus's *"Nil nimium studeo, Caesar":* "I shall not raise my hand to please you, Caesar, Nor do I care if you are black or white."

I brooded on that, and the next day telephoned him to say that I had made a better version: "I couldn't care less about pleasing you, Caesar. You can be white or black—it don't make me no never-mind."

There was a pause. Mack asked, "And did you introduce the ungrammatical expression in order to conform to the original?" I said loftily that I had employed an American idiom to render in a contemporary mode the unbuttoned impertinence of the original. "I see," he said. "Would you repeat the lines for me? I'd like to write them down." So that one missed fire. I doubt that it will stop me, though. I have observed that experience does not teach, though it may canker.

But what it comes down to is that, with less reason to do so than Avrahm Yarmolinsky, since he has not like Yarmolinsky devoted a good part of his life to a scholarly investigation of Chekhov, and with equal lack of concern for the possible consequences to me, Rosenthal has concluded that I am mistaken, and in an unimportant way, about the authorship of the Chekhov story. That, from a close friend, strikes me as cavalier. On the basis of an investigation that could not, in the nature of the case, be systematic, let alone exhaustive, he has decided that I am not to be believed on this point—indifferent to him, capital to me.

Now, the trouble with being alone in the world, in the sense that no one agrees with you and the world's experience does not ratify your instinctive feelings, is that you go crazy. I do not mean in a statistical sense. Since no one agrees, you repeat, you exaggerate, you shout. And at last you shout not from outraged conviction but from terror, from distrust of your feelings, since they are coin that does not pass current and you cannot rid yourself of them. At that point you understand that you are crazy. And a man is a social animal. How can you believe that you are in the right when everyone knows that you're crazy?

When I was second mate on the *Ulla Madsen* I invented a method of finding longitude at noon. It came to me suddenly on a day when I was taking the usual noon sights to establish the latitude—just as once, when I was a child riding on the subway and seeing the lights of the tunnel slide by, it came to me that motion in space was the graph of time, and time elapsed the measure of motion. For hundreds of years men had been measuring the angular distance of the sun above the noon horizon, applying a correction for the date, and setting down the result as their latitude. Longitude was a very different matter. To arrive at it one worked cumbersome problems in spherical trigonometry, or, more recently, with one's sight entered volumes of tables and in about ten minutes could hope to come up with a "line of position" that gave an estimated longitude that was close enough for the purposes of a vessel that could not run into danger any faster than fourteen knots. But a dozen or so entries on a form are required, and petty calculations, and there is plenty of chance for error. It came to me that at one moment of the day—noon—one could find longitude almost as one finds latitude, almost by inspection.

Every deepwater ship carries two timepieces, the ship's clock that is set approximately to local time, and the chronometer that is set as precisely as may be to Greenwich time, with its rate of error written down in the log every day after comparison with radio signals. You start to take sights a few moments before noon by the ship's clock, and note the time of each sight with a watch set to local time. The sun is climbing to its greatest altitude, and the successive sights show a larger and larger angle with the horizon. At last the sextant shows a smaller reading—and you know that the sight taken just before that one represents high noon. From it you get your latitude, as usual. Then, by comparing the ship's clock, allowing local time, with the chronometer, set to Greenwich time, correcting only for the moments elapsed since that penultimate sight, you have your longitude. The sun passed over Greenwich before it passed over your head, and the difference in time between those two transits is the measure of your distance from the prime meridian at Greenwich—which is longitude. The only calculation required is to change time to degrees and minutes of arc at the rate of fifteen degrees to the hour, for that is the speed of the sun's apparent motion through the sky.

At first I wondered why the books did not mention it. I must be wrong. Or perhaps it was because the method is usable only at noon, when the sun is on your meridian. But that did not seem a sufficient reason, since the navigator's "day's work" required him to shoot the sun at noon in any case.

Well, I never had a skipper who let me use that discovery. There had to be something wrong with it, though it sounded right. I used the method secretly because it was quick. And since it is inherently more accurate than the method of looking up tables and making entries and manipulations on a form, every day I had to nudge my noon position on the chart and ease it over toward the old man's. But that is an old sea-custom anyway.

Many are the persons I have told of my discovery. Always they looked sympathetic and skeptical. The more they knew of the subject the more careful they were to look sympathetic—*on ne badine pas avec l 'amour*— but they were skeptical. I bore it all. Then, last summer, I picked up a yachting magazine on a newsstand, for I love boats and shall never have one now. In it there was an advertisement for an electronic pocket calculator that would solve various problems in navigation and piloting. My eye went down the list of problems disapprovingly: I detest those machines. All at once my heart jumped. You know how it is when you miss your footing on the stair. The first you know of it is that your hand has seized the rail–your body knew the danger before you did, and your heart has jumped. One of the items read, "Longitude by Meridian Altitude." The technical term means one thing only. My method, my rejected method is now so much a matter of course that it is programmed on a pocket calculator. And for thirty years I had thought myself mad.

So when my friend Mack Rosenthal adopts with me the tone of a man visiting a sickroom, and says it sounds as if it might be Chekhov, but it appears after all that it isn't, he cannot possibly know that his tactful tone is an exacerbation. He is driving me to the verge of recklessness, something to which my unfortunate temperament lends itself in any case. So, too, is my other friend who is nameless here because he does not properly figure in the foreground of the account I have to render–the one who tells me, "In these matters no one has absolute pitch." After these excitements of my reason and my blood, and given a certain instability which is after all my business alone, though it is probably patent to that small portion of the world that knows of my existence, I think it will be understandable if I do something characteristic and out of character. Then who will be mad and who will be sane?

The third person whom I must introduce here for the sake of his testimony is Mr. Monroe Engel, who is well enough known as a scholar and man of letters, I trust. He is quite as well-known as is agreeable with honesty, and no grander notoriety would serve my particular purposes. I met him three years ago, when both of us served on a literary jury. We had two prizes to award. One of these went, as of right, to the foremost American novelist–now in his dotage but who served the Republic well while he still had all his marbles. The question was, what younger deserving writer should be granted the second award? It had been decided by a kind of unofficial consensus to bestow it upon one who deals in the necrology of our dead world, taking his cue from a hint in T. S. Eliot regarding rusted iron, stonecrop, merds. And that made me think of another and most gifted writer who was still blindly evoking memories of life, the possibility of tragedy. Then I did something unseemly, for I know how to sway a committee: a child's heartbroken insistence, or the calm lucidity of the paranoiac, or a new proposal put forward with manly firmness when everyone is looking at his watch and thinking of his luncheon engagement–these are features of my armamentarium. I think none of my fellow committee members understood the willfulness of my filibuster in favor of vanished hope, except a young woman–herself a notable writer—the youngest member of the committee. She understood because she is hostage to death by reason of her youth, with her teeth set against vain sentiment. But she was outvoted.

After the formal session there were a few minutes of conversation, and Monroe Engel spoke to me. He was cordial, as if I were a man and a brother rather than a person secretly convinced that his literary passions had more than a tinge of defensiveness. And we are a social animal; Mr. Engel's manner made me feel readmitted to human converse. Our discussion before the vote had provoked the mention of Chekhov, and Mr. Engel told me now that he was editing a collection of the stories. I told him of my Chekhov story. I asked if he was acquainted with it. In putting the question I tried to disguise my eagerness to be delivered of the burden it has come to represent to me. He said he hadn't come across it, but that he would be reviewing the entire corpus, and he would let me know if he found it.

People say those things, but life intervenes, and you do not hear from them. So I was touched to get a postcard from Monroe Engel some time afterward. I have it before me now—the only physical document in the case:

January 8

I've not been able to find the Chekhov story you described. Perhaps it will turn up in the one volume of stories (the stories of 1894) that has not yet been issued. If not, you have a collector's memory.
Sorry not to be more helpful.
Sincerely,
Monroe Engel

A collector's memory. That is an interesting coinage. Under other circumstances I suppose I should think it pleasantly witty, signifying the substance of things hoped for that cannot possibly exist. I am in any case very grateful to Monroe Engel for his courtesy, and I hope he will not think it an ill return that I hale him before the public on my business without asking leave. For my need is great. I am too old to imagine that the volume containing the stories of 1894 (my father was at that time a child of five) will sustain my claim. Besides, more than two years have passed. Mr. Engel has no doubt finished his review of the Chekhov corpus some time ago. I am sure that he would have let me know if he had come upon the story.

Now, that puts me in a very difficult position, though I might appear to have sought it. I may resent—not on trivial grounds, but on grounds that are scarcely avowable nonetheless—Avrahm Yarmolinsky's ukase in the matter, and the pronouncement in the same sense of my friend M. L. Rosenthal. The fact remains that I appealed to their special knowledge, and they answered me according to their understanding of the case, as they were bound to do. Marshalling their testimony in this account has been painful to me, but I have gone through with it doggedly. Monroe Engel's report I cannot resent at all, though he has delivered the latest blow to my hopes. The problem is severe, and it is not simply a matter of my having been hopelessly wrong about a literary ascription that has had special meaning for me. I have been wrong in worse cases and survived. I mentioned how Mack came to the defense of a foreigner—unknown to the man himself, simply on principle, because that man was the stranger within our gates. Well, I have had very different relations with foreigners in my time. I shall not dilate upon an incident in a Latin-American port where, one night, drunk and about to be arrested (for cause), I snatched the policeman's saber from its sheath, foined at him with the point to gain a moment's start on him and his companion, ran along the wharves in the darkness, came on a providential *lancha* with oars in her whose painter I cast adrift, pulled away towards the anchor lights of the shipping in the roadstead, made my own vessel at last, having run into the stage at the foot of her lowered accommodation ladder, discovered the accursed sword still beside me on the thwart—the pommel gouging my hip and the point jammed under the stretcher against which my feet were braced— hurled it away from me into the water and from the stage spurned off the *lancha* to drop down-current, all with no thought of the policeman answerable for that saber nor the waterman whose livelihood was that boat. That happened far away, in a far-off time, and I had the excuse of being drunk and frightened. But not long ago I was crossing Seventh Avenue from the west, and the traffic light changed before I had reached the sidewalk. Immediately I heard the baleful blast of a highway horn at my back, and the car passed so close that I had to jump for the curb. The driver shook a fist at me as he sailed around the corner into Bleecker Street. I began to run, and I pressed on until I caught up with the car at Sixth Avenue where it had stopped for the light. It was livercolored. When I pulled the door open the driver shrank away as far as he could without letting go of the steering wheel. He was a dark man. At that moment he looked as if he had been hit with a singlejack. I thrust my head and shoulders inside the car and said murderously, "The pedestrian has the right of way in this city. You cross with red light." Cars that had come up behind us sounded their horns. I felt disgust and savage pleasure at his fear. "In your country, no doubt, a man in a car can run over any man on foot. Don't ever try that again here." I slammed the door, exulting in the noise. The livercolored car moved away and the next car sounded its horn indignantly at me as it went by. I could scarcely see for a few minutes. I found it hard to walk because I was shaking, and as that began to leave me my satisfaction too ebbed away. The business took on an ugly look. I was ashamed.

No one, I trust, will imagine that I have described here the worst actions of my life. I have done worse things. And the swan's breast stems the turbid flood and takes no stain, but the things of man are otherwise disposed. Every act of prepotency or cowardice has left a sediment in my spirit that darkens for me the stream of life. But somewhere I keep a measure, as they say a meter stick is preserved at Paris to try the truth of all the others. Even in this city that offers no horizon I find out a level and a perpendicular. In the end I know how much things come to, which way is up. To suppose that I would be ashamed to acknowledge that I have been dim-wittedly ascribing to Chekhov a story of which he is innocent, would be to deny me all sense of proportion, as if I could not tell the difference between footlessness and faithlessness. It's true I can't say how it comes about that I should be so mistaken, but I long ago resigned the childish passion for knowing the inessential—if I want to be fully informed I can always read the *New York Times*. It is something else that troubles me. For even as I loathe with all my soul the waitress's musky aura, her hoarse voice, the matter-of-fact brutality that informs her brisk, awkward movements, so I hate the artist's mountebank suppleness of self-exposure, his gift for uniforms and posturing, for being all things to all men, for taking on willingly the tincture of the stream of his times. I know there is in it a certain temporal majesty, marked with grime, as there is grimy majesty in empire or in the vulgar power of Concorde. But it troubles me exceedingly to confess what at this point the reader may already suspect. It was not what I intended at the outset, I could swear to that. But do I know what I intended? And to take responsibility is one thing; to feel myself complicit is another. Nevertheless it appears, against all likelihood, that in a certain season, when day was drawing off, the brown air taking the creatures of earth from their labors, all alone I girded myself for the journey and its pain, and composed—magisterially—the myth of our times. It was a signal and thankless effort, but the mere mention of it has persuaded men of judgment to consider for a moment its admission to the canon. It seems certain now—in my own despite—that I am the author of the Chekhov story. What genius I had then.

CALYX, A Journal of Art and Literature by Women

༺༺༺

Choosing "Sheets"

Micki Reaman and Beverly McFarland

Since its birth in 1976, *CALYX* Journal has been a collectively minded organization. *CALYX's* mission to promote the art and writing of diverse women, to provide a forum for *all* women and their concerns, visions, and perspectives, is ensured by a collective process. No one person's assumptions, preferences, biases define the journal–and by extension no one aesthetic, arena, agenda. This, of course, is the ideal, the hope. In reality, attempting collectivism demands energy and time, time often reflected in how long a writer may wait to hear about the status of her work. In reality, conflicts arise. Consensus is not reached. Subjectivity is still, in the end, the difference between accepting or returning a manuscript. In reality, representing diversity is a challenging endeavor.

The process of publication at *CALYX* Journal hinges on two open reading periods each year during which manuscripts are accepted. *CALYX* Journal publishes solely unsolicited manuscripts. We read every manuscript received, sometimes two thousand each reading period. Before the entire collective reads a manuscript, submissions are screened. One editor can decide to hold a manuscript for the collective to read, but two editors must agree to return a manuscript. After this initial reading, each manuscript that is not returned is read by the seven members of the Journal Editorial Collective. The manuscripts are then discussed at weekly meetings over a period that can be six months long.

Editors who have been involved with *CALYX* from the early years have seen an increasing number of manuscripts dealing with urgent, traumatic issues that touch women's lives: domestic violence, rape, harassment, incest. This is a shift from the earlier presence of writing about power, anger, and rediscovering women's culture. One of the ongoing challenges for the Editorial Collective is to maintain a balance between feminist issues and quality of the art. *CALYX* is a forum that validates and publishes the *voices* and the *subjects* often ignored, ridiculed, trivialized by mainstream literary tradition. Sometimes the work we read does not take for its subjects the spheres confiningly defined as "women's"—we publish it for its literary quality. Sometimes it sings with a voice we haven't heard, or focuses on a vital subject, but is not refined—we often work with and encourage such authors in order to publish their work. Occasionally, a piece achieves elegance *and* weaves a subject of intense emotion and trauma with unusual beauty. "Sheets" by Beth Bosworth is one of those stories.

Most editors of the collective were very enthusiastic from the beginning about "Sheets." Even when there is no obvious disagreement, no strong feelings against publication, stimulating discussion ensues about a manuscript like "Sheets." Because *CALYX* editors read a large number of manuscripts about issues such as incest, we are well aware of how overwhelming the subject can be. Our commitment to publishing fine literature and art and to providing a forum for the concerns and visions of all women cautions us to be aware of an immediate "another-incest-story" reaction and to consider each piece with the care it deserves. In the case of "Sheets," the issue of its subject was raised, but the theme was so artfully handled that the editors' questions involved not the subject but the story's form. "Sheets" deals with incest without being polemic and while being artful. Not a story about "incest," "Sheets" nevertheless gives voice to the issue.

The editors examined and discussed the experimental form of the story, and agreed that the ambiguities seemed in keeping with the form and that the stylistic choices were consistent. We chose "Sheets" for its elegant writing, for its experimentation with form, for its textual layering of the story within story, for the way it combined life and fiction. Beth Bosworth in "Sheets" provides a new perspective on an important, troubling issue, with an engrossing balance of subject and artistic quality.

As feminist publications, publications by people of color, and political publications all know, functioning on the margins of the literary establishment can be discouraging and alienating. At *CALYX* Journal (and at other organizations no doubt) the experience is uplifting, encouraging, and inspiring as well. The need for alternative forums is clear; the necessity of publishing voices that are more inclusive of our diverse culture is even more clear.

Sheets

Beth Bosworth

In a hotel room near Paris my mother lifts from her suitcase a story of mine about a father and a daughter.

I want to know, she says, if this is true.

Mom, I say. It's a story.

I have a right to know, she says.

In the story the father has bright blue eyes like my own father and the daughter also has blue eyes and my sallow skin and some of my own questions about the world, about the unknown country through which the two, father and daughter, are traveling. They travel to Mexico City and home again and the pattern of their trip is determined by his desire for her, a zig-zag of rooms and beds. First there is her disheveled room in New Jersey where he asks her to journey with him, his palm spread between her warm shoulders; then the cool beds in the motel room where he tells her that she looks like her mother and that this stirs him; then the big white room in Mexico City where he says that no, it is not only because she looks like her mother. Her mother, for instance, has big dark nipples. He asks her to lift her shirt then and he points out, gravely, that she does not, that her own are rosy and smaller.

Will they change later, he wants to know? He speaks with the same search for honesty, the same grave voice with which years later (but before my mother lifts the story from her suitcase) my own corporeal parents will announce their separation from twenty-seven years of each other.

You look just like your mother from behind, he says in the story. And I miss her so much. That night or another night he says, I'm so cold. Could you come in my bed and warm me up? And that same night or another night in Mexico City he slides his fingers into her underpants and, sucking in his breath, up into the warm lips so that for many years she dreams about intercourse with a fat man whose penis is deliciously swiveled. In the story she remembers kicking him away. She remembers this while she is folding her clothes into her suitcase. They have been traveling for many days now and her mother's neat piles of shirts and shorts and underclothes have come tumbling down. It is not clear to her when this happened, when they all began to drift. She pats at a sprawl of socks and, standing, says, Daddy, that wasn't very nice, what you did last night.

You didn't seem to mind.

I pushed you away.

You pushed me the first time. You didn't push me away the second time.

I was asleep.

Children often pretend to be asleep when they don't want to accept responsibility for something they do.

The daughter frowns and walks into the other room where his parents are waiting. In the story his parents are playing chess and they lift their old heads and smile above the glinting chess pieces, rook, pawn, king, and queen. In the story I linger too long on the old, reptilian features of the grandmother, and, later, on the great love with which the grandfather lifts his grey head and shouts, Esther, you see, she beats me at chess! The child beats me! He lifts his palm to the white, white ceiling in wonder.

This does not really belong in the story at all.

I want to know if this is true, my mother says. Her face glows pale beneath dark hair.

Mom, I say. I am twenty years old and she has flown to Paris to find me and bring me home because I have written to her that I am pregnant and that I mean to keep the baby. That is why we are together now in this hotel room, because after dinner with Pierre, after she has cried and spilled dark wine across his carpet, she has asked me for five minutes of my time. Alone. Pierre stiffens at this. He cannot understand this need of hers to pull me away from him. He says it is the way lovers behave, not parents.

In this hotel room dark metal *volets* cover the windows. When I can no longer stay there with her I twist hard on the knob and swing the v*olets* open and holler down to Pierre, who is waiting, *J'arrive!* He shrugs. What is he thinking down there? I can never know. I will never, ever know what Pierre is thinking as he smokes his Gauloise and watches the smoke curl and remembers the morning that I told him that I was pregnant. I stood in his small bathtub and my face felt hot. I'm going to buy cigarettes, he said, and he walked in after a while to say that he had called his mother.

What did she say? I asked. I was dry and sitting on his bed among the rumpled sheets. He dipped his cigarette into the grey pool of the ashtray.

Maman? She wanted to know if you were upset. I told her no.

So?

So? If you're happy, she's happy. You know her. She's always happy to have another baby in the family.

What about you? I ask. Aren't you happy?

I, in life, want a daughter so badly that I spend the many months of pregnancy looking for the perfect name for a boy. I want the boy to have the Jewish names Abraham or Jacob, but Pierre laughs hard at the sound of Abraham in French. We sit on the cool sand and Pierre cups his palms and drips sand across his bare feet.

He would be ridiculed, the poor boy, he laughs. *Abrahm! Abrahm!*

He throws a burst of sand into the air.

Well, then, I say. What about Isaac?

Isaac! Isaac! Why not Moses? He twists it into the French name, *Moise.* Why not *Moise!* Ha! Ha!

That's a fine name, I say, sniffing. I draw a letter M in the sand.

Moise! He gurgles in the back of his throat. I hobble toward the water with the briny air and bright cold sky and I squat down, looking away from him. On this beach I am always writing this story in my head about the pregnant girl who liked, as she grew rounder, to sit near the water that was wrapped around the globe just as she was wrapped around the child who swam inside her. I rub a clear patch in the sand and I draw another M. Then I snake the ends of the letter around above its two peaks.

Moise! laughs Pierre from behind. He stands, pressing against my bent back with his thighs. Why not God? Why not *le bon Dieu* himself?

I have a right to know, my mother says. She holds up one palm.

Why now? I ask. Why do you want to know now?

Because. Because he was my husband for twenty-seven years.

What difference can it make now?

Her face splinters and her lips stretch out.

Some of it is true. But it isn't finished. It's a story, Mom.

What about this? she asks. She turns the page.

On the page the father and the daughter ride a bus which rocks and plummets across the continent and north, north to their home where the mother waits for them, and now as the bus rocks around a curve and its coiled springs gasp he asks the daughter to sit on his lap.

Why? I don't want to, she says.

God, you're becoming such a bitch, he says. I don't even know if I can love you anymore.

She shrugs. A hot tear drips from her cheek to the window pane. She watches it drip and flatten and disappear where air vents stripe the cool sill. Why can't you, she wants to say. Why can't you love me? The words are like stones in her mouth. Finally she climbs onto his knees and sits, leaning into the seat ahead. He pulls her closer.

I want us to know each other better, he says. Can you feel me growing?

What?

Can you feel me growing?

No.

That part is true, I say. Well, almost.

The bastard, she says.

I tried to tell you.

You did? When did you try to tell me?

I said to you, Can't you tell your husband to keep his hands from between my legs.

You said that? Those words?

Yes. Yes.

When I said that, she was standing over the washing machine, her head bent, her hands reaching into its flecked bowl. She turned to look at me. Her eyes were flat and dark. They were not the eyes of my mother at all.

What did I say? she asks.

You said, you said, He wouldn't do it if you didn't fawn on him.

I said that?

I think to explain how a person can use words without understanding but then she says, I would have had to divorce him, and I wasn't prepared to do that yet.

She waves little fists. I want to kill him! she cries. I just want to kill him!

Behind her a dark chair hugs the wall. The bed is narrow. She has slept here one night, two nights, looking for me in Paris while Pierre and I have slept at his mother's house by the sea, walked along beaches, thought about names. In this room she has written notes to me and then walked down the broad boulevard and taped them to our door. Looking for you, been here two days, she writes. Then she returns to her hotel room and she rifles through the pages of my story and she—what does she do? She clutches the skin of her throat. She slides under the stiff grey blanket and warms her hands between her thighs. She shuts her eyes. She wonders how often they wash these bedclothes and whether or not she will catch fleas. She does not like the French with their unwashed bodies. As the days pass and I still don't come for her she begins to feel, she says, as though something is terribly wrong. Then Pierre and I drive up to his door on Sunday afternoon and he hands me the note. We walk quickly to the hotel. Pierre speaks to the dark man behind the desk. I sit on an armchair. There is sand in my shoes and one broken shell in the pocket of my full-bellied dress. I smell of the ocean. My mother spills from the elevator.

My daughter, she says, I have spent two days looking for you. I was about to call the police.

Pierre, this is my mother.

That is what I have thought, he says. When he speaks English his voice is like gravel.

Welcome to France, he says.

What do you want to do? I ask.

I finally found you, she says. I don't care what we do.

Would you like to see the *Tour Eiffel?* Pierre asks.

I don't care what we do.

We can go to Luxembourg, he says.

Fine with me, she says. So we walk along the narrow *trottoir* again to his building, and he opens the car door for her. I sit in the back.

Look, I say, when we pass through the Porte d'Orleans. Now we're really in Paris.

I've never found Paris to be a terribly pleasant city, she says. The French in general are not a terribly pleasant people.

Pierre, hunched over the steering wheel, snorts and whips his hair off his face and his brown eyes fill the mirror.

You do not want your daughter to marry a French man?
Are you going to marry her?
No.
Good.

Pierre decides that my mother wants to see the Eiffel Tower after all. It is very popular with tourists, he says with a laugh. So we park the car and walk past the green lawns and we go right up inside the Eiffel Tower and out into the wind. Pierre points monuments out to us: That is Montmartre, where are the artists, he says, and that is Sainte-Chapelle. The wind blows my hair into my face and across Pierre's cheek and he puts his arm around my shoulder and I smile at my mother as if she were taking our photograph.

I think you are doing something very wrong, she says. Both of you. Pierre brushes his cold lips against my cheek. We walk a few times around the steel tower but I cannot possibly, now, describe the city stretched out before us, the red mansards and stovepipe chimneys and white cathedrals. The truth is that in those months and years I only see the rooms and beds of our life and perhaps the view from each of our clouded windows—a parking lot, a goat tethered beyond it. We sleep each night naked on his mattress on the floor, in his rumpled sheets, surrounded by our lives, and behind us rises a mural of ocean and sand and blades of bright grass, a bright, bright beach. That evening my mother says to Pierre, How do you feel about this? How do you feel about having a child now?

How do I feel. Ha ha. It is all right by me.

I have some responsibility, she says. This child would be my grand-child and I have a responsibility, not just to you. Have you thought about what you would be doing to this child?

Will be, I say. Will be your grandchild. She knocks her wine glass over. He leaps to sponge up the spreading red stain. She watches him and she begins to weep. Now she is weeping still through the dim panicked air.

I want to know whether or not you and your father have fornicated, she says.

Mom! No!

Do you promise me?

Of course, I say. God. Then I smile as if she will understand that the verb, fornicate, is a good joke.

Don't you see? You're doing this to get back at me, she says. You're doing this out of anger at me.

No.

Yes, yes. Because I didn't help you, you're ruining your life.

I cross to the window and throw open the curtain and twist up the knob and push out the *volet* and call down to Pierre, *J'arrive.*

I have to go now, I say. He's waiting for me.

He can wait.

I really have to go now.

Why? she cries. Why are you doing this?

We walk home, Pierre walking silently ahead of me on the narrow *trottoir.*

What did she want? he asks.

In the morning we leaf through a book of names. We start at the beginning of the alphabet: Alain, Albert, Alfred, and we laugh at some of the names and some of the names make only Pierre laugh (Clovis) and some of the names make only me laugh (Bertrand, Nathan). We go through many letters of the alphabet and although I will never know what Pierre is thinking, so that when he leaves me in three years I am very surprised, I know nonetheless even now, today, the spry hairs which curl above his brown nipples and the tobacco smell of his skin. I also know that he is growing a beard to match my belly. By the time we have chosen the boy's name, Simon, his father Pierre wears a great dark beard like an anarchist. By this time also I make weekly, hulking visits to the public clinic where I wait with other foreigners for the nurses and the doctor to examine me. They ask me to spread my legs and the doctor, a man, slides his sheathed hand up inside me and with the other hand on my belly he pushes down until I wince. *C'est parfait,* he says. His glove, as he removes it carefully, is coated in white clouds of semen and my own viscous secretions and afterwards, walking home, I feel the warm rush of his lubricants into my underpants. All of my underpants are stained like this now. I wash them out and hang them, still yellowed, from Pierre's shower stall.

When I waddle past the hotel where my mother stayed I think of her still in her hotel room, where I have left her. And although I have taken the story from her she is still holding it out to me. Why are you doing this? she calls.

What's that? asks Pierre.
It's a story.
Where did you get it?
She gave it to me.
What is it about?
My father.
Can I read it?
It's not finished yet.

In the story, in New Jersey again, the daughter and the father argue at the dinner table and when she heads for the stairs he kicks her hard in the back, so that she falls and scrambles to look at him. Then she walks down the stairs to the bathroom and she cuts the skin of her forehead in two places, like horns. He walks into her room when she is dabbing the trickles of blood with a tissue and his face changes when he sees her. Oh, he says. He takes a step forward.
But I plan to change all this.

When I go into labor I climb the stairs of the hospital. I climb the six long flights of stairs and then I turn around and walk down to the bottom of the stairwell and I turn around and climb again. I climb and climb. Are you sure you aren't tired? Pierre asks.

No, I say, I could not ever be tired.

When they force me to a room and into a bed, I wait until they leave and then I slide my feet to the floor and walk in slow circles around, around. When the pains grow sharp I touch the cool, white wall with one insistent fingertip. I spread my legs and step a bear dance, a kind of bear dance and I hear myself saying through gruff lips, Open, open. Later I pant and pant and the nurse says, Look at her! She is wild!

I'm wild! I cry.

I look up and yank hard on Pierre's beard.

I feel sick, he says.

The doctor tries to slide his hand inside me so I kick him in his soft stomach, hard. I have to push, I have to push, I say. He threatens to put me to sleep and only then do I let him touch me. Finally he nods and I push once; I push a second time and its big wet head pokes through. *Ho la la,* croons Pierre, it pokes through. Through the membranes and blood they spy the swollen genital fold and say, It's a girl, and I say: Pierre, Pierre, it's a girl, a girl—my mother will be so happy.

Her name is Sarah, I tell them. I name her Sarah after a Dylan song about a man and his wife whom he has left, and the children as he recalls them, playing on the bright beaches of their childhoods. Sarah, Sarah, he sings. Loving you is the one thing I'll never regret.

At the day care center at the end of one year, the teachers say to me: It's better now. She isn't so unhappy. At first we were going to tell you, because it was so sad to watch. But now it's all right. And this seems true to me now: that after Pierre leaves us she is very sad and then she is all right. People give her nicknames and each nickname tells a short, short story. When we are still in France, they call her *Sarouille.* By now we have all left the broad boulevard on the outskirts of Paris although in my mind my mother still waits there for my answer. She is waiting for me even when I walk into the day care center and Sarah, who sits, hunched, on the low bench around a tree, looks up and her face bursts into life. She ducks her head, smiling gently to herself. I push her stroller down the street in this other city where we live now. I push her the long way around the *centre-ville,* looking away from the cafe windows behind which I think that Pierre and his girlfriend sit and talk. I want them to notice us as we wheel by on our way home.

We live in a series of rooms and beds high up above this last city, Nantes; from our last, round rooms I hold her up to the window and we can see the entire Place Graslin, the Opera and the statues of the Muses on its roof and their mother, Memory. In fiction this won't do at all, I know, but in life there she actually stands, white and solemn and symbolic. And I know something more, already, about metaphor, that first, primitive definition of self. Because at first, in this round room, Sarah will only sleep in my bed. She falls asleep only if I let her shove her feet between my thighs and when she stretches out her toes, I think with despair that she is trying to climb back inside. I pull the sheet between my legs then so that her toes claw rhythmically only at the sheet, cool and bunched. And she comes to love this feel of soft cotton. She makes me tie a knot in a pillow case and she tucks this under the covers, down between her ankles. Then she reaches down and pulls it up and wets it with her lips and slides it down again. Then she names it. She names it her *doh-doh,* after the verb, *dormir.* Sometimes we lose it in a corner of the room and she cries out, *Où est mon doh-doh? Où est mon doh-doh?* Sometimes I make her let me wash it, and then she squats and wraps her hands around her knees and watches as I wring out the pillow case and drape it across the small electric heater that hisses and glows. Then she trails around the room, restless and unpleasant, until I tie the knot again and hand the doh-doh to her, almost dry.

Why are you doing this? my mother calls. She goes on calling to me even after we fly back to New York. She calls to me every time my child cries and she rattles the pages of my story. She has made it her own story, too, in some way that I try not to think about; I notice that the ink has come off on her dark fingers.

On Saturdays, now that Sarah and I live in New York, we load our cart with great black sacks of laundry and we navigate the few blocks to the laundromat. When the weather is fine, like today, I let Sarah balance on the tilted cart and she reaches over and pats our sacks. She is four now and experienced. At the laundromat we breathe in the hot air and listen to the shouts of other mothers and fathers and their children. When a machine is free, I lift Sarah and she places the quarters in the round slots. Then we walk up and down the avenue. We stop at gum ball machines or sometimes in the coffee shop for hot dogs and milk. At the laundromat again, behind the round glass, our clothes begin to slow in their whirring around and around so that Sarah sees first a red shirt that belongs to me, then the yellow, faded flowers of her pillowcase. She is old enough to let me wash it now but we are happy to see its folds crumple and stop. We like to put it in the dryer. Then we load all of our other clothes into the dryer too. We like the sound of buttons slapping on its walls. Sarah kicks her heels against her chair. She watches the other children. I watch the other women and their men and once, one Saturday, a tall man wanders in and tends to his own small load with such careless grace that every Saturday for a while I think that perhaps he will return at that same hour. When our clothes are clean and dry, we fold them together on the long wood table. We are always surprised to find which stains have been removed and which have not. There does not seem to be any logic to it. I am still trying to fold shirt sleeves the way my mother could, and Sarah is learning to fold two socks together. We fold everything. Then we stack our sacks again, carefully, the doh-doh tucked on top of them, and we walk out with our heavy cart and we go home.

At home I sit on my bed and make piles of clothes. Sarah rides by on her red truck. She has loaded the back of her truck with her belongings: a bear, a pillow, a box of raisins. She is on her way somewhere.

Hello, she says, Excuse me. How do I drive to First Street?

Turn left at the table, I say. She scoots around the corner and she looks up at me. Her eyes shine bright blue from this distance. She reaches behind her and pats her bundle.

Is that all? she asks.

No, I say. This is a one-way street. You'll have to drive around the table again. There's no parking over here anymore.

There's no more parking?

Not over here.

So she drives around the table and when she reaches the door to the hall she looks back.

You made it, I say. That's First Street.

Later I fill her drawers. Because she has missed her nap today, she lies down and smells her laundered doh-doh and watches me. If I am lucky today she will fall asleep like this, and I will sit on my bed in the other room and look through the curtains at the street below. Then, although I have always been stronger on character than on plot, I will plan for our future. I will say that in years to come I am a teacher and she is a student in the same school and when we feel like it, we eat our lunch together. My salary will permit me to buy her fresh, bright overalls and even some dresses with lace which she will only occasionally agree to wear. We will meet in the cafeteria and she will slip her hand into mine and I will bend to pull up her white socks from around her ankles and both of her socks will match. At lunch she will stare and smile at a man who resembles the man from the laundromat and he will say, What a pretty little girl you are, and she will say, I'm not allowed to talk to strangers. The man and I will laugh about that. We will also agree to meet for lunch another day and then we will marry. In the luxuriousness of our union we will shower her, Sarah, with gifts, with clean, bright clothing and toys and trips to the sea, and names. We will call her Sarah-Bearah, and Boo, and Molly or Molly-coddle, and even sometimes Louise for no reason at all, so that when she is almost a woman suddenly she will turn around at the water's edge, on this bright beach where we have taken her, and with the wind whipping her hair and her blue eyes flashing, she will say to me, her mother, who chose with such care. Why don't you ever call me by my own name? If you didn't like it, you shouldn't have picked it.

Then perhaps the telephone will ring and my mother will say, Hello daughter. You have a hard life. Are you ever sorry?

Am I ever sorry? That is not a question. Mom, what kind of question is that?

Or I will say nothing and look around this room while silence crosses the telephone wire. In this last room I have a bed and the small, round table where we eat and in the corner an old desk, like a schoolchild's desk, where I have put my typewriter and next to them the black trunk which we brought home with us from France. I remember that I have yet to revise my own story, that old one. But now I have more questions. Such as:

How can it be that this father turns so suddenly into a villain?

Would he really use words like bitch?

Wouldn't he worry, on the bus ride, about the other passengers?

And who is he? I have left out so much. I have left out the fact that he is a physicist who has always tried to teach his daughter about the world. He has struggled for many years to find a new language to describe it. Perhaps he has gotten all tangled up in language, so that when he tells his daughter that he wants to carry her to bed and rock her back and forth, gently, crooning the same song that his own mother once sang to him, when he tells his daughter that he doesn't want her to grow up unloved, it may be that he persuades himself of the truth of these words. He may even persuade himself that they will always sound true.

It may be that in the story, when the father has carried the daughter down to bed and is cradling her, crooning, his arm presses warm against the cotton of her underpants and she lets it. She even inches down so that his fingers touch more of the cotton. His breath catches in his throat and then he begins to hum again, slowly, softly. Again she inches down so that his hand lies, each warm finger spread flat against the cotton, pulsing.

Then her mother walks into the alcove with a pile of folded linens, and he jerks his arm away and he stands up and bends down and kissing her gently whispers, You're very brave. But she has understood this sequence of events: the mother's appearance, the father's withdrawal. Because she has understood this and because some stories seem to have inevitable and natural resolutions, she glances up and she whispers, Never again. She whispers: Never again.

In life, when I leave my mother in the hotel room, she sits on the edge of her bed and she weeps. Then after she has wept she begins to pack for her return trip to New York. She folds her clothing very carefully and she talks to herself. A fine business, she says, You ought to be ashamed. She lets her voice trail on like a broom, sweeping: a brave one, you are, she says. That is enough. You should be ashamed, a grown woman. Then she goes downstairs to pay her bill. After that she goes upstairs to her room and she lies down until morning.

When she gets home she unpacks her suitcase. She empties a bag of dirtied clothing into her hamper and she puts her hand beneath each clean, folded blouse and slides it into a white drawer. She wipes her palms. She examines her cuticles. She walks through this cool, white apartment. She turns on and off the television set. She opens the refrigerator door. She sees one can of grapefruit juice and a wrapped cheese. This is the first time that she has left and come back to this new apartment, and the return makes it seem for the first time like home.

So it is only in my own fiction that I have left her in her hotel room, waiting for me. She has cleaned the old house after the years of marriage and she has found the story where I left it for her to find, and now she has so many questions. And these years later I have come back, after all. I have come back to answer her although no word or words will quite suffice.

I want to tell you something, I say.

She is older now. Her face is fuller and her jowls hang loose. Her lips turn down at the corners. Over the years I know that she has taken my story and given it to her friends, out of her own mouth, in restaurants, with tears and vocabulary. Every now and then she calls my father on the telephone and he cries, I'm sorry. I'm sorry. How could I? Was I such a bad man?

Today, in the hotel room, the *volets* are thrown back and we can hear the sounds of a woman who squats on the stairs, scrubbing. She grunts and her big brush hisses. We step into a shaft of light. In those months of pregnancy, I remember now, the sun barely shone at all; I remember also that when spring finally arrived in Paris the rains went on, and the new leaves on the trees sagged wet and sad, everything was grey or dull-colored like wet earth. My mother's face quivers in the dim room. What should she do? What has she done? Her marriage has not been what it seemed and her divorce must now be bitter and total. She is relieved at least to find that my belly is almost flat. There is still time to change this, she thinks. At least this. She tilts her palms to the low ceiling. But why? she asks. I reach to take the story from her hands which are thin and veined. I kiss her cheek, wet and too soft like the pulp of fruit, and I touch the edges of the papers, lightly, to her still-black hair.

But why did you do it? she asks.
Oh Mom, I say, because now it's done.

~~~~

First Evidences: The Work of Young Writers in Little Magazines

Amber Vogel

These stories, first printed in the Spring 1955 and Summer 1964 issues respectively, were chosen to be reprinted in the Summer 1993 issue of *The Carolina Quarterly*, which marked the forty-fifth anniversary of this little magazine. Both stories are the work of young writers, apprentices in a tradition of apprenticeship that editors (often, themselves, apprentice editors) of *The Carolina Quarterly* have through the years maintained. Lloyd Shaw's "The Disillusioned" was written for a composition class at the University of North Carolina at Chapel Hill and submitted to the magazine by his teacher; Robert Morgan's "A Fading Light" was written, as far as he remembers now, in a creative writing class at North Carolina State University, and published later, when he was on this magazine's editorial staff. Though they are apprentice works—and at such a remove of time might seem to their authors imperfect *juvenilia*—both stories are nonetheless skillful, evocative, remarkable. In the context of this book, which is intended to explore the motivations of editors of literary magazines, these stories are remarkable for the fact that, almost thirty or forty years after they were first chosen for publication, they are still sufficiently representative of choices that fiction editors at *The Carolina Quarterly* have made over the years to be chosen again.

In 1948, the first editors of *The Carolina Quarterly* stated that "In a chaotic time such as ours, in which standards rise and fall at a moment's persuasion, the *Quarterly* gives the young writer a place where he may express himself and where he may reach an audience whom he may in some small way, benefit." In view of that bold, hopeful statement, it is gratifying to discover after forty-five years that back issues of this magazine are repositories of early work by Russell Banks and Doris Betts (published while they were students at Chapel Hill), by Wendell Berry, Rosellen Brown, and Raymond Carver, by Annie Dillard, George Garrett, and Barry Hannah, and by many other fine, young writers whose reputations were not then established widely. Indeed, when his work has not yet been printed in hard covers by Random House, and praised by *The New York Times Book Review*, and added to the syllabi of American literature courses, a little magazine's editors, who must be persuaded only by the quality of a manuscript and not by its author's fame, can offer encouragement of real worth to a young writer. It may be the only encouragement he receives for a long time; it may be the last of that sort he seeks. Larger success can draw a writer out of the small orbit of the little magazine, the editors of which are left to boast of their prescience, of their previous acquaintance. Then again, publication in a little magazine may be the particular fulfillment of a writer's ambition, which will then be redirected to other worthy goals. Robert Morgan, whose publication in *The Carolina Quarterly* in 1964 was his first anywhere, has continued to write and publish fiction and poetry and contribute his work to the magazine. His newest book, *The Hinterlands*, has been praised by *The New York Times Book Review* for its wisdom and eloquence. Until its republication in the anniversary issue, Lloyd Shaw's story marked the only appearance of his work in *The Carolina Quarterly*. After 1955 he published fiction and poetry elsewhere (including the marvelously wry short story "The Judgement of Paris" in *Spectrum* in 1967), but over time turned his attention to reviewing and academic writing.

It is probably true to say that, had they not been printed in *The Carolina Quarterly* or a similar magazine almost thirty or forty years ago, "The Disillusioned" and "A Fading Light" would not exist outside some desk drawers to the back of which sheaves of yellowing typed pages had been pushed. Such is the fate of innumerable early efforts by innumerable young writers who, growing older and wiser, come to doubt the first evidences of their talents. The choice, then, to reprint "The Disillusioned" and "A Fading Light" after so many years happily focussed editorial attention on why they had first been chosen for publication and on what their enduring value might be. Apart from extrinsic features (the mockingbird and pine of their Southern settings, the themes of race and regret revisited by their North Carolinian authors) that they share with much other fiction published in *The Carolina Quarterly*, these stories have an intrinsic quality not necessarily related to geography. To achieve this quality, evoking in the reader a recognition that some early and necessary drama of human life is being played out, seems to require of the writer not only verbal skill and keen attention, but also youth. Each story, taking place in a span of time less than a night or a day, manages carefully to describe all the essential details of its young hero's political or emotionally life that lead him, at the end, to a moment of profound darkness. A bare light bulb is turned off in a small house with a rusted tin roof, night falls on a rural road to a creek far from Asheville, and in the dark the hero, the reader knows, must feel acutely the fear and pain of *not knowing anymore* that come with the beginning of new wisdom. Perhaps it is a moment described best when the author is nineteen and not when he is twenty-nine or fifty-nine; when he can first express what he has been paying close attention to all his life; before what he can express becomes a motif polished then dulled by reconsideration and use. It is an aching moment that deserves not to be forgotten. A fine story by a young writer may be its perfect expression; the pages of a little magazine may be its perfect gallery, eventually its poignant museum.

The Disillusioned

Lloyd Shaw

It was nearing midnight when he turned off the road and started down the dusty path between the hedge and chicken-wire fences and the railroad track. The signal at the railroad crossing stopped blinking as the light of a train faded in the distance. A line of cars was turning into the chair factory parking lot. In a few minutes the whistle at the factory would blow, and a new shift would start to work. A mile away in Oak Hills the lights of the country club went off, and headlights could be seen intermittently as the cars came down the hills that made up the town's wealthiest residential section.

There was a decrepit insomnious woman sitting in her rocking chair humming spirituals on the porch of the first house in the row. Somewhere in the darkness of the rows of houses that ran parallel to the track he heard the shrill laugh of a woman and the sound of Negro jazz. The music made him wonder why there was no intermediate in his people's music, why it was either very sad or very gay.

Further down the tracks, behind a hedge entangled with honeysuckle, was his house. Its rusted tin roof dipped in a gentle angle over the walls to form the roof of a porch running the width of the house. Four posts rising from the plank porch supported the roof, and boards were nailed between them to form a rail on which sat his mother's begonia plants. Underneath the porch was the heavy black pot which his mother would wash in until the Monday before she died because she did not understand machines. She would drag the pot out to the pile of ashes that only the wind removed; build the fire to heat the water; wash the clothes in the boiling liquid with her homemade soap; and then hang them on the line between the chicken house and the hedge. On the windy days of late winter, when the trees were still bare, he could stand on the loading platform at the factory and see the clothes flapping above the hedge.

There were trees in the yard, but they were not oaks. They were chinaberry trees which dropped their shriveled waxy berries on a yard of Bermuda grass and chicken dropping.

He opened the screen door and walked across the room. In it were the reminders of religion and family that his mother was bound to and the simple furnishings she was content with. In a corner of the room he had built his study, enclosing the two open sides with curtains. When he was within the curtains he was cut off from the flypaper, dusty tintypes of his grandparents, and multicolored shawls covering the chairs, and could live vicariously the life he dreamed of. His books were there, on a polished bookshelf. Sophisticated wallpaper covered the pine wall–the wallpaper ending at the curtain–and there was a rug on the floor. His desk, which had cost him two weeks' pay, his record player, and his lamp were here. All the material symbols of the life he wanted that he could possibly obtain he had put in this corner, five feet wide and nine feet long.

He sat down at the desk and took a notebook out of a drawer. It was only on nights like this, when he could find nothing but depression in his surroundings, that he used it. He wrote swiftly. He knew that he must express somehow the difference between chinaberry and oak.

"I have been to the movies tonight and sat in the colored balcony and listened to those below laugh at the appearance and actions of the African natives in the movie, applauding when their white hero shot or knifed them. My people and I in the balcony were strangely quiet. The Africans in the movie were funny and villainous, but I felt and I think my people felt that by laughing at the natives in the movie, those below were indirectly making fun of us.

"I felt because I could not stand their laughter and because I was afraid, whether it was of them or life I do not know. I walked for hours. I looked at their homes (the wealthy ones, the important ones) and remembered how once I had thought I would be accepted there someday, and how I was going to work and work and take advantage of every opportunity until I *was* accepted. I was going to be an example of what my race could achieve, but my ambitions have become passive desires. I do not believe anyone can achieve what I want through work, because I know now that they will never accept me or any of my race. The work I am trained for they give to their sons and to the sons of their friends. To a Negro, they only give 'nigger jobs,' the kind that offers no advancement. With intelligence and education, I shall spend my life loading trucks and returning home to the railroad tracks, the chinaberry trees, and the chickens that scratch in the yard."

Laying down his journal, he looked up at the framed copies of the Declaration of Independence and the Declaration of Human Rights hanging above his desk and the faded square in the wallpaper where until six months ago had hung the Soviet Constitution of 1936–which he had taken down, though he still believed in the ideals it set forward, because the faith he once had in its proponents was gone, taking much of his optimism with it; and because it was not good for such a document to be found in a Negro's home. He had lain awake many nights trying to determine which reason was dominant, lying awake with something of the feeling he had in college after being introduced to the works of Freud, when he lay awake trying to decide what were his dominant desires.

After lighting a cigarette he walked onto the porch and looked across the tracks at the lights in the chair factory. The muffled droning of machines vied for the position of laborer's companion that the spirituals once held, and the smoke from the factories moved like an endless veil over the moon. There were no lights inside the analogous houses along the track. These were as dark as his skin, but the orange porch lights, which are supposed to keep the insects away, uncovered the darkness and the ugliness of their unpainted fronts, as the glow of his cigarette revealed what was happening to the education and culture of the whites he had acquired, revealed what he was: a black house that must stay by the railroad track under the chinaberry trees, because the smoke and dust of their trains and their factories caused the paint his people tried to use to fade and peel and without paint the house cannot be moved.

Beyond the factories where the roads became asphalt and the white homes began, there were fluorescent street lights that colored everything within their range a deep purple, but there were none to color the houses along the dirt roads.

A mockingbird, which sang far into the night like the old woman down the row, was moving in the hedge. Once when he was small, his mother had taken him to work with her one day, and the young son of the white people whom his mother cooked for showed him his birthday present, a canary in an ornate cage. So that night, without telling his mother, he trapped a mockingbird and the next day built a cage for it. Proudly, because he had captured the bird which the oldest people in the row said never slept, he took it to the home where his mother worked to show his new friend, but his white friend's mother took the bird from them and let it loose, because, she said, there was a difference between keeping a canary in a cage and keeping a mockingbird in a cage. Tearfully, he had run home and never returned.

Along the road across the tracks, a car passed, and he distinctly heard the word, Negro. Two years ago, he would have thought that they were discussing his people's plight, discussing means of helping them. But now, their voices only made him wish there was not a light in the door behind him, revealing him to them. He wondered if the people in the car were like the white girl he met in college who said with enthusiasm that his people's suppression would soon cease and the world would open up to them, and shook his hand, and left saying that she enjoyed talking with him; but then, as she went out the door, wiped her right hand on her dress, clinching it as if it was unclean.

Perhaps that was when he began to break, when he began to become as fearful of the men who talked of the Negro's great progress as he was of the Ku Klux Klan. He knew he should not be, but he could not regain his once ambitious and outspoken self. He was a cross-tie that could not lift the rail and end the sounds made by the trains that kept him from sleeping.

He backed slowly into the house closing the door quietly because he hated—or perhaps feared—sudden harsh sounds that broke the silence, and then he reached for the string controlling the bare light bulb and picked his path through the darkness to his bed, undressing without a light because in the darkness the eyes of those he feared and envied could not see him.

⌒⌒⌒

A Fading Light

Robert Morgan

Yesterday was my birthday, and as I am thinking about the party and presents I had, I am proud to be a year older. More than the rifle, or the books, or the clothes, I am proud of myself, of my age and maturity, and most of all my newfound freedom; I have discovered what it means to be in love.

Frieda and I are sitting in the creek, and I am holding her to keep her from sliding off the rock into midstream. She is afraid of the water because it is fast and cold, and if I let her go for a second she will scream and fall and splash me, and I must pull her back up beside me to keep our peace. I hold her under the shoulders and she has her hands behind her, and when I pull her closer I can feel my heart beating against her narrow back. She is soft beneath my hands and moves inside her wet blouse, and where my fingers touch her it is warm. Our feet drag in the water and make a trail of bubbles behind the rock, and its coolness belies the heat of the July air.

Now she turns to me and says, "I'm falling," and she pulls and I let her go, and she hits the water with a splash that wets both me and her, and the sun makes the drops in her hair sparkle like diamonds. She screams, "I hate you; you're mean like Svengali," and she climbs back up out of the water and I pull her against my lap. Touching her now I am almost as wet as she, but the dampness is welcome, and we sit and I can feel her breathing.

From on top the rock we can see beyond the bank to the pasture, and beyond that the wire fence and then the end of the corn rows. The stalks and leaves are tall and dark green because of the heavy rains in the spring, and now they are sprouting their first July silks and moving slightly in the late morning breeze. We can see the white pines on the hill beyond the corn, and beyond them Old Pinnacle rises dark and hazy against the sky. The air between shimmers with heat, and we can feel the warm air moving across the pasture and drying our arms and faces.

"Last week Daddy said we're going to move to Asheville to be closer to his new job," Frieda says. I am looking down the stream to where the maples are and the picnic tables and the rock grill and I say, "No, you told me that before last year and then you didn't move, and now I don't believe you." She is about to slide again and I hold tighter, and I put my chin on her shoulder and can feel the blood pushing in and out on her neck. "It's true," she says, "Daddy told me again last night that we are going to live with Grandmother until our new house is finished." She has lived in the white house beyond the church since I was four, and except at school she is my only companion.

Frieda is darker than I am. I have been outside all summer and my hair is bleached by the sun like straw, but my skin will not tan. Frieda's hair is short and black like a pony's mane, and soft, and her skin is brown and smooth. Her white blouse makes her look even darker, and I used to hate her because she tanned well without making freckles. Last summer I told her she looked like a Melungeon and she cried, and I said I would never say it again. I am in love with her skin; it is soft and tan like I imagine the underside of fawnleather, and she has a brown mole beside her navel which we call a bullet wound when we play cowboy. Last fall my Dad killed a deer and had the hide tanned to make me a jacket. When I got it for Christmas I sat for hours and rubbed its leather against my face, but even it is not as soft as Frieda's skin. She says she is stronger then I am because she has more hair on her legs, and on her arms is a fuzz as soft and limp as milkweed whiskers. I put my face against her hair and my ear against her ear and we laugh, and she says, "Let's go finish building the pond."

We wade up the creek a hundred feet to the mouth of the branch and I hold Frieda by the waist to keep her from sliding on the mossy rocks. There are trees over the creek where the branch runs out, and it is dark and cool after coming out of the sunlight. There is the swish of a limb over our heads and a thin snake falls into the water and Frieda screams and grabs my shoulder, and I must tell her for the hundredth time that water snakes are harmless.

Last week we started a dam on the branch a few feet from where it runs into the creek and today we will finish it. It is made of sticks and rocks and mud which we have carried with our hands, and this time we hope to make it permanent. Every summer for the past three years we have built a pond here and every time it has washed away when the first rain came. Now we have a hoe that I took from the barn, and Frieda carries the sticks and piles them against the line of rocks across the branch and I rake mud against them to make it watertight.

In thirty minutes we have built it over a foot high, and we stop and take off our clothes to play. Lying flat on the bottom of the little pond I can submerge my head and I play that I am drowned. I can hear Frieda crying and she hits my back with the hoe handle to see if I am alive. The water is muddy and it is in my eyes and ears and I almost strangle, and then I get up. She is gone, and is sitting under the laurels on the bank, and I would go to her, but the water is beginning to run over the dam. Already the trickle has washed a crack in the dirt, and I grab the hoe and furiously pull dirt from below the dam to fill it. But it is too late because the stream becomes wider and the sticks and dirt give way and in a few minutes nothing is left of the dam but the row of rocks. I go over and sit on the bank beside Frieda and I put my arm around her shoulders, but she pulls away because I am still muddy. We sit for several minutes, and finally she looks up and I can see her eyes are blue and shiny where she has been crying. I look at her and her lips are twisted, and then she begins to laugh. "You *do* look like Svengali," she says, "with your face muddy and your hair wet and sticking up." I go wash in the creek and she rinses the mud out of her green shorts, and we put on our clothes. They are still wet from the splashing, and we wade back down the creek and lie in the grass by the picnic tables.

We lie on our backs and look straight up, and the maples are above us on one side, and the sky, and the fence and pasture on the other. Then we lie with our eyes closed and the sun looks red through our eyelids. Her head lies on my arm and our legs are entangled, and as always when she lies in the sun, she talks:

"This year I won't be here when the leaves fall," she says, "and we can't slide down the mountain on a board into the piles of pine needles together." She speaks as she thinks, and she rambles on and on about the winter and snow, and about waiting on the school bus on cold mornings when we have to dance around the mailboxes to keep our feet warm. She will be in the second grade this year and I will be in the fourth, and she talks about how I will be alone now since no one else lives on this part of Willow Creek. "That's alright," I say, "because Dad says I can use the .22 this fall and go squirrel hunting with him on Old Pinnacle." I know she is teasing me and I laugh, and she doesn't say anything more.

Her forehead is damp with perspiration and she is beginning to doze. I wait until I know she is asleep and I slide my arm out from under her head because it is becoming numb. There are patterns in my arm where the grass blades have pressed against the skin. The ground is warm, and I move my face away from the sun so that her hair is in my eyes and I can feel the softness of her neck and chin.

She awakens me and says that our clothes are dry and that it is lunch time, and we fasten our shorts and shirts and I am sunburned, but she does not seem to notice. We run along the edge of the pasture toward the field, and the plowed ground at the end of the corn rows is hot and soft and burns our feet when we sink into it. The Junebugs buzz out of the grass and off the leaves and silks and I would catch one if I had time.

Above the corn is the road, and we are dazed from the sleep and sudden running. Everything looks white and flat and faraway for a few seconds, the road, and trees, and even the mountain beyond. The whitepines are dull and motionless in the bright light. It seems to me that it's later than noon and I know that Dad will be angry.

Frieda turns toward her house which is a quarter of a mile down the road past the church, and I take the shortcut home and run up the bank through the pines. She calls something after me, but I do not stop because it is late and I have promised Dad that I would tie bean strings in the bottom this afternoon.

It is supper time and Dad is sitting across the table watching me; I know something is on his mind by the way he slowly butters the cornbread and waits as if he is about to say something. I worked hard all afternoon to make up for being late and he was pleased. I wonder what he is going to say.

"Troy, have you seen the new hoe lately? I have looked all over the barn and tool shed and can't find it; it was brand new."

He is waiting for an answer, but I go on eating, trying to think what to say. It occurs to me that he will find it sooner or later all rusted and lying somewhere on the creek bank no matter where we hide it, so now I tell him, "Frieda and I thought it would be alright if we borrowed it to build a pond on the branch." He is mad because he puts the bread down and says, "You bring it back this very evening before it gets all rusty and broke." We eat again in silence and I wish now I hadn't taken the hoe at all. The road to the creek goes through the pines and is dark and spooky, and I am afraid to walk it alone. I am going to beg him to let me wait and get it tomorrow, but he is already speaking:

"I guess you'll miss your old buddy Frieda," he says. I ask him why he says that, and he says, "Didn't you know that they were going to move, and that her father took them over to Asheville this afternoon to stay with her grandmother until their house is finished?"

It is dark on the road to the creek, and I stop by the fence and look across the pasture. The katydids are singing in the trees down by the creek, and only the maples are outlined against the sky. Below them I can see the white cement picnic tables reclining like two ghosts in the darkness. I walk along the fence and smell the damp watersmell and it makes me think of Frieda. The lights are out in the house down the road, and I walk toward the trees where the branch runs out. I will probably never see her again. Something scrambles in the bushes ahead and I wonder if it is a snake, or a partridge, or maybe a rabbit. I listen, but it does not come again, and I stop by the edge of the gully to pee.

The night air is cool and I can feel my sunburn under my shirt; I wonder if I will ever tan. Toward the east there is a glow in the sky which Dad once told me was Asheville. It looks like a light behind the mountain, or a sun coming up from the other side of the world, and I wonder if I will ever go there. Around me the katydids are now chanting full blast and I can hardly think; according to the saying it means that summer is half over.

Fiction in Disguise(s)

Sonia Raiziss

What to make of this? The writer who submitted three successive "pieces" described the material as fiction. And that is how we were beguiled into viewing the work–which we published with alacrity. But the format, the style, the recalcitrant language, its speed and backtracking, the argumentative nature were stubbornly contrary to the rubric under which they appeared. The would-be fiction had no visible plot (or even the shadow of one); the characters consisted ostensibly, in one instance, of interrogator and witness (professor and student). In the course of the question/answer dialogue, a kind of conversational plot dialogue emerged–that of the unwilling emotions and half-hidden happenings in the life and mind of the student revealing herself, *malgré lui,* in the process of taking an oral exam. Here is an example of her erratic responses to a direct question, or any ordinary quotidian contact.

1. Why did you take this course?

You know how in *Erosion,* Jorie Graham's words crumble and slide down the poem, making an ant hill at the bottom there? The way in *Three Poems* Ashbery leaves a thin slick of water on concrete? The way "The Burning House" feels like "13 Ways" with the center missing? Well, it doesn't matter. There was no vocabulary to talk about this. I slithered into art reviewing in search of a language that might describe three-dimensional surfaces in contemporary American poems. And fiction.

If not a story, then what? Certainly not an expository exercise, hardly a memoir, an unlikely prose poem (though the style and passion had elements of that roving form). Perhaps pages of a diary now allowed out into the indiscreet world: mordant memories of a soul's adventures. But fiction, of course, has had a most mixed and intractable history, especially in modern and post-modern times. In our day, the French novelists—Natalie Sarraute, Alain Robbe-Grillet—took a brisk, brave turn off the well-traveled road of the story/novel mission: telling a tale, but more explicitly exposing the interior characters in their experimental trackless situations. These writers and their colleagues clustered as a school that reached a plateau and left visible options to imitate or disregard them.

But the "fiction" in question follows no apparent school or recognizable influence which is easily labeled. I was troubled that the work eluded my identification and yet invited my acceptance of its selfhood as the author unreservedly presented it. This was something well off the beaten track: intelligent, even intellectual (though not off-putting), certainly original in its content, approach, development. . . Not a story at first encounter. So what? Call it what you will: it catches your interest. Not a page-turner in the common book-review terminology, but a mind-turner.

Elizabeth McBride had offered us three such "fictions." Each time, the shape or shapelessness of the form (if you could apply that term) played a variation on the wild, personal, wholly off-beat view of this writer's fulminations regarding her contacts with life: father, husband, friend, sexual partner, scholarly mentor—each psychological stumbling block, passing or profound experience.

Not only did this writer produce a saucy variation on fiction, but she seemed to challenge the very notion of that form, any configuration that would willingly lie down in a Procrustean bed. The history of fiction covers the familiar novel (from novella to trilogy, etc.), narrows from a Borges "ficcion" to Cervantes's adventures, vacillates from the vulnerable Raymond Carver's "minimalism" to *Ulysses*, that classic/modern "stream of consciousness" which encompasses the vagaries of a lifetime. Parables, fables, legends, lies . . . all are fiction. The word bewilders. Formulaic impositions merely restrict.

Are McBride's pieces fictions then, exposition, expostulation in mad paragraphs, thesis, antithesis (sometimes in question/answer minuet), simultaneous declarations of love and hate, experimental avowals of internal turmoil, struggling to be expressed, undressed—cluttered field of personal implosions?

Fiction, so-called, has been in a tentative, innumerable state since it first acquired its elastic label. Writers themselves eschew markers to direct the critic or reader. Fiction finds ways to lurch around corners, wear masks. Distinctions blur, standards topple, mirrors cheat . . . We accept cross-breeding, tolerate stylistic *ménages-à-trois*.

Another piece is a Proustian effort in personal recall, as idiosyncratic as the first and third of her contributions. This is perhaps an arbitrary, equivocal pursuit. Maybe there is an area of prose that means to be nameless, so elusive that it is vain to stalk it, slap a color on its seachange skin. Anyone is welcome to restrict or expand so recalcitrant a life: that lovely and startling chameleon.

Of the three fictions we have to date published by McBride, I chose the second entry by this maverick writer (poet and columnist for *ArtScene*). She has entertained us in the deepest, widest sense, leading us into her realm: personal, worldly, otherworldly, style-rich, natural—mysterious and self-contained as a rain forest.

Chelsea plays no favorites stylistically as to author or material. Apart from solicited work, the eventual choices lean obviously in the direction of the general character of the issue or of a section we plan to stress. Sometimes it is simply the striking appeal of the writer's self. In this case, both the surprising, even agreeably disconcerting, manner and contents won us over in the end. I personally was at once captivated by the expressive language of a singular voice that did not hesitate to challenge the conventions.

✣✣✣

Final Exam: History of Art 321
Elizabeth McBride

1. Why did you take this course?

You know how in *Erosion,* Jorie Graham's words crumble and slide down the poem, making an ant hill at the bottom there? The way in *Three Poems* Ashbery leaves a thin slick of water on concrete? The way "The Burning House" feels like "13 Ways" with the center missing? Well, it doesn't matter. There was no vocabulary to talk about this. I slithered into art reviewing in search of a language that might describe three-dimensional surfaces in contemporary American poems. And fiction. Only to find I had disappeared. Just think: to discover the subtle rockings of *Houseboat Days,* identify the swells in the water, use a Marshallese navigation chart made of woven palm leaves to navigate from Bikini to Kwajalein. I saw one of these in the Primitive Modern exhibit, decorated with cowrie shells. We are speaking of Metaphorical Structure, and Ashbery, the most impoverished master, starved for a window into a true passion. I wanted to take notes. I wanted to see slides. I hoped the professor could zero in on my slack thoughts, gifting me with a sound base for the flighty superstructure of my intellectual life. I wanted to knock some of the hard out of my head. I had another reason to take this class. That was my grief. I had heard that it wasn't about art, it was about the professor, who was a latter-day shaman, and that it would feel religious. As a reincarnated pre-Bronze Age fertility goddess, I'm more at home with Marxist lingo than with Derrida. The professor keeps the room kind of dark, but he's probably just a reincarnated pre-Bronze Age cave artist. It's okay because I wanted to make amends, I wanted to pray.

2. What is Modernism?

If there's no skywriting, why would we want to look up at the sky? With Modernism the artist could play with the symbols at will. Because if you buy the concept of a secular world, it's naive to accept the existence of a transcendent being. At its best, Modernism was pure, stingy, expressive, private, a public display, an elegant blueprint of artistic secrets. At its worst, it kicked us out and sealed the windows behind us. Purity's okay, I guess, Kant liked it, but people got tired of playing hide and seek, searching for something the artist misplaced on some other canvas. Or wiped off. Or left in the tube of paint. It wouldn't be fair to envision only harsh puritanical angles, fingerprints on the stainless steel, because occasionally Modernism pushed itself to a lyric, emotional stance, a marriage of sensuousness and rationalism. (Goldberger on Mendelsohn's buildings.) It might be true that Modernism rendered the object makers as privileged, leading indirectly to the commodification it tried to protest, but it was an act of democracy, not of elitism, which propelled Yves Klein out of the window. Because it was photographed, mechanically reproduced, although there is no difference anymore. (It was an act of fate which propelled Maria out of the car to her death.) "You can make people swallow anything," said Duchamp. "That's what happened." If he had put horse manure on the canvas, said some cynic in *Artforum*, we would have to accept it. The Modernists fostered the myth of the autonomy of the work when everyone knows it cannot hang itself on the wall. I was reading Kant last night, my husband was lying beside me reading *The Skeptical Inquirer,* sucking erotically on my little finger and biting my nail for me. He can bite my nails in such a smooth arc that I don't need emery boards. Then he got frisky. "I'm busy," I said. "You're doing my nails. Besides, I know you're a fan of Klein blue, but how, in this runaway time warp, can we halt the process of commodification and fetishism which drives you to string blue paper clips around my neck when you want to make love to me?" "Color," he said, "is the most spiritual of all qualities."

3. Discuss: Is Modernism Dead?

Is this a trick question? The name of the book is *Has Modernism Failed?* It's by Suzi Gablik, and she does indeed think it's dead. If your idea of a work of art, like Gablik's, is when a Hasidic Jew shakes hands with all the Brooklyn sanitation workers, that's fine, but I've avoided taking the garbage out my entire life and I don't want to get involved with that. Besides, aside from color, odor, texture, and weight, shit and garbage are all the same.

4. Define Conceptual Art.

Mythic structures carry with them a certain divine promise. And so we are saturated with content, we refuse to look at it, we try to scream it out of existence. (Maria's body.) Conceptual art relates to values of wit and critical insight, I was thinking this morning, gluing my eyebrows on, sliding the water slide of life. I had such a thought. It went like this: "The values of wit and critical insight," I thought. But I would just like to break open the sanctum sanctorum by forcing the realization of the relativity of certain aesthetic feelings. Habits arise. Subjects, verbs, objects, dependent clauses. There could be no accounting, however, and the readymades were designed to be unaccountable. Even Duchamp said, "It's very difficult to choose an object, because, at the end of 15 days, you begin to like it or hate it." Duchamp was a man of many words which, when accounted for, amounted to silence. I was still reading Kant–it takes a while–and my husband was reading *Quantum Electrodynamics* (by Feynman) and he said to me, "Why you read that corn flake Kant is beyond me; he didn't know diddley-squat about mathematics; he can't even think straight." "Kant had a notion," I said, "of a sense of taste, through which we respond to art." "I'll show you a sense of taste," he said. "I have a headache," I said.

5. Discuss content, which you mentioned above rather cavalierly.

I didn't know you were listening. Sometimes I wonder. Content arises from contradictions between levels of content. A woman loves her child.

She neglects to buckle her into her seatbelt. The very sort of contradiction which creates content, weight, gravity, earth, the sort of contradiction which leads down a curved gravel path to the tiny child-sized grave. My sister was hard, jerky, constantly shaking, like a Tinguely machine drawing a picture. My parents were stiff and silent and ripe with grief. My older brother could not be stopped from muttering "seatbelt, seatbelt." He thought he was still in his helicopter in Vietnam. When the undertaker embalmed Maria, the fluid missed a stretch of her leg and she was soft there, lying still in the small coffin. Go ahead, it's all right, my sister said, pick her up if you want, and I picked her up and held her and felt her leg and thought that just there she felt as she had when she was alive. At her grave we played a tape of Mozart's Piano Concerto #17 in G Major, released twenty-five colored balloons filled with helium and watched Maria climb the sky. When I think about her I think of her black eyes, how they opened and closed like a doll's, how soft her hair was, and how, when my father tickled her, she collapsed on the rug laughing.

6. How many copies of Duchamp's fountain are there?

Fortunately, Edward Ball and Robert Knafo (writing in *Artforum*) have clarified this situation. In Spring of 1917, Walter Arensberg of Boston and New York was said by Marcel Duchamp and other witnesses to have purchased a porcelain urinal at the J. L. Mott Iron Works, New York. Then the fun started. New York, 1941, Duchamp produces twenty-five replicas and then ninety more for *The Box in a Valise*. New York, 1951, Sidney Janis commissions the first full-sized simulacrum for his *Challenge and Defy* exhibition. This was before Jean Baudrillard published *Simulations*. Then, in Paris in 1953, a second full-sized fountain. We now have one hundred and seventeen fountains, but the original has disappeared. Sixty more versions in Paris, one more in Stockholm, one hundred more in Paris/Milan if you can visualize that, and then in 1964 in New York, two hundred and fifty lithographs. In October 1964, a copy or two and the fountain becomes a generic form. Duchamp declares the object as immaterial, lost to inscription, and his last reflections disclose nothing about the Byzantine teleology of the vanished object. Art has a way of undermining aesthetic theories, but we are involved in ordinary causality here. You do not fasten the seatbelt, you lose the child. The car crashes, the door opens, Maria is thrown into the night. In life, there is no simulacrum. My husband was reading the book reviews in his ACM, then he looked up at me and saw I was sad. "There is only one thing to do," he said, wanting to cheer me up, knowing how desperate I was becoming. "You must be recycled. I will reduce your body to its component parts and spread them over the earth. Think. You may end up part of a silver mine, or a single molecule on the shuttle, being propelled out into space." "Shut up," I said. "It's not me that's dead, it's Maria. You need to bite my toenails."

7. Steady. Back to the topic. Are you sure you know what this course is about?

At first I thought, just another superficial graduate-type seminar of a Marxist persuasion. The lectures were pretty, simply sparkling with little jewels, information that slips so quickly through the strings of the hammock. This course is about the professor. I think I told you that. What else would it be about? It's a metaphoric structure of the professor's mind which, I had the impression at first, was about an eighth of an inch deep and a mile across. But the central character has a set of values, so although the structure here is contemporary, the discussion circles, reentering repeatedly on a different plane. It begins as a spiral and he fills it in. What this course looks like finally is a coffee can, or a tall cylindrical building, slanted at the ends. The point, though, is not simply to build a shape, but to open the can, to take out the coffee, subject it to an examination. We're expected not only to understand what it is that we're drinking and to describe how it tastes, but, furthermore, to articulate how we came to that decision, and what other decisions we could have made. It's easy to write a review of the coffee because taste is, after all, according to Kant, in some way universal, so if we all agree that it's good, it's good.

8. Have you read the reading?

As of this moment I have read the Kant. My husband says that was a foolish act. It will contaminate me like nuclear waste. I've read the Burke although the sublime and I have a previous history. I've read the yellow book. I'm reading the Kinko packets. The yellow book provides a critical stress: I would never have felt at home without stress. Also I would never have realized that abstract expressionism was an arm of the cold war. Living in Europe in 1957, wishing like all the other fourteen-year-old female dependents of the American Armed Forces that I was Priscilla, I thought Elvis Presley had handled that. This reading has made me think about Marxism in a more disciplined way than when I was actually studying Marx. Everybody's the same: give me a small country, I'd probably take Central America and manufacture glassine bags.

9. So right at this moment. Where do you stand?

On the scaffold. My language has gotten a little silly and slack. I need to tighten the cord but it's around my neck, I suspect.

10. What do you think of the class?

I'm going to assume that you're asking me to take a little phenomenological tour here. The students revolt me. They are rude and they smoke too much and it irritates me when they talk or leave the room when the professor's talking, although he doesn't seem to mind, and the seats are comfortable only for the first hour. Sometimes in his almost religious devotion to screwing our heads off and screwing them back on right, the professor talks through the break. Then when I get home I have a backache and I take a Vicodin.

11. Come on. What do you think of the class?

Right. I believe this is one of the three significant experiences of my intellectual life. The first occurred when I was a college freshman taking Physics Lab. While completing the forms for error analysis lab, it crossed my mind that physicists who must teach each other how to analyze errors must make a lot of mistakes. Until that moment I wanted to be a physics major. This was the end of my love affair with science. I started a love affair with my labbie who consequently excused me from class. The second such experience was reading *Quantum Electrodynamics* and learning that light does not always travel at the speed of light. (I sneaked the book away from my husband while he was sleeping.) My alienation from scientific disciplines increased as I realized I could never again believe anything a scientist taught me. This may be important; it may endanger my marriage. But it made me free because I no longer had to believe in death. I want to think that my niece Maria is floating brightly above us like a beam of light, aware and happy. I want to think she will return to us if I pray enough, or if I turn the lights off at night. Last night I turned off the light. My husband turned it on again. He was doing my toenails and threatened to bite off my little toe if I didn't cooperate. He has a book somewhere, I've never seen it, he calls it the *Marriage Manual*. He has it memorized; it says I'm supposed to cooperate. Like when your husband's tired you rub his back. You can imagine what follows that. "You would do that?" I said, fascinated. "You would bite off my little toe? Would you

chew it up? Would you taste it? Would you swallow it right down?" "Only
if you will wear blue," he said. "I love you in blue, you taste good in blue,
I love the feel of the blue cedar needles against the blanket we spread on
the ground, your blue blue jeans, the sight of your blue silk shirt and the
way you removed it." "Your blue bruises," I said, "when I get through
with you. If you bite my toe. The blue satin ribbon I'll choke you with."
He turned the light out and went to sleep.

12. Pick a central issue and spin a narrative.

The role of the artist in prehistoric times. The artist as mere function,
magical but not idolized, ensuring fertility, the success of the hunt, and
sharing in what is gained. This professor believes there was no such thing
as tribal art—only religious artifacts. I believe that all artifacts are religious,
that all human activity is creative, in spite of Maria's death. According to
letters in *Artforum* this professor's primitivism is romantic, expressive, and
fantasizes total escape; it has disturbing undercurrents that are grossly
authoritarian in their implications. I can identify with the idea of reaching
for the sublime, that strange cocktail of peace and excitement when all
your nerves lie down in the same direction. But ultimately I come back to
Marx. In his highest moment (in *The German Ideology*) he dreamed of a life
when men could hunt in the morning, farm in the afternoon, write poetry
by the light of the fire. I think we can get to that if Maria returns. Meanwhile I'll grind the corn, as if that were a kind of prayer. Which it was to
the Anasazi Indian tribes. As to being in service to the ruling class, there
seems to me no way that a person can step outside of his culture. We
serve our culture even when we are carrying pickets. Inclusive, emic,
organic parts of that which surrounds us. In that sense, in terms of the
cultural baggage we carry around, wear on our backs, we're all emic. If
history is really cyclic and if we may have faith in that, it is possibly true
that the world, by coming close together through media, travel and wars—
after all, think how many people in Houston are now using chopsticks and
eating Vietnamese—will suddenly magically transform into an emic
culture. The nature of such a culture might be startling. Perhaps we could
tackle population. There might be an upper limit on the number of
people who can live peacefully in an emic situation. I know in my family,
nine was too much to live peacefully in one house; in fact, before the kids
were born, just my parents were too much. Which is why the ruling class
rose from the pottery shards and the burnt wood about the time of the
Bronze Age. To put a stop to marital discord and sibling rivalry, and
transform emotion into world wars. It might be a matter of numbers as
well as a matter of surplus.

13. You haven't mentioned Hegel. The concept of Historical Progress. They're the three musketeers, remember, Kant, Hegel, and Burke.

Progress. I've always worried about the microwaves. On November 23, 1945, *The New York Times* (a popular new divinity) quoted atomic scientists as saying that nuclear fallout was not harmful. Tell that to the natives in the Marshall Islands, the former residents of Bikini, where the first bomb was dropped. Discuss it with their thyroid glands. Ask them about the radiant beaches. Remember those funny machines with the green lights we stuck our feet into in the fifties? Remember how zingy we once thought asbestos was? It's hard not to get paranoid, scared of our TV's and our microwaves, our electric can openers (I don't have one). I have a hard time believing in progress much less the general progress of history. I call myself a Marxist. But here is my dream, the vision I have: living along the Mimbres River one thousand years ago in New Mexico, which in America's case is like living before the Bronze Age, hoeing a little, grinding corn, making classic black on white Mimbres pottery, watching my small daughter play in the shallow water. I would teach her how to paint the clay. She would probably drown there or die of disease as so many did or fall off the mesa, and might come back to us as Maria. I would never know, then, that I didn't have a microwave. While I was reading the Kinko handout, my husband came into the room carrying a new book I had bought him called *Chaos*–fractals, Mandlebrot equations, those secondary metaphorical incarnations of the Second Law of Thermo-dynamics. I'd been hoping this would keep him busy on the computer, but he began to get frisky again. My grief had left me empty and numb. "You're greedy," I said. "You're always wanting something. We did that last year, remember?"

14. Discuss Derrida. Discuss Baudrillard.

I read that little green and black book. *Simulations.* Beaudrillard. "Facts no longer have any trajectory of their own, they arise at the intersection of the models; a single fact may even be engendered by all the models at once." There is one fact. Maria is dead. Baudrillard knows nothing about the relationship between time and space, he demonstrates that when he talks about Einstein, so how can he be an expert on *simulacrums?* He needs to consult Bertrand Russell, *The ABC's of Relativity.* He needs to read *Conversations with Alfred North Whitehead.* Old books. Reliable books. Until then, he's not fit to doodle on Einstein's junk mail. As for Derrida, if his mother had let him take the docks apart and unwind the fishing line and

waste the scotch tape, like any good mother should, none of this difference would have taken place. Life is not art. I hate to disappoint Peter
Halley and George Kubler *(The Shape of Time)* but I cannot reenter that
night in history and save Maria. My sister was driving the car and a three-
year-old child was killed because she was not wearing her blue and silver
seatbelt. Because she was thrown from the car and the back of her skull
was crushed, her neck was broken. My sister has many wrecks and my
opinion is she should not be allowed to drive. Do you really think the
connection between the signifier and signified is arbitrary?

15. You're losing your control of tone.

Tone. That means an attitude. To the material. One might take an attitude
to the yellow book, that it was authoritative, reliable in terms of discus-
sions of cold wars and conspiracies since it was objectively picked, that it's
just an accident that it sounds like *Gravity's Rainbow* and is therefore
probably pure paranoia. Personally, I find paranoia a defensible intellectual stance in "today's world," as my students put it. I do remember the
yellow book has a remarkable clarity to it for something so deep and
written by so many people. Having attempted collaborations, I know how
hard this is. *Stop.* I want to bring this back, salvage whatever spirit I
started this with. But it's a serious topic. I have Maria's picture on the top
of my bookcase. My mother has a video of her but I'm afraid to watch it,
afraid I'll fall in love with her. She's really cute in it, my mother says, she
was always a funny kid. We can start out laughing but these are crucial
issues. And crucial issues can make you lose your tone. If you give a
damn, they can hurt.

16. What is this paper about? You didn't take the course, you're only
sitting in? Why are you taking this test?

This paper is about the fact that I wanted to force myself to respond in
writing to this course, and I was tired of writing papers in the same way.
During the process, I discovered I wanted to talk about Maria's death.
Because there was no reason for it, just as there's no reason for art if you
think about it, except that with art it's nobody's fault. And I keep wanting
to ask Nance WHY she bent over to pick up a piece of paper and crashed
the car into a tree.

17. I'd intended only to ask 15 questions. But you're a judgmental person. Did you know that? You're a blamer. It's disgusting really.

Yes. As I grow older it seems to spread through my system. I've seen it do that—make its little ole way into every artery, every vein. It's only my fault that I was mad at my sister and I never knew her daughter enough to even know she was funny. But if Robert Smithson's essays control the interpretation of his work, why don't my explanations control how you think about me? I do believe that to remove my faults would be like removing all of the "e's" from this exam. My faults are increasingly all I have. How can I give them up? The faults, the weaknesses, the silly games? Last night my husband came into the bedroom carrying two aspirin and a glass of water. "Do you think it's true," I asked, "that it's nobody's fault about art?" He shook his head, grinning in that tired way, like he's thinking "I'm *so sick* of her intellectual poses." "What's that?" I asked, pointing to the glass of water, the two aspirin. "It's for your head-ache," he said. "I don't have a headache," I said. He said "Aha!" and set the glass down on the bedside table. And then, because I was tired of grief, because even grief must at times release you, because I love him, and because he's the only one who still loves me, I am so obnoxious, I said, "Here," and I threw him the box of blue paper clips.

Getting into *Fiction*

Mark Mirksy and Allan Aycock

Asking me to pick a single story as an example of *Fiction's* editorial process is to set me an almost impossible task. Every story at *Fiction* has a different genealogy, and the stated policy of the magazine in combining the well known, the hardly known, the forgotten, and the unknown in each issue, immediately sets one as an editor to the riddle–from which category should I choose? As an essayist, I would find many pleasant hours in anatomizing Harold Brodkey's story about T.S. Eliot, "Eliot," in Volume 10, 3, or Donald Barthelme's fiction, "Three," in our first issue.

It takes no courage, however, to publish writers whom one already recognizes in the golden circle. At least half of the magazine comes from our unsolicited pile, despite *Fiction's* commitment to stories in translation and to regularly publishing writers who are established but want a place to experiment. Before I discuss selecting Mary Clark's "The Red-Headed Man," I think it's important to mention why this story was picked out of over twenty years of publication. I wanted a story that both the present managing editor, Allan Aycock, and I had collaborated on selecting, so that we could collaborate on an essay. This immediately limited me to the years from 1990 to present in which Allan has been part of the editorial process.

We both felt that we should choose a story which came strictly from the non-solicited pile. Some stories come to my attention through the graduate program in Creative Writing at The City College of New York in which I teach. Two of my favorites are by Gabrielle Selz and Martha Upton, but I felt that although still relatively unknown, they were part of a circle close to the magazine. We wanted to make clear that *Fiction*, as opposed to some literary magazines, though it has very specific tastes, is not dominated by a group of insiders. So we even excluded from our field of inquiry those writers who came to my attention on the recommendation of other writers.

What I like about Mary Clark's story is the riddle of dream and reality. It is this surreal snaking in and out of fantasies that has always characterized the stories we select for *Fiction*. From the very beginning, under the hidden baton of Donald Barthelme, whom I consider the foremost stylist of American fiction through three decades, from the 1960's to the end of the 80's, the magazine was founded to find and to publish such fiction, stories, and passages of the novel that ran against the prevailing grain of naturalism in the American narrative tradition. The Europeans of our first issue, Max Frisch, Thomas Bernhard, Peter Handke, were masters of a metaphysical riddling that American fiction could rarely embrace in its commercial heartbeat.

Not only the structure of Mary's story, but the language, not abstract, but precise, moving from strands of red hair, to red shading into orange, cantelopes, fields of red grass, drew me to the narrative. Line by line the whimsical laughter mocked the heartache of the dream inevitably to fade. For the moment it even promises solutions, the door back into childhood, sexual bliss, before the car drives off, jilting the narrator. In reading it again I seemed to hear echoes of Dorothy in *The Wizard of Oz* evoked in the playful circling between the storyteller and her red-headed fantasy. This gives it a certain resonance as an American narrative, drawing on those common memories of movies which have become the stock of our nightmares.

I remember Donald Barthelme's praise of John Hawkes, a writer whom I loved but towards whom Donald had a certain reserve, not entirely convinced by his fiction. We were arguing in Donald's living room, and he cut the conversation short with, "But Hawkes writes a tight line."

Mary Clark writes a tight line. When I hear that, I sit up at my desk and pay attention.

–Mark Mirksy

It is easy to discuss what makes Mary Clark's "The Red-Headed Man" a good story. I have read the story many times, worked on it with Mary, discussed it with her, and the story holds me. But what is it about the story that captured me on first reading? What spoke to my intuition?

I am the first or second reader on nearly every manuscript that comes unsolicited to the *Fiction* office. That's several thousand stories every year, of which I pass along a couple hundred to the editor. Why do I pass on one story and why do I return another? We don't have a critical agenda at the magazine, we don't have strict stylistic guidelines, and we don't have a thematic program. Although we do have a distinct proclivity for the fantastic, and we rarely publish strictly naturalistic fiction, these are hardly restrictive guidelines and, therefore, are not terribly useful in approaching the mass of submissions. And even if I could give a prescription as to what makes a story right for *Fiction*, I wouldn't want to. Nothing could be more deadly uninteresting than handfuls of stories written to someone else's specifications.

The most I can hope for as reader is to approach each manuscript with an openness to being captured by its world. This is impossible, of course, for I am moody and often recalcitrant. Still, what most of us read for, I think, is to lose ourselves for a few moments in someone else's dream. And whatever my mood may have been when I picked up the story, this is what happened when I first read "The Red-Headed Man."

Mary's story came to me with a scribbled comment from a reader that said something like *Strange. Take a look.* Elliptical, yes, but not unusual among our editorial comments. Although it sometimes happens, we don't encourage lengthy analyses of manuscript. Our editors have a wide range of tastes, but they know the magazine well and we rely on their intuitive, visceral reactions.

My personal taste in fiction is for work that is grounded in the concrete, in detail, in the real. When a writer can evoke the fantastic through the portal of the real, I am most deeply affected. This is what is so compelling about Mary's story, and, I think, what first captured me as a reader and drew me into her dream. The story begins with a very cautious, partially recalled dream and the narrator's halting effort to find the details from her real life that she has taken "from the waking to the sleeping world." The story progresses likewise, cautiously, farther and farther into the dream, which is described with a gathering of detail, emotion, narrative. As the narrator gives herself to the dream, where everything is recognizable, everything strange, she leaves behind the waking world only to find it again at the end in the elusive correspondence of memory.

This tenuous negotiation between the two worlds is what the story is about. And the method of the writing is not to define the distinction between them with aggressive or pyrotechnic effects; rather, it is to explore the infinite, subtle, mysterious connections with clear, precise language. The "dream" is marked only by a slight skewing or syntax and by a slight adjustment to the odd internal narratives of the dream fragments. Without strenuous motions to be dream*like*, the story becomes the thing itself, suggestive, slippery, haunting.

Finally, what I can say about Mary's story is that it finds a unity of voice, language, and narrative that makes all three disappear as separate elements; in the unity the writer disappears, the artifice disappears–there is only the dream, and the reader enters.

–Allan Aycock

⌒⌒⌒⌒

The Red-Headed Man
Mary Clark

Early in November, Julia began having dreams about the red-headed man. In the dreams he was her boyfriend, and when she was with him, she had the feeling of being so deeply loved that it didn't matter if he wasn't real. On the subway the day the dreams started, a stranger with red hair had asked her if he was traveling in the right direction. Thinking back on the dream the next day, Julia could tell that while she explained how the underground pathways corresponded to the streets above, a part of her collected his red hair as something to take from the waking to the sleeping world. Other than that, the man in the dreams did not remind her of anyone she knew in real life.

She didn't remember the first dream until she was in her kitchen making her breakfast the next morning. She cut a cantaloupe in half and when it fell apart and she began to scoop the seeds out over the garbage can, she remembered driving in a very small car with her new boyfriend who had red hair. She was able to hold on to that memory enough to recall that she had told him his hair was the color of cantaloupe—as if she had also been thinking about her breakfast while dreaming—and was taken aback when she saw a pale peach-colored fruit rather than the brilliant orange she remembered from the night before. The only other memory she had of the first dream was that after telling him about the shade of his hair, he replied, "It is tremendously clever of you to say so." Then the feeling of being loved poured over her, making her clothes feel a little damp for a while afterward.

His hair was the clearest memory she had of him. She had never been close to a redhead. If not for the unusual color of his hair, Julia was convinced that she would not have felt so enlivened while dreaming. It was thick and straight and cut short, so that when she pushed it all one way it was bright orange, and when she pushed it another it was burnt rust, like the nap in a carpet. But his hair was not the texture of carpet, it was the texture of cut grass.

"Your hair has a grass-nap in it," Julia told him the very next night in the second dream.

"Yes, I know."

"Let me make a design."

"If it suits you to do so."

She made a J in his hair with her fingers, using short, brisk strokes at the top cross and the rounded part of the letter. "There, now you are a dreamboat."

"Thank you. May I erase my hair now?"

"Yes, you may. You are a dreamboat, but not a brown-haired one like in the Mystery Date Game."

"Thank you, and you are a beautiful woman who is slightly nervous," and when he said this, his arms around her became a wool blanket she was wrapped in.

In the second dream she remembered that they drove down a narrow residential street in an old city she couldn't identify. His car was the size of a book; that's how she thought of it, the size of a textbook, a textbook that held a catalog of animals. She didn't know, but perhaps she had such a particular sense of his car because they had to shrink to that size whenever they got in.

The dream reminded her of the Mystery Date Game, a board game she played as a girl wherein players advanced their markers by landing on squares that brought them closer to, or further away from, being dressed and beautified for their dates. When each became ready, she opened the plastic door in the center of the board where, underneath, a dial had spun and positioned on an unknown picture of one of five possible dates: the Sporty Guy in shorts who leaned on a tennis racket; two others whom Julia couldn't remember; the Dud—the consolation prize of a date—who slumped in the doorway, seedy and unkempt; and the Dreamboat in a white tuxedo, who held out flowers and stood up straight, right in the center of the doorway. Girls on the commercial for the game successively opened a real door to actors portraying each of these men. Then the camera held a few seconds on the real men in the real doorway. Julia knew that if there was anyone who looked like the red-headed man, it was the man who was the Dreamboat in the Mystery Date Game, although that man had brown hair.

By the evening of the third dream she had forgotten about the pleasant dream she had the night before and went to sleep thinking about a meeting she had the next morning.

"My, it's a windy day," the red-headed man said.

"Lovely." As in the waking world, the dream showed fall colors, though some trees took on blue leaves. Besides a streak of chill in the wind of a certain height, there was something else about it that she noticed. The wind was . . . the wind was separated into parts of wind . . . it was . . .

"Just don't let it get inside of you."

"What?"

"The wind."

"Oh, I won't."

"Once inside, you can only get it out in a way I don't know of yet."

"Oh, I won't then, especially."

"See the trees change color."

"Exquisite." The view was bright and clear and exaggerated from the angular late-afternoon light.

"The grass doesn't turn like a maple does, except in one place I know."

Then they were driving up a hill in his tiny car. "Only a small amount of mileage and I will show it to you," he said. "There." At the top they could see a whole field of red grass.

"If this grass were enough," she said, "it would be red hair on the planet. Now it's only a tiny, tiny tuft."

"There he is now." He pointed to a man in overalls, who appeared from behind some trees, mowed across the red field, and emptied bags of cut grass from the lawn mower attachment onto a pile in the center of the field.

They must have run down to that pile, because in the next moment Julia dove into it as if it was water. When the worker heaved another load on, she had to go deep under the same way she survived waves at the ocean, letting them pass before surfacing.

"Your hair is so cold it's making me numb," she said, confusing his hair for the grass that was like the ocean around her.

"The Red Sea," he called it, which came off in the dream as an intellectual joke.

He swam over to her. "I love you so that I've put you inside of my hair this way. I knew I could always do this for someone, and I've waited to do it for you."

"I feel like Venus, but with arms!" This image of herself accentuated the actual radiance she felt and continued to feel for a while when she woke.

Julia could never really see the face of the red-headed man; however, the dream led her to assume that he had a kind face. Likewise, his build was vague, his skin tone blurry, and she could not acquire a sense of his height since he grew and shrank to accommodate the events in the dream and to correspond with what he said. But her mind selected other features to push to exaggeration. She had an especially precise memory of his hands. The skin of his palms and fingers was the smooth skin of a woman's back rather than the usual skin ridged by fingerprints. The balls of his fingers and palms, padded with the consistency of foam rubber, received the pressure of holding hands and reformed quickly when she moved her hand away. And just under that padding, she could tell, the hard muscles there gave his grip restraint. Holding hands with him felt like lying down at last after a day at work.

Julia could barely recognize a certain side of herself in the dreams, and would not have seen that woman as herself if not for dreaming's way of letting the dreamer know personal perspective. Her behavior and the corny things she said embarrassed her, even though the only witness was an invented man. She accused herself of girlishness when she strolled along the river with him and said that the stars reminded her of sequins on the evening dress of the night, and that the moon was the scoop of vanilla ice cream fallen on that dress when the woman of the night was not careful enough with her cone. And to think it was her creation to have herself strolling with him along the river looking at the moon as well!

But the red-headed man did nothing and said nothing for which he could be embarrassed. Roller skating on the river, close like a waltz, she fretted that they were going to fall through any minute, but he gently reminded her that he had turned on the very cold water faucet just before stepping on, and that the river should be freezing up in no time.

"You think of everything."

"Oh, do I? I thought I was thinking only of you."

"Let me see your face." She stared and stared at it and described his features in words to herself to try to root the image of him in her memory. "Every time I try to remember some parts of you, it won't go in."

"That's a good thing."

"I am also embarrassed about what I said about the moon."

"You only said it because you're so homesick." With that he twirled her until she lifted up to the bridge. The motion gave her the distant feeling that something was not right with her.

"Look how very cold my elbow is from skating." He was on the bridge too then, pointing his elbow at her. She could see that the elbow of his coat was frost-covered.

"My poor darling, let me warm it for you." She cupped her hands around his elbow and breathed her warmest air—that's how she thought of it, her warmest air, calling it up from the warmest part inside of her.

"It's no use, really. My elbow won't be warm until you're no longer homesick."

"But I don't feel homesick at all; I rarely think of my parents. Anyway, silly, I couldn't be homesick, I have you."

"You'll know you're not homesick when my elbow's warm."

That dream ended with her breathing and breathing onto his elbow, but it still stayed cold. She woke from breathing so deliberately, and once awake her breathing seemed more like panting. When she had located herself from the lost feeling of not knowing why she was breathing so, or where she was, she sat up in her bed and cried.

Going down the elevator to lunch with a co-worker the next day, Julia asked her if she ever had a dream that wasn't so much recurring as continuous, like a sequel each night.

The woman answered no, that she didn't dream much, or rather, didn't remember her dreams.

Julia decided it wasn't fair to tell her dreams to someone who didn't have so much pleasure herself. She worried that describing them would make them sound dull and haphazard.

But Julia felt grateful for their return each night. To bring them on, she practiced the method of willing them by not trying too hard. Before sleep, she lay flat and still and tried to think of nothing. She waited like this until she saw splotches of dull light behind her lids shift slightly, and then soon after shake. That shaking had frequently been her last memory of being awake, and a signal of the transition into sleep. So when it started, she thought only of a color: red-orange.

"Get into my Match Box; get in quick." He was holding open the car door, leaning across the passenger seat to do so. "You'd better hurry because the tornado will arrive in our presence."

She shrank fast and got in.

Even though they were tiny, the approaching wind did not blow them off the road because they maintained their actual weight. He pulled right, got out, and opened her door. Taking her arm, he led her to the elevator that delivered them onto ditch-level of the field.

"Lay flat for now until it passes."

The tornado blew over them resembling the black smoke off a train. It sounded like a train–something Julia remembered reading about tornadoes.

"Do you hear that?" he asked her. "It's the eye." It sounded like a sweet, spiritual chord held by many voices. "It's nice now, but you know it comes again."

When the winds returned, she knew they had returned, but did not feel them around her. She looked at the sky but could not locate them. She grew desperate, feeling that the wind was going to sneak up on her.

"The wind is blowing hard inside me now. Will you help me, please?" He was shouting above the wind inside him.

She panicked. She grabbed him and held him, but his hair blew wild, as if from inside his head since there was still no wind in the air around them. She pushed him down and made him small so she could put him in her sleeve, but even small, his hair shifted like a tiny wheat field–the color of a wheat field at dusk–in a storm.

She put her hand on his head, but she could feel his hair trying to move underneath. When she lifted her hand, his hair switched even faster, like when a child releases hold of the legs of a wind-up doll whose legs scissor fast until the backlog of the turning crank reaches its actual pace.

"It has wound down for now," he said, human-size again, "but look!" He showed her his elbow, covered in ice.

"My stomach," she said, because the worry she had for him had clawed at her inside until the pain was too much to sleep through, and she woke.

The sixth night, just after falling asleep, she was wakened by the telephone from what she could tell was the beginning of the next dream. The intensive conversation that followed stirred her, and its lack of resolution made her too angry to sleep. She tried to calm herself by fixing on a certain shade of orange in a cloth on her dresser.

"You must pay just the right amount of attention to the wind, or it will get inside of you. It's always been my mistake to do so." In the sixth dream, they were flying above the city, supported on the stronger part of the wind. Julia could tell that they were able to fly because the wind had been inside him so long that he could use it to his advantage.

"Just be sure to stay on the level of wind that can hold you. Don't go to a weak level."

"Oh, I won't." She felt the mix of fear and liberation.

In the dream she saw a goose flying right beside her. Close up, she could see how hard it worked to fly, bobbing a little from each stroke. It was sweating, and its mouth was open. It turned its head to look at her and then looked ahead again.

"The best thing is the rooftops. It's how I got red hair, by looking at rooftops from above."

"I knew it was from some such thing."

"Don't you look too long, because your hair is the best color I can think of."

For him to think of her hair color as better than his when she so adored him being a redhead made her whole body warm from inside out.

"Are you ready now? To go to bed with me?"

She couldn't answer, so aroused by his question; she could only exhale a long breath.

Next, they were in bed in the sky. She recognized the bed as her own because it had the same headboard and footboard.

"I have wanted to make love with you since on the subway I saw you, but I didn't want to be regarded as too attentive." He kissed the inside of her forearm. "Your skin tastes like sweet milk."

With her lying there, exactly as she was actually lying, he went under the light down quilt to please her.

His tenderness startled her and kept her longing until she came in the dream and, as far as she could tell, in actual life. This was something she had experienced only one other time, as a teenager. Afterwards she lay awake curled in her bed facing the space next to her where she had last seen him.

The next night Julia wanted to call up the red-headed man for that evening's dreaming. But the dream that night was very slight and set between other dreams. She did remember being in a house behind a screen door, looking out. The red-headed man was walking down the sidewalk, away from her.

"I'll miss you." She called to him in slow-motion.

"I'll be all right."

She knew when he got into the cab that it was really an ambulance because the light on top of it wasn't yellow but blue.

She couldn't sleep that night and got up to watch late-night television. On the show, she noticed that one of the men in the talk-show's band had red hair. She got up close to the set to look at him in the background while the band's leader talked to the host. She waited through the next guest for him to appear again, but the camera only flashed on the band for a second before cutting to a commercial.

She turned off the TV and made a sandwich. She sat by the window and ate, looking out at her sleeping residential street.

She felt a tired ache in her body the next day at work, and went to bed early that night.

"How's the space in the broccoli?" the red-headed man asked her in the candle-lit restaurant.

"It's so good." Julia had the pleasant sensation of eating something light and warm and a vanished green.

"I come here because the food has tremendous space in it."

"Delicious." She was inside of the experience of tasting, which had expanded to an enclosure bigger than herself, making it that much more interesting.

"To your liking?" He cranked the pepper mill above her plate, and—when he did so, nodding forward a little, she saw that her letter still sprawled across the crown of his head.

"I thought you erased your hair a long time ago."

"I did."

"But the J's still in it."

"Of course."

"But I don't want it in that long." Terrified, she swished her hands briskly in his hair till she was almost slapping his head.

"It will go away when a dog walks by me," he said.

"Hurry. Hurry, hurry, hurry." They were running down the alley trying to find a dog. In the back yards, none were out.

People's gardens were dying from the approaching cold, just as they were dying from fall in the waking world. Marigolds stood brightly above brown rubble, but the sunflowers had turned to cast iron and could no longer be picked.

From far down the alley came a small black dog.

"There's one."

"Come here, please," said the red-headed man. The dog went to him and licked his hand, and as it did so, gradually the J left his hair and appeared in the nap of the animal's fur.

"A little J dog," Julia said as the dog trotted off.

"He'll lose it one day in the stones that wash into the sides of the alley after a storm. Everything rubs off eventually."

"You rubbed off on me."

"Impossible."

"Yes, you did. Yes, you did. You did rub off on me."

"I'm afraid that's outside of possibility, Julia."

"Yes, you did. Yes, you did."

He was fading. His car grew to normal size. He got in without her and drove away. In the distance, the shadows on his hair made it look brown. Still in the dream, she stood in a place she thought of as the corner of the alley and repeated his last sentence to her, but it became more and more unfathomable, as the knowledge of something that happened to a person everyday as a child—something that influenced all of everything that person was and is now—becomes, as an adult, the one thing too hard to remember.

~~~~~

Finding the Real Thing
Stanley W. Lindberg

During my twenty-five years as an editor, I've participated in several hundred fiction-writing workshops and sessions where I've been asked to field queries from aspiring authors. Some of these questions are perennial and pose no problems. No, I explain, you don't have to live in Georgia to get published in *The Georgia Review*. Yes, we read all stories that come in–even if the author is completely unknown to us. No, you don't need an agent at the start; most of what we publish is unsolicited and comes directly from writers. Yes, we pay–more than most quarterlies, but not nearly enough for any of you to quit your current day job. Cover letters? Well, some editors seem to give them more weight than we do, but . . . And on it goes–until someone hushes the room completely by raising THE QUESTION: *Tell me, exactly what is it you're looking for?*

"There's no secret formula for acceptance," I say quickly. "It's true that we almost never publish translations or portions of novels, but beyond such announced exceptions, we give open consideration to an amazing range of fiction. Sure, I can suggest that you avoid anything that fits neatly into such genre categories as detective, science fiction, western, or romance, but I really can't offer you a recipe for success. Look at what we've already published in *The Georgia Review*–that will probably give you a better sense of the qualities we're seeking than anything I say here."

Any listeners actually going to our back issues will gain at least an appreciation for the editorial range and the variety of our fiction. Take, for instance, the length of our stories: we've featured one single-page story, a couple running more than fifty pages, and just about everything in between. We're equally difficult to pigeonhole in terms of authorial reputations: we've presented a healthy number of writers' first-published efforts (more than twenty-five in my tenure here), but we've also devoted space to previously unpublished fiction by Robert Louis Stevenson and William Faulkner, as well as to new work by such acknowledged masters of the short story as Frederick Busch, Louise Erdrich, Ernest J. Gaines, Joyce Carol Oates, and many others.

Still, an editor's advice to read the magazine itself—no matter how well-intentioned and pragmatically sound—is seldom heeded by those looking for a shortcut to fame and glory. "We seek only the best stories, and the best are almost always unpredictable," I stress, but even as the audience nods its agreement, their eyes keep asking: "OK, so what are you *really* looking for?"

For years I've tried to answer that question, but lately I've become increasingly uncomfortable with definitions of taste and judgment that lack specific referents. I can honestly say, for example, that I'm looking for fiction that engages me personally, that really *insists* on being published—but how far does that take anyone else toward the concrete? Besides, I'm also searching for other key elements: genuine emotional depth, a distinctive voice, a fresh angle of vision. What I want, in other words, is a story that somehow clearly distinguishes itself above hundreds of competitors, one that appeals convincingly on both an intellectual and a visceral level, one that arrests and holds my attention initially yet also invites me back and sustains later readings. But let's face it: since fiction with that much vitality is by nature capable of *surprising*, it tends to be easier to recognize than to describe.

One such defining example, in my opinion, is "Manly Conclusions" by Mary Hood, which arrived at *The Georgia Review* in late 1982. As the sole editor at that time, I screened all the manuscripts and then (after inevitable delays) read the survivors against each other before making final judgments. (An enormous increase in the volume of submissions received soon after this led to changes in our staffing and editorial selection process. Manuscripts are now screened by others, primarily by my associate editor Stephen Corey, and—of necessity—I seldom serve as first reader of new work received.) I was already familiar with Hood's writing—indeed, *The Review* had published several of her earliest stories—but I was on the verge of accepting another, longer work she had revised at our request, so I didn't initially give this quiet little tale much thought.

But I obviously couldn't forget it, either, though I can hardly reconstruct now all the reasoning that went into my decision to accept "Manly Conclusions." I didn't have time then to rationalize my preferences and prejudices to the extent that I am attempting here, but I can clearly remember the way the story haunted me, the emotional impact of later readings, and my growing sense that, in its telling, Mary Hood is demonstrating a kind of authority writers rarely attain.

The story opens with a marvelous economy of expression, weaving background exposition into action already in progress. We are not *told*, for instance, that it's an early spring morning; we *see* Valjean–identified/defined as Carpenter Petty's wife by the story's first two words–standing in "the year's first growth of grass" and speaking "to the greening forsythia" as she "shook the tablecloth free of breakfast crumbs." Although we do not immediately meet Carpenter Petty himself, we are set up for that introduction by learning character traits via his chosen bumper sticker ("I don't get mad, I get even") and his wife's apparently practiced defense: "He's always been intense. It wasn't just the war. If you're born a certain way, where's the mending?"

In the course of the opening paragraphs, Carpenter's wife reveals much more about herself and the setting than she may realize–including some aspects that the narrative voice reinforces with lines like "Valjean knew the value of a light hand" and (later) "Valjean kept on praying and preventing." At the same time, Hood is establishing Valjean as a reliable set of eyes through which to see and to judge the story's action–authenticating her character both through convincing speech patterns (listen again to "If you're born a certain way, where's the mending?") and through such small details as the pride she clearly takes in Carpenter's praise for her biscuits and her "old-fashioned willingness to rise before good day and bake for him."

There's not a lot of surface dazzle in Hood's telling of the story–not, at least, in comparison to many writers today. In some respects she seems to put as much weight on common things like Carpenter's boots as on a pistol that later turns up missing. The boots get muddied in digging the grave for their son's dog, and Valjean cleans them–"not that he had left them for her to do; he had just left them." Yet even in apparent stasis Hood's writing holds reader interest. Unlike some minimalist writers who never leave the first-person present tense, Hood can be stylistically quiet without being flat:

> Dennis so much like Carpenter that the two of them turned heads in town, father and son, spirit and image. People seemed proud of them from afar, as though their striking resemblance reflected credit on all mankind, affirming faith in the continuity of generations.

And she regularly shows just how well-chosen action verbs and verb tenses can serve both to intensify dramatic moments–

Valjean's cup wrecked against her saucer. He hadn't told her that! He had held that back, steeping the bitter truth from it all day to serve to the boy.

—*and* to enliven even slow spots in a narrative:

Carpenter crouched and pulled on his stiff, cleaned boots, then hefted one foot gaily into a shaft of sunset, admiring the shine. "Good work, ma'am." He tipped an imaginary hat and strode off into the shadows of the tall pines.

Only lately have I come to notice how closely this story resembles a Greek tragedy, with all action occurring during "a single revolution of the sun" and all violence taking place offstage. Purists would argue, of course, that the Petty family lacks "heroic stature," but it's clear they have the respect of Mary Hood, and there's no question that their fates are being determined by their own characters. Few readers will note how the dramatic unities operate here, I'm sure, but most will sense the author's steadfast adherence to the classic truth of these particular human characters caught up inexorably in this particular situation.

There are numerous things to admire in "Manly Conclusions"—including the masterful ending and its insistence that readers draw their own—but more than anything else I respect its integrity. Hood doesn't try to make the story something other than it is in an attempt to be fashionable. The dramatic power here is far richer than best-seller sensationalism; it derives from Hood's unflinching psychological insights into characters who, in the hands of a lesser artist, might very well have been trivialized, sentimentalized, or exploited. It's *their* story, she seems to say, and she does nothing to upstage them by calling attention to herself as author.

Those are some of the main reasons why I have selected "Manly Conclusions" to define the kind of story we seek to publish in *The Georgia Review*. It is true to itself. It has that feeling of *necessariness* that Elizabeth Bowen identified as a prerequisite for good fiction. It holds up. As an editor, I can ask no more of a story or from its author. I found "Manly Conclusions" to be compelling writing. I hope you will, too.

∿∿∿

Manly Conclusions
Mary Hood

His wife, Valjean, admitted that Carpenter Petty had a tree-topping temper, but he was slow to lose it; that was in his favor. Still, he had a long memory, and that way of saving things up, until by process of accumulation he had enough evidence to convict. "I don't get mad, I get even," his bumper sticker vaunted. Fair warning. When he was angry he burned like frost, not flame.

Now Valjean stood on the trodden path in the year's first growth of grass, her tablecloth in her arms, and acknowledged an undercurrent in her husband, spoke of it to the greening forsythia with its yellow flowers rain-fallen beneath it, confided it to God and nature. Let God and nature judge. A crow passed between her and the sun, dragging its slow shadow. She glanced up. On Carpenter's behalf she said, "He's always been intense. It wasn't just the war. If you're born a certain way, where's the mending?"

She shook the tablecloth free of the breakfast crumbs and pinned it to the line. Carpenter liked her biscuits–praised them to all their acquaintances–as well as her old-fashioned willingness to rise before good day and bake for him. Sometimes he woke early too; then he would join her in the kitchen. They would visit as she worked the shortening into the flour, left-handed (as was her mother, whose recipe it was), and pinch off the rounds, laying them as gently in the blackened pan as though she were laying a baby down for its nap. The dough was very quick, very tender. It took a light hand. Valjean knew the value of a light hand.

This morning Carpenter had slept late, beyond his time, and catching up he ate in a rush, his hair damp from the shower, his shirt unbuttoned. He raised neither his eyes nor his voice to praise or complain.

"You'll be better at telling Dennis than I would," he said, finally, leaving it to her.

She had known for a long time that there was more to loving a man than marrying him, and more to marriage than love. When they were newly wed, there had been that sudden quarrel, quick and furious as a summer squall, between Carpenter and a neighbor over the property line. A vivid memory and a lesson–the two men silhouetted against the setting sun, defending the territory and honor of rental property. Valjean stood by his side, silent, sensing even then that to speak out, to beg, to order, to quake would be to shame him. Nor would it avail. Better to shout Stay! to Niagara. Prayer and prevention was the course she decided on, learning how to laugh things off, to make jokes and diversions. If a car cut ahead of them in the parking lot and took the space he had been headed for, before Carpenter could get his window down to berate women drivers, Valjean would say, "I can see why she's in a hurry, just look at her!" as the offender trotted determinedly up the sidewalk and into a beauty salon.

She was subtle enough most times, but maybe he caught on after a while. At any rate, his emotional weather began to moderate. Folks said he had changed, and not for the worse. They gave proper credit to his wife, but the war had a hand in it too. When he got back, most of what he thought and felt had gone underground, and it was his quietness and shrewd good nature that you noticed now. Valjean kept on praying and preventing.

But there are some things you can't prevent, and he had left it to Valjean to break the news to Dennis. Dennis so much like Carpenter that the two of them turned heads in town, father and son, spirit and image. People seemed proud of them from afar, as though their striking resemblance reflected credit on all mankind, affirming faith in the continuity of generations. He was like his mama, too, the best of both of them, and try as she might, she couldn't find the words to tell him that his dog was dead, to send him off to school with a broken heart. The school bus came early, and in the last-minute flurry of gathering books and lunch money, his poster on medieval armor and his windbreaker, she chose to let the news wait.

She had the whole day then, after he was gone, to find the best words. Musing, she sat on the top step and began cleaning Carpenter's boots–not that he had left them for her to do; he had just left them. She scrubbed and gouged and sluiced away the sticky mud, dipping her rag in a rain puddle. After a moment's deliberation she rinsed the cloth in Lady's water dish. Lady would not mind now; she was beyond thirst. It was burying her that had got Carpenter's boots so muddy.

"Dead," Valjean murmured. For a moment she was overcome, disoriented as one is the instant after cataclysm, while there is yet room for disbelief, before the eyes admit the evidence into the heart. The rag dripped muddy water dark as blood onto the grass.

They had found Lady halfway between the toolshed and the back porch, as near home as she had been able to drag herself. The fine old collie lay dying in their torchlight, bewildered, astonished, trusting them to heal her, to cancel whatever evil this was that had befallen.

Carpenter knelt to investigate. "She's been shot." The meaning of the words and their reverberations brought Valjean to her knees. No way to laugh this off.

"It would have been an accident," she reasoned.

Carpenter gave the road a despairing glance. "If it could have stayed the way it was when we first bought out here. . . . You don't keep a dog like this on a chain!"

It had been wonderful those early years, before the developers came with their transits and plat-books and plans for summer cottages in the uplands. The deer had lingered a year or so longer, then had fled across the lake with the moon on their backs. The fields of wild blueberries were fenced off now; what the roadscrapers missed, wildfire got. Lawn crept from acre to acre like a plague. What trees were spared sprouted POSTED and KEEP and TRESPASSERS WILL BE signs. Gone were the tangles of briar and drifted meadow beauty, seedbox and primrose. The ferns retreated yearly deeper into the ravines.

"Goddamn weekenders," Carpenter said.

They had lodged official complaint the day three bikers roared through the back lot, scattering the hens, tearing down five lines of wash, and leaving a gap through the grape arbor. The Law came out and made bootless inquiry, stirring things up a little more. The next morning Valjean found their garbage cans overturned. Toilet tissue wrapped every tree in the orchard, a dead rat floated in the well, and their mailbox was battered to earth–that sort of mischief. Wild kids. "Let the Law handle it," Valjean suggested, white-lipped.

"They can do their job and I'll do mine," Carpenter told her. So that time Valjean prayed that the Law would be fast and Carpenter slow, and that was how it went. A deputy came out the next day with a carload of joyriders he had run to earth. "Now I think the worst thing that could happen," the deputy drawled, "is to call their folks, wha'd'ya say?" So it had been resolved that way, with reparations paid and handshakes. That had been several years back; things had settled down some now. Of late there were only the litter and loudness associated with careless vacationers. No lingering hard feelings. In the market, when Valjean met a neighbor's wife, they found pleasant things to speak about; the awkwardness was past. In time they might be friends.

"An accident," Valjean had asserted, her voice odd to her own ears, as though she were surfacing from a deep dive. Around them night was closing in. She shivered. It took her entire will to keep from glancing over her shoulder into the tanglewood through which Lady had plunged, wounded, to reach home.

"Bleeding like this she must have laid a plain track." Carpenter paced the yard, probing at spots with the dimming light of the lantern. He tapped it against his thigh to encourage the weak batteries.

"She's been gone all afternoon," Valjean said. "She could have come miles."

"Not hurt this bad," Carpenter said.

"What are you saying? No. No!" She forced confidence into her voice. "No one around here would do something like this." Fear for him stung her hands and feet like frost. She stood for peace. She stood too suddenly; dizzy, she put out her hand to steady herself. He could feel her trembling.

"It could have been an accident, yeah, like you say." He spoke quietly for her sake. He had learned to do that.

"You see?" she said, her heart lifting a little.

"Yeah." Kneeling again, he shook his head over the dog's labored breathing. "Too bad, old girl; they've done for you."

When the amber light failed from Lady's eyes, Valjean said, breathless, "She was probably trespassing," thinking of all those signs, neon-vivid, warning. He always teased her that she could make excuses for the devil.

"Dogs can't read," he pointed out. "She lived all her life here, eleven, twelve years. . . . And she knew this place by heart, every rabbit run, toad hole, and squirrel knot. She was better at weather than the almanac, and there was never a thing she feared except losing us. She kept watch on Dennis like he was her own pup."

"I know . . ." She struggled to choke back the grief. It stuck like a pine cone in her throat. But she wouldn't let it be *her* tears that watered the ground and made the seed of vengeance sprout. For all their sakes she kept her nerve . . .

"And whoever shot her," Carpenter was saying, "can't tell the difference in broad day between ragweed and rainbow. Goddamn weekenders!"

They wrapped the dog in Dennis' cradle quilt and set about making a grave. Twilight seeped away into night. The shovel struck fire from the rocks as Carpenter dug. Dennis was at Scout meeting; they wanted to be done before he got home. "There's nothing deader than a dead dog," Carpenter reasoned. "The boy doesn't need to remember her that way."

In their haste, in their weariness, Carpenter shed his boots on the back stoop and left the shovel leaning against the wall. The wind rose in the night and blew the shovel handle along the shingles with a dry-bones rattle. Waking, alarmed, Valjean put out her hand: Carpenter was there.

Now Valjean resumed work on the boots, concentrating on the task at hand. She cleaned carefully, as though diligence would perfect not only the leather but Carpenter also, cleaning away the mire, anything that might make him lose his balance. From habit, she set the shoes atop the well-house to dry, out of reach of the dog. Then she realized Lady was gone. All her held-back tears came now; she mourned as for a child.

She told Dennis that afternoon. He walked all around the grave, disbelieving. No tears, too old for that; silent, like his father. He gathered straw to lay on the raw earth to keep it from washing. Finally he buried his head in Valjean's shoulder and groaned, "Why?" Hearing that, Valjean thanked God, for hadn't Carpenter asked *Who?* and not *Why?*—as though he had some plan, eye for eye, and needed only to discover upon whom to visit it? Dennis must not learn those ways, Valjean prayed; let my son be in some ways like me . . .

At supper Carpenter waited till she brought dessert before he asked, "Did you tell him?"

Dennis laid down his fork to speak for himself. "I know."

Carpenter beheld his son. "She was shot twice. Once point-blank. Once as she tried to get away."

Valjean's cup wrecked against her saucer. He hadn't told her that! He had held that back, steeping the bitter truth from it all day to serve to the boy. There was no possible antidote. It sank in, like slow poison.

"It's going to be all right," she murmured automatically, her peace of mind spinning away like a chip in a strong current. Her eyes sightlessly explored the sampler on the opposite wall whose motto she had worked during the long winter when she sat at her mother's deathbed: *Perfect Love Casts Out Fear.*

"You mean Lady knew them? Trusted them? Then they shot her?" Dennis spoke eagerly, proud of his ability to draw manly conclusions. Valjean watched as the boy realized what he was saying. "It's someone we know," Dennis whispered, the color rising from his throat to his face, his hands slowly closing into tender fists. "What—what are we going to do about it?" He pushed back his chair, ready.

"No," Valjean said, drawing a firm line, then smudging it a little with a laugh and a headshake. "Not you." She gathered their plates and carried them into the kitchen. She could hear Carpenter telling Dennis, "Someone saw Gannett's boys on the logging road yesterday afternoon. I'll step on down that way and see what they know."

"But Carpenter–" She returned with sudsy hands to prevent.

He pulled Valjean to him, muting all outcry with his brandied breath. He pleased himself with a kiss, taking his time, winking a galvanized-gray eye at Dennis. "I'm just going to talk to them. About time they knew me better."

She looked so miserable standing there that he caught her to him again, boyish, lean; the years had rolled off of him, leaving him uncreased, and no scars that showed. He had always been lucky, folks said. Wild lucky.

"Listen here now," he warned. "Trust me?"

What answer would serve but yes? She spoke it after a moment, for his sake, with all her heart, like a charm to cast out fear. "Of course."

Dennis, wheeling his bike out to head down to Mrs. Cobb's for his music lesson, knelt to make some minor adjustment on the chain.

"I won't be long," Carpenter said. "Take care of yourselves."

"You too," Dennis called, and pedaled off.

Carpenter crouched and pulled on his stiff, cleaned boots, then hefted one foot gaily into a shaft of sunset, admiring the shine. "Good work, ma'am." He tipped an imaginary hat and strode off into the shadows of the tall pines.

A whippoorwill startled awake and shouted once, then sleepily subsided. Overhead the little brown bats tottered and strove through the first starlight, their high twittering falling like tiny blown kisses onto the wind-scoured woods. It was very peaceful there in the deep heart of the April evening, and it had to be a vagrant, unworthy, warning impulse that sent Valjean prowling to the cabinet in the den where they kept their tax records, warranties, brandy, and side arms. Trembling, she reached again and again, but couldn't find the pistol. Carpenter's pistol wasn't there.

Not there.

For a moment she would not believe it, just rested her head against the cool shelf; then she turned and ran, leaving lights on and doors open behind her, tables and rugs askew in her wake. She ran sock-footed toward trouble as straight as she could, praying *Carpenter! Carpenter!* with every step. And then, like answered prayer, he was there, sudden as something conjured up from the dark. He caught her by the shoulders and shook her into sense.

"What's happened? Babe? What is it?"

But she could not answer for laughing and crying both at once, to see him there safe, to meet him halfway. When she caught her breath she said, "I was afraid something awful–I thought–I didn't know if I'd ever–"

"I told you I was just going to talk with them," he chided, amused. She gave a skip to get in step beside him. He caught her hand up and pointed her own finger at her. "I thought you said you trusted me."

"But I didn't know you were taking the gun with you . . ."

Angry, he drew away. Outcast, she felt the night chill raise the hair on the back of her neck.

"I didn't take the damn gun! What makes you say things like that? You think I'm some kind of nut?"

"But it's gone," she protested. "I looked."

And then a new specter rose between them, unspeakable, contagious. For a moment they neither moved nor spoke, then Carpenter started for home, fast, outdistancing her in a few strides. Over his shoulder he called back, edgy, unconvinced, "You missed it, that's all. It's there." He would make sure.

She ran but could not quite catch up. "Dennis has it," she accused Carpenter's back.

"Nah," he shouted. "Don't borrow trouble. It's home."

When he loped across the lawn and up the kitchen steps three at a time he was a full minute ahead of her. And when she got there, Carpenter was standing in the doorway of the den empty-handed, with the rapt, calculating, baffled expression of a baby left holding a suddenly limp string when the balloon has burst and vanished. The phone was ringing, ringing.

"Answer it," he said into the dark, avoiding her eyes.

All We Ever Wanted to Say

Peter Stitt

The Gettysburg Review did not actually exist in October of 1987; the first issue would not be published for another three months. We had tried to
spread the word of our imminence, however, and some writers did respond by sending manuscripts for us to read. Indeed, the magazine had
only one manuscript reader in those days, its editor, and on October 9 he
found in his mailbox a story, along with a cover letter beginning: "Here is
a story, 'Father Pat Springer,' for your consideration for *The Gettysburg Review*. I determined that I would send it to you after I read your article in
the *AWP Newsletter*–I love this article that talks about love being so 'important a component of the equation.'" I have just tried to find that article,
but think I failed. I did find one called "Love-Hate Relations: Writers, Re-
viewers, and Critics," but it was published in the *Newsletter* in 1980. The
one Deborah Larsen referred to must be the one I published there later,
the one about relations between theorists and creative writers. Love, of
course, is not a part of the equation between theorists and writers; that is
one of the things wrong with literary criticism in our day.

Anyway, we have always liked cover letters at *The Gettysburg Review*,
and you may be sure that we liked this one better than most. Flattery is always welcome to anyone who writes, even though an editor who writes
must not let himself be swayed by it. Many wonderful letters are accompanied by utterly undistinguished poems, stories, and essays; if we were to
publish those materials on the basis of their cover letters, we would look
foolish indeed, perhaps even to the point where no one would compliment us anymore. The only thing an editor can judge for publication is
the work itself; the cover letter must have no more bearing on his decision than two other factors that one might be swayed by: the reputation of
the author and the fact that he or she might be a friend. Occasionally, in

fact, one's friend is an author of considerable standing, but if the submitted work is not strong, it must be rejected anyway. This is, alas, one of the ways friendships end.

But Deborah Larsen was not a friend when she wrote this letter and sent this story; she also had almost no standing as an author, having just taken up residence as a Wallace Stegner Fellow at Stanford to begin her study of creative writing. And since we were not going to accept her story solely on the basis of her charming and insightful cover letter, we found ourselves obliged to read the story itself. In the same issue in which the story was eventually published, I find equally strong, but very different, fiction by Frederick Busch, Ed Minus, and Tony Ardizzone. The primary difference is that all of these other stories are serious, none of them relies primarily—as does Deborah Larsen's story—upon humor, or whimsy, for its success. And that strikes me as slightly odd, since I as a reader of fiction probably value humor above all other things.

The humor in "Father Pat Springer" emanates from its speaker, Addie, whose take on the world and whose way of expressing it are so wonderfully her own. She is a bit of a ding-a-ling, a little ditzy, a little goofy, in the things that she notices and the spins that she puts on them. The fact that there might be a priest in her aerobics class is of enormous interest to her, though it most definitely bores Ray, the other significant character in the story. Joanne is interested, but for a different reason; she is taking instruction from the Father. But why does she tell Addie about him? Perhaps because she thinks the priest's interest in the absurdities of life is equal to Addie's own such interest. Addie is so interested in the insignificant fact she has been told that she ends up creating a life and a personality for the priest, whom of course she never meets, never even sees.

We might wonder why Addie is so interested in the priest—much more interested, for example, than she is in Ray. One of the mysterious moments in the story occurs when Addie tells us of Ray: "And he said what he always says, 'Call me, Addie.' But I never want to. I never do call him." Does his request mean that he is interested in her? And if he is, then why doesn't he call her? Why does he only ask her to call him? Perhaps he is just that kind of person: from the story we deduce that he is a regular kind of guy—unreflective, unsubtle, direct in everything he says and does. His only cunning act is always to wear a dirty apron while working at the Fullbelly Deli, because it makes it seem that he is working hard.

In any case, though our speaker seems to enjoy talking with Ray, she never calls him; but she is obsessed with the unseen Father Pat Springer. I think this is because, though she does seem to long for affection, she wants it from a comforting father figure rather than from someone her own age, someone who might want to offer her more than a reassuring hug. She is a person who has been abandoned at least once in her life, perhaps by someone like Ray—perhaps, in fact, by Ray himself: perhaps the reason he won't call her, but wants her to call him, is because he wishes to resume with her the relationship they had in the past; he did her wrong and then apologized, and she told him not to call, that she would call him if she wanted to start seeing him again. I suppose I should say that I do not believe what I just said; I think Ray tells her to call him because he is just that kind of guy. But it is a possibility.

In dwelling, however briefly, on why the speaker is obsessed with Father Pat Springer, I am making the story seem more serious than it actually is. To correct this impression, and to show the whimsy that I think is the most significant quality of this work, I will quote my favorite paragraph in it. Ray wants to know which of their fellow students Joanne identified as the priest, and Addie cannot answer:

> "Well, didn't she point him out?" He sounded exasperated. And it made me wonder, because Ray doesn't seem to be the least bit interested in religion. "You die, that's it," he's always saying in a flat voice and making, with a forefinger, a slitting motion across his neck from ear to ear, making a clicking sound with his teeth.

These sentences reveal the speaker beautifully, her uniqueness. Her interpretation of Ray's question is so exquisitely odd, so wonderfully unexpected, so completely unRaylike, that we know immediately that it is she who is interested in religion, that the fact of religion has a lot to do with her curiosity about this fellow aerobics student, Father Springer. Meanwhile, Ray's way of expressing his theology is marvelously funny; this is a wonderful paragraph.

In my letter to Deborah Larsen accepting the story, I find these sentences: "I love the story, which is so beautifully wry and understated; your narrator is completely lovable. And the ending, where Dorothy appears in such economical fullness; this is very fine work." Dorothy is another projection from the mind of Addie, an invented character who serves to express the kind of affection for which Addie herself seems to long. The notion of love, of loving literature—my idea that an editor, or a critic, must love the stuff first and foremost, or seek another line of work—comes full circle in Deborah Larsen's response to my letter. She wrote back: "I am delighted that you will publish 'Father Pat Springer'; I was *as* delighted by your letter and your comments. The fact that you loved my story and said so is of enormous importance to me." In an unusually full way, this correspondence illustrates why we like cover letters at *The Gettysburg Review,* while many magazines do not like than at all: they establish a personal connection, however tenuous, between the author and the editor. They reveal character, and character is what "Father Pat Springer" is all about.

All that was in 1987. We still like humor in the stories we publish in *The Gettysburg Review*, though whimsy is perhaps the better word. Lately, however, I find another tendency in our pages, one that favors a kind of oddness that is not necessarily funny, though sometimes it is. I am thinking of stories like "The Good Farmer," by Andrew Hoffmann, "Benjamin," by Naeem Murr, and "Jim," by G. K. Wuori. Character is the fundamental thing in each of these stories as well, and at a certain level it is also a mystery. But then character always is a mystery. Later today I will meet with my colleagues in the English Department, each one of whom is, beyond an obvious surface familiarity, a mystery to me. I know how mysterious their lives must be because I know my own life so well, and I know that my life is almost a complete mystery to them, however hard I try to make it clear. We will be discussing candidates for positions in the department, people whom we have been interviewing. Mysterious characters, every one.

Two other changes at *The Gettysburg Review* are that we now get lots and lots of manuscripts and the editor is no longer the only person who reads them. Everywhere I look in this office I see huge piles of manuscripts that are in one phase or another of the reading process. Jeffery Mock, our assistant editor, screens the approximately four hundred fiction and poetry submissions that we receive each month and passes about fifteen percent of them on to me. Emily Ruark Clarke reads the essays and essay-reviews, makes evaluatory comments, and passes them all on to me. I make the final decisions, accepting perhaps one of every ten manuscripts that I read. Our acceptance rate therefore falls somewhere between one and two percent for creative work, and is about ten percent for nonfiction prose. Because of this immense volume of reading, we find that we are sometimes unable to respond to some of our writers for a considerable length of time. The biggest irony in this situation is that the writers we are likely to keep waiting longest are the ones whose work we are most interested in, the ones who make the first cut. Therefore the writers we are most likely to offend are the ones we least would want to offend. Sometimes we wish they would realize that the delay is a good sign, not a bad sign.

But our slowness does sometimes offend writers—and sometimes writers offend us, whether they mean to or not. We have a policy of not reading manuscripts that are being simultaneously submitted elsewhere. Most writers seem aware of that policy, but occasionally someone will become exasperated at not hearing from us and will send their manuscript elsewhere. That is fine, as long as they first withdraw the manuscript from our consideration. Not long ago we commissioned an essay-review from a writer. When he accepted the assignment, we ordered the books we wanted him to write about and then sent them to him when they arrived here. When his piece arrived, we were busy with other things and unable to get to it for almost three months—but it had been commissioned, and the acceptance was almost automatic, so we did not worry much about the delay. Eventually we read the piece, liked it well enough, and proceeded to spend a couple of days copyediting it; relatively heavy copyediting is the rule, not the exception, with essays and essay-reviews. But when we sent the results to the author, he said that, after so long a wait, he had assumed that we were not interested in the piece; he sent it to another magazine, which had accepted it immediately. It is easy to understand the frustration of the author; even the editor who caused that frustration can understand it. Clearly, however, that author does not understand the frustration of the editor.

It is not like we were sitting on the beach all that time, eating kumquats and kiwi fruit. No, we were working our usual ten-hour weekdays, half that much each day on weekends, trying rather desperately just to *get to* his essay-review. And the work that an editor does, the time that he spends on manuscripts rather than on his family, his tan, his tennis game, his desire for rest, so much of that work and time are done for the primary benefit of the writers. Think for a moment about the nonexistent fame of editors; think of the NEA fellowships for which they cannot apply; think of the many awards and prizes that will never come their way (there is only *one* monetary award available to editors, the PEN/Nora Magid Award). These are the things we think of when writers withdraw manuscripts that we like, or when they write, many in asperity, wondering why we have not decided on their manuscripts yet: we understand your frustration, we want to say; can you understand ours? Can you possibly understand this one crucial mystery of our lives? That's all; that's all we ever want to say.

Father Pat Springer

Deborah Larsen

A woman named Joanne told me that there was a priest in our aerobics class. And I said, "a priest?"

We have this huge aerobics class at six o'clock on Mondays, Wednesdays, and Fridays at the University. This class is through Continuing Ed and I suppose there are about a hundred and fifty mostly good-looking younger to middle-aged people in it. The reason I know Joanne slightly is that she has the job, in this class, of checking at the door of the gym to see that we all have the little orange tags marked "Fitness" laced into our shoes. It makes it hard, that way, for anyone who hasn't paid to sneak in.

When Joanne told me this, about the priest, it was early, there were only a few people in Gym D standing around stretching, and the priest hadn't arrived yet so she couldn't point him out. She said, "I suppose he'll be here any minute."

"I'd really like to see," I confessed, "what he looks like."

If you don't know much about aerobics you'd wonder what Joanne was doing in this class because she's slim, slim. She wears these little skimpy loosely-belted shorts and a halter-style top over her narrow chest and you can always see a lot of her small bare back. She has frizzy auburn hair around her thin face and she looks really fierce, lion-like. But she smiles sometimes. And she's good at aerobics, you should see her. It seems to me she always does the exercises perfectly, can always reach down and grasp her toes or the backs of her ankles without bending her legs. I mean she seems like a human gyroscope when she runs and leaps, dripping sweat onto the floor. Every time I see her and ask her how she's doing, she says, "I just got up," and looks fierce. But she's always there early, watching at her station, there at the door, glancing at all the feet.

The other thing she told me about the priest was that she was taking instructions from him, in religion. She said, "It's interesting." And she said, "He's wonderful. He's so wonder-ful," is the way she said it. "He has an eye," she continued, "for the odd things in this life. I mean, he sees these things everywhere. In the human part of the Church. Even in this class he sees some, you know, absurdities." But since he hadn't arrived yet, and I didn't know what else to say I went over to my side of the gym and started stretching.

I was all by myself, stretching, when this acquaintance of mine, Ray, showed up. He has this tin star that says "Menace" and today he had it hanging from the front of his red T-shirt. "Ray," I said, "do you know Joanne? The one who stands by the door and checks our shoes as we come in? The one with the halter and navy blue shorts?"

"Uh, huh," said Ray. "The one, that reed who always eats nothing but honey on wheat." Ray works at the Fullbelly Deli on campus in the afternoons. You can always spot Ray at Fullbelly by his dirty apron. He says all the smeared ketchup and mustard shows how hard he's working.

"Well," I said, "she told me there's a priest in this class."

"Which class," said Ray.

"This one," I said. "This aerobics class."

"This class?" Ray asked.

"This class."

"Well, which one is he?" Ray asked.

"I don't know," I said. I looked anxiously around. The gym was filling up.

"Well, didn't she point him out?" He sounded exasperated. And it made me wonder, because Ray doesn't seem to be the least bit interested in religion. "You die, that's it," he's always saying in a flat voice and making, with a forefinger, a slitting motion across his neck from ear to ear, making a clicking sound with his teeth.

"He hasn't shown up yet, Ray," I said.

Somebody had turned up Willie Nelson, "On the Road Again," and we were getting ready to start. Walt had just jumped up onto the platform in the center of the gym. Walt Reusch is our aerobics instructor and he has a class in Seattle, too, and one at Washington State in Pullman as well, and he drives a BMW. Once my step-brother, who is a good baseball player but who hardly ever says a word, got a look at Walt through the door of the gym and said, "Whoa, that guy looks more like a football player than an aerobics instructor."

One reason I like to watch Walt lead aerobics is that sometimes he talks seriously to the different parts of his body. If he figures things aren't going absolutely perfectly, say, when he's doing the floor exercises, he decides it might be the fault of a foot because he cocks his head and shakes his finger at one of his feet the way Mark "the Bird" Fydrich, while he lasted in the Majors, used to shake his finger at the baseball. Well, Walt's scolding his foot is what I think he's doing. Telling it to contribute or else, to the whole body. And sometimes, during aerobics, I think Walt's looking right at me and I see him open his mouth and say something but of course I don't know what it is because I'm so far from him with my back to the wall of the gym and "Every Breath You Take" is so loud. But I think he's talking right to me but I don't know whether it's encouraging or scolding he's doing. Sometimes I even think the funny pointing he's doing is aimed right at me, and I can feel my face getting hot and the carotid pulses in my neck beating even faster than usual.

But Walt never talks to me outside of class. He just chews gum fast and walks by me fast, chewing, as if he's in a hurry.

But now he was making a sign with his fingers pinched almost together but not quite, a sign you might make if you wanted to tell somebody that something is little, tiny, and in this case, if you know what he's saying, the sign meant that he wanted one of those big, beautiful, young women in the shimmering exercise suits who always stand near the sound system, to turn the music down. And Walt started shouting, you have to shout to be heard in Gym D with that crowd, that Father Springer had a question. "FATH-er SPRING-er," he yelled, and waved one arm wildly toward that half of the gym opposite where I was, "has a QUEST-ion about the FLOOR exercise where you FLEX your HI-ips and bend over and GRA-ASP your TOE-OES. And he wants to KNOW-OW what if you CA-AN'T stretch your arms FAR E-NOUGH to RE-EACH your TOE-OES. Now the important THI-ing is to keep your legs STRAIGHT! and DOW-OWN against the FLOOR and BEND from the HI-IPS but if you can't quite reach your TOE-OES, that's OK-KAAY. Stretch the HAMSTRINGS is the MAIN THI-ing. It doesn't matter if you CA-AN'T hold on to your TOE-OES, OK-KAAY? OK-KAA-AAY!"

I side-stepped over to Ray. "Father Springer."

"What," said Ray.

"Father Springer must be the name of the priest."

"Why," said Ray.

"That question," I said. "That question about not being able to reach your toes was Father Springer's question. I think Walt said, "FATH-er SPRING-er has a QUEST-ion.""

Ray shrugged. "I can't understand a word Walt says. That guy. It all just sounds like gibberish to me."

Then one of those women turned up the music again and we began taking big goose steps and then we swung our arms back and forth as hard as we could. The thing is, I have never been able to grasp my toes in those floor exercises without bending my knees a little. I think it's because I'm long-waisted but not very long in the arms, if that makes any sense, I'm not sure. But whatever the reason, I couldn't do it. And now I knew that someone else was having a tough time with it, too. Father Springer, the priest who had asked a question, the only one who had ever asked a question in this class.

And then I really started looking for him, looking hard while doing jumping jacks and then running in place, bent forward making little tripping motions, waving my arms like Charlie Chaplin. I was looking all around at men one after the other, on the side toward which Walt had pointed. I could feel the sweat starting down the back of my neck.

I figured Father Springer must be slightly middle-aged and there were several middle-aged men on that side of the gym. The thing is a priest's training I knew was long, so he must not be any kid. There was a big, tall man with light, thin hair and a really, really black moustache who reminded me of my cousin Hunt, who has a Ph.D. from Stanford in something like aeronautics/astronautics, and I thought he might be Father Springer because he was tall and composed-looking like Hunt. Hunt, in a crisis, always says, "It seems to me we have three options here." But there was another man who was also fairly tall who might be Father Springer. He didn't look quite so composed but he had, well, longish shorts on. And I thought that somebody who was Father Springer might not be so composed and could have longish or baggy shorts on, to be modest. Aerobics shocks you a little until you get used to it–there's all this skin, some smells, body hair sticking out like scarecrow's straw, and sweat. Once I was in back of a man whose shoulders were all burn scars. Here, you even notice light rashes on people's arms and legs. And sometimes when we throw our pelvises forward in one of the exercises you can see that some shorts are really too tight. But this man in the longish shorts had on a T-shirt with words printed on the front of it which I couldn't quite make out, my eyesight is bad, but it looked as if the words might be missing vowels. I wondered if a priest would have on a T-shirt with words on the front.

I looked at each middle-aged man, one right after the other. But I couldn't decide, in this class, which one was Father Springer. I wondered if it would work to imagine starched white gleaming collars around the necks of all of the middle-aged men for the purpose of sorting them out. I was getting a little desperate, to see what he looked like.

When aerobics was over I looked for Joanne but she had already left, so I walked down the stairs with Ray. And he said what he always says, "Call me, Addie." But I never want to. I never do call him.

But I did, on the way to work, remember a story Ray had told me about what a man dressed in sweats said to Dr. Harris, our cellular biology professor, the other day at the bottom of the stairs to the River. (Ray calls Gym D the River because of how all the perspiration rolls off everybody onto the floor during aerobics. "That place, that's a real River up there," he always says.) According to Ray, he, Ray, had just finished telling Dr. Harris that he should try aerobics sometime when a man standing there dressed in sweats and a headband said, "Oh, Richard here goes to a pretty fancy spa to get his exercise and he gets massages, too. And from what I hear about those massages—how he's treated and how he treats the personnel—I think he needs to go to confession." And the man laughed, according to Ray. When I asked him what Dr. Harris, who's always prepared in class and who wears a wedding ring, had done then, Ray had said, "Huh, him? He just smiled. Hey, call me, Addie."

I wondered, on my way to work at Saga, Saga Foods, if that could have been Father Springer, a man in sweats who said to straight Dr. Harris that he might need to go to confession.

That night, after I got home from work, I found out what Father Springer's first name was. His name was Pat. I read practically everything in the local paper because when I get home from school and aerobics and work I'm so tired I can, once I sit down in the chair, hardly get up again to go to bed. So I even read the obituaries and this one obituary especially drew my attention because there was this little blurry picture with it of the deceased talking on the telephone. I mean there was this little white telephone receiver that the deceased had up to her ear in the photograph. Maybe that's the way this woman's kids wanted to remember her, maybe she was always on the telephone trying to talk to people, but I thought it was a little crazy to have a picture like that in the paper. Her name was Florence Wachter and she had died at eighty-seven after a long illness, memorials to the Kidney Fund of N.W. Washington. And her funeral would be next Wednesday, two days from now, and then I read "the Rev. Pat Springer, officiating." Not Patrick, but Pat. The newspapers wouldn't use a nickname for a priest in an obituary notice.

And I began to think of Father Pat Springer conducting a funeral service, though I couldn't imagine his face nor the details of the service, but I just imagined how he might carry himself. And I thought about how he would be in good shape from aerobics so that he could stand for a long time at the side of the casket and probably make a vigorous sign of the cross so you couldn't mistake what it was. And I wondered if aerobics gave him the strength to stand it, even when he felt like groaning inside, to talk, at all the funerals, to the boring young and old relatives standing around, including the ones who take pictures of their mothers on the telephone. And then I wondered if he ever put his arms around any of them who might need comforting, any funny smelling ones, people who usually never came to Church or ones who heard voices and who came and sat in the pews in spurts in the summers with bandages on their perfectly good hands and feet and with their faces wrapped in scarves. Some ones like that who you don't know what they'll do next.

And I thought maybe he did, that he put his strong arms around, say, Florence's old sister, a spooky one whom he'd never met before that day but whom he'd watched, from time to time during the service, out of the corner of his eye. What he did was, at the graveside, he just folded her up in his arms, this old girl in a coat, Florence's sister. She just let him fold her up in his hairy, chaste arms, this stiff girl whose breath makes you want to jump back, who lives above the Oasis tavern near the train station, who you could never convert in a million years, whose cookies taste like her apartment smells. And then he said something in a voice so low I could barely make it out. What he said was, "O.K., Dorothy, now we're not just going to walk away today, don't worry, we're not just going to all walk away and leave you standing here by yourself."

꙳꙳꙳꙳

A Story Like the World:
The Selection of Louis Gallo's
"Bodies Set in Motion"

Jim Clark

I distrust first impressions. The story that dazzles me on an initial reading immediately goes back to the readers. And this is exactly what happened to Louis Gallo's story, "Bodies Set in Motion." "Not Bad," I told my fiction editor, Julianna Baggott, who had first read the story and then brought it to my desk with much enthusiasm. "But I like a little more story in my story. Get some other readings on it."

At *The Greensboro Review*, we have a fiction editor plus two or three editorial assistants, all second-year MFA students, who are first readers on the 700 or so stories we get for each issue. Some fifty stories (about one in seven) make it back to my desk after receiving positive comments from an editorial assistant and the fiction editor.

I build deliberation into our editorial process. If a story is strong, I ask for arguments against it. If a story got mixed reviews, I ask for someone to argue for it. In addition to MFA readers, I have undergraduate interns (including this year a young Russian woman, a remarkable short-story writer herself). I have a managing editor who is a science fiction writer, and I have a poetry editor (over the years I have found poetry editors, writers of fiction or not, to be invaluable readers of stories when we get down to copyediting questions). A top-50 story on my desk may have received nine diverse readings before the fiction editor and I sit down to select the half-dozen or so we'll run. Most of the time we agree. If we don't, I win—unless the fiction editor is willing to die or kill (me) for a story.

These many-voiced deliberations make for better stories and provide some insurance against accepting a story that emerges as a ball of technical problems when we come to the line-by-line editing. Then too I feel I've earned my money if we've anguished over a story for weeks. A story like Louis Gallo's makes things too easy.

So I was pleased to see his manuscript returned to me in its mailer covered with readers' comments, including, "A little overdone. . . Really, what happens here? This guy, Pepe, can't sleep. He thinks and thinks and thinks. Then he wakes. He decides he shouldn't go to work and develops a theory around this impulse. . ."

Now I had some backup to really go at this beguiling story. Witty, sure I explained, but I like my humor bolted to a narrative drive that makes me reach for my seatbelt. Give me an anarchic jokester, not a mere stand-up (or in Pepe's case, a sit-down) comic. And then there's this entropy notion. Didn't Thomas Pynchon already do this subject in his story "Entropy" some thirty-five years ago (long before Jeremy Rifkin made the term a household word), and didn't Pynchon himself confess the topic led him into overwriting? Aren't entropy stories as common as all those other stale tales of kids trying to figure out their lives via algebra homework and depressing old dying geezers (most often cancerous jungle priests)? How do these overdone topics catch on? I asked, working myself into a harangue worthy of Pepe himself. Remember those anti-beef days and the resulting "chicken fiction" issue where there was a chicken in every plot? And what about all those damned angel stories we're seeing?

By now I could see editors scurrying from their flippant infatuation with "Bodies Set in Motion," but I couldn't resist a few parting shots. Don't we tell undergraduates not to open a story with the protagonist waking in bed? Don't we insist on knowing up-front the where and when of a story? We don't get the vaguest sense of place until the end, we don't know the season, except it's cold, don't know if we're in a house or a log cabin. And if work's so important, why don't we learn what Pepe and Faye do for a living?

So the Gallo manuscript went back into my stack as we read the remaining hundred stories and began copyediting stories we were accepting. The *Review* office is large, with desks for the staff and a desktop publishing center. Unlike in "Bartleby," there are no dividers, and at the height of production, the space is a cafeteria of noise: fingers tapping keyboards, editors arguing points of style, usage, and lineups with teams of proofreaders droning away. Such work is dry, hunger-inducing effort, and there's a lot of munching on leftovers from visiting-writer receptions. Jokes abound. Still, I was disconcerted at how often I found staffers sitting alone, smiling. What? I'd ask. "That Pepe, I can't get him out of my mind"–that's the answer I'd get. "I'm sorry," my fiction editor confessed. "That story just makes me laugh out loud." Contagion was afoot.

And so I went back to "Bodies Set in Motion," noting that even the most reserved readers' reports concluded, "But I *really* like this story." And, I finally had to admit, so did I—not just for the hysterical energy of the story, but for its immensity.

Ever since our MFA faculty editors Robert Watson, Peter Taylor, and Fred Chappell put together the magazine's first issue more than a quarter century ago, the *Review* has been asked what we look for in a story. Our stock answer: "The best being written regardless of theme, subject, or style." If I have my notion of "the best," it's this: there's a *story*, and somewhere in its narrative floor is a trapdoor that, once discovered, leads the reader below the surface to a big room filled with a richness of stuff: allusive artifacts, bits and pieces of our collective history on this planet—even some Garpian muck the sump pump of editorial cleanup can't totally remove.

But in Gallo's story Pepe paces a thin floor with little under it. Even the furnishings are sparse. There's a bed and a sofa, and we know from his piddling that the living room contains an ornate plaster frame and a lamp. A bowl of fruit sits atop the refrigerator, a woodstove hisses and pops throughout, and there's a stereo. But I was so busy looking for my theoretical room in the deep structure that I just never saw the really big things.

Like, well the *Titanic* in the first paragraph. And Mahler. Music fills this story, from Barber's mournful *Adagio* and Verdi's *Requiem* to Prokofiev gone graphic, "piecing together an alarmingly vivid nightmare, goblins rushing me with hacksaws and ice picks." But it's Mahler's "eerie flights" which help Pepe filter out global injustice: "lawyers with saber-teeth and sewerage for entrails, massacred peasants, thieves, butchers, the gleaming white teeth and sinewy smiles of hypocrites, liars, traitors . . ."

Mahler once said, "A symphony is like the world—it must embrace everything." And it is precisely this reach that Gallo attempts in this story. Pepe's Job-like harangues pinball from Methuselah to Lazarus, from the fantasies of Disney to the horrors of Hitchcock, scanning human wanderings from Odysseus to Chaplin. There's the pop psychology of Dr. Joyce Brothers, the protests of Luther, Victorian cupids, multinational team playing, and Teen Angel. We move from London to Hong Kong to the Tunguska Crater in a single bound. The cataloguing of the world's good things and bad things is as encyclopedic as Whitman's, as fast-paced as Billy Joel's "We Didn't Start the Fire."

It's not that Pepe's conflicts are too little in this story. They are just too big to be seen at first glance. After all, this is a man who wants to be "God for a day," wants to punch out the second law of thermodynamics, and calls time a tattooed street hooligan.

Before accepting a story, we raise copyediting questions with the author. We're not dictatorial. If we have serious reservations about a story, we suggest the author send it elsewhere before trying us with a revision. My only substantive question to Gallo had to do with tense, and we had an extended discussion about how time works in the story, whether the classical unities are still sacred: how time can stand still and, if you believe in Superman, even reverse itself. I'm satisfied now with the shift past tense when Faye steps out of Pepe's little world, how there is no present when she's gone. And I accept that when she returns, demoralized and burned out from work, present time returns, moves forward: "Under my feet I can almost feel the planet rumble on its axis."

We are, says Pepe on Faye's return, bodies set in motion in Eden, cursed to work and age and die, but always desiring comfort and warmth in this cold universe moving toward heat death. All we can do is live by hope, carry fruit in our pockets to remind us of Paradise. All we can do is keep the home fires burning, and if we can't actually embrace the world, at least we can embrace each other.

As he heats almond-scented lotion for her homecoming massage, Pepe feels "vibrantly alive and on to something big." But it's doubtful Pepe in his "minuscule patch of Blue Ridge" will ever be able to articulate this news of the universe, except maybe by sharing with her his vision of the blazing pyracantha or by putting on Mahler.

Lest it seem the *Review* craves stories glowing with hope and joy, let me note that Gallo's story is one of the darkest we've published: good comes only in low wattage, ideals are "slimy reptiles," truth is "ugly and wet like a mucous membrane," and life itself is "slime and ooze, ultraviolet rays bombarding primeval pools of sizzling amino acids." There are some old geezers in here too, but Gallo's geezers are not dying in the world's back rooms; they are prowling the sun-drenched beaches with metal detectors looking for Civil War submarines and ingots while fondling bikini-clad volleyball players.

When I called Gallo to praise this absurdly funny tale and to tell him he had won our 1993 Literary Award, he said the story is one of several Pepe and Faye stories in a collection titled *Dead by Tuesday*. "These are comic voice stories. I want the audience to laugh. If we lose our sense of humor, then what's left?"

Nothing in the world, I guess, but Pepe's impossible dream: "The *Titanic* has risen and we're all on board."

I don't mind finally admitting that a story won me over on first reading, if I feel we have engaged the piece in some editorial tag-team wrestling. In fact, looking back over our recent stories selected for or cited in the anthologies honoring "the best," I see that most of them floored me in the first round. Take, for example, Larry Brown's "Kubuku Rides," appropriately subtitled, "This Is It." The *Review* stories that got the most notice were those evoking the most heated discussion before (and after) we published them. Every one of them did things we thought a story writer shouldn't or couldn't do. But they did them, going into the deep waters, winning our hearts by doing so, and making us shout, "This is it!" on first reading–even if we didn't want to.

Bodies Set in Motion

Louis Gallo

We're asleep, or rather, we were asleep, a splendid oceanic dunk, warm and syrupy, limbs helixed like ancient jungle vines. Suddenly I'm lurching off my side of the bed, awash in not sweat but adrenalin, crying something like "Alarum! Alarum!" in midair. Naked and unarmed I whirl about the darkness of our bedroom, a reluctant dervish with raised fists and cocked bloodshot eyes. Cozy sloth, violent frenzy–who can fathom the vicissitudes of a single moment? The *Titanic* has risen and we're all on board.

Faye too has roused by this point, though awake or asleep, Faye is always conscious, perhaps even most conscious when she sleeps. She can report the most specklike details that occur throughout a night–how many trains passed, how many dogs barked, how often I snort, that kind of thing. She can tell me if I've slept well or fitfully, which sometimes I need to know for peace of mind. I feel cheated if I learn I've slept poorly. If I brag about what I regard as one of the most memorable oblivions of my history and Faye reports that in fact I had really writhed all night, I both reject the news and crumble at once, crave a nap, become a crotchety and infirm Methuselah. Thus I've learned that sleep is a most precarious Balkan state of mind.

"What's the matter!" Faye cries. Already I'm piecing together an alarmingly vivid nightmare, goblins rushing me with hacksaws and ice picks, the old story, Prokofiev's music gone graphic.

"Nothing," I pant, "a dream. Go back to sleep."

She turns on the bedside light. "Jesus, Pepe, you scared me. Don't *do* that."

I realize I'll be up for a while, so I grope for the robe I last saw bundled on a chair across from the bed. "Sorry, Faye, didn't mean to scare anybody. Who doesn't dream?"

"You were thinking about injustice again, weren't you? You wouldn't dream if you stopped thinking about injustice. I've told you a dozen times you can only think about injustice in the morning."

Poor Faye, I'd really terrified her. After great false scares, we get pissed. It's only natural. All that frightful rush and hair standing on end– for nothing. But she isn't remembering straight in her groggy muddle. What a treat, Faye stuporous! I'd better take advantage of this.

"What you always tell me, Faye, is that I can't think about injustice at night if I want to get to sleep. I *was* sleeping. Injustice keeps me awake. It wasn't an injustice dream; it was more Pascalian, you know, the horror of a black empty universe. I only said goblins for effect. It was much more abstract than goblins. Second law of thermodynamics. Entropy. Gödel's theorum. Uncertainty principle."

"You were trying to punch the second law of thermodynamics? Sure," she smirks. "It was goblins, Pepe, little green, scaly monsters with bulging pop eyes. You're just ashamed to admit you had a goofy kid's dream."

"I was punching space-time," I declare solemnly. "People my age only wish they could have kid dreams again. It might give some feeble hope. When 1 was your age I could lift not one but two boulders, now–"

"Oh, I see, we're on the age routine again. You're the only person in the world who's aging."

"Well," I shrug, "not the only one. Let's just say I take it more personally. To me time is a street hooligan, not so bright, crude, lots of tattoos and proud flesh. Somehow he gets you cornered in this back alley and there's no way out. I know if I could just reason with the creep, he'd see the light, or if I could roast out his eyeball like Ulysses and the Cyclops, you know, I–"

"Pepe, you're delirious, it's late, have mercy."

"You asked," I say, "didn't you ask?"

"I'm going to sleep." She pulls the covers over her head and pretends she is already sinking. But I know Faye. She will lie there and brood even if she doesn't writhe as I do. I brood viscerally. Faye has more finesse, calm as shrubbery through it all.

Darkness penetrates every crevice of the room, my own crevices as well. A curse upon everyone safely snuggled upon the waterbed of Morpheus. The robe is still bunched in my arms. Time to slip it on, go downstairs, and mourn the death of sleep. Time to relieve stress by sniffing the apples and peaches we keep piled in a wicker basket atop the refrigerator. Fruit therapy, according to *Psychology Today*.

I'm so sad maybe I'll put on Samuel Barber's *Adagio* and mourn myself as well. I imagine insomnia is like missing the last bus out of the Tunguska Crater, not that I've ever had that desolate thrill. I haven't been to hell yet either, though sometimes when guilt and regret claw at me like rakes, I feel the heat.

Guilt never touches Faye because she never does anything wrong, never unloads her venom on anyone, never pilfers someone else's slice of pie. I confess I have not only pilfered slices of pie but savored their meringue at the very moment of pilfering. Perhaps the truth is more modest. I haven't really stolen anyone's pie, ever, but I might have if given the opportunity. And it's this potential guilt, along with injustice and outer space, that gnaw me ragged late at night. You could say my mind churns like a sturdy dishwasher but that no plate emerges spotless because we ran out of Joy. So wrap me in a total body poultice, apply the leeches, this is no party. Faye remains whole and, as they say, well-integrated, despite a twinge of poetic misery, because she has been blessed with the almost sublime gift of accepting life for what it is. As far as I'm concerned, life is never what it is. There's always something missing or something egregiously extra, the lint on your cashmere overcoat. That I admire Faye's philosophy or talent or knack or whatever it is goes without saying. She foams with the froth. I sink like a construction block. Evanescence is too complicated for me.

I must resolve to stop thinking about pilfered pies.

And, yes, I've put on Barber and will sit through Mahler next, maybe Verdi's *Requiem*. What could be worse than an Italian requiem? The Germans never quite caught on to this. There's always something cool and threatening in Mahler, but listen to Verdi and your very organs and glands weep. Of course the Lutheran in me resists such shameful displays, marches onward in full battle gear to tack Theses upon a wall. The point is, as my fifteen-year-old cousin George once told me on the very day he tried to commit suicide, you've got to appreciate the good things, not dwell on the bad. After imparting this bit of advice George swallowed an unknown quantity of mothballs and spent the afternoon having his stomach pumped.

Appreciate the good—such optimism! Who could be more optimistic than the old geezers I so admire prowling beaches with their metal detectors? I read somewhere that one of them actually found a Civil War submarine right beneath a flock of bikinis playing volleyball on the sand. Suspect, if you ask me. Can't exactly fondle a barnacle-encrusted submarine, can you? I have always, in fact, appreciated the good, which for

some reason always comes in low wattage–how fondly I recall the spec-
tacular berries on our pyracantha bush (or is it tree?) back on Columbus
Street, those glorious waxen globs of lime, pale yellow, burgundy and
fiery orange, or a day when the sun beats down on you like bucketsful of
butter. It's the thorny labyrinth we wander between times that douses the
spirit, reduces Eden to Knossos. I've never quite got the hang of mazes,
collide with walls at every turn.

Faye's secret is not that she minds colliding with walls but that she
expects it and prepares, sports a nifty little Red Cross emergency kit in
her purse. I never expect the walls that keep rising out of nowhere; each
new one is a surprise. My adolescent cousin said he didn't care whether
he lived or died. Faye says it's no big deal one way or another. But I care!
Anything but life is preposterous. Good old life, its slime and ooze,
ultraviolet rays bombarding primeval pools of sizzling amino acids, God
breathing soul into Adam's lungs (wouldn't God have to kiss Adam on the
lips for that?), the whole fucking splendor of creation. I drink to it even if
my drink is Pepto-Bismol. Sign me up despite the boils and locusts and
sieges of pure panic. What I don't get is why we have to pay for everything. Faye doesn't argue, whips out her coin purse, and lays out the gold.
I cry, "Hey, wait a minute! Fifty dollars for a cupcake? Outrageous!"

Guess who winds up with the cupcake?

So I lie on the sofa in the back room listening to the wood stove hiss
and pop between Mahler's eerie flights, a glass of apricot nectar in my
hands. Okay, I think, this is okay. Will cost a little finger maybe, but I'll
give them the arthritic one. Yeah, injustice prevails, lawyers with saber-
teeth and sewerage for entrails, massacred peasants, thieves, butchers, the
gleaming white teeth and sinewy smiles of hypocrites, liars, traitors . . .
but the music, like fine gauze, somehow filters them out. The peaches and
apples help too; pop psychology aside, it makes good sense to carry an
apple or peach in your duffel bag. We've got to lift ourselves by our own
beatitudes.

And who should drift through the door, sleepless, soft as cotton, limp
in her flannel nightgown, but Faye? Her hair is straight, the way I like it;
she looks delicate as a soap bubble, eager to reconcile, though we haven't
fought. It's a trick we learned along the way: make up even if no viperous
words or homicidal silences have passed. I should report our success to
"Can This Marriage Be Saved?" On the other hand, secrets are secrets.
I've never told Faye about pyracantha. I've never told anybody. It's just
there, buried, ready when I need it, blazing in black outer space, immune
to time, silent as an atom.

Faye crawls on top of me and we listen together. "We'll remember this
moment in fifty years," I whisper.

"We'll be dead in fifty years," Faye mumbles, always the supreme realist.

"Impossible!" I say. "I'm going to fix it, make deals, do some hard-core negotiation."

She shifts her body so we fit snugly in the right places. "Deals with the Japanese, Pepe?"

I clear my throat. I'm being crushed but it feels good. "No, with God. It's about time somebody did. This sort of shit has gone on for millennia, dying when you least expect it or want to, rushing about like manic little insects, constant battles with your own species, not to mention microbes, the insidious bastards—"

But I'm not up to the harangue. It's too late and we're tired as rusty old anchors. Best of times, worst of times–they're upon us again. I'm veering toward worst myself although Faye's cautious optimism, which I otherwise reject on principle, keeps me gliding, makes me smile in a goofy saintlike way. Faye has this effect even if I don't want to admit it; left on my own I'd probably explode like a spore swollen with rage or anguish or disenchantment. I'd point fingers, that's certain, get myself excommunicated though I belong to no church, wind up in some institution for the hopeless. Instead she's on top of me with her eyes closed and I feel her breath on my neck. Best, worst, eenie meenie minie moe. They're the same.

We wake up the next morning side by side on the skinny sofa. I vaguely recall falling off a few times, and my joints are stiffer than usual. I'd been sleeping on the crook of my arm and there's no circulation. I try to move it but have no control. It's as if you go to sleep with an arm and wake up without one. Bad sign. Faye has been mashed against the back of the sofa and is trying to squirm free. "Whaaaa?" I mumble in my enormous resistance to waking at all.

"My God, Pepe, we're late for work! What time is it?"

She bolts over my lump of a body, straightens her nightgown, and rushes for the stove clock in the kitchen. Then she returns rubbing sleep out of her eyes. I'm aware of what's going on but don't want to be, would pay handsomely to stay curled where I am now that I have a little more room. But the Lutheran in me, that shrewish Jiminy Cricket, squawks, "What's the time, what's the time?"

Faye stretches while gazing out of the window, and I cannot help even at this hour but admire the contours of her body. "It's only seven o'clock, imagine. Go back to sleep. I'll take my bath."

"Come back," I plead, "it was so nice. We've got time. Let's not go to work at all."

"Do what you want," she says. "I've got to go, all sorts of reports due and meetings."

Now I'm up too, or partially up, my good elbow propped on the pillow, my head resting upon the flat of my hand. "See what I mean, Faye, this is classic. One of our really fine moments and we're foiled by clocks. Kibbles 'n Bits, Kibbles 'n Bits. We'll regret this when we're in our graves. Well, you'll regret it; I'm being cremated."

"I thought you said you'd fix it," Faye cracks as she gathers a handful of kindling to throw into the stove. "A little chilly down here today."

"Negotiations take time," I sigh, watching her move. There is something heavenly in the way women move. Nature seems to have endowed them with effortless grace. A man would not load kindling into the stove gracefully. There would be stomping and clanking and maybe a fart or two. When she passes the sofa I make a grab– "C'mere," I say, pulling her over by the hip, a wonderfully soft hip full of Victorian cupids I might add, not one of those bony anorectic plates. But I'm using the dead arm and it's not cooperating. Neither is Faye, who is struggling to get loose so she can bathe. "Let me go, Pepe," she demands, "or I'm really going to hurt you."

"You're weak," I laugh. "You can only hurt me if I let you hurt me. A little thing like you–"

I hate the way sudden pain always takes you by surprise. I actually screech as Faye bends my fingers back almost to the wrist. "Now will you let me go?"

"I'm just letting you think you're hurting me," I gasp. "If I wanted–" She gives my fingers the old heave-ho, and I'm screaming again. "You're free," I cry, "go, go, go!" I'm inspecting my wounded hand as she moves on toward the doorway. Finger movement okay, wrist fine, still some tingling from blood loss but getting better all the time.

"I'm going to kill you, Faye, when you least expect it," I shout at her. "I'm coming up when you're in the shower and make you grovel. Remember that movie *Psycho?* You hear me, Faye?"

But she's gone and our brief little party's over. Why are our brief little parties always over? My friend Winston would say you need the ugly to know the beautiful, you need opposites to know anything at all. I say caca. I say our brief little parties are always over. No more macaroons and punch. Time to break out the old sledgehammer and chisel. Time to get sucked back into the punctilious world. Time to succeed and amount to something and oil the gears and do whatever it is we're supposed to be doing. So I pull myself together, toss a match into the kindling, throw on a log, and prepare to prepare for the day. The truth is I'd much rather just piddle around, though there's no money in it. I recently read the classifieds in *Advertising Age* and came across a high-paying job notice. "Wanted," it said, "aggressive, creative, energetic, decisive, competitive copywriter, a team player not afraid to take risks, willing to uproot, confer with agents in Amsterdam, Hong Kong and London at a moment's notice, consult with industry giants, assume executive status." I cringed as I read, folded the paper carefully, and set it down. I think what appalled me most was the idea of winding up a team player in Hong Kong. I rejoice that there's no chance in hell anyone would hire me for such a job. But let's imagine some colossal personnel blunder. You still couldn't pay me enough. I'd become a team player in Hong Kong on one condition only: immortality as a fringe benefit. And then I'd quit on the spot. Since when do the immortals work? Talk about piddlers.

Faye has already outfitted herself for the day's buzz. I hear high heels clicking, valises being zippered, the efficient, abrupt transactions of someone who has shifted gears. I'm still lolling in my cloud, can't seem to keep up with time's arrow or get revved up enough to make the transition. Current realities don't seem worth the trouble, which my friend Dr. Assad regards as a sign of serious despair. I've told Dr. Assad that serious despair is stitched not into people but into the situations people find themselves in. There is, for example, serious despair in Hong Kong team playing. Give me a Jacuzzi, some good music, a bowl of juicy strawberries, the dream massage of my highest yearning, a sufficient bank account, assurance that the universe won't begin to contract while I'm in it . . . you get the point. We do not, I think, flow with the proverbial river but, rather, leap like electrons from one high-energy state to another until we finally lose energy altogether and decay in our rigid shells. This has got to stop. No more clicking heels and urgent telephone calls. Up with lazy hammocks and white pristine beaches and emerald oceans. Elect me God for a day, my fellow organisms, and you'll see changes. Not for nothing do I endorse the campaign slogan People for Paradise. What astonishes me is that we haven't all rebelled already, torn up our contracts, erected the barricades. Dr. Assad at the clinic says I score low on reality testing. Faye says I'm immature. Winston says we're already in Paradise but don't know it. I say bravo, they're undoubtedly right, I'm unrealistic, immature, ignorant. But who could argue against Paradise, settle for less without at least filing an official complaint? Life is not yet what we make it; it's what we think we ought to be doing to save face. Peace with honor, remember? Gross national product be damned, I want to lie on the sofa and snuggle with Faye. I feel the lance materialize in my hands, see windmills in the distance. Time to conquer something!

When Faye has finally finished getting ready, she comes in to tell me good-bye. She looks sad-faced and pouty. By this time I have created a blazing fire in the stove and the room is womb-toasty.

"Well, Pepe," she shrugs, "hi ho."

"You don't have to go," I say. "I'm not."

"You're not going to work?" she asks.

I stand erectly, holier than a kid with his first driver's license. "No," I announce, "I'm taking a stand. Somebody has to."

"Some stand," she sighs, "millions of people don't go to work every day. You're just like everybody else, Pepe, face it."

Faye has a sharpshooter's eye for bursting bubbles, but theoretically she has missed my point. The point about points is that they're so small, so mystical, so misjudged. We're far too fond of briar patches and periodic tables and IRS forms to give the simple point its due.

So, "No," I say, "everybody is taking off work for trivial reasons–they have the flu, they're tired, trying to catch up on errands, need a day off here and there, have appointments with plumbers, the array of excuses, whereas I am taking off to protest the insanity of work itself. The Bible says it's a curse, what happened to Adam and Eve after they got kicked out of the Garden."

"You don't believe in the Bible, Pepe. Look, I've got to go."

"Wait, Faye, just a minute. Ok, I don't believe the Red Sea parted and Lazarus came forth, unless he was in a coma and suddenly revived, although I grant some general truth along the way. But over ninety percent of everybody out there believes it's the direct word of God. So I'm making my point for the believers, the ones who go to work and randomly take off every now and then. You could say I've become a surrogate martyr."

Faye twitches her nose as if to detect an ever-expanding sea of guano. "The only *mortar* you'll make is the kind they put between bricks, Pepe. I've *got* to go. It's getting seriously late." So she marches toward the door and is, in effect, off to work except that she sticks her head back in and asks, "And what do you plan to do today anyway?"

I'm ready. "Absolute Rest, Faye, that's the agenda. A body set in motion tends to remain in motion. A body laid to rest tends to remain at rest. That last one didn't sound right, but you get the idea. I will do nothing at all, not because I want to do nothing but because nothing is symbolic in this case."

She closes the door, and I hear the heels click up our brick walkway like dainty horseshoes on cobblestone, hear the car door open and slam, the ignition grind, then silence.

Well, once I'd approached my third hour of Absolute Rest I had to admit privately it wasn't all the second law–or was it the first?–had cracked it up to be. I simply could not sit still and started piddling. The varied piddlings took on a chilling resemblance to work. I could not help, for instance, trying my hand at restoring the ornate plaster frame in our living room. It needed general refurbishing, cleaning, a new paint job. I worked like a maniac and had the thing sparkling in less than an hour. Then I Brassoed away the green fuzz on a standing lamp in the same room. The TV needed a good dusting as well. By hour five I'd also fixed leaks in both upstairs and downstairs faucets, which included rushing off to True Value for the proper washers. When I tried just sitting again I got antsy, felt imaginary hives breaking out all over my body. So I looked up imaginary hives in the *Merck Manual* and discovered there's no cure. You catch my drift, don't you? I would either die or live to a ripe old age. Thus it was time to sort through my sock drawers and discard those with holes or worn spots. Since I still own every pair of socks I've had since college, the task was formidable. The screen latch needed repair, the furniture craved lemon oil, the plaster could have used some spackling, the silver was black with tarnish, the doorknobs loose . . . entropy had infiltrated our household in a major way. By the time Oprah came on– Faye had not yet returned from work–I'd whipped through the entire place like a crazed popular mechanic waving screwdrivers and dusting rags. Home looked good after I'd finished, I must say. In fact, I couldn't wait for Faye to return and applaud my enterprise. As for Absolute Rest, feed it to the maggots.

While it is no small setback to grasp that one's philosophy has been ravaged by experience, I felt wonderful, brimmed with energy and housewifely pride, even self-righteousness. A pox upon the malingerer who never rises off his can. Put wash buckets and Brillo pads in thy pocket. Work while you whistle and all that. Naturally, I could admit none of this to Faye, who would taunt me mercilessly for having abandoned my noble plan.

And it was noble, I maintain, as grand a social experiment as any, in league with emulating Jesus. Because we fail in no way detracts from the ideal, right? No shame in routine confusion over policy and procedure. Alas, a burning smidgen of doubt has begun to glow in my dark brain like some lone firefly trapped in a cave. Suppose ideals themselves leave us more lonely and brokenhearted than the departure of Teen Angel? Suppose ideals, our grandest accomplishment, destroy us in the end? I'll have to consult Dr. Joyce Brothers on the matter. To learn that I've squandered most of life in pursuit of what doesn't exist would be a gruesome reckoning indeed. The good part is that I haven't squandered any life at all because I've never been able to live up to my own ideals, the slimy reptiles. Success by default. O happy day!

And naturally, when my speculation has reached what can only be described as its hysterical pitch—the highest C on a piano—when, ironically, to any casual observer at least, I'm paralyzed by Absolute Rest in order that my pinball of an idea might crash through the machine and set off all kinds of buzzers and bells and flashing lights, in walks Faye. She looks edgy, jagged, has had a rough day obviously. I'm sitting in the same spot I was in when she left. This could not fail to infuriate even the most patient of Penelopes. I'm tempted to cry, "I've only been at Absolute Rest for three minutes, and, besides, thinking counts too!"—but I say nothing as our eyes meet. She'll see soon enough that I've been busy. All she has to do is look around.

She lowers herself beside me, stiff and awkward in her business suit, another Faye entirely. "You know, Pepe, you were right," she sighs. "Work sucks. All I did today was redo other people's mistakes. I'm tired and burned out and very disgusted. I wasted every moment doing nothing that meant anything to me and probably no one else either. So . . ."

She trailed off, winked, and I took the cue.

"So?"

"So I'm taking tomorrow off, like you. You're right, we have to take a stand."

I'm gulping wildly now. "Uh, Faye," I begin, "leisure isn't exactly a picnic, you know. I struck out. You'll see in a minute. Maybe we're doomed to work after all. I think we like it. Never imagined I'd hear myself say such a thing, but truth is ugly and wet like mucous membrane."

Faye's eyes widen with surprise, and she actually looks startled. "But you said . . . Absolute Rest—"

"Bodies set in motion," I reply sadly. "We've all been set in motion. Can't stop it now. Can't evade the laws of physics."

"Maybe we should kill ourselves," she murmurs, the way she talks when I concur with her worst fears. I envision the old folks and their metal detectors. Thousands of miles of beach to cover with a feeble instrument. Maybe they'll find a few ingots, maybe nothing at all. And all that team playing in Hong Kong. International markets, profit margins, losses, capital gains, R&D, P&I, the metaphysics of shifting capital. No deals with God in the cards. We're stuck with what we have or don't have. Paradise is the night we don't dream of goblins or universes without pension plans. And yet I'm mildly happy–the roof hasn't caved in, I've taken the day off and got a lot done, Faye is home (irritable, true, but alive and well), we've beat back entropy for a while, we're still solvent.

"Take the day off tomorrow, Faye," I tell her as I massage the back of her neck, the sinews of which are taut as violin strings. Her hair smells like apples and peaches. "Just call in sick or something. No big deal. Get out of that armor you're in and I'll rub your back."

"Really?" she asks. "I'd love that."

"I'm ready to conquer only the next moment, perhaps the next second," I mumble. "My lance has shrunk to a toothpick. Where's the lotion you always use that smells like almonds?"

She's already unbuttoning the blouse as she goes upstairs to put on her robe, or my robe, which she prefers. "In the hall cabinet," she cries merrily at the prospect of a massage.

I find the stuff and warm it up in a basin full of hot water. It will be a pleasure to rub the knots out of Faye's back, knead her slender shoulder blades and make her purr. At this particular instant of space-time, here in our minuscule patch of Blue Ridge, I'm vibrantly alive and on to something big. I want to break the news to Faye but don't know exactly what the news is. It's coming, though, the way you know the phone is about to ring or somebody wants to kiss you. Under my feet I can almost feel the planet rumble on its axis. Somewhere in the empty universe pyracantha has bloomed again. Life is only sometimes what it used to be.

~~~~~

The Resurrected "Mother"

Cara Diaconoff

W.B. Pescosolido's story "Mother," which ran in the Fall 1993 issue of *Indiana Review*, was first submitted to us around January or February 1992. At that time, the fiction staff was composed of the associate editor–acting as head of staff–plus four fiction editors, of which I was one. All the editors, incidentally, are graduate students in creative writing or literature at Indiana University. Our procedure, basically, is to circulate any manuscripts which make it past the first and second readers among the fiction editors; if at least two of them feel that the manuscript is worthy of further consideration, it is submitted to the associate editor and discussed at the next staff meeting.

When I first read "Mother," I was struck first of all by its wit and by the lightheartedness with which it handled its theme of the mysterious disappearance of a mother. There was a sense that the story was making fun of its own theme, its own conceits; indeed, that the narrator's very capacity to amuse himself was the force propelling the narrative forward. Secondly, I couldn't help but note that the attitude toward traditional "realistic" narrative techniques was decidedly less reverential in this story than is the case in the vast majority of our other submissions. I appreciated the way the story seemed to be satirizing traditional plot structures even as it partook of some of their most familiar devices. One of the fiction editors compared it in theme and treatment to Donald Barthelme's *The Dead Father*, which I found to be quite apt. In some ways, Pescosolido had written the "mother's" response to Barthelme. When the fiction staff met, however, none of the other editors shared my enthusiasm, and one in particular was strongly against accepting the story. I allowed myself to be swayed by the arguments that it was *too* light, that the satire was too predictable, and that the narrator and family members were undercharacterized–a charge which is easy to make against work that is not traditionally "realistic." The story ended up getting an encouraging note from me.

A year passed, and the author sent us another story, a satire along the same lines as "Mother," but one that didn't work as well. Indeed, I felt that its failures served all the more to underscore "Mother"'s successes. The story was circulated among the fiction editors, received lukewarm comments, and was sent back to the author, along with a whimsical request to resubmit "Mother," if by any chance it was still available. Much to my surprise and delight, it was. In the interim, the previous associate editor had finished out her term, and I had taken her place. I was now in a better position to act on my editorial impulses, so I proceeded to reread the story and happily to accept it.

I think one of the facts the editorial history of "Mother" makes clear is exactly how subjective even a well-discussed, fairly voted-on rejection can be. Many writers never know just how close their story came to being accepted; one more point, one more minute of discussion, one editor being in a more or less confident or belligerent mood on a given day, can mean the difference between acceptance and rejection. Months after we first rejected "Mother," the associate editor at the time was still musing on the decision, to the point where she finally wished that she had gone ahead and accepted it. This points up another important truth of the whole business, which is that the taste of any given editor can change over the course of her or his tenure. The business of editing, by definition, is one of learning, of constant change and growth. In the case of this particular editor, both her editorial taste and her own fiction writing had become more and more experimental over the course of her time at the magazine; she was moving steadily farther away from an aesthetic that privileged realism and narrative. My advice to writers, therefore, would be to keep a file of encouraging rejection notes and continue submitting to those magazines until they either publish you or beg you to cease and desist. If an editor has bothered to pen a note and has given you encouraging words, your chance of being published in the magazine is very real. If you take their comments to heart and continue sending them work, your eventual acceptance for publication may only be a matter of time.

Mother

W. B. Pescosolido

Mother's gone. She's been gone for about a week. I don't know where, and Dad doesn't worry.

I went over to my parents' house to borrow the vacuum to clean my new apartment. Dad was at the office as usual, but Mother wasn't there. I looked around for her, in the kitchen, the living room. Her car was in the driveway. I became worried.

I began to look in the places one would expect her to be. I looked in her bedroom and bathroom, in the den where she likes to read by the bookcase, in the laundry room. I called Dad at the office to ask if he knew where Mother was, but he was on another line, so I left a message. I went down and searched the basement, opened the storage closets in case she was hiding, playing a joke on me, pushed aside the musty winter coats. I looked in the cedar chest, under the down comforter, the afghan.

Then I looked further afield, out in the garden, beneath the juniper bushes along the driveway, in the garage. I climbed in my car and drove into town, checking for Mother at Rose's Beauty Boutique. I asked Rose if she'd seen Mother. She was leaning over Mrs. Atkinson's large, plastic draped body at the sink, rubbing her fingers through Mrs. Atkinson's soapy hair. "Have you seen Mother?" I said. "No," she said, pushing a stray piece of hair away from her face with the back of her hand. Mrs. Atkinson gave me a sidelong grin, a little wave from under the plastic. I nodded back to her.

I walked up the block. I checked at Nickels Payless, at the Jiffy Mart, the Video Vault, at the Kaweah Chuckwagon. She wasn't there. I went home to my apartment.

I drive back to my parents' house to see if Mother's returned. She hasn't, so I call Dad again. I ask him where Mother's gone. He says that she's around, about. "You know how she is," he says.

"No, I don't," I say.

I'm sitting in the den in the chair by the bookcase. I sit so that I can see the front door, just in case. Dad tells me he has another call on hold and has to go. "I've got to go now, son," he says. "I'll talk to you later."

"But, Dad . . ." I say.

"Got to go," he says.

"But . . ." I say.

He hangs up; I hang up.

I look through a photo album that I've found in the filing cabinet, bottom drawer behind the folder with last year's tax returns. There's Mother in black and white sitting on Dad's shoulders. I was told it was her, sitting there, smiling and looking at the camera. She looks different, younger. Dad looks fit in a tank top and gym shorts. He must've been about eighteen and on the high school track team. That would make Mother sixteen. She's smiling at the camera, wearing shorts and an Oxford cloth shirt, her hand resting on Dad's head. She looks like she's about to say something to the camera, to me. Dad looks determined. They have the same birthday, October 18th, National Dog Whipping Day, easy to remember. Cuts down on the costs of cards and gifts, a new toaster oven for both, an orange-juice squeezer. They have the same wedding anniversary, too.

I have dinner at Leonard's house, my oldest brother. We sit on the plaid couch and sip beer. I don't really like beer, but I just turned twenty-one, so I feel compelled to drink it. My other brother, the middle brother, Dan, is there too. He chugs his beer. Leonard's wife is cooking burgers in the kitchen, ripping open a bag of potato chips. She's already put the kids to bed.

My brothers tell me I am worrying needlessly. That Mother's just sowing her wild oats now that the kids are all well out of the house, having a fling of freedom. When the kids are away, Mom will play. Leonard tells me to quit this silliness. He says, "Go back to work or you'll lose your job."

Dan says, "What, Momma's boy scared to be all alone?" He tells me to chill out, have another beer. They're obviously not concerned. They tell me not to worry, and I try not to.

Perhaps I should call the police, check hospitals.

I wonder if I should call Grammy Cooke to ask if she has heard from Mother. But then I remember that Grammy Cooke is dead. She died six months ago. Perhaps Mother has been overcome with grief, a delayed reaction. It's not everyday you lose your mother. But this doesn't seem likely.

Is there anyone I could call? Anyone who would harbor Mother? Is Mother right now sitting on a chintz love seat sipping tea and talking about the news of the world?

It is the King that Mother talks to, and his wife. She's driving me along the shore in her gold Cadillac convertible for a picnic. The spring breeze blows in over the surf. The little plastic dog I gave Mother sits on the back dash. Normally, its head bobs up and down, but the wind popped the head off five miles back. Jenny, Mother's Shi-tzu dog, pants and drools in my lap. Mother talks to famous people to pass the time, to keep me amused, just for fun. Today it is the King and Queen.

She glances over her shoulder behind my seat and says, "Such a fine day we're having, isn't it, Your Majesty?" She smiles at me and winks.

She hums "My Country Tis of Thee," glances behind me to address the cooler that has deviled eggs in it, and bologna and ketchup sandwiches. Fluffernutters, and a thermos of Kool-aid. "How is the situation in the Middle East developing, Your Highness?" she says.

She asks me if the Queen is feeling fine. I look at the blanket behind her seat. I say, "I think so."

I sit on the floor of my apartment and think about Mother. It's a small apartment, one room. I have no furniture yet, just a mattress and a TV. It's not really a home. I drink iced tea, watch *Lost in Space* reruns, eat macaroni-and-cheese dinners late in the afternoon. An hour ago my boss called to ask why I haven't been to work. He said the books were backing up, the debits and credits were becoming confused, debits becoming credits and vice versa. He told me that I shouldn't start off a new job on the wrong foot.

I told him I wasn't feeling well. "I don't feel well," I said. And it's true, losing your mother is an unsettling experience, hard to know how to feel.

I try to picture Mother. How she looked when I last saw her, last week, the week before. She's of medium height, five foot four, a good, stocky build . . . motherly. A round face with cheeks pink from the sun. She looks like . . . like a mother. Sort of like Betty Crocker; the old one, not the new one. She has gray hair, or graying. . . . No, she had Rose dye it for the Elks' Club Christmas Dinner Dance. No, that was two years ago. . . .

Mother reads bedtime stories to me. She reads me a story about hedgehogs and gophers. I curl up against her warm hip. Then one about stuffed animals who walk and talk, about a wicked stepmother. A different story every night.

I sit in the den of my parents' house, looking at the photo album and listening to the radio. It was set to the station Mother listens to, KJUG, a country & western station. I didn't know Mother liked country & western. She doesn't seem the type. At the break for the local news, the announcer says that the number of mothers utilizing local day care facilities has dropped. He cites changing demographics and an aging population base. He says that experts project a twenty percent decrease by the end of the year. That two day care centers have already closed down. "This is due, partly," the announcer says, "to the decreasing number of mothers in the tri-county area."

Mother shouts in the middle of the night, and Dad kicks my bedroom door open. "Get up, there's a fire!"

I grumble and tell him I don't want to, I want to go back to sleep, it's only three. He yanks me out of bed and tells me to get outside. I'm thirteen; I can be grumpy. Smoke fills the room.

I get up and pull my pants on. By the time I get outside, Leonard has put all the silverware on the lawn, the TV and stereo. Dan and Dad have carried the sofa out of the house and have gone back in for the grandfather clock. Mother has her jewelry box under one arm and the dog under the other.

"It's a good thing Mom woke up and smelled the smoke," Leonard says looking at the house. "We all might've died."

I don't see any flames, just smoke pouring out of the crack where the roof meets the walls.

Later, near dawn, I sit in the car and watch Mother. The neighbors stand on the curb across the street, lining the street like they're waiting for a parade. The house we've lived in my whole life has now burned almost to the ground. Dad still tries to salvage the lawn furniture with a garden hose. The fire roars like a waterfall. The dog sits by Mother's foot, leaning against her ankle, and I would give anything to be that dog. I watch as Mother cries.

She walks around the house in her bathrobe. I try to catch her before she's gotten out of bed. Try to sneak up and yell "Boo!" to wake her up. But she's never there. No matter how early I slink into her room, the bed is empty. And then she surprises me at the top of the stairs in her fuzzy, lavender slippers and gray robe. Standing looking plump and comfortable with a cup of coffee in one hand, the Shit-zu by her foot.

"No, no," she corrects me. "It's Shi-tzu, SHI-tzu."

How does she do it? Always awake to cook breakfast before me and my brothers are up. Dad too, he's never around, does he ever sleep?

I look in Mother's closets and on her bookshelves, in her desk, for clues as to where she might have gone. Something out of the ordinary. Some half-hidden common denominator . . . a pattern.

In the closets I find twenty-two pairs of shoes, countless skirts and shirts, paisley seems to be a favorite. A coat made from the skin of an undetermined animal. And in the back, I find a horseshoe, upside down so all its luck has drained out.

In her desk I find a checkbook, recent checks written to Gump's, Macy's, Nickels Payless, the electric company. An address book, a letter opener, a desk calendar, stamps.

In her bureau, I find socks, shirts, some rather unmotherly underwear. There are blue jeans and khakis folded neatly in the bottom drawer.

Mother takes pictures of me and Lynn Carpenter, all dressed up for the Junior-Senior Prom. Lynn is wearing a long, light-blue evening gown. Blue high-heeled shoes and a corsage. I'm wearing a baby-blue tuxedo, double-breasted with matching shoes. "Cheese," Mother says. "Jarlsberg, Limburger!"

Mother is a very good cook. Her specialties are, in descending order of my preferences: Eggs Goldenrod, Sour Cream Twists, Cream Cheese Pie, Portuguese Sweet Bread. . . .

On the bookshelves I find books. But it is at the bookshelves that I notice a pattern developing. I go back to check my figures, review the data. The pattern is clear—a country & western theme. Mother has placed a Louis L'Amour book on every shelf in the house, I counted forty-three in all, mixed in with the cookbooks, murder mysteries, the *Encyclopedia Britannica*. The one by the dictionary is called *Jubel Sackett on the Haunted Mesa* . What does this imply? Is Mother a closet cowboy, or rather, cowgirl? Has she gone off to ride the range in chaps and boots, to punch a few doggies? Will I find a pair of pearl-handled six shooters in the basement where we store the the Christmas lights, the little glass angels? Should I go check?

I pick up the dictionary. *Webster's* defines "mother" as: a female parent. A woman in authority. An old or elderly woman. A slimy membrane composed of yeast and bacteria that develops on the surface of alcohol liquids undergoing fermentation.

I go to the Public Library to contemplate Mother's whereabouts and do research. Mother told me she used to like libraries, their smell. She used to come to this library. She said she picked which books to read by their bouquet, walking the aisles sniffing to find the books that smelled just right, that had that perfect mix of musty moldiness, paper, leather and knowledge. She'd pull them from the shelf, inhale the aroma, nod to herself, and then check them out.

This is how she chose Dad. She said that he smelled good, better than any other man she'd ever met. That he had the redolence of royalty.

I don't have a good nose. I spend all day reading foreign-language dictionaries. *Where is Mother? Ou est Maman? Wo ist Mutter? Donde esta Madre? Gde je Mati?*

I've had a nightmare about a wild puma chasing Bugs Bunny, trying to eat him. So I go into Mother and Dad's room, in my pajamas with the slippers attached. A little hood with droopy mouse ears. In bed they're not sleeping, they lie on top of each other. They've taken their pajamas off. They're making noises, moaning. They sound sick. I curl up and try to go to sleep on the floor, but I can't sleep. I can feel my heart beating in my ears.

I find a werewolf mask in the back of the guest-room closet. The last time Mother wore this was when she and Dad went down the street to the neighbor's costume party. Afterwards, she snuck into my room and woke me by howling like a wolf at the moon.

"Howl!" she said. "Snarl."

I pulled the blanket up to my nose.

"Woof," she said. She kissed me good night, licked my cheek. "Sleep well," she said.

I'm in the upstairs hall when the telephone rings. It's a wrong number, but the caller refuses to hang up. She asks for somebody named Pete Doffelmyer.

"There's nobody here by that name," I say.

She says that she knows she dialed the right number, and that I should go get Pete for her. "Go get Pete," she says.

"I'm sorry," I say.

She asks me if I'm Pete just pulling her leg. "Are you just pulling my leg, Pete?" she says.

Who is this Pete Doffelmyer? I want to go back to searching the linen closets. But perhaps this is Mother, just testing my filial devotion and instincts. "Is that you?" I say. "Mother, is that you?"

She hangs up the phone.

Mother tries to play my trombone.

"I've paid for the lessons," she says, "so I have a right to try it out."

She blows and blows, trying to play it like one might play a balloon, or a plastic baggie. She gasps, blows, gasps. Her cheeks turn red. The trombone trumpets. She hands it back to me and goes into the kitchen.

Mother had told me that she went to a Catholic school for girls, then two years of college. She said that she dropped out to get married. That she worked as a secretary while Dad finished up college. That by the time he graduated, she was pregnant with Leonard. She told me that Dan was planned, they were trying to have a daughter. Mother wanted to have a daughter.

"You were the big surprise," she said at the kitchen table over a bowl of Fruit Loops. "A good surprise." She grinned and held her hands on either side of her face like a vaudeville dancer. "Surprise!" she said. "Surprise!"

In the stereo cabinet, I find the music Mother listens to, a collection that shows unsuspected range: Lots of country & western, Hank Williams, Jerry Jeff Walker, The Flying Burrito Brothers. One album has a song on it called "Red Neck Mother." There is Maori Folk Music, Maasi Religious Hymns.

I decide to give up searching the house, no telling about this country & western thing. Instead I go to the store to prepare for her return. I don't know that she'll return, but I hope. I want to make her return pleasant. I stock up on things that Mother likes. I buy artichoke hearts (canned), diet soda (creme), corn chips, bean dip and tortillas. I buy her a new tooth-brush and toothpaste. Mouthwash, Q-tips, cotton balls, rubbing alcohol and shampoo. I am perplexed over the sanitary napkins. Does Mother use these anymore? Has menopause struck? I find that I am completely ignorant of the female physiology behind these questions. Can one tell by looking, assuming she will come back so I can look? A different glow on the cheeks, a different walk, like the proverbial non-virgin strut? I decide to play it safe.

My father and brothers don't worry, which I find disturbing. They say she's in and out, she's around, she's here and there. Here and about doing this and that. Could it be that they are right? That she is here and I keep missing her? Perhaps she was weeping by the sink when I came home with all the groceries, wondering why her youngest son looked through her. Perhaps she rushes about the house slamming doors and dropping potted plants on the brick floor of the conservatory in a vain attempt to get my attention: the pothos, the gold spot croton. The variegated, heart-leafed philodendron. If this is the case, then it is I who have gone away. Perhaps for good. But then why don't my father and brothers mention this to me? For fear they will hurt my feelings?

Mother's back!

I had come over to the house to look for a copy of her birth certificate, and there she was in the bathroom putting on mascara. I'm not really sure if she ever left.

She asks me, "What do you mean left, gone?" She puckers her lips and applies lipstick.

I can't seem to explain. Where has she been? Is this really Mother? Or has Dad married some other woman and is now trying to pass her off as the old one? She doesn't really look like a mother, she looks too old, too much like a woman. As she bends over the sink to check her eye-lashes in the mirror, I can see her freckled cleavage. She doesn't look as I remembered her looking. I could be mistaken. The photos . . . there is a similarity to be sure, but is this woman Mother?

My brothers arrive for dinner. They talk like nothing's happened. "Mom," they say, "you sure can cook!" She has made them a huge skillet of eggs goldenrod and a basket of sour cream twists. Dad reads the paper, the business section, as they all sit down at the kitchen table. Leonard's brought his wife and kids.

Mother tells me I am looking thin and pale, which I admit is a motherly thing to say. She tells me she has cooked my favorite dish. She says, "I've made you your favorite." Mother smiles at me. She brushes a piece of hair away from her face with the back of her hand. I realize I don't know this woman, and this is my mother.

"Thank you," I say. I sit down to eat; after all, it is my favorite. But it doesn't really taste like I remember it tasting.

I look up. Mother is puttering by the sink, cleaning up some of the dishes before she sits down to eat, which seems to be an odd thing to do, something that could wait until after dinner. She looks over at the table and smiles at all of us sitting and eating, wipes some splattered water off the counter.

She seems to be a rather tidy woman. . . .

Breaking the Rules

David Hamilton

With Norman Sage we broke all our rules. Here we are a magazine that reads 2000 unsolicited stories a year, prints say fifteen of them, "half" of which will be by writers totally unknown to us, with half of those remaining likely to be writers who were in that same unknown position a year or three before. We rarely solicit anyone, nor do we often invite in acquaintances and friends.

Norman, however, is a friend. He is one of several small press printers in the area and sometimes sends around chapbooks of poems under assumed names to selected readers. Having a collection of those, and liking them well—"my heart leaps up/when I behold/your Honda in my drive"—I once put a small gathering of his work in an issue under one of his pseudonyms. Mary Hussmann, my associate editor, thought that he might be working on his memoirs and that perhaps we could coax something interesting from him. So we went to see him one afternoon early in the summer and pushed him to fess up to what he was doing. We drove to his small house on the edge of Lake MacBride, fifteen miles north of Iowa City, where he lives among books and papers, prints and paintings by his diseased wife and one of his daughters, writings by the other daughter, photos of grandchildren, files of correspondence, special printing projects completed or in some stage of process, for he has printed many more writers than himself, and an aging black dog named Beauregard. The water was rising in the lake. It was to be a summer of flooding. The park beach across from him gave us a blank stare; it was closed. His own small dock was entirely under water. Finches and sparrows darted under his north eave, narrowly averting disaster against a large, almost wall-length window. And yes Norman had been writing, but not memoirs. "Stories."

How much writing, I finally asked. Norman was silent for a moment, then, holding his hands in front of him, he lifted one above the other to at least the height the water must have risen from its normal level to cover not just the floor but the railing on his dock. Apparently he had put in many years at his desk, writing story after story and completing five manuscripts of novels. Mary and I coaxed a handful of folders from him and departed. Over the next couple of weeks, we read forty stories each and decided to put together a portfolio of his fiction. These stories are not long. The longest is twelve pages, the shortest are four pages each. Memoir is part of them, but there is enough variation and invention to leave a reader, even a reader who knows the writer well, uncertain of particulars.

The one we placed first seems the most autobiographical. It is set in a small town, perhaps Washington, Iowa, where Norman grew up, and recounts adventures with the girl next door who could in many critical activities outdo him. The fourth in the sequence, however, is written as a journal prescribed by a psychiatrist and records, along with the speaker's taking up, trying, and abandoning the writing project, his shifting relation with one Llilly, who seems to have mislaid her virtue, which the narrator tries to return in a beribboned box, while he carps about her profligacy with "els," and while hearing occasionally also from an absent wife who writes or calls from Mexico, speaking as if it were China. We suspect that was mostly imagined. Then there is a story of a father who watches and overhears his own father giving instructions in the meaning of words and in signs of life and death to his two grandchildren, the narrator's children. The grandfather is said to be a retired professor, which Norman's father was not; nor is Norman. He is too well read to be a professor. The setting though is clearly his house by the lake with its broad glass window into which sparrows sometimes crash, as one does in the story, giving the grandfather material for his lesson. Another story has to do with the swift passage of time, on how the sense of its slippage varies with situations, being in the arms of a willing young woman in a parked car in that hometown, for example, or being on the wrong side of a gun during an attempted holdup of a bank. It has also to do with enigmatic gifts made by a younger woman to an older man—plastic flowers, wilted zinnias, or seven blackberries in a paper cup, an image that gives the story its title. The final story, the most bittersweet of our collection, is an account of the narrator's giving himself a birthday party at seventy, inviting co-workers from his office, all of them young people, providing an enjoyable party for them and diversion for himself, though through the greater part of the story, which is a foretelling of the party rather than a later recounting, he absents himself from the party, takes a walk around the lake, and remembers his dead wife. The story balances memory with imagination, just as it balances his honest-seeming admission that he will be attentive to the young women while trying politely to ignore their husbands or boy-friends, and that he will even daydream of one immoderately, with remi-niscences of the wife that are tender, wry, bewildered by evidence of cos-mic disorder, and guilt producing.

I say what Norman's stories are about but little of the quality of their being. I have said they are short. In a case or two, he might prefer to call them sketches, though in fact I think they are not. Each begins some-where and moves somewhere else. There can be seeming drift in the story, as in the party giver's walking alone around the lake, giving himself to reminiscence, but it is drift that acquires the shapeliness of direction. There is action that tightens and releases. There is texture, layering, and complication. Several strands of the lives rendered gather to each story, and each ends with a feeling clarified. I think of Frost's "momentary stays against confusion." The prose, always cultivated and clear, can veer to the colloquial, while remaining aware of the promises it is making, and keep-ing them. His values seem modest, human, and demanding. Modest be-cause the writer never shows off. Human because they are accounts of love, mostly, and its attendants–disappointment, humor, tenderness, death, and loss. And demanding because a certain grace is asked of us, if we would live in the fragile company of these stories. Here is the opening paragraph of the middle one in our gathering, "Reflections":

> At certain times of the day, when the light is just right, the birds seem to think that our house, which is mostly glass on the lake side, is wide open, and they bang themselves to death on the windows. We have tried various means of preventing these catastrophes: we have criss-crossed masking tape on the glass, we have painted designs on it in washable poster colors–nothing seems to do any good. Aside from the really shabby appearance of these disfigurements, the birds, used as they are to darting between the branches and leaves of trees, simply head for a spot between the lines of the designs and bash their brains out anyway. We regret this carnage–not always fatal, of course–for we love birds and know that there are few things more wonderful to see than a bird in flight.

The first thing to catch me, usually, is voice. This one is civilized, bal-anced, and attentive. It is not afraid to say things as they are–"bang them-selves to death," "catastrophes," "shabby," "disfigurements," "Bash their brains out," "Carnage." Language that avoids euphemism is more compli-cated than that as it sways between the graceful and the foreboding. It seems that of a man who is shy neither of the world nor of his education. There is a relaxed air about the beginning of this story as if the speaker assumes he has time enough, and enough of our interest, to qualify and thicken without becoming a bore. Then he delivers much in four pages. The end of the first paragraph, after its frank foregrounding of sudden death, gives us an image of life at its most glorious. Then, too, we are looking at that beautiful bird—a sparrow, not a raptor or a lark—through a window, an image of separation, of distance that may allow us to see, and of, as the title suggests, "reflection."

I hope it is clear that Mary and I, and our assistants, as they also read these stories during various stages of production, found reason enough to favor them. Reason becomes reasons that incorporate many things, but it all begins with confidence in a human voice, in this case understanding but not pompous, very likely wise, and gifted with humor. Humor is suggested in the accuracy of "disfigurements" and "carnage," words that carry a sense of measure that will recognize the humorous. In "Reflections," it is quite delicate, living mostly in the differing registers of diction, of grandfather and grandchildren, when the former, with a dead sparrow in his hands, tries to tell the latter something of the mystery of life and death while also explaining words like "articulate," "adjectival," and "skeleton." At the end of the story, the narrator sees in his mirror what the sparrow must have seen an instant before colliding with the window.

These stories have another value as well: they render a vision of our future, should we too be so fortunate as to experience growing old. It is often said that literature should give voice to the voiceless, and our literature is not rich with the experience of aging. One of the virtues of Norman's work is that he is a deft guide toward the future into which we are headed, he himself being guided by the virtues I have listed and by extended experience. When at the end of the party-giver's story, the narrator returns to the young people saying, "And seventy is quite beyond their comprehension," I felt he, looking back on that, had got it just right because he had given me a glimmer.

"Seven Blackberries," however, is the story we will offer here, for the simple reason that when we went on the air locally earlier this year with selections from *The Iowa Review*, that was the story Norman preferred that we read aloud. So here it is again for a different audience.

Seven Blackberries

Norman Sage

I would like to put everything on hold, for I fear running out of string–it is being hacked away in snippets, some too small to remember, surely, but it worries me nonetheless. Snip goes five minutes here, five minutes there. Time does not, as some say, serve us; we are slaves to *it*. It nibbles us away in stealth, thinking we won't notice. But I notice. I worry. I fear. I say to myself, Stop! but time has slid through the word while I say it–even before I began to say it–while I was just thinking of saying it. Most of the time we all idle away five minutes now and then, here and there, and don't even realize that those moments are forever gone. If we could recall those little five-minute chunks of time and recycle them, we'd be rich. I can recall many lost moments–not necessarily idle ones–the kind which seem to have lives of their own. I can call them up now and then for re-examination, but not for reuse. Some are pleasant to recall, some not. Although I do not enjoy the process, it is necessary to get inside oneself to remember. Heaven knows I can't get inside anyone else, which is suffi-cient excuse for using the confessional first person, and if any object, may their pumpkin pies become cowflops.

What I fear, of course, is that eventually I will indeed run out of string, with this incessant snipping and all, and knowing that we all must, sooner or later, is no comfort. I fear that, and he who says he doesn't, lies. I try to think of it all in everyday terms, such as being fired from a job–depressing, but in the long run probably for the best. It's that long run which worries me; I would like to know more about that. I try not to think of these things, but they rise in my thoughts often and without bidding. Audie ran out of string, and so will I, one day, and it depresses me and makes me look like death on a soda cracker. I am not what you'd call a happy person much of the time.

Once, long ago, I was in a small bank in a very small town when it was robbed by men with guns. One of the guns was pointed at me, and looking down its barrel was like looking at the end of a culvert. All the time this holdup was going on, I commanded time to pass swiftly so it would be over, knowing full well that time does not take orders and that no one, in any way, can mess around with it to any satisfactory extent. One can *beguile* time, but its content and flow are not at all disturbed. I remember thinking, God! I'll be glad when this is over. And I remember trying to beguile time by thinking that only a few miles from where I was in mortal peril was the place where Dvoràk wrote his *American Quartet* and sketched out the *Ninth Symphony*. There were Indians around this place then; now thieves with guns. But most of the time I was thinking, Dear God, please bring me through these next few minutes so it will be only a memory and not going on right now.

As you see, I lived through it. The whole experience didn't actually take five minutes, although it seemed to have drained away half of my life expectancy and to be lasting forever, going on and on. I knew it was over when the young woman who had her feet in my face as we lay on the floor gave a long quavering sigh and said, Well, that was quite a thrill, wasn't it?

I was very brave then, when it was over. The shaking began later. I didn't call Audie in that distant city where we lived, because our first daughter was about to be born and I didn't want to worry her. She read about it in the paper the next morning and called me early at the hotel and she was mildly hysterical about it. You might have been killed! she said. But I wasn't, I said. Don't worry—it was nothing. It will be a good story to tell our kids, I said. But I was sweating and shaking as I said it, even though it had happened more than twelve hours before, that few moments of undiluted fear. It took only those few moments to be held at gunpoint and survive. There was little comfort in that, and even less in the realization that it would have taken even less time to shoot us all. That bit of string I remember.

Another time, longer ago than the bank robbery, I was in a car with a girl in Sunset Park in our home town. It was the girl's car, and we had known each other all our lives, but not as well as we were about to. She was not the woman I truly loved, and I was cheating a little because that woman was in a town at some distance, but this one was right here, and anyway, the one I truly loved didn't know that we would be married at last—nor did I, although I hoped so, even while all this with the girl in the car in the park was going on.

Our clothing was in joyful disarray, and we were getting better acquainted with each passing moment and in some detail, too. She was breathing noisily and so was I, and she kept saying, Oh God! over and over and so did I. Then, in less time than you can imagine, even taking into account its constancy of flow, there was the town marshal shining his flashlight on us, saying, See here now, we don't allow this sort of thing, and you'd better get yourselves together and get out of here or I'll run you in and call your parents! He called me by name, I being the one most guilty, I guess, and I knew he was not just blowing hot.

That was all over in a very brief time, too, and I hated that marshal and his intrusion, for there was an overpowering need between us. But I have also learned to be grateful, in a small way, because I did not wholly cheat on the woman I truly loved and later married–the one who called me in that little town after the bank robbery. I was glad for that. I was within a few moments of cheating, and perfectly willing to do so, but I was saved–not by choice, to be sure, but by inadvertence–as later I was spared in the holdup. Some would mention a kindly Providence; I think it only chance, but I learned then that a negative experience is often as salutary as a positive one.

Of course, the girl in the car in the park was intent on cheating, too, and I think it would have been worse in her case, for she was soon to be married. But there she was, within moments of a really monstrous job of cheating– in another minute or two we would have done it, and we would have been either glad or sorry or a little of each. There was no thought of compromise there, before the marshal stopped us. I often wonder if she thinks of those few moments, as I sometimes do.

It is possible that the woman I truly loved cheated on me, too, or wanted to, or was about to, when she was in that distant city and I was in our home town. I don't know. I always wanted to ask, but didn't. And I wanted to tell her about the night in Sunset Park, too, but didn't. We might have wounded each other deeply.

The idiot–now dead, I presume, and good riddance–who first said that time heals all wounds made the mistake of sounding off without full consideration of the possibilities, and a lot of people have been saying it ever since and it chaps my ass. Some things never heal–there are at least four, and love is one of them. Sweet agony that it is, it leaves scars, at the very least: the girl in the car in the park; the woman I truly loved–both left wounds that do not completely heal. The one is deeper than the other, of course, and was opened forever, never to heal, when her string ran out.

While the wounds, large or small, bleed, one can beguile both time and the wounds by deliberately putting oneself in a position in which the chances of being wounded again are excellent: we are such fools, after all. Be warned that falling in love again, even if not quite in the same way or with as great intensity, is perilous in the extreme.

Yesterday Vicki Versa, my backward friend, brought me the gift of seven blackberries in a small Dixie cup with daffodils on it. I regard her highly as to both intelligence and charm, but each of her gifts carries with it some kind of warning or wonderment, an implied unanswered question. The blackberries: does she love me only seven blackberries' worth? Another time she brought plastic flowers. How does one deal with a gift of plastic flowers? I remember thinking to myself, Well, I guess that puts me where I belong—in the ranks of world-class dinks. Another time she brought zinnias. They were wilted, but she gave them—*bestowed* them— solemnly, as one might a gift of rare magnificence. Was she telling me that I, too, am drooping, my days numbered? Was she saying, in her oblique way, These wilted flowers, and you, are nigh unto death? Is she being playful, wry, cruel? I never know. On my last birthday she brought me a cactus. I wish I knew an old gypsy woman who reads cacti. If she is telling me to hold my ground, to know and observe my insignificant place in her life, to come no closer, why doesn't she simply say so? It would make another wound, but I live with wounds—we all do.

Perhaps she is giving me, in these strange gifts, forlorn parts of her own hopelessness. If that is the case, I wish she'd let me help. I could—one doesn't live as long as I have without learning at least something about such matters. It may be that there is a kind of love there, one which includes faults as well as virtues. If *that* is the case, I would be pleased; but as these thoughts weave their way through the tangled cobwebs of my reason, I remember the terror she thinks she hides deep in her eyes. Even when she laughs, it is there. I wish she would ask me about terror—I know about that; I know a great deal about terror. But I don't know what she fears; I know only what I fear, and most certainly I do not fear love, wounds or no. What I fear at this moment is her knowing so much about me as to decide that I am worth neither regard *nor* affection. That would rip my string right off whatever it's attached to. I wish I could persuade her that no part of love is either evil or dangerous. Even an interior, unspoken love is healing and pushes all terrors into the darkness where they belong. I am aware that this is not new information.

I wish only that the snipping would stop—for just five minutes, so we could lean back and consider, between us, her gift of seven blackberries, honestly and without any mental or emotional reservations. I suspect she might say, Just eat them, dummy, and shut up. What I'm *afraid* she thinks is this: Seven is just the right and magical number; eight would appear to promise more than I intend to offer.

Meaningful Fiction
and Women's Lives

Marianne Abel

"Good Shabbos" by Pamela Walker is so typical of the fiction that appears in *Iowa Woman* magazine that it could have been written from our submission guidelines. It has two strong women of different ages and backgrounds, it centers on women's experiences, and the author uses language and narrative technique effectively. There is also a moral to the story, without being preachy, and it has the traditional, appealing air of common storytelling. Perhaps the close focus on ethnic life from a woman's perspective made it stand above other fiction submissions we received at the same time.

"Good Shabbos" is also an example of a story that would be unlikely from a male writer. The sudden turn of events–the intimate exposure of Mrs. Goldstein's brassiere and body in the dining room–is probably not an experience that would be shared by a woman with a man. The problems and little humiliations of shopping for and wearing women's clothing are not generally a part of men's lives and so may not occur to a male writer as a literary scenario.

This exclusivity makes "Good Shabbos" part of telling the stories of women's lives that is one of our agendas in publishing women's writing and visual art. Ms. Walker renders private moments compassionately public, without voyeurism or gawking. Information about how women exchange their life stories and how women help each other through tough times adds a didactic element that is not unwelcome. We see how widowhood, old age, and urban isolation are woven into a particular life. Regardless of gender, we learn what it means to be a good neighbor in the city, how to respect our elders, and how to appreciate others' lives without judgment.

The story's central characters have quiet independence and strength of spirit. Neither woman is dependent on the men in her life for her sense of self or fulfillment of her needs. No white knight comes shining through to save the day for anyone. Many stories we reject have this cliché as the primary resolution and it just doesn't suit our manuscript readers. Selfish as it sounds, our readers would rather have their own aspirations reflected somewhere in the fiction they read. Dreams about being saved by a man are rare.

Our readers prefer self-actualizing women who are three-dimensional, just as they prefer well-characterized men who have depth and complexity. Many stories we reject have central women characters but the men appear as cardboard meanies, cardboard saviors, or just plain cardboard fillers without energy, vitality, or direction. In this story, men play supportive roles and the women think and act independently. Yet their interdependence with others—men, as well as women, children, animals, and rituals—is obviously important in their lives. This portrayal of how life actually is gives an inclusive tone to the piece, even though the primary characters are women.

Women become actual props in the story, one of the many intriguing uses of narrative technique in "Good Shabbos." Far from being objectified, the minute details of women's shoes, breasts, bras, embraces, gestures, hairdos, to ways of opening doors and approaching others, ways of sitting alone and together, ways of talking to dogs—these features become part of the stage on which several small human kindnesses are mutually shared.

The multiplication effect—one woman's breasts recalling all women's breasts, one passionless grandmother who "would turn away from a child's kiss"—is a rhetorical device that is used to advantage in "Good Shabbos." More than fourteen women are mentioned by name or role title in the short space of the story, and hundreds of others crowd the wings. By picking out the "telling detail," as the how-to fiction writing books tell us, more emotional power can carry the story's undercurrent than by speaking generically.

We see all brassiere sales clerks and all women fitting their breasts into the cages of bras, all the miscarried children, all schoolgirls, other nuns, stone-faced English Department heads who have their own tragedies. Women from the synagogue stand next to Megan's Irish relatives; we grieve for all the grandmothers and their sisters buried in their clunky brown shoes. Even all the altar boys in Catholic church are herded together through the phrase "head bowed like an altar boy," describing the holy way Mrs. Goldstein lights the Shabbos candle. The gesture mixes both faiths, and pays homage to all the Catholic girls who wanted to be altar boys—or play some important, recognized role in the church—but were denied simply because they were girls. Mrs. Goldstein enacts the Shabbos ritual herself and shows how many women are the faith keepers in the absence of men.

Other how-to writing rules are evident here, especially the interweaving of sensory impressions. The smells of birth and death mingle with the textures of food, furniture, and clothing. The odd juxtaposition of a crumpled bra in the silver tray next to the Shabbos food is the kind of surprise mixture of things that—as in real life—gives depth to the scene. The foreboding cast by a New York apartment hallway makes readers suspect something violent might happen to these two women. Fear is unwittingly called up from the depths and yet a surprisingly different resolution unfolds. The situation becomes even more intimate, but without the violence we expect. No harm is done; in fact, there is healing. We are relieved that even in New York, gentleness occurs.

Fear, treachery, and a sense of universal anguish lurk below the story. The "authority" of the non-Jewish white woman who writes a good note leaves an unpleasant aftertaste of class and ethnic prejudices. The yearning of many people for many lost things is just feathered in by mentioning how the Goldsteins' fled their homeland without naming the country, by making a passing reference to the Korean vegetable stand and its implied Korean immigrant owners, and even by Megan's longing remembrance of herself "as a girl aching to leave the Plains."

If the story has a "negative," it would be the use of Hester Prynne and *The Scarlet Letter* as thematic elements. Hester Prynne as another heroic woman with a child on the pyre casts almost too gloomy and tragic a feeling for the incidents that follow in the lives of Megan and Mrs. Goldstein. But more important, it's a kind of intellectual snobbery. Readers who aren't familiar with *The Scarlet Letter* are left out. It also takes up room in the story that could be occupied with something else. Compared to another story by a writer who creates her own fiction, this particular feature might be enough to choose another selection that is more inclusive of more readers' lives or has something else that pulls us out of our shells.

Ms. Walker, a native Iowan who fled the Mississippi River town of Burlington for New York City twenty years ago, said she was delighted to have her one "New York story" appear in *Iowa Woman.* She'd subscribed to the magazine for years and sent the story to us after it was rejected by several other magazines. Her familiarity with our work, her portrayal of character and feeling, and her sense of the rituals of daily life had something to do with why she sent us the story and why we published it. We hope other readers will find some redeeming image in each short story we publish that rewards them for the time they've opened in their lives to read contemporary fiction by women.

Good Shabbos

Pamela Walker

for Mireille

The winter day fell charcoal beyond the bare windows as Megan curled up on the sofa, an old wool blanket across her lap, five stacks of blue-books beside her. The week was done, another first semester ended. As quietly as dusk crept into the room, Megan marked a decade teaching English at Brewster Day Academy in Riverdale. Her companion of those years, a cocker spaniel she called Moon, snuggled against her thigh.

Megan felt content with the simple niche she had carved for herself in the city. She never longed for glamour; an afternoon in the hush of the Public Library's reading room was greater luxury than any she imagined as a girl aching to leave the Plains. When Megan met Jeff at the wedding of mutual friends, both had lived single for years. Jeff left his apartment in a fashionable brownstone for Megan's spacious quarters of faded elegance in a prewar building further uptown. He brought his cats, they set up home and became a family.

The head of Megan's department delivered the blue-books that morning. For the only time in her years at Brewster, Megan had not proctored midyears. She spent the week recuperating from a miscarriage. Though she felt well enough by Wednesday to make the trip to Riverdale, she could not face her colleagues' sadness. Even Jane Newton, the chisel-faced English department head, was softened at Megan's door, handing over the exam booklets.

"I was so sorry to hear your news." Jane touched Megan's hand. "You can't give up."

"We won't. We're hopeful, really."

"It happened to me when my girl was three, and it was such a disap-pointment." Megan never knew Jane had a daughter. "But I became pregnant again. Of course, I was scared to death, but it was good and our son was born."

"I'm glad."

"I'm sure you'll be successful."

"I'm sure too. Thanks, Jane." Often this past week, Megan found herself assuring others of hope she had not mastered.

Megan chose her best class to begin with, her brightest freshmen's essays on *The Scarlet Letter,* the tale with which she wooed her freshmen every fall. Slipping the rubber band over her wrist and resting the booklets against her knees, she hoped for a jewel, a line, a phrase so true she thought the student must be possessed to feel such depth.

Megan thought of Hester Prynne, her strength, her youth, her arrogance—that haughty smile as she emerged from prison, the A emblazoned on her dress. She stood alone against the world beneath the austere sun. Megan envied Hester, child clutched at her breast, upon the scaffold. The infant blinked, twisting from the vivid light, its cheeks flushed pink as the fragile blossoms of a wild rose bush. Megan's jewel was lost. In the deep night of the hospital as she eased off the gurney to the bed, Megan saw the tiny body cradled in her blood, its back a perfect curve at peace. She wondered had it been a girl like little Pearl.

When the bell rang, three hard, insistent blasts, Megan knew it was the Rabbi's wife. It had become her habit to hurry next door for Megan to solve her daily crises when her door would not unlock or if she needed parsnips from the Korean stand. Megan put aside the blue-books and padded in stockinged feet to the door. Her dog tick-tacked across the hardwood floor, ears perked, a quizzical rumble in her throat.

Mrs. Goldstein stood in the hall holding a bottle of kosher grape juice. A shock of gray hair sprang from beneath her stiff brown wig like Sister Superior's white hairline revealed below her wimple, a sight laced with the fear and excitement of a world forbidden to Megan as a schoolgirl. The Rabbi's wife wore a dark timeless dress of good wool.

"Mrs. Goldstein, how are you?"

Though everyone called Mrs. Goldstein the Rabbi's wife, in fact she was his widow. The Rabbi had been dead six months. Now Mrs. Goldstein brought bottles of seltzer and borscht next door for Megan to open as the Rabbi had done for her when he was alive. Mrs. Goldstein looked up at Megan, a grin out of place on her wizened face. She bobbed her head like Megan's Grandma Quinlan, who died back home the year that Megan had come East.

"Open?"

"Sure." The bottle sighed as Megan uncapped it.

"Come," the rebbetzin tugged at Megan's arm, "and bring your doggie."

Moon slipped out and ran ahead. Megan left her door unlatched and followed through the chilly hall. The Goldsteins' apartment had been painted before the Rabbi died. Its walls glistened under bright foyer lights. Mrs. Goldstein led Megan into the kitchen where a small sterling tumbler sat on the plain table, solitary in its beauty, etched with dainty filigree.

"Pour." Mrs. Goldstein gestured from the bottle to the tumbler. "To the top—the top!" she insisted when Megan stopped an inch below the rim.

Mrs. Goldstein picked up the brimming cup with both hands and carried it close to her bosom into the living room. Head bowed like an altar boy following the gaspy cadence of an organ, she did not spill a drop but set it on the table beside a shiny platter where two thin slices of chocolate roll lay head to head. Megan and her dog were invited for Shabbos, the Jewish Sabbath. Megan wondered if Mrs. Goldstein had intended from the start to make the invitation, the uncapped juice her ploy, or had she cut the cake and placed it with such care upon the serving plate for someone else? A woman from the synagogue perhaps had taken ill.

Silver candlesticks stood upon the dining table draped in white, the cloth embossed with swirls and flower baskets like Megan's multitude of linens, her Irish legacy along with handmade lace, doilies and hankies and antimacassars, starched stiff and wrapped with lavender. The etchings on the candlesticks matched those on the sterling cup. Slender candles sputtered, the frantic flames reflected in the windows, six flamencos dancing against the night.

The Rabbi's chair had been removed from the head of the table where he used to stand to say prayers and cut the challah bread which lay untouched beneath a blue velvet cloth, edges trimmed in braid, Hebrew symbols in its center, the golden threads as rich and sensuous as Hester Prynne's scarlet letter. Megan stood at the right hand of the Rabbi's wife as she mumbled a Jewish blessing over the chalice, then drank from it.

"Eat." Mrs. Goldstein jiggled the platter.

Megan broke off a nibble. The cake left a dry lump in her throat, but she did not dare sip from the sacred juice.

"Sit."

Megan sat on the chair's edge, crossing her leg and pointing her toes; a stretch buzzed up her shin bone. Moon sniffed the baseboards. Her collar tags rang like bells on a child's shoes.

"Ai, God," Mrs. Goldstein lamented, lowering her frail body onto the chair. She wore tie shoes with a chunky heel, the type the old women on Megan's Irish side had worn.

Grandma and her sisters were buried in those shoes. Mrs. Goldstein's thick calves hinted at the larger woman she once was. In pictures she showed Megan, she stood beside her solemn husband in his Amish coat and flat-brimmed hat. She was not tall but strong with broad shoulders and the ample hips of one who had borne children, though Mrs. Goldstein was barren from the war. Her full, healthy face in the snapshots belied the years she and the Rabbi had survived beneath a Catholic farmer's hog barn.

"Ai, God, what is my life without the Rabbi?"

"I know, I know," Megan cooed her refrain to Mrs. Goldstein's sorrow.

"My nephew say, 'What you think? The Rabbi live forever?' I say, 'I never think.' " Mrs. Goldstein pursed her lips and shrugged. " 'Woman with your brain,' my nephew say, 'you are naive.' I say, 'Who should think, the Rabbi first? It's me, I have the heart.' " She touched her breast.

"We never know."

"They say it's God's way."

"Yes, they do."

"Have more." Mrs. Goldstein pushed the cake closer.

"Oh, that's okay, you have some." Megan pushed the platter back.

Mrs. Goldstein made a face. She had no stomach for the cake—for any food. "Where's your doggie? Give the doggie."

"Moon," Megan called and Moon came eagerly, knowing she would have a treat. "You want to give it to her?" Sometimes Mrs. Goldstein liked to feed the dog.

"No, no, you. You give." Mrs. Goldstein watched and smiled and bobbed her head. "More." She touched the plate when Megan stopped. Moon sat rapt, her black eyes wet, a hopeful twitter in her nose. "He is so smart. He want more. His eye say so."

"No, that's plenty for her."

The dog heard "no" and made a nest, circling twice before curling up on Megan's feet, her body warm and reassuring

"A genius, your doggie. Now he know it gone. Wise eye, your doggie." Megan worried on Moon's eyes, grown cloudy with the passing years. "You know brassieres?" Mrs. Goldstein jolted Megan.

"Brassieres?"

"Yes, brassieres."

"Well, yes, I know brassieres."

"So then you see." With one deft move, Mrs. Goldstein popped hidden snaps and let her dress fall to her waist. She stood revealed in a new white bra from chest to below the midriff. "The Town Shop, you know the Town Shop?"

"Yes, I know the Town Shop."

Megan squirmed as though she were partaking of a sacrilegious act to see the Rabbi's wife disrobed.

"She say it good, but it no good."

"Mrs. Goldstein, it's fine. It's beautiful."

"Fine?" Mrs. Goldstein looked down her bodice, pulling the bra tight.

"Yes, just fine."

The old woman pulled her dress back over her shoulders. The front lay open, a pink rosette peeking from between her breasts.

"Mrs. Goldstein, do you have to go to synagogue tonight?"

"Pft," Mrs. Goldstein dismissed the thought. "I don't go to shul, not tonight, not tomorrow."

"Oh, that's good."

Megan relaxed against the chair's padded back. If Mrs. Goldstein was not going out, if she expected no one else, what difference did it make if she sat half-dressed at home?

"No, no, you must see." Mrs. Goldstein grew agitated. Her feet clopped the floor and she slipped out of her dress as smoothly as before, turning sideways where her breast protruded like a lump of rising dough, then backwards. "Look, look. See?"

The last two hooks of Mrs. Goldstein's bra were not closed. Megan pulled but the fabric resisted.

"Oh, you're right, Mrs. Goldstein, it's too tight."

"Now, you know."

"Yes, I do."

"She say it good, but it no good."

"No, it's too tight."

"I take it back."

Mrs. Goldstein reached behind, unhooked her bra and slid out, more facile than a young girl in gym class. Her breasts were long and tubular, meaty breasts that had lost their fat. Irish women started small and ended up with nothing. Grandma Quinlan hid beneath a pink chemise, even as she slept. On Megan's German side, the women kept full busts in age. Megan's breasts were young, firm though small. Someday she would be old with a flat Irish chest like Grandma Quinlan. Mrs. Goldstein handed her folded bra to Megan, which she set beside the platter on the table, while Mrs. Goldstein stood naked and made no move to cover herself.

"Let me help you, Mrs. Goldstein."

Megan lifted the garment and the old woman slid her shoulders in.

Her skin was soft and cool. She plopped on her chair and her broad feet popped off the floor with new vitality. Snapping her dress, she bobbed her head, victorious that she was right and those who thought she lost her sense were wrong. The candles had grown smaller. They flickered orange and yellow.

"You tell her?" Mrs. Goldstein asked coyly.

"Tell her?" Megan feared Mrs. Goldstein foresaw them walking to the Town Shop first thing Monday morning to exchange the crumpled bra.

"Write it. She believe you."

"The woman at the Town Shop?"

"Yes."

"You want me to write a note about the bra?"

Mrs. Goldstein nodded, a mirthful glint in her gray eyes.

"Oh, sure. Do you have a pen and piece of paper?"

"Yes, yes. For you I get it in the kitchen."

Megan had her doubts the shop would want the bra. The threads had sprung along one stay. Yet Mrs. Goldstein could not see the damage, and she believed quite urgently that a neighbor's note would put an end to her predicament. She returned, handing Megan a pen and pad.

Megan wrote quickly but legibly:

Please let Mrs. Goldstein return this bra.

It is too tight. Thank you. Her neighbor, Megan Schaefer

"Now, it's done."

Easing onto her chair, Mrs. Goldstein held the pad and read with narrowed eyes. Her hands were wide and worn, the fingers marred by bulbous knuckles like Megan's peasant hands.

"Good. Thank you."

"You're welcome."

Mrs. Goldstein set the note aside with an air of finality. Sinking further in the chair, arms limp in her lap, she seemed to grow smaller. The green velvet back rose regally above her head like a mosque topped by a smooth wood ball. Her shoulders drooped from the relief of reaching safety for another night. Megan would go home and put up dinner soon.

"You must have baby."

"Oh, we will."

"Try again."

"We will. They make you wait."

"Oh, the doctor make you wait?"

"Yes."

"One child and you are not alone. You are not too old."

"No, not yet."

"If you cannot have, adopt."

"We will."

"Ai God, I should listen to the Rabbi. The Rabbi say adopt. I say no."

"Why, Mrs. Goldstein?"

The old woman shirked as if she would forget the reasons of her youth. Her rheumy eyes steady, Mrs. Goldstein pulled up her shoulders with some kind of pride or maybe defiance for that which led her to deny the only man she ever knew, though she was left to doubly mourn. Megan thought of her own pungent odor in the hospital, an acrid sweat of fear and death. She lay in bed and smelled beneath her arms the strange, strong odor of her loss.

"Mrs. Goldstein, I have to be going."

"Your husband will be home."

"Yes."

"You must go."

"Yes."

"He is good husband, your husband."

"Yes, he is."

"Always friendly."

"Always."

Megan followed Moon into the kitchen, sweeping the dog into the crook of her arm.

"And you good neighbor, the best."

"Oh, that's okay." They were at the door. "You have a nice evening, Mrs. Goldstein."

"And you. With your husband."

"We will."

Moon sat in Megan's arm like a baby, eyes full of wonder on Mrs. Goldstein's wrinkled face.

"You good doggie." Mrs. Goldstein petted Moon's nose, gentle though tentative. She and the Rabbi had been scared of the dog. Now the deep crow's-feet crinkled around her eyes. "I like your doggie." Moon licked Mrs. Goldstein's thumb.

"And she likes you." Megan backed into the hall. "Good night."

"Thank you." Mrs. Goldstein stood at her door, the foyer brilliant behind her. She murmured, "You good neighbor," and she smiled a sly smile of the secret they shared, forming a kiss on her lips as Megan's grandmas never did, not the German, not the Irish, cold women bred of harsh winters and hard work, women who could turn away from a child's kiss.

The rebbetzin's door closed and the lock engaged as Megan hurried on tiptoes to her apartment, the cold of the tiles penetrating her thick socks, Moon's weight solid in her arms. Shouldering open the door, she kissed the dog's head and set her tenderly on the rug. Moon took Megan's love in stride, shaking her body and stretching, then toddling to the kitchen to slurp from her water bowl. The lamp cast a warm glow over Megan's sofa spot, the rumpled plaid blanket, bluebooks fanned over leather, beckoning her to read and believe in her students' words. Jeffrey would be home soon.

~~~~

Our Lady of No Consolation: On Eileen Pollack's "A Sense of Aesthetics"

Devon Jersild

The fiction I most appreciate undoes my sense of the world; it challenges me to rethink and reevaluate, and shows me my own limitations. I suppose it might seem rather masochistic to like fiction of this sort—it means I'm happiest when I'm most upset. Yet this is the perennial paradox of art.

When I was a teenager reading C.S. Lewis's *The Problem of Pain*, one point in particular made an impression on me; Lewis says that once you have thoroughly examined your conceptions of God and come to a clear sense of who you think he is, all you can say for certain is, *God is not this at all.* I mention this here because it seems to me that the dislocation or disorientation of the reader that I mention above is at heart a moral task: the best fiction prompts us to stop projecting our own assumptions, to resist fixing people or cultures into forms of our own making, and to start *listening* to other voices.

Of course any fiction relies on certain conventions, which can work against the possibility of truly challenging or surprising a reader. For the most part it seems true that the writers who transcend this fact—whose fiction reflects the flux and randomness of real life—are those who have thoroughly understood these conventions. Yet mastery of form is no guarantee of originality or hard thinking. The thriller, for instance, has as its goal to upset us and overturn our expectations, and it accomplishes this through the manipulation of certain tropes; yet the thriller is of course a formulaic genre, entirely predictable in retrospect, and in the end most likely to confirm the sets of prejudice we bring to it.

As I read story after story for *New England Review*, the contours of the conventions of fiction become increasingly apparent, and the more apparent they are, the harder it is to respond to the work's dynamic center. And so the fiction that gives the impression of enormous freedom, that brings the process of change and discovery into the act of writing itself, has the power to make me suddenly alert. This impression of freedom, of a broad range, is ideally established in the very texture and rhythm of the prose. I find it exhilarating when such a story goes on to achieve certain perceptions and revelations only to undo them and insist that they are not enough; they will not do; the world is larger than that.

This was my experience in reading Eileen Pollack's "A Sense of Aesthetics." It's written in the energetic voice of a teenaged girl named Marianne, who hates hypocrisy and injustice and is determined to fight them wherever she can. In the course of the story she comes to recognize an hypocrisy of her own, and in so doing she transcends her black-and-white vision of the world.

Within the first few paragraphs Eileen Pollack establishes the complex feelings of her narrator—her sassiness and sensitivity, her rage and compassion all vying with each other. Though Marianne claims she "hates" the poor girls at school who are allowed in early to shower in the locker room, one infers her sympathy from the quality of her attention, as when she describes how they "rinsed out their panties with gritty yellow soap pumped from dispensers over the sinks, and put these back on, the cloth damp but clean next to their skin." Even the first sentence communicates her sympathy and anger, as the school first seems charitable for allowing the girls in, then measly and shabby for inviting their humiliation, as they "dry their hair under the blowers for hands"—the image of the stooping girls providing a literal figure for the grovelling attitude such charity inspires.

On the same page we're introduced to the ludicrous Miss Stark, the chief object of Marianne's school-girl satire. Miss Stark, we are told, used New York State history as an "excuse to tell us how her family had stripped bark from hemlocks and boiled it with boots, which they sold to Abe Lincoln to help free the slaves." How much is accomplished in this brief sentence. In it the narrator communicates Miss Stark's grandiose sense of herself and her family, her awareness of how "official" versions of history tend to reinforce the status quo, and her own irreverent attitude. It seems especially fitting that the Stark family "sold" the boots to Lincoln—charity, once again, at a price.

Miss Stark is a persecutor—making the poor kids feel poorer, enjoying her sense of *noblesse oblige* when she offers her camera to Marianne, who couldn't otherwise afford to take pictures for the Photographic Essay of the History and Resources of Lenape County she's assigned. She's nicely echoed in the figure of Solly Gipps, who feels sorry for Marianne's mother because her poor drunken husband has disappeared, and gives her "boxes of candy that could not be sold because they'd gone stale, expired cosmetics, wilting bouquets, and slightly soiled clothes." To Marianne, Solly Gipps gives a brand new camera (with a broken flash), and in spite of herself, Marianne falls in love with it—"My chest loved the weight of the camera," she says, "my neck, the bite of the strap." She decides to photograph the contrasting poor and rich communities of the town of Paradise to show "how sinful it was that some human beings were miserably poor while others were rich."

First she photographs the gray-shingled building where the Puerto Ricans live. Then, because "the churches in Paradise were the biggest, and fanciest, and therefore most sinful buildings in town," she works her way down Main Street taking shots of the elaborate and ornate structures. Finally she wanders into Our Lady of Consolation, where she discovers the gaudy statue of a beautiful woman—the Virgin Mary standing on a starry globe, wearing a blue-and-gold cape "like the hood of my mother's parka," and "stretching her arms from the folds of her gown, hands turned palms up, asking for something I didn't know I had." When Marianne pushes the button, red bulbs light up and bathe the statue in "a ruby-red glow." When she steps back to take a picture—her last shot—she knocks over and shatters a statue of Christ. She flees from the church in fear and guilt, worried that if anyone finds out, her mother will spend the rest of her life repaying the debt.

Yet there in the church which offends her sense of morality, in front of a statue which offends her sense of aesthetics, the angry young girl for the first time experiences *gratitude*. Soon after this, when her lovely mother asks her if she feels poor, Marianne suddenly understands that poverty is not her problem: she is angry because her father has gone away and left them. Later she has another revelation: Miss Stark offers her roll of film and Marianne sees that the woman is afraid of her—she's desperate for *gratitude*, and she, Marianne, has the power to bestow or deny it. Then, when the Puerto Ricans' building catches fire a few days later, Marianne does not take arms against the landlord who neglected to build a fire escape; instead she remembers the beauty of "a woman in a black-and-gold kimono, watching her nephew go up in flames." It's a wonderful touch that the cape on the statue of Mary reminded Marianne of her mother, for it helps prepare us for her final revelation: "I knew, to my shame, that I wouldn't spend my life searching for evidence that the world was unfair, but for beautiful things to lay before my mother as an offering of love."

By now the ground of the story has shifted, and all the polarities are called into question. The charity giver becomes the beggar, and the equation of rich vs. poor becomes so complicated by matters of the spirit that it no longer "computes." In the gaudy statue of Mary, Pollack links the grotesque with the beautiful. Then there is the Mexican mother, Anita, who has earlier insisted that her son have "*nada* to do with those [Puerto Rican] pig," but when her son objects to her giving his bathrobe to a victim of the fire, she turns and slaps him; Pollack writes, "He looked at her as though everything she'd taught him, except for that slap, was revealed as a lie." In many ways it's these smaller touches that reveal the imaginative depth and coherence of "A Sense of Aesthetics." When the Puerto Ricans' building burns down, for instance, the reader remembers that amid those gray shingles Marianne had watched "the ugliest toddler I'd ever seen . . . pressing her face to a window." How much more moving, this rush of regret and sadness, than if the narrator had passed a doe-eyed child in that window.

I should point out that, in retrospect, the archetypal pattern underlying "A Sense of Aesthetics" is apparent: an angry, self-righteous girl with a ravenous hunger for justice experiences grace; her anger turns to compassion, and her obsession with the law transforms to an impulse toward beauty and worship. The narrator sees her own transformation as a way into maturity and greater wisdom—and it's clear that she achieves a deeper self-knowledge—but it's interesting that she also feels "shame" about her love of beauty over justice. The shame is at least in part a recognition of her own hypocrisy, but the story also leaves room for the possibility that Marianne goes on to work for a "slick magazine" and uses her money to help her mother move to Main Street—the radical young girl has become mainstream. Just below the surface of the text, new questions simmer: what *about* that negligent landlord, and the fire inspector who hadn't turned him in? Does Marianne's conversion entail a loss of energy for social reform? Where is that saucy, irreverent girl who described Paradise "as a soggy old mattress with all the poor people jumbled together in the trough down the middle?"

A lesser writer would have left out the messy details and allowed Marianne to congratulate herself in peace. But Eileen Pollack has a restless energy equal to her narrator, and she doesn't edit out the jagged edges that keep a reader from settling in to a cozy afternoon by the fire.

⌒⌒⌒

A Sense of Aesthetics

Eileen Pollack

Most of us had to wait in the schoolyard until the first bell, but five or six girls were allowed in each morning to shower in the locker room and dry their hair under the blowers for hands. They rinsed out their panties with gritty yellow soap pumped from dispensers over the sinks, and put these back on, the cloth damp but clean next to their skin. Then they shuffled through the halls to the Home Ec department, where the nurse doled out oatmeal along with advice about avoiding V.D.

I hated those girls—for looking both ways before slipping into school through the door by the gym, for bowing their heads even when their hair was shiny and fresh. If I'd seen a classmate mouthing "B.O.," I'd have punched that boy's nose.

But I lived in town, where everyone had sinks and toilets indoors, and it wouldn't be my smell that revealed I was poor. It would be Clara Stark and her Photographic Essay of the History and Resources of Lenape County.

Miss Stark was a Scot (" 'Scotch' is a beverage, an *inebriant*," she said). The pattern on her skirts was the tartan of the Stark clan. "I'm the last living Stark," she announced the first day. "No one can wear it after I'm dead."

The topic that year was New York State history, with an emphasis on the county we lived in, and she used this excuse to tell us how her family had stripped bark from hemlocks and boiled it with boots, which they sold to Abe Lincoln to help free the slaves. The Starks used their profits to set up a bank, the Paradise Dime, and to build a block of stores in the middle of town. The word STARK was carved in stone above the windows of my teacher's apartment. You almost could see the same letters traced on her dusty white forehead.

The assignment always started on the first day of fall, so we knew what was coming. While Miss Stark took attendance, the room buzzed with words that sounded like weapons—"telescopic lens," "light meter," "tripod." Harry Hooper said "f-stop" and "aperture" in the same lustful tone that I'd once heard him use to describe a French kiss.

"Juancito!" I whispered to the boy on my left. "Remember, you promised."

He folded his hands and shook his head no. Then he looked toward the front with a beatific smile on his delicate face.

"You coward," I said.

He turned in his seat. "You watch what you say, girl."

Miss Stark rapped her desk. "Let's have some de-cor-um!"

"It was her fault," he said. "She crazy. She don't–"

"It was me," I told her. "Why do you always right away blame–"

"Never mind whose fault it was. If you don't quiet down, I'll bring out the muzzles."

This was the story: Her Scotties had died and she kept their old muzzles in a drawer in her desk. She would fit a mangy muzzle that still smelled of dog drool over my face so I couldn't talk or bite.

"All right then," she said. "Shall I continue?"

No one said no, though the rules of the essay were something you knew by this point in life. You couldn't just go out and snap pictures of anything. You needed a theme. You had to write captions to explain how each photo showed a part of your theme. Finally, you had to narrate your essay in front of the class; this would give you a chance to practice your poise.

Before she was done explaining about arranging your photos on a piece of white oaktag with those sticky little corners from the five-and-dime store, the kids in the front were waving their hands. She pulled back her face. "If I wanted to see waving palms," she said, "I would go to Miami."

Only Lisa Chernov kept her hand in the air. "Miss Stark?" Lisa asked. "Could I please do my essay on the old tanning business in Lenape County?"

I turned to Juancito and gagged in my hand, but he'd changed into stone.

"Why, of course," Miss Stark said. "Come see me after class and I'll give you some hints as to where you might explore."

"Miss Stark! Oh, Miss Stark!"

I waited until all the questions were asked. Then I held up my hand, straight as a spear. I didn't call her name.

"Marianne?" she said.

I stood by my seat. This wasn't required, so everyone looked.

"We can't afford a car. Besides, my mother can't drive."

"Well," she said, stroking the lace at her throat, "the town is a part of the county, now isn't it? I'm sure you could find many an interesting theme without leaving Paradise."

I was ready for this. "I don't have a camera. And I don't want to ask my mother to buy one. A camera is a lux-u-ry." I drew out the word as Miss Stark liked to linger on words like de-cor-um. "And she works hard enough to buy our ne-ces-si-ties."

At this point Juancito had promised to say: "My mother does too. The essay isn't fair to poor kids like us." But he seemed to be staring out the window at the lawn, where one of the janitors was down on his knees, scraping mud from a mower.

"Your mother can't afford a camera?" she said. She looked for advice to Franklin D. Roosevelt, who hung by her desk. "You could borrow one, couldn't you? If not from a friend, then from Mr. Deeds, in art? And if those options fail, I myself have a Brownie that I would be pleased–"

"I don't accept charity." I had practiced these words. "Besides, there's the film."

"Oh dear," Miss Stark sighed. "The quality of your pictures matters, of course. A sense of aesthetics certainly counts. But not nearly so much as the content of the essay. Perhaps you could draw? Your mother is something of an artist, I've heard?" Her eyes, which were usually harsh as two tacks, shone with new warmth. "Doesn't your mother teach art at the church?"

Years later I read a novel whose heroine was called "genteel poor" and I realized Miss Stark had thought that my mother fit this description, a well-bred young woman forced to clerk in a store and teach ladies art. But I didn't know that then, and my plans were thrown off by her tender regard for my mother's hard work. I sat in my seat, despite having vowed to stand there until Miss Stark had promised that she'd never assign her essay again.

Every morning, when my mother walked to the store, people from town would offer her rides.

She would pump her arms. "Heart! Lungs!" she would shout, as though peddling these organs from the rucksack she wore. "It helps move the bowel! You should try it yourself!"

On days when it snowed, she wore a blue parka with fur on the hood. She loved that word, "parka," and sang out its syllables, as foreign as Eskimo in our town at the time, to the people who tried to convince her to ride. At the store she would trade her parka for a smock. But she wouldn't wear a red plastic badge with her name. Instead, she embroidered JEANNE on the pocket in graceful red loops. My mother was short and the counter where she worked cut her off at the chest. In the cold fluorescent light of that colorless store, only her lined, earth-colored face and braid of brown hair seemed living and warm.

The counter enclosed her, the long panes of glass held together by chrome that would give you a shock on a dry afternoon. In her spare time she polished bracelets and rings that were locked in the case like flowers too finicky to grow in the wild.

I considered real jewelry an immoral waste of money. But buying the fake stuff, which hung from steel gallows on top of the glass, showed that a person had no sense of . . . aesthetics. Under the merciless lights of the store, the heavy chains and earrings glinted like handcuffs, dog collars, bolts.

For the young girls, to whom beauty and love weren't yet weighty things, the jewelry counter offered filigree hoops and ceramic blue pansies to wear in their ears, and paper-thin charms with BEST FRIENDS engraved on a heart cut in half, so that each friend could wear half the heart on her wrist. The girls who bought this jewelry treated my mother with enormous respect. They said: "Mrs. Augustine, if you have the time, please. . . . " But I didn't like the way they asked her for help in running their lives. Some girl would be watching the waterfall of watches in the Timex display, and the next thing you knew she'd be asking my mother: "What should you do if your boyfriend won't love you unless you put out?"

Even I knew the answers to the questions they asked. But more than her answers they wanted her voice.

When I think of that voice I see the big landscape she was painting that fall—a river that flowed around big mossy rocks, the foam flying up. She had lived in America since she was ten, but she still couldn't pronounce three-syllable words; her low, fluid voice would break into eddies as it passed by those words, though some other part of her voice would break free of language and rise like that bright foamy spray.

"I never could talk to my mother like this!" The girl would lean over the counter and give my mother a hug.

Why did she waste her time on these girls? I knew them from school. They were flighty, I said. I saw them as birds that had flown in a window and were flapping around, primping and screeching and making a mess. Their mothers had women who came in to clean, their fathers earned tens of thousands a year. How dare they ask for sympathy from a woman who'd been working since she was thirteen?

That day after fighting with Miss Stark in class, I walked to the store and found her advising her boss, Mr. Gipps. For most of his life Solly Gipps had sold eggs. Then egg prices fell and he'd been obliged to take a job here. He would stop by each counter and coo to the salesgirl, "Come, come, you can sell more merchandise than that." His wife had run off and he'd gotten in the habit of asking my mother: Should he let his daughters date non-Jewish boys? Should he pay the school nurse to teach them "the facts"? In return for this help, Mr. Gipps brought my mother boxes of candy that could not be sold because they'd gone stale, expired cosmetics, wilting bouquets and slightly soiled clothes. He was pleasant enough, with a square, kindly face and shiny black hair combed back from his brow. But I hated him because he had asked why she'd never gotten divorced.

"In Jewish law," he said, "if a man leaves his wife, a posse of rabbis goes to track him down. They twist the bum's arm until he comes back, or at least says she's free to marry again."

I was glad when she told him that, rabbis or not, she'd promised to wait for my father's return. He'd left her a note that said he'd come home when he learned not to drink. He was careful with words, my mother explained—he had, after all, worked many years taking down telegrams over the phone—and he wouldn't have said "when" if he'd really meant "if." (This gave me great comfort. I imagined he'd been sent to deliver a telegram, then drunk too much beer. Even now he was wobbling around some city on his bicycle, peering at street signs and asking strangers the way.)

When I got to the store, Mr. Gipps clucked: "How can you frown on such a fine afternoon? A pretty girl like you . . . . If you were my daughter, I'd see you had something to smile about. Wouldn't I now, Jeanne?"

If only she would tell him: My daughter is frowning because you are here.

Instead, she said: "Hints! What Mr. Gipps is meaning is now is the time I should give you his gift." She took a white box from under the counter.

His face had that overly vulnerable look of a grown-up who hopes that his present will buy the love of some child.

"Marianne," she said, "why didn't you tell me that you needed a camera for this class that you take?"

I was afraid that you'd buy one, I thought.

"I didn't need to be told," Mr. Gipps said. "I saw Jeanne this morning and something just clicked. I said, 'Marianne is in seventh grade this year.' Then I went up to Cameras. And as it turned out, a man had returned a little Instamatic whose flashbulbs wouldn't flash. He browbeat Miss Dowd into taking it back, which she oughtn't have done. So what could we do except give it away?"

He seemed pained at my silence, my refusal to smile.

"My daughters did their essays on the Egg and Poultry Business in Lenape County. What do you mean to do?"

I meant to do nothing. I couldn't draw worth beans. The other kids would have their photos of forts and I would have pages of squiggles and blots. I had come here to ask my mother for a note forbidding Miss Stark to cause me this shame. But now I couldn't ask. She nudged the box closer. Her face said: I promised that you wouldn't have to suffer for how I have lived.

The Styrofoam squeaked as the halves came apart. The foam had been hollowed so the sleek metal camera, black with gray trim, fit neatly inside. In separate compartments were the strap, plastic case, and the useless plastic cube with its four tiny bulbs.

Until then I'd never imagined that an object could call out your name.

I'm yours, it said. Yours. I have special powers. Don't give me back.

I cradled it in the palm of my hand. I couldn't help but run my finger around the rim of the lens.

"There! Didn't I tell you! Solly Gipps knows how to make a pretty girl smile!"

My fingers took joy in winding the film so the next number showed through the small yellow hole. My chest loved the weight of the camera; my neck, the bite of the strap. But no matter how much I polished the lens and tried to invoke the genie inside, my camera wouldn't give me a picture that showed how sinful it was that some human beings were miserably poor while others were rich.

This theme wasn't quite original. Browsing through *Life,* I'd come upon photos of babies with bellies as swollen as lunch bags you blow up and pop. They were stretching their hands through the gate of a mansion, curled up to sleep by a temple wall, crowding a gold limousine. I knew right away that I'd steal this idea, but I wasn't sure how. Maybe the kids who lived in the trailer parks on the outskirts of town had bellies that swollen, but here in the village poverty hid. Except for the drunk who slept in front of Town Hall–snapping his picture, I assured myself that my father would sleep in a tent–the most likely candidates were the Puerto Rican families who lived in the big gray-shingle building not far from my own.

When I walked by the building, the ugliest toddler I'd ever seen was pressing her face to a window. She saw me and shrieked, then disappeared inside. I got up the courage to go down the alley and poke around back. I focused my camera on a trashcan, then a wall with the paint peeling off, but the fact was the building didn't look that bad. I was sure the apartments were furry with rats; holes in the ceiling let in the rain; toilets flooded the halls with vile-smelling slop. But I didn't have a flash, and even if I'd had one I couldn't have explained my reason for using it to the people who lived there.

I tried to persuade Juancito to help. We were sitting in his kitchen, upstairs from my own.

"Girl, I'm from Mexico." He nibbled a fritter, then wiped his fingers on a pink paper napkin. "What I got to do with them dirty P.R.'s?"

His mother was scraping the skin from a chicken foot. "*Nada!* You got *nada* to do with those pig. I hear you got somethin' I make sure you don'!" Snorting, she pitched the foot in a kettle.

Anita regarded her cooking as magic. The aromas from her stewpots and her cave of a stove made you feel famished. You would promise her anything just for a taste.

"You know Spanish, don't you?" I said to Juancito.

"Yeah. Maybe. So what?" Did I mean he had anything in common with the kids who sat in our classes chewing their thumbs? Didn't he always get A's in science and math?

"So couldn't you explain that I'm doing my essay on how they shouldn't have to live in that dump?"

He rolled his eyes. "Girl, you don't know a thing. Those dirty P.R.'s, they think a dump's better than where they been living on that island of theirs."

"Um-mm, that so *la verdad, la verdad.*" She accompanied this chant by shaking more pepper into the pot.

My eyes filled with tears. Imprisoned in that building were babies with pussy sores on their cheeks and bugs in their hair. "I don't understand why you're not on my side. You don't have a car and your father is dead. What kind of essay can you do with no car?"

His mother turned to face us, her waves of fat whooshing a moment behind her. "Mi *hijo* gonna do A-double-plus essay! His *tio,* he drive him around so he look . . . so he take picture of . . . What you say, *hijo?*"

"The railroad." He lifted his nose in the air. "The title of my photographic essay will be: 'All Aboard, All Aboard!: The History of the Railroad in Lenape County.' "

"Jesus," I said.

"No swear in this house!" Anita had said this hundreds of times, but I could not remember that "Jesus" was as bad as "hell," "damn" and "shit."

"Juancito," I said, "that's what everyone does." He wouldn't even have to narrate his captions; Miss Stark would take over and tell us about her great-great-grandfather buying the land that the railroad would need and selling it back at three times the price. At the end she would say: "I am *so* pleased the memory of this transportation link, so vital to our country's economic development, is being preserved in this photographic essay," and she'd give him an A.

I was deeply ashamed of my best friend. And jealous. I would have loved to take pictures of the trestles that hid in the hills around the county like shy, skinny dinosaurs, and the tracks that went nowhere, lost in the vines.

"Brown-noser, brown-noser, Juan's nose is brown." I flicked the tip of his nose, which really was brown.

"You call my boy name I sendin' you home!" She was waving a carrot; the greens brushed my face. "And don' you go gettin' my boy in no mess. *You* make a mess, one thing. But a boy, he ain' white, *he* make a mess, that it, that his chance, bye-bye, *adios.*" She tugged at her girdle through her polka-dot dress. "Why you so rile' 'bout bein' poor? You ain' never live in no box at the dump. Ain' never been hungry you chew up some leave. Ain' never been poor so the worm get inside and whatever little thing you scrape in your mouth just feed those worm."

Juancito said, "Mama! When you say things like that it makes me have to throw up!"

"*Mi hijo* got stomach made outta paper." She was shaking her head, but she seemed to be proud. "So who gonna taste this stew here and tell me, is it too hot, or ain' hot enough?" She wafted a ladleful under my nose. I couldn't help but open my mouth and lean forward. "Okay now, you promise you ain' gonna mess with this lady no more. You promise Anita you gonna be *good.*"

Imagine our town as a saggy old mattress with all the poor people jumbled together in the trough down the middle. On the lump to the west the rich Christians lived in Victorian houses three stories tall; on the eastern lump, Jews, in vinyl-sided ranches with brick and stone trim. In the yards on both hills were rose gardens, willows, swing sets and pools. The cars in the driveways looked like beached whales.

I shot a whole roll of film. But several days later, when the pictures came back, I was so disappointed that I tore them in half. To save my mother's money I'd used black-and-white film; to avoid being caught I'd shot from the road. What would anyone think of these tiny gray houses, with their tiny gray trees and tiny gray pools, except that the people who lived in those houses were tiny and gray?

I punished my camera by leaving it in my underwear drawer. I sniped at Juancito for crowing about some field that he'd found where a train had blown up; he and his uncle had poked around for hours looking for bones. When my mother asked to see how my essay was going, I said: "It's not done yet," afraid she'd find out that I'd wasted her film.

But the next afternoon, as I walked by the synagogue on my way home from school, I saw the word TEMPLE on the billboard out front. I'd thought there were only temples in India, but we had them right here.

"Temple" meant "church," and the churches in Paradise were the biggest, and fanciest, and therefore most sinful buildings in town.

I'd once asked my mother what religion I was and she'd said that I'd have to decide for myself.

"Well, what are you?"

She showed her gold tooth. "When I married your father, he was a Catholic and I was a Jew. We decided to change to be the same thing. But the only religion we could agree on was pagan."

I wasn't sure then what a pagan might be, but now I can see that my mother was right. Each apple she painted, each root, tree and rock glowed with a life that was more than its own, the life of some idol, or maybe a god, trying to escape its flat canvas world.

"You must keep this a secret." My mother turned serious; her gold tooth disappeared. "If the Reverend finds out that a pagan teaches art in the basement of his church . . . He already has suspicions"–the word had three syllables, it came out a blur–"that I bring naked people when he is not there."

I didn't want to be a Christian like the ladies in pink pantsuits in her class at the church. But I couldn't see the point of being a pagan. I had better things to do than paint pictures of fruit, or even naked men. If God existed, He must be the principle that Life Should Be Fair. Spending money on churches was a theft from the mouths of babies in rags. So many thieves . . . and no one but me to bring them to trial! What truth have I since seen as clearly as that, what purpose in life so pure and profound?

I scrounged enough money for a roll of color film. The churches in Paradise stood along Main Street. I started at the south end and worked my way north. I took a picture of the star tacked to the synagogue; I didn't know for sure what metal it was, so I said it was gold. The Methodist church had a slender white steeple with a silverfaced clock and a weather-vane angel whose puffy cheeks blew the wind from a horn. Paradise Baptist was shaped like a castle, and First Congregational had pink marble arches, a four-headed gargoyle and a tower so high, with the clouds rushing past, that the stones seemed about to fall on my head.

It was Indian summer. Everything–the sky, the marigolds in pots near the Lutheran church, the pears on a tree on the library lawn–seemed to be made of the same fruity gems as the rings in the store. I got carried away and took photos just because I liked how things looked. By the time I reached Our Lady of Consolation, I had only one picture left on the roll. This was too bad. The Catholic church was bigger than the others combined. Two gigantic evergreens had stood by the steps, one on each side, until they'd gotten so bushy that they'd smothered the saints perched on the roof. The trees were chopped down, but their outlines still showed, and in my mind these shadows had something to do with the words Holy Ghost.

I circled the church. Enormous white underpants hung from a line– for the nuns? for the priest? I tried not to look. At the rear was St. Mary's, grades K through 6, squat and unadorned except for a statue of Christ near the playground. He looked like a misfit who'd been teased by the kids and left behind to mope.

A window shade snapped up. A woman in a head cloth peered from the glass. Before she could see me and ask what I wanted, I ran back to the church. I was tired and hot. I walked up the steps to the huge blood-red doors. Every other church I'd tried had been locked. Not that I minded. I didn't have a flash, and I wanted to say that they kept the doors locked so that no one could steal the treasures inside.

But Our Lady was open. I found myself standing in a room of blue light so quiet and cool that I felt I was floating in a very still lake. The pews were rich brown. Scattered on the seats were mossy-smelling prayer books and mimeographed pamphlets with a faint purple drawing of a mother and child. "Blessed are you among women," it said.

The blues, greens, and purples from the windows played across the white plaster walls. The first window showed Jesus Christ as a baby. A plaque underneath said GRACIOUSLY GIVEN BY THE MISSES STARK. The next several windows showed Christ growing up. He got caught by the soldiers, mocked and lashed by the crowd, then nailed to a cross. This upset me so much that I turned counterclockwise and made time go backwards: He unfastened the nails and explained to the soldiers he was leaving their town, rode backwards on his donkey and returned to his home, then got younger and younger until he was a baby in the stable again, with his parents and lambs.

On the altar stood a table covered in white. There were candles on the cloth, and peach-colored blossoms on slender green stems. Above, on the wall, was a large wooden cross with a yellow-skinned Christ. The cloth around his waist had fallen away to lay bare his ribs and the hole in his side. He had holes in his feet and the palms of his hands.

Poor tortured soul. My mother had described my father this way. "That a poor tortured soul could capture such joy with a few strokes and dabs . . . No one could paint a nude like your father, so luscious with life."

Now, in the church, I knew that my father would never come back, no more than the man asleep on that cross would pull out those nails and climb down and save the poor from the rich.

I took refuge in an alcove off to one side. A beautiful woman stood on a globe; her head was a little higher than mine. She wore an apricot gown, and a blue-and-gold cape covered her hair–like the hood of my mother's parka, I thought. Someone had hung a wreath of yellow flowers around her thin neck. She was stretching her arms from the folds of her gown, hands turned palms up, asking for something I didn't know I had.

Maybe she asked other people for things like believing in God or helping the poor. But she asked me for gratitude–for the blue starry globe under her feet, her beautiful face, the fine yellow flowers laced around her neck.

In front of the globe were three rows of candles with red bulbs like flames. DONATE $1 AND PUSH BUTTON, the sign said. I didn't have a dollar, but I pushed all the buttons and each one lit up until Mary was bathed in a ruby-red glow.

I lifted my camera. I thought it might work. I twisted the lens, but her face was still blurred, so I stepped back a little, and a little bit farther, and I knocked against something–a coat rack, I thought–and it fell to the floor.

Remember how you felt as a child when you broke some wine glass or vase–the queasiness, the chill so violent you shook. Then let the crash echo in a cavernous church. Picture Christ at your feet, the thorns of his crown like so many teeth strewn on the floor, two fingers snapped from his right hand and lying in a pool of red light.

Did I think of admitting what I had done? The priest lived next door. I'd seen him on the street, a jittery man with bristling red hair. I knew he would rage and tell me that I owed some awful amount. I couldn't even guess how much a statue of Jesus might cost. Maybe if he'd let me spend my whole life repaying the debt. . . . But I knew what would happen. My mother would take the debt on herself, and how could she pay for a statue of God?

I righted the crucifix. How ugly it was! The cross was too small for such a large Christ, and his face was a blob, as though being divine meant you were above needing a chin. The artist had taken no care with the fingers; they were plain as two chalk sticks.

I stole a last look at Mary. She was reaching toward her son, the distance between them still glowing red. Please let me hold him. Please let me put him together again.

"I'm sorry," I told her. I hid the fingers in an urn. This reminded me to wipe my prints from the statue and the pew where I'd sat. A block down the street I removed the film from my camera and buried it under some trash in a can.

My hunger for justice had grown to be ravenous, feeding as it did on the sins of the world, but now it turned inward and satisfied its appetite on my sin alone. I had destroyed not only a statue, but also my sense of myself as invulnerable, the blue starry globe under my feet.

My mother was worried. "What is it, Marianne? Has some boy upset you? Maybe you have gotten in trouble at school?"

I'd never kept a secret from my mother before.

"It couldn't be that essay with the camera?" she asked.

I still had some photos of the Puerto Ricans' building and the carcass of a cat I'd found on the sidewalk near my house, but I needed a contrast, some photos of the rich to round out my theme.

When I started to explain this, my mother looked puzzled. She tugged at her braid. "You think we are poor? You feel that your schoolmates have something you lack?"

"No, that's not it. I don't think we're poor." And suddenly, I didn't. What I lacked was a father. He had gone away and left us. That's why my mother needed to work. How could I do an essay on my father being a drunk?

I might have come up with another idea, but I was afraid that my mother would ask Solly Gipps to drive me around the county in his Pontiac. "Smile!" he'd keep saying. "A pretty girl shouldn't frown!"

What was the use? The nun who'd seen me lurking in back of the church was even now studying the pictures in the yearbook, trying to fit my name to my face. Any moment the cops would knock down our door. My life would be over, and my mother's would too.

Miss Stark's was the last class of the day. A big roll of oaktag or a yellow box of slides sat on each desk. Miss Stark stood in front in her heavy plaid dress, pleased as a goddess who knows that her acolytes are ready to lay their best at her feet. Since "Augustine" came second after "Appelbaum," I practiced what I would tell her. "I didn't do the assignment. I can't explain why. I accept the consequences." At least I wouldn't have to suffer through another five days.

"All right people," she said. "Just to be fair, why don't we start with the end of the alphabet and go backwards this time?"

Every day that week we gathered around small blurry photos tacked to a poster or squinted from our seats at big blurry slides smeared on a screen. I tried not to care that the exposures were wrong, tried not to think what I could have done if given the chance to focus my lens on the rusted red caboose in Juancito's green field, or the old bluestone quarry so deep that the bodies of drowned little boys could never be found (or so said Brick Davies, whose essay this was, and Miss Stark confirmed it—the quarry had belonged to an uncle of hers).

I found myself hoping that some other poor kid would put up the fight I'd intended to make. But even Donna Mott, who came in each morning to shower in the locker room and rinse out her clothes, had pictures of the dairy where she worked after school.

Only the three oversized boys in back of the room mumbled "Don't got one" when Miss Stark called their names. But they didn't stand and fight. And Miss Stark didn't scold them. She just marked an F next to each of their names. Three years from now, none of the kids who got F's on their essays would be sitting in school. None except me. I could get an F and it didn't mean I'd fail for the rest of my life. What it meant was Miss Stark looked at me, startled, and said, "Really, Marianne? Is something wrong at home? Come in and see me after school, we'll discuss this."

A half-hour later I walked through the empty school to her room. I paused at the threshold to gather my courage. The chairs behind the desks faced every which way, and this made me realize that each class escaped as soon as it could, leaving Miss Stark behind. The time-line that ran from the Prehistoric Era to the Modern Age never added a year while the woman who sat beneath it got old.

The light from the windows was cloudy with dust, and Miss Stark herself, her white hair and powdered face, seemed little more substantial than the motes in the air. It took her a moment to recall why I'd come, but she seemed glad to see me. She teaches because she's lonely, I thought. Talking about all her dead relatives makes her feel they're alive.

She motioned me over. "You don't have to tell me what is bothering you," she said. "Unless you think that talking will make you feel better."

She took me around. I didn't pull away. I remembered her saying, "It's the content that matters," and I pitied her because her wool dress seemed hollow, except for some ribs.

"I certainly understand your wanting your privacy." She opened her drawer. "But I wonder if this might have something to do with. . . . At any rate, I always keep an extra roll of film in my desk. If you need to start over. . . . Perhaps you had trouble finding a theme? You might let me suggest one. I have always thought that someone ought to do an essay . . . This used to be quite a prosperous town. The churches reflect that. Some of their artifacts, well, they're true gifts. The Catholic church, in particular, has some of the finest stained glass in the East. The windows were executed by Wendell Hunt James. Your mother would know all about him, I'm sure."

I jerked away. Tricked! Why else would she lure me to her room after school, mention the church and the word "executed" in the same breath?

"As it happens," she said, "those magnificent windows were given to the church by some great-aunts of mine. They scandalized everyone by turning Roman Catholic. Oh my, what a tempest! The family was terrified they might become nuns!"

The windows! I'd forgotten. A coincidence, that was all.

She placed the film in my hand and curled my fingers around it.

"Thank you," I said.

She patted my hair. "You're a well-bred young lady. Tell your mother I said that."

Well-bred? Did she think I was one of her Scotties? But oh, she was right. I'd even raised my hand and stood by my desk.

I ran to the door. I wanted to shout: "Keep your damn charity!" But I couldn't form the words. The look on her face . . . where had I seen it? Her expression was the same as Solomon Gipps's when he'd given me the camera. Why, Miss Stark was scared that I'd give back her gift! Miss Stark scared of me! She wanted my gratitude, maybe even my love, and if I withheld it. . . . I let myself imagine hurling the film, spitting out hateful words, watching her face crumble to chalk. But the scene was so ugly that it gave me no pleasure.

"I've got to be going," I said very politely. "Thank you again."

I saw her relax. She smiled at me, and waved. "Good-bye, Marianne. Do be sure to give my regards to your mother."

"I'll do that," I said. Then I turned and made my exit, as poised as a queen.

I didn't want to go home to our empty apartment, so I walked to the store. The light was gold-red and the leaves like stained glass, millions of fragments, solid, yet transparent when the sun hit just so. I passed the Catholic church, and the Stark Block, and the building where the Puerto Ricans lived. I would never be caught. Someone could break a statue of Christ and still other people would talk to her kindly, even give her a hug. The rich could be rich and the poor could be poor, the guilty unpunished, yet these sins would be covered by a tapestry of light.

Several days later the Puerto Ricans' building somehow caught fire. My mother and I saw flames from our kitchen and ran down the street. I would have grabbed my camera, but I'd used up the film taking pictures of churches for my new essay.

Standing at the barricade was a woman in a nightgown, its fabric so thin the bumps around her nipples made bumps in the cloth. The woman was crying, as was her husband, a skinny young man in red pajama bottoms with tufts of hair bursting from under his arms.

Juancito walked by on his way home from a concert at school. "What all this commotion? What you done now, girl?" He'd been insufferable since he'd gotten an A+ on his essay. He put down his clarinet and loosened his tie in the manner of a man who enjoys such a gesture. Then he noticed the woman. His eyes touched her breast, fled in disgust, wandered toward it again.

His mother said something in Spanish to the couple. They didn't seem to hear. Then she and my mother went home and came back with slippers and robes. The skinny young man was slight enough to fit into Juancito's bathrobe, the one with the trains running every which way.

Juancito said, "Mama! What you doing, that mine!"

His mother turned and slapped him.

He looked at her as though everything she'd taught him, except for that slap, was revealed as a lie. She'd extracted those promises about being good to keep him from harm, as she would have restrained him from dashing in the fire to save someone's life, all the while hoping that he'd break from her grasp and run inside anyway.

"You hit me!" he said. He picked up his clarinet and wandered down the sidewalk. He sat on a bench, stroking his cheek.

My mother wrapped the woman in her black-and-gold kimono. She repeated the phrase Anita had said—*Ven a mi casa*—and tugged on her arm, but the woman wouldn't budge.

"They don't want to come," my mother said, surprised that someone had declined to take her advice. A few minutes later the bristly priest, fussing with his collar, led them away.

"Well," my mother said, "if they think he can give them something I can't . . . ."

I watched as a fireman carried out a body in a green plastic bag. Who was inside it? The girl I had glimpsed at the window that day? I tried to recall what was ugly about her, but the face I kept seeing was smeared with black tar.

We read in the paper that the building, by law, was required to have a fire escape, but the landlord hadn't bothered, and the fire inspector hadn't turned him in. I should have been angry. But already I had given up my black-and-white view of the world: rich vs. poor, wrong vs. right. I had begun to acquire a sense of aesthetics. I had come to believe that the image of a woman in a black-and-gold kimono, watching her nephews go up in flames, was a beautiful thing, more deserving of attention than a matter of law.

The building was leveled. The lot was paved over. I left home at eighteen and moved to New York, where I worked as a stylist for a slick magazine. Eventually I was able to help my mother rent a nicer apartment on the hill west of Main Street. While she was packing she came across an envelope.

"There were pictures of a building and a dead cat," she said. "They did not look special, so I threw them away."

After leaving Miss Stark, I put her film in my pocket and walked very slowly by the edge of the road. The colored leaves, the pigeons, even the cars seemed panting with life. When I got to the store I paused by the registers, blinking against the absence of sun. I watched as my mother tried on a necklace of very blue stones. She swiveled the mirror on the counter so it faced her, put her hand to her throat. Light from the ceiling flashed from the mirror, the necklace, the chrome of the counter, the glass, the fake charms and chains.

Mr. Gipps strolled by. He nodded his approval and gave her some compliment, but he didn't say to keep it. As soon as he'd left, she unclasped the necklace and ruefully locked it back in its case.

I knew I was safe then. My mother wouldn't marry Solomon Gipps. What was the privilege of staying home and painting compared to the insult of living with a man who never gave you anything but secondhand gifts? And I knew something else. I knew, to my shame, that I wouldn't spend my life searching for evidence that the world was unfair, but for beautiful things to lay before my mother as an offering of love.

∾∾∾

Choosing Fiction for Publication

Robert Stewart

Save us from competent writers.

The editorial process at *New Letters* involves, in part, a group of pre-liminary readers, community associates, we call them, who are well-educated, professional people; mostly, they are already accomplished writers, themselves, when they join our staff. Yet, the most consistent reaction each has after reading manuscripts for a while is to understand for the first time, perhaps, the enormous banality of competence.

New Letters' single interest in its fiction is literary excellence. It has no other "agenda," cause or concern. We take on all subjects, genders, races and creeds, in search of the transcending, distinctive voice. Among the dozens of manuscripts that waft in on the mails each week, certain patterns become apparent to those shovelling hefty loads of prose into the editorial sieve: humorless lamentations on relationships, bar scenes, an occasional cross-country trek, all in a kind of flat Ameri-jargon. All the unities are in place: point-of-view, pronouns and tone consistent. Correct, careful, dull.

Commonly, a manuscript reader will say to us, after a time, "Now I know what happens when my own writing fails." For writers, reading manuscripts is a great education, and we let them do it, if chosen, for free.

We learn nothing from bad writing and dismiss it quickly. Great writing teaches, excites and gives life. Competent writing, on the other hand, wastes time. It gives the impression of skill while containing no reward. This is not to say that we hold competent writing in disdain. Editors exist, partly, to offer writers the chance to test their stuff. To give it a try. To get it back, knowing that it didn't measure up, or did. Sometimes, unknown to the writer, a story will become the cause for celebration among our small staff (many of whom know each other only by their initials, signed beneath their comments on evaluation sheets).

This is not to say, as well, that community associates "vote" on stories or that *New Letters* chooses its writing democratically–this is an editorship, a form of administration in which the editor takes responsibility for all final decisions. That's why the story of Victor Travesti suits *New Letters* so well: It has an edge, a character whose arrogance gives it distinction and life.

The opening raises this story above competence. Right away the main character takes charge of events. Even though the story has a third-person narrator, that narrator's job is to become Travesti, too, not some generic drone. The story begins, then, in authenticity, with a copper Mercedes 450SL and a "silver suit," and then the verbal tension established by Travesti standing at a bus "shelter," with its haunting contrast and implications of poverty.

More important, Travesti, himself, dives into his role, blaming "Jewish people" for his descent; "the (divorce) judge had been a Jew. Silvermann," he remembers. Right away we are out of bounds, working with character in a way unallowed by the politically controlled media. He names names. Yet is Kennedy, the author, insulting Jews? No. We know, as sophisticated readers, that when Travesti curses Jews or "the Irish fornicator" who married his ex-wife, Travesti is really, bit by bit, dismantling his own self. This is what pop-culture cannot account for, and why it removes from its audience the chance to do its own thinking.

Travesti, rather than being one-dimensional, has that quality of being both consistent and complex at once. He behaves with gallantry toward two women on the bus, while carrying his disgust for their simple lives in his heart.

"Just think of all the families who planned to go on picnics," says one woman, looking at the rain.

"Let them eat grief," thinks Travesti. He charms them to their faces yet averts his eyes from the rolling masses of their flowered backsides.

The manuscript reader knows immediately that a living creature has appeared here, that the possibility exists in this story for a complex vision. It is the kind of joy readers of *New Letters* expect from fiction, the kind of joy they trust editors to supply for them.

Travesti is a character revealed from the inside. The heart of conflict is between the two poles of his spinning needs: to hold onto his image of dignity and yet to be taken care of, as well–to be mothered. Each time his dignity is assaulted, he returns to the position of boy, literally, by returning to his mother's house; and, at the end, in the presence of the infinity of God, he asks for money, for a loan.

Travesti's dignity is only the trappings of dignity; and, like all wounded creatures, he attracts predators to him, those who sense his charade, his deep frailty, and can't resist the impulse to finish him off. In a nice moment of irony, Travesti's feigned generosity–his travesty–becomes the actual moment that sets in motion, the author tells us, his physical death, as well. It is nothing more than bird shit that soils his outer garments, a chance moment; but it is part of a series of dichotomies set up by the author: dignity and frailty, chance and reason.

What happens from this point is a matter of progression, not direction. We readers are beyond saving. We search in stories for others like ourselves. In this case, it is the Italian character that confronted me, in particular. Whether on the "Hill" in St. Louis, the northeast in Kansas City or North Beach in San Francisco, something fundamentally grand and reckless, proud, reminds us of what is emblematic in this story, too.

In my own wandering, recently, a stranger in a cafe on Columbus Avenue, San Francisco, directed me to an anonymous hotel down the street. Only a number identified the door to me; but after I had been buzzed in, I followed the aroma of neck bones cooking in the kitchen of the building's owner, Grace Iribarren. She had me sit at her table and explain to her why I needed a room. Where did I come from? What was my business? In what seemed, at first, little more than a flop house, a transient's hotel, I tendered my nervous application for a $12-a-night room. At some point, I began to feel a little like Travesti–that my dignity were of little weight, that a slight mistake, an instant's chance, might bring some new misfortune, *disgrazia*. When I finally went to see the room, it was spare but clean; the old yellowed curtains blew in the never-ceasing breeze of the city. Dignity.

Good writers, such as Kennedy, establish in their stories recognition of contingencies, as they exist in life; yet they shape those events toward a climax that is both inevitable and surprising. It is not that structural element, however, necessary as it is, that will light up an editor on first reading; it is the recognition of a vital human life in the story, of connection, whether crude or grand, eccentric or steady, that sets such a story above the level of mere competence.

What Does God Care
About Your Dignity, Victor Travesti?

Thomas E. Kennedy

He shall fly away as a dream,
and shall not be found, yea,
he shall he chased away as a vision
of the night. The eye which saw him
shall see him no more.

Job:20:8

Happy is the man whom God correcteth:
therefore despise not thou
the chastening of the Almighty

Eliphaz:Job:5:17

Victor Travesti stood beneath the bus shelter, tall, hands easy in the slash pockets of his trenchcoat. The coat hung open on him, exhibiting the hand-stitched lapels of his silver suit. He watched for the bus, thinking ruefully of the copper Mercedes 450SL that Jewish people had sent an ape to take from him.

Seated on the bench at his back, two women in their late sixties chatted. Rain drizzled from the grey sky onto the pavement and slicked the road.

"It's sad for all the little boys who wanted to play ball today," one of the women said.

Let them drown, thought Victor Travesti, watching for his bus.

"And just think of all the families who planned to go on picnics," the other woman said.

"Such a shame."

Let them eat grief, thought Victor.

The broad glass face of the bus appeared at the corner. The vehicle slid in alongside the curb, wheezed to a halt, clapped open its doors. Victor Travesti turned and with his arm swept a gallant, imaginary path toward the bus to usher the women ahead of him.

"Ladies," he said, and bowed to them.

"Such charms," said one. The other giggled, fluttered her eyelashes, plumped up her thin, red-black hair. "Sidney Omar *said* my stars showed a tall dark handsome fella," she said.

"Your Stars Today," pronounced the first dreamily, with a smile of mystical ignorance.

Victor Travesti winked, poker-faced. Then his strong white teeth flashed as he guided the ladies up the steps of the bus, averting his eyes from the rolling masses of their flowered backsides.

"My mother always said to beware the Latin charm," the balding red-headed woman said, glancing sidewise and up into Victor's dark face, which replied with graceful forbearance.

Yes, he had charm. And scorn, too. He knew how much hand to give, and to whom, and how. For the upstart, for the Irish fornicator, two fingers, while the eyes look elsewhere. Full clasp for peers, for men of respect. He had all the tools of a good *paisan*. His people had been *Calabrese*. He thought it sad that a man of his dignity should have to ride the public bus with balding old ladies.

The reek of a rainy Saturday hung over the seats and passengers inside the bus—wet corduroy, yesterday's onions, breath. Victor Travesti sat by a window and watched the streets and neighborhoods of Queens roll past. Corona, Jackson Heights, Woodside, Sunnyside, the chintzy optimism of a people who would call their main road "Bliss Street." He watched the shops and houses and apartment buildings of people who were doing better than he, people whose dusty shoe shops and dry cleaners hung on, decade after decade, despite the neglect and sloth of their owners, while to Victor, who rose early and worked hard and bore himself with the dignity of a *Calabrese,* fate had dealt failure as a crown upon his efforts.

Victor Travesti signalled his stop and rose, thinking of his wife and two boys and the Irishman who now lived with them, sleeping in bed with the woman who had pledged herself to Victor at the altar of God, sharing her marital bed in the same house where his children slept, eating food at the table with them. Victor's family. With whom a court had told Victor he had no right to be except twice a month at a time chosen by the wife who had violated her pledge. This they called justice. A woman spends afternoons in secret meetings, becomes drunken in public in company with a lecherous man in a business suit, and the court gives to her Victor Travesti's sons.

The judge had been a Jew. Silvermann. A tuft of dark hair jutted from each of Silvermann's nostrils and his eyeglasses had been dirty, speckled with dandruff and grease. When he informed the family of his decision concerning the fate of Victor Travesti's sons, Victor had clamped his jaws tight and risen. He had gazed upon the woman and her Irish lawyer in his shiny three-piece suit, forced them to observe the smouldering of his eyes, his dignity in the face of indignation. He raised his index finger to his eye and smartly drew down the underside of the eyelid: *I see this outrage. I see your deceit. Victor Travesti sees.*

Things had not gone well for Victor Travesti. Tribulation was upon him. His business had failed. He had had to go out begging to work for other men, companies. Victor Travesti had had to offer his skills and wisdom for money, payable by the hour, by the day, the week, to offer himself as a laborer in another man's vineyard, and even that was denied him. No one was left whom he even could beg. He had had to return to live again as a boy in the house of his mother. To see his sons, he had to ride in a public bus and wait with his hat in his hand in the foyer of the Irish fornicator who had cheated him of his family. A man named Sweeney with green creases between his teeth and the red veins of drunkeness across his nose.

The bus slowed. One of the old ladies, moving toward the rear doors, weaved off balance. Victor Travesti's hand leapt to her aid, steadied her by the elbow. She fluttered her eyelids at him. He nodded, dealt her a small, firm smile, held her elbow while she descended before him to the street.

The instant's delay that his courtesy produced decided the course of the brief remainder of Victor Travesti's life.

As he stepped off the bus, he heard a strange sound, very slight, yet somehow foreboding, a kind of hiss, a plop, and there was something familiar and strangely taunting in the sound. He heard the wings of a bird shiver overhead, and the mocking scream of a gull, as he stood at the curb, hands in the slash pockets of his trenchcoat. Two men standing beside a carpet truck laughed raucously. Lettered on the side of the truck were the words *Kipling Karpet Ko.* The men were thick and red-faced. The one smoked a cigarette and smirked. The other wheezed with laughter. Pointing a thick, hair-knuckled finger at Victor Travesti, he said, "I want to sing like the boidies do, tweet tweet tweet."

Victor Travesti clamped his jaws shut. The old woman he had helped off the bus was pushing a fistful of tissues at him.

"You poor dear," she said, "Don't you pay them no mind." She daubed at the lapel of his raincoat. Victor Travesti tipped his chin toward his throat and strained his eyes to see. Something green and white was sketched down its front. Victor grimaced, looked about him with chill fury. The red-faced man stood with his palms on his thighs and wheezed.

Victor Travesti took the Kleenex roughly from the woman's hand, wiped at his lapel. He pitched the crumpled, slimey paper into a refuse basket, shook his hands as though to shed water, fumbled into his pocket for his handkerchief. The stuff was streaked on the lapel of his silver suit as well as on his Sardinian silk tie. The old woman was shoving more Kleenex at him.

"Please!" he snapped, palming her hand away from him.

"Well!" she said. "Some people."

The hand-stitched lapel of his silver suit was blemished with an ugly stain even after he had scrubbed it with his handkerchief, spit on it, scrubbed more. He could carry the raincoat over his arm, but the jacket and the tie were just as bad, worse.

The carpet man watched with unconcealed pleasure. Victor Travesti looked at his freckled, pugged nose, his sandy-red, close-cropped hair. The man seemed to be laughing on behalf of all of Victor Travesti's enemies and tormentors: Judge Silvermann, the Irish fornicator, his adulterous wife, those who had taken over his business, those who had forced him to demean himself requesting permission to labor for their enterprises at a wage and then sent him away with no work. The blood raced to his face, his temples. A brilliant pain seared his skull.

Victor Travesti stood his full height and gazed with chill ferocity from the one carpetman to the other. The smirking one shrugged his shoulders and turned away, but the thick, red-faced man met Victor's gaze with a fury of his own. Victor found it necessary to avert his eyes, to turn away and walk from them.

A bitter taste rose to his mouth as he heard the man speak viciously to his back: "That's right, Salvatori, just keep walkin. That's what ginzos are good at: walkin."

"And fartin," the other added.

"Yeah, that's right: And fartin."

Victor's face burnt with shame. It was difficult for a man of culture and dignity to deal with rabble. Personally, he felt no shame over it, but he had begun to imagine how his sons might have felt had they witnessed the mockery of these orangutans. That they were strangers frightened him vaguely. That strangers should laugh in his face, select him as their target. Why? On what basis? He remembered the woman at the bus stop with her smile of weird, dreamy ignorance: *Your Stars Today.* He kept walking, quickened his pace toward a sign in pale red neon script that said, *Fortune Dry Cleaners–French Method.* Inside, a tall Negro in a white short-sleeved shirt worked the presser, while a man in a lavender mohair sweater did paperwork at the counter.

Victor Travesti laid his coat and jacket on the counter, unknotted his tie and removed it carefully, trying to avoid touching the stain. The man in the mohair sweater took up each garment, examined the stains, laid them gingerly down again. He thrust out his underlip and shook his head. "I don't know about this," he said.

"I need it right away," Victor Travesti said.

The man laughed, tongued the backs of his upper teeth. "You can have them next Monday."

"I need them now," Victor Travesti said. "As soon as possible."

The man looked at him with a smirk. "I could bulk them for you. You'd have them in a hour. But you'd need to pay a surcharge of twenty-five percent. Standard for a rush job. And no guarantees on that there Eyetalian necktie."

"Do you mean I have to pay a surcharge of twenty-five percent," Victor Travesti asked, "And still get no guarantee?"

The man shrugged. "Take 'em somewhere else."

"I need them *now,*" Victor Travesti said.

The man said, "The labor's the same whether I succeed or not."

Victor Travesti emptied the pockets of his jacket and coat. He could not allow his wife or the Irish fornicator to see him like this. It would kill him.

"Come back in an hour," the man said and returned to his paper work.

The Negro drew down the lid of the presser; steam hissed out around the edges.

Outside on the sidewalk, Victor Travesti lit a cigarette. The carpet men were feeding a long rolled-up carpet onto a pile of similarly rolled-up carpets in back of their van. Victor Travesti turned his back on them, walked past an Army & Navy Store, a cake shop, a glass doorway at the foot of a flight of stairs. Lettered across the glass was:

MadameEsth r
Fo tun s
While U Wait
One $/One F ight Up

Victor Travesti looked at his watch, flipped away his cigarette, opened the door. He didn't believe in such superstitious nonsense, although he had an aunt who could predict the weather by flinging drops of scalding olive oil across a scrap of red silk. He just wanted to get off the street, to sit, to have a woman hold his hand and purse her lips and touch his palm with the tips of her fingers and care for a moment or two about his fate. The miraculous medal around his neck jangled as he climbed the wooden staircase two steps at a time.

On the landing were three doors. The first two were locked. He turned the shaky knob of the third and entered a room that was empty but for a ladderback chair in which an old man in a flannel shirt and mustard colored necktie sat gazing out the window. His hair was white and trimmed close at the back and his body looked as though it might once have been powerful, barrelchested, his hands thick and large, the skin now freckled and puckered with age. The room itself looked as though it were in a building that had been bombed. Plaster had fallen away from the walls in several places, showing the woodwork beneath. The floor was covered with dust and plaster flakes from the ceiling and rubbled with bits of wood and glass, broken bottles, a newspaper that looked as though it had been soaked in water and dried and yellowed in the sun.

"Pardon me," Victor Travesti said. "I was seeking Madame Esther."

The old man said, "I can't ever bear to look at it anymore. It's no good. There's no pleasure left in it." He rubbed his eyes with the heels of his hands, then ran a palm over his entire face. "I could as well put it all to the torch." He signed, clasped his hands across his stomach, closed his eyes. A tubular flesh-colored wart hung from one eyelid.

Victor Travesti waited for a moment to see if the old man would say anything further. He glanced around the room. Apart from the rubble, it was empty. No chair, no other furniture. Against one wall was a gutted yellow plastic radio with a crack in the casing.

As he began to turn away, the old man said, "Shut the door. There's a draft."

Victor Travesti hesitated. "I cannot stay," he said.

"Young men are impatient," the old man said. "It makes them uninterested and therefore uninteresting."

Victor shut the door, put his hands in his pockets, jingled his change, considering how he might amuse himself with this old man. He said, "Thank you for the compliment, sir. In fact, I'm hardly young."

The old man's eyes turned upon him in their pouched lids. "Ha!" he said. "You're all of what? Forty-two."

"Good guess."

The old man snorted, reflected, looked sad. He said, "I had such hopes for you."

Victor Travesti inclined his head in dignified query.

"You were so much greater than the monkeys," the old man said. He hawked gravel from his throat, spit it into a handkerchief, which he returned to the pocket of his khaki trousers. "The monkeys were so stupid," he said. "All they ever did was fiddle with themselves and giggle and throw their crap at each other. Never much cared for the monkeys. What can you do with a great ape that does a crosscountry hike just to find some bamboo to eat? Stupid, vulgar creatures. Beauty," he said and smacked one palm with the back of the other hand. The report was startlingly loud. Victor Travesti flinched, wondered if the old man might get violent. Old as he was, he looked like he still might have some power in his body, and Victor wasn't in the mood to wrestle him down or call an ambulance. "You and all your kind. You had advantages. You had capacities never *seen* before."

He rose from his chair, crossed the room, retraced his steps, stared out the window down over the elevated train tracks. Without looking from the window, he said, "What good does it do me? What can you do? You try your best, and it all goes bad. Then you start to question your own motives. Who or what was it for? It was sport, too. I was young. It seemed exciting. I liked them to be brave. I liked the men to be brave, and the women to be nubile. They were men, not rodents. I liked them to make spears and run after the tigers." The old man's deep blue eyes lit for a moment, staring into an invisible past that Victor Travesti could see only in the reflection of sudden vivacity on the man's face. "You should have seen them. Three men, naked in the woods, holding big javelins over their heads and chasing one of those great big tigers right through the trees. *This* was sport: See that big cat go *down* roaring and the three of them waving those bloody spears in the air, yelling out praises. *Praise to the Lord! Hosannah on highest!* That's how it was then. That's how it was back then. Once there were such gods . . ." The old man paused, and his eyes grew distant as his mood seemed to slide downward. His eyes were very blue beneath his white eyebrows, his eyesockets deep in sculpted pouches so that his gaze was like a pale blue shadow. The old man sat again, turned his chair toward Victor Travesti.

Victor Travesti's mind had begun to work hard as he listened to the old man's story. Slowly it had begun to occur to him that everything that had happened to him today, all his life, from the instant of his birth, every chance turning and decision, had been leading him to this moment.

When the old man had ceased to speak for some moments, Victor Travesti dug his handkerchief from his pocket, dusted a spot on the bare wood floor. Then he genuflected onto the handkerchief and bowed his head.

"My Lord and my God," Victor Travesti said with humble dignity.

The old man wet his thin purple lips with the tip of his tongue and watched this man on one knee before him.

"Dear Lord," Victor Travesti said. "I have a favor to beg of you. I have been to the courts and have had no satisfaction. My wife is an adulteress, and the man with whom she fornicates has been given to live with my children, my fine young boys, and I can receive no legal satisfaction. Now I am on my way to visit my children, and I cannot let them see me as I am. I must have some clothes. And if I could rent—or buy—a car, could show up in an expensive car, it would win their respect. It would refresh my dignity. But I have no money, dear Lord. Dear Lord, I need money, very badly. I'm really on my backside."

The old man gazed upon Victor Travesti, and the light blue shadows of his eyes darkened.

"You. Ask. Me. For. *Money,*" he said, his voice faint with incredulity. "You *ask me for money?*" As he repeated the question his face began to grow larger, his eyes burned, and his hands swelled. The old man's face became the face of a radiant beast, huge and furious, blazing.

Victor felt his underpants get wet. He began to weep and dropped his other knee to the floor and clasped his hands together to beg for mercy, but the old man's rage continued to grow. The ceiling lifted above his head to accommodate it, and the walls bulged outward as the waves of fury radiated against them.

"You ask me for money?"

He was on his feet now, bellowing. Victor slipped onto all fours and crawled wildly toward the door, but the old man caught him by the seat of his pants and the scruff of his neck, lifting him with enormous hands, his voice now a wind tunnel of rage, the words no longer distinguishable. Victor was flung against the door, knocking it off its hinges. It toppled, smacked the floor with a hard flat report. Dust rose in small clouds around its edges.

Victor tried to scramble to his feet, but the old man was on him again, picked him up by his shirt front like a suitcase and chucked him down the stairs. Victor Travesti tumbled, feeling the wooden edges of steps punching his kidney, his ribs, the bones of his cheek. He rolled to a stop against the entry door, which shattered, raining shards of lettered glass upon him. In terror, he looked up the staircase, but the old man did not pursue him. He only stood on the top landing, glaring with enormous eyes of fury down upon the heaped body of Victor Travesti.

Victor crawled out the door, took hold of a fire hydrant and hoisted himself to his feet. His one hand was pulsating. He cradled it in the palm of the other. The middle finger lay at a sharp angle from the middle joint and throbbed painfully. He tucked his shirt into his pants, buttoned the collar at his throat, tried to smooth down the torn flap that hung from his hip pocket.

Cradling his injured hand, he shuffled toward the bus stop, uncertain what to do. He would go home to his mother. She could call Dr. DeAngelo. Dr. DeAngelo would splint Victor's finger. He would drink an expresso and anisette and eat some stella dora bread. He would take a nap and when he woke again, his mother would have baked some zitti for him, and he would be calm.

The carpet men stood in his path.

Victor Travesti drew back, tried to circle around them, but they stepped to the side to block his way again. "Leave me alone," he whimpered. "I broke my finger."

"Oh," said the thick-bellied red-headed one to the quiet, smirking one. "He broke his finger."

"Yeah, gee, poor guinea broke his finger. He wants us to leave him alone."

"Have you no culture?" Victor Travesti inquired icily. "Are you *animali?*"

The red-head cupped a hair-knuckled paw behind his ear. "Come again, Salvatori? You said *what* to me?"

"That is not my name," said Victor Travesti. "Leave me alone. My finger."

The carpetman reached for Victor Travesti's lapels. "I'll leave you alone," he said. "Come 'ere, Salvatori."

Victor shrieked with indignation and fear as he was dragged down, kicked in the thigh, shoved and stuffed by the two men into a half-rolled, synthetic Persian carpet. He flailed, was kicked hard in the buttock, the arm; he caught his injured finger, cried out with exquisite pain. The thick man knelt with one knee on Victor's gut, pinning him, as the other, snuffling with laughter and excitement, began to roll the carpet. Victor kicked and twisted, and just before the carpet roll closed over his face, he saw, watching from the window above the street, the old man's blazing eyes.

Then the carpet was over his face, was lifted and tossed onto the stack of other carpets in the back of the van. Victor could not move. He felt another carpet tossed on top of his. The air was very close and tight. He could not fill his lungs. He realized—even as he heard the ignorant muffle of the laughter outside, as he heard the van's rear door smack shut, as he heard the ignition wheeze and catch, and his consciousness slowly began to dim from lack of oxygen—that he was going to die. He realized that he was going to die and that these two carpetmen, when they found his body, would be stricken with terror, would be baptized with a terrible guilt that might change the rest of their lives. All because of their stupidity in not realizing he would die if they did this to him.

It hardly seemed fair. Any of it. He had done nothing to deserve this. Nothing. Perhaps it was stupid of him to have asked for money, but he needed money. Very badly.

His eyelids lowered in the woolly airless darkness, and the tight gasping fury of his lungs stilled, and he knew that he was crossing the border to whatever awaited him— nothing or something, disintegration or the reflection of spirit for a time or forever—as the humming motor of the van faded off into a sleep that slowly ceased to dream him.

Fiction and Politics

Robley Wilson

We claim to be eclectic in our choice of fiction, and our guidelines for authors insist that we have no prejudices with regard to subject matter—that excellence is our only criterion (though we admit we are less drawn to longer stories on the simple ground that we would rather publish more stories than fewer). Whether or not the *NAR* succeeds in its public intentions, or whether there is in fact a "*North American Review* story" whose trademark is obvious to everyone but the editor, only a regular and careful reader can tell us (and it's true that once in a great while we'll receive a letter castigating us for too many stories in present tense, too many stories told in first person—the most commonplace of today's fiction techniques).

In any case, we *believe* we are without prejudice and, if nothing else, we have the advantage of continuity: twenty-five years of the same editor choosing all the fiction; no guest fiction editors, no editorial panel, no committee whose diversity attenuates its decisions on the near side of the border of risk. We think of our single focus as an enlightened tyranny, one additional virtue among those others enjoyed by non-commercial magazines: no catering to advertisers, no bending to the tastes inferred from the demographics.

The *NAR* offers prospective contributors a quite narrow window—we consider fiction only between January and the end of March—and receives between three- and four-thousand submission a year. Of those, in our six issues we publish between thirty-five and fifty stories—forty in 1993, twenty-three of their authors appearing in our pages for the first time. Many of the fictions are short-shorts, a form we've been especially friendly to for more than a dozen years, which we call "four-minute fictions" (originally after the time barrier of the mile run, now long-since broken), and which others call variously "sudden fiction" or "flash fiction." (We once considered calling our fictions of fewer than 1500 words "quictions," but wiser minds dissuaded us).

Forty stories a year is a healthy quantity–perhaps only *The New Yorker* publishes more–and even an editor with erratic judgment might be expected to turn up a gem or two in that number. The story following, Norman Lavers' "The Translator," is from the September/October 1992 number of the magazine, and we think it is as unusual and excellent a fiction as any editor could ask for. It is literary, it is political, it is a compelling and moving expression of individual freedom overcoming blind despotism, and it conveys with marvelous economy the almost quirky depth of cultural and philosophical disjunction between East and West. That the story is told in present tense only makes the nobility of Shakespeare's translator more immediate and wrenching.

The Translator

Norman Lavers

Noshi Bei Wattapornpet drags the beat-up cheap piano bench one step away from the tacky old piano, its deal finish peeling, and places it up against the 900 year old rosewood table and sits down. The lovely smooth wood of the table has two deep rounded valleys where generations of scholars have rested their elbows. Even Noshi's tiny feather-light elbows have contributed. She is 89 years old, and was trained by her father to be a scholar from the time she was nine.

The two-room flat has only a narrow pathway in from the front door, circling the room, exiting into the next room, and circling it. Only one as tiny and narrow-shouldered as Noshi can walk the pathway facing straight ahead. The remainder is piled to the ceiling with boxes and parcels wrapped in cloth or paper, and tied about with string. The rosewood table itself is stacked high with books and dictionaries and papers, leaving only a small square workplace where she sits, with her brush and the little tray in which she mixes soot and oil to make ink.

She is translating *Hamlet,* re-forming its gorgeous blank verse into the sweeping and elaborate script of her own language, so that her nation, her people, can have this masterpiece. She is working on the great final scene, culminating in the treacherous duel between Hamlet and Laertes.

"We defy augury," Hamlet is saying.

She needs to think about that line. How can she convey it into her culture without the reader thinking Hamlet is a fool? How can an educated man, especially one who has studied philosophy, defy augury? It is like snapping your fingers in the faces of the gods, challenging them to do their worst. It is a senseless and unnecessary thing to do. (She has had a candy bar for breakfast, and now she taps a king-size cigarette out of its package, breaks off the filter, and lights it, inhaling deeply.) When she had her four beautiful husky young sons, she told everyone how ugly they were. Who would not do the same? Even with her saying that, the gods looked and saw how handsome they were, and killed every last one of them, one by smallpox, one by tuberculosis, one fighting the Japanese, one fighting the communists. Just as she had spoken poorly always about the two strong husbands she had had in her life, telling everyone they were so weak they could not even beat her properly, and did not even have mistresses, but the gods had found them out anyway, and killed them both fighting the colonialists. And her four brothers—always in twos and fours, lucky enough numbers—and always males (except her), which showed how much good luck there was in the family (that's why she is so unlucky, it suddenly occurs to her, because she is so cursedly lucky)—her four brothers, impressed into various armies of various warlords and killed fighting on one side or other. The gods, of course, had never noticed, had never needed to be jealous of her, so little and insignificant with her frail bones like dry sticks, and no muscles anywhere in her body. Her nickname is Sparrow. And that's what she is like, too, so easy to crush that nobody bothers, able to live on grit, and missing nothing with her sharp eyes.

She will skip that line about auguries for the moment and get on to the duel itself, because a duel is something understandable in any language. She drags the bench the step back towards the piano. Playing Western music gets her blood into the proper rhythm for translating a Western language.

She bangs at the piano vigorously, and sings in her piping bird voice:
Mia-tsee dotes an do-tsee dotes
An ridder ramzee divy
Uh kiddery divy too
Wooden yu
Then she sings:
Yu ah mah des-tiny
Yu ah what yu ah to me

Now she feels ready to begin, and drags the bench back to the table. She has given up trying to translate word by word, since that seems to make no sense in her language, and of course there is no way blank verse can be duplicated–she had learned that when she made her translation of *Paradise Lost*–since most of the words in her language rhyme with each other. Nor could she write it as a play, for in her country plays are only music and dance and beautiful costumes and go on for hours, while the audience eats and visits with friends, no one listening to the words of the songs. So she is writing it as an epic novel, trying to capture the spirit and render it into something intelligible.

The demon king Claudius (she writes) went to visit Ophelia where he was holding her captive in the Kingdom Under the Water. He was smitten sorely with love of her, but she was Prince Hamlet's number one concubine. He ordered her to put her raiment aside, and took his pleasure from her young body–how could she resist a mighty king?–but she despised the odor of his aging body and the simpering expression on his wrinkled face, and in her heart she stayed loyal to her youthful lover. Claudius sensed her coldness, and ground his teeth with frustration. He had offered her half his kingdom and joint rule and everything her heart could want if she would agree to be his voluntarily, but she quietly resisted. He had tried to stay away from her, and Gertrude, his number one wife, and all his concubines and pleasure girls did what they could to make him forget her, but he kept coming back.

If this coldness is out of loyalty to Prince Hamlet, he said, then you are a fool. Prince Hamlet is not going to save you. In fact by tonight he will be dead. Then you will have no one but me.

She bowed before him in bodily submission, but in her heart she was steel.

King Claudius was depressed returning to his castle, but he felt better the moment he looked at the forces he was marshalling against Hamlet. The ghosts of Rosencrantz and Guildenstern had been converted into mighty demons, each with four heads and eight arms, each arm carrying a weapon. Laertes, mounted on a giant war elephant, was carrying a bow the size of the mast of a ship, and in it was nocked the magic arrow that could not miss. The ghost of the sledded Polack, wearing a magic armor that could not be pierced, and sending out a blast of icy cold that froze and shattered anything he touched, had gladly come to fight the son of his hated old enemy. And there was the ghost of Polonius, master of curses and deceits. Finally, King Claudius had purchased with gold the services of Fortinbras and his entire Army of the East.

Noshi pauses. In a traditional novel she would now outline Prince

Hamlet's forces, and they would be equally grand and magical. But in fact, there is no one to be in Hamlet's army. There is only himself, not very brave or very strong, and with no special weapons. Horatio, his friend, who is not a warrior but a Buddhist priest. And Ophelia, but Ophelia is tiny and slight like Noshi herself, and a prisoner.

(Noshi stops chewing the end of her brush—a bad habit!—and lights a new cigarette.) She is thinking of the many times when she was herself a prisoner. Her status changed every time the government changed its policies. One time she would be a professor at the university, and have her precious rosewood table and her books and manuscripts and dictionaries, and a commission to translate a great work. Then she would write something wrong, and all her things would be taken from her, and she would be put in prison or on a work farm in the bitter north of the country. That had happened when her prizewinning translation of *Paradise Lost* had been published. First the colonials had arrested her, when she seemed to be saying the great powerful God from the West had sought to keep the native people in their tropical paradise naked and ignorant, preserving for himself the best fruits of their forest, and how the tireless Satan, with his forces in the hills, had got the people on his side, and dressed them and tried to bring them into the modern world. When the communists had thrown out the colonialists, they had released her and made her a hero. But then when they looked again at her treatment of Satan, they decided that what she was really saying was that Satan and God were fighting each other for their own selfish motives, and using the people as their pawns, and the people's land as their battleground, and that the people were just as bad off either way. At that point she was put back in prison. Then the new more liberal and open government said that the past governments were wrong, and all praise should be given to the truth tellers, who were only loyally trying to make the country stronger with their intelligent and constructive criticism. The new government actually asked for, desired criticism, the harsher the better. So she was released, given her books and her rosewood table back, and commissioned to work on *Hamlet*. All of her generation were dead, either killed by the emperor, or by the colonialists, or by the communists. They were all stronger than she was, but not as patient. Now she is out again, and has quietly picked up her work where she left off.

All the people are saying these are the good times, it won't go back to the old bad days again, it can't, the government would no longer dare. The government will listen to the people's demands now, and the people have plenty of demands to make. (Some of the young people came to Noshi's apartment last night and advised her that they would be gathering in the streets today to voice their protests, and she has been hearing the rising murmur of their voices outside her second-floor window all morning.) Noshi says nothing to discourage the people, but they are all so young they have not seen the pendulum swing as many times as she has. For herself, she is writing as fast as she can, eating her candy bars and smoking her cigarettes while they are available to her. As the Westerners phrase it, she is saying "Hey!" while the sun shines.

She has been reading *Hamlet* all her life, but had always been afraid to try to translate it. Because the more she read it, the more it seemed to consist only of its beautiful words, and since she could not translate it word for word, she would have to render it into equally beautiful words in her own language. In short, she would have to be Shakespeare at the top of his power.

But while she was in prison this last time, she had got an insight into one of the themes, and thought she could weave her translation around that. She was watching the young people around her dying of starvation and tuberculosis and despair, and watching, without listening, as the aging cadre came to give them their reeducation lectures every day, and she was looking at the posters everywhere of their leaders, more ancient and doddering than she was. In a flash she understood the play *Hamlet,* and the character Prince Hamlet.

The big question had always been why he was such a coward, why he hesitated for five long acts to kill Claudius when in the first he promised to sweep at once to his revenge. When Noshi was first trying to puzzle out that question, she used to think, Why didn't Shakespeare just put Othello in the part of Hamlet? And then she realized: because the play would have been over in the first act, Othello either killing Claudius or being himself killed in a reckless head-on charge against the palace guard. But that couldn't be the only reason a great writer would make Hamlet hesitate, just to fill out the length of the play. Nor, for that matter, was Othello necessarily right and Hamlet wrong. For, look, if Hamlet had been put into the play *Othello—he* never could have been duped into killing his wife. That's the answer, Othello was a rash fool, and rash fools are manipulated by the clever evil people. Laertes, after all, was hasty and rash, and Fortinbras was hasty and rash, and Claudius played them like instruments. He would have done the same to Othello.

The question was answered the moment you realized the play was a battle between youth and age, the old and doddering but rich and powerful and clever playing the young for fools, using wealth and cunning to get the young to fight each other, in order to preserve power for the old. Only Hamlet, by using patience, by holding back, by thinking and testing, could not be played for a fool. After all, he had first to be certain the ghost of his father was not a sort of supernatural Iago. And he had to be sure he killed Claudius in a way that would truly punish him. And finally, because Hamlet was young and full of imaginings and loved a beautiful young girl, it was only fair that he did not rush off at once to save his country, but had a moment to enjoy the attractiveness of life.

The gods had taken pity on Ophelia (she writes), and freed her so she could fight alongside her lover. On the plain beyond the river on the edge of the mountains, the two armies met.

Claudius was furious that Hamlet and Horatio and Ophelia could dare to challenge his authority, but he gloated when he saw how weak and unprotected they were. (Noshi can hear the crowds down on the street two floors below beginning to shout and chant. She has not looked outside, but she can tell by the sound they are in tremendous numbers.) First he sent Rosencrantz and Guildenstern, converted into eight-armed monsters, against them. Hamlet and his party threw stones and sticks at them, but could do nothing against the dazzling curved blades of their swords. Guildenstern chopped off Hamlet's head with a single swing. Hamlet made a groan, quickly silenced, as his head went rolling, and his body, shooting up a geyser of blood, dropped lifeless. Rosencrantz swung with one sword against Horatio, and another against Ophelia, and they both similarly dropped, spouting blood. For fun, the two monsters stripped Ophelia's clothing off, so they could ogle the private parts of her headless corpse. But suddenly the heads swelled up, and new arms and legs dangled out of them, like a crab coming out of a shell, and Hamlet and Horatio and Ophelia jumped to their feet with their new bodies. At the same time a nub appeared on the severed neck of their original bodies, and new heads quickly grew up. Now six friends were facing the monsters. Again the monsters swung, and now there were twelve, and then twenty-four. The monsters looked back at Claudius, worried, their arms growing tired. (There is louder chanting on the streets below, and a loudspeaker is ordering everyone to go home. Noshi hears the rumble of heavy vehicles slowly approaching in first gear.) Claudius called them back and now sent Laertes in with his giant bow, and his magic arrow that could not miss. He pulled the bow back and let the arrow fly. It whistled on its way, then curved, and weaving back and forth, went through the chests of all eight Hamlets, then curved and went through all eight Horatios, and all eight Ophelias. They cried out with the pain of the cruel jagged barb ripping their flesh aside, skewering their organs.

But soon they had risen, and flocks of sparrows began to fly out of the holes in their bodies, then the holes themselves closed. The sledded Polack sent out his cold, and the friends were fractured into pieces, but more sparrows flew out, and the body parts grew back again. There were thousands facing Claudius's embattled army. Claudius saw the hatred in their eyes and could not believe it. I was always told that everyone loved me, he lamented. He staggered back to the castle on his cane. Kill them all, he ordered his army, then went into his room where he would not have to see any more. (She eats quickly the candy bar she has been saving for lunch, and takes the cigarettes out of her package and secretes them in the hem of her shapeless old housedress.) His army was weary, and beginning to feel sick at what they were doing. (Suddenly there is shooting, and she hears the people screaming, and the pounding of their feet as they run. She stops then for a moment, and closes her eyes, and thinks to herself how beautiful all the young people are. Then she begins writing again even faster.) Fortinbras's army had sailed in, chopping and cutting, and at first the easy victory, the smell of blood, the thought of how much money they were being paid, thrilled them. (She hears heavy booted footsteps running up the stairs.) But after the first surge of excitement, the blood began to smell repulsive to them, and besides, the people were coming on in bigger and bigger crowds, and even sticks and stones, when there were so many, began to hurt. And everywhere that there was blood, sparrows flew out, thousands and thousands, and fighting them was like fighting the drops of water in the sea.

The soldiers only have to hit her thin door once to knock it to splinters. She sits quietly looking straight ahead while one of them turns sideways and squeezes through the crowded room towards her. He jerks her hands up and puts manacles on them, which of course immediately fall right off her skinny hands and wrists. The soldier glares at her, then orders her to get up and accompany them down the stairs. She does not even glance behind her, so no one will notice how hard it is for her to give up her table and her manuscripts.

"This time you won't be coming back, old woman," the soldier says. It is at this precise moment that a new insight, a new understanding comes to her, which is why she raises her hand and snaps her fingers at her astonished captor, and answers him in English.

"We defy augury," she says.

~~~~~~

"Trinity Doughnuts"
and the Openness of Life

Hannah Wilson

"Trinity Doughnuts" is Amber Dorko's fifth story in *Northwest Review*. Although stories by past contributors land at the top of our reading pile, being a past contributor in no way guarantees publication. For one, staff turnover, though slight, means that a different mix of readers might well be evaluating someone's second or third submission, bringing new critical slants and changing tastes to the discussion. And as most editors and writers know, quality control eludes even cat food manufacturers. In the four years I've been with the staff, only two other fiction writers have doubled in our pages–actually doubled; none by Dorko appears more than twice. We publish Dorko because her work pulses with qualities we admire: she introduces us to real people who move and talk in memorable, often idiosyncratic ways; she evokes pathos without making her characters victims; she makes us laugh. And she's willing to revise.

Few of the stories we accept come to us in their published form. Sometimes a scene or an ending slips into cliche, a stretch of dialogue seems stilted, a character trips into the rut of the expected or goes too far beyond. But if the writer has moved us to live for a while inside the fiction, if we come to recognize some of our own pain or joy there, if the prose sings un-self-consciously as if from the next room, then we believe the story is worth more work and hope the writer capable of revision.

"Trinity Doughnuts" went through three revisions. After the first staff discussion, I wrote:

> We admire the way this story about a casual genius becomes a story
> about the neighborhood's hopes, illusions, and realities–but we sense

that the end dissipates what comes before, just when it needs to resonate. . .We're puzzled by the return to Nathalie. Was she supposed to be a genius too and turned out "only" a mother? Or is Obie resigned to his not being able to create life as his sister did (only God can make a tree; only a woman can give birth)? This seems too simplistic for the story and for you.

The ending of the story *NW Review* published wasn't radically changed from that first version, but the few changes made a huge difference. The friends' talk towards the end about Obie and his family, including the lines about "the Projects" where Obie grew up, absent in version one, now pulls the reader back to view the whole neighborhood, to see the importance of class and social rifts that the characters had seemed indifferent to earlier.

In Dorko's second treatment, she shifted from first to third person. From my letter about that version:

We like the way you've focused more tightly on Obie's relationship with his "audience," on his fan's perception of his genius. We like that at the end we're not at all sure he is a genius.

The point of view troubles us—and I think your shift to third accounts for some of us liking the first version better. This is and is not Obie's story. It is also the narrator's, and if we get closer to some of the narrator's perceptions, we'd know more about Obie, know how to come to our own view of him.

Dorko then shifted back to first person and sent us essentially the story we published, brimming with the qualities we've come to associate with her work, ones we find enormously appealing in any writer.

Within the first few lines, she creates a distinct voice that we hear all through the story. In "Trinity Doughnuts," her narrator is an on-looker, someone who knows who and what he loves, but who doubts the worth of his own judgments and talents. Three times in the first paragraphs, he needs to tell us that his friend "Obie Vance was a true genius." That voice doesn't change, but his insights do. Towards the end, when the band breaks up, he says, "What would it make me, sitting along with Obie in his bedroom, under Nathalie's ugly God's Eye, listening to him strum? I was a hanger-on, a fan, who hadn't thought too much about the person involved." He had wanted to bask in Obie's light, but at the end, led both by Obie's acts and his own heart, he knows himself to be a friend, not a fan, as perhaps he also knows that Obie's genius is in going his own way.

The narrator's vulnerability could make him pathetic or even irritating, but the voice subtly controls our reactions. This is a quick, observant narrator. In swift phrases, we get whole pictures: "a bad-tempered guy named Dougie Rutecki"; "Obie spent his nights flapping around in the batter and sugar and those huge cloth funnels full of shiny lemon filling"; "Dougie's girlfriend Liz was there and had her legs stretched out all over the place." Dorko, of course, is throwing his voice—note the harsh sounds of the mean-tempered Dougie Rutecki's name; the humor in Obie's revising, "My Cousin Lives on A Sheep Farm," to "My Cousin Has a Prosthetic Arm," and Missy's defense of Obie's songs, "You gotta listen to the words," when even the narrator knows "Well, you also had to be able to understand the words." We know by the flat, tasteless song Chris Traiman writes, "Hepatitis Vaccine," that Obie has a kind of genius the others lack.

Dorko's shift back to the first person helps her structure the story as well as give it its lively pacing. Many stories we read try to avoid textbook structure—exposition, rising complication, climax, denouement—but in doing so, their writers often fail to create any line of tension along which the story can move. Here, as we follow the line of Obie's genius from the opening to the final phrase, "Obie is not in the picture," we also come to care about how the narrator's loyalties will play out. And so the seemingly random return to Nathalie roots Obie in his family, and both Obie and the narrator in the neighborhood, in a community.

Reading Dorko's work, even her stories which aren't yet ready, we come to quickly care about the characters. Too often, we get stories in which writers have created characters they don't seem to know very well or care much about, and if *they* don't care, why should we? Even the minor characters in "Trinity's Doughnuts" receive attention: Kerry, Obie's co-worker, "raising his dough-covered hands and pantomiming handcuffs"; Obies's "macrobiotic" parents; the nasty Doug who eats "Goober Grape . . . with a plastic spoon." Even the two who have the same name, Missy and Missy, *because* they have the same name, immediately become recognizable as long-time friends whom we're likely to mix up because they react so similarly.

At a workshop once, I heard Grace Paley urge writers to "Bring other characters into the story. It's an act of generosity," she said, "to give more people life." Later, she added, "It's not bad to have an outline, especially if you don't plan to follow it. Everyone deserves the open destiny of life."

Amber Dorko's work has that openness of life. So, too, do the many other stories we work with that are quite different from hers, from the surreal and almost allegorical through the magically real to the more traditional stories set in real places populated by people we wonder if we haven't met somewhere. What we keep looking for is a story where something happens to somebody we care about, something that matters to the character and to us, where the reading offers us pleasure in the language, in the humor, in the surprise of emotion.

Trinity Doughnuts
Amber Dorko

Obie Vance was a true genius. "You're a true genius," I kept telling him one night while we were sitting around drunk in Seth Traiman's bedroom. Obie's band, The Screaming Mimes, used to practice in Seth's bedroom. It was Obie, Seth, Seth's brother Chris, and a bad-tempered guy named Dougie Rutecki. Then there was me and Gary Dutka, friends of the band, who sat around on Seth's bed to listen. Obie was restringing a popped A when I told him.

"Obie," I said, "You are a true genius."

"Nah," said Obie. He grinned, forty, blinding white teeth in a huge pumpkin head, and stabbed himself in the thumb with the discarded string. "Ow," he said. He squeezed the tiny puncture so that an equally tiny welt of blood rose up. It looked like one of those old Close-Up toothpaste commercials. "What makes you say that anyway, man?"

There are a handful of Obies in every neighborhood, kids whose parents came in to school occasionally to do special slide presentations in the Auditorium on the years they spent in the Peace Corps, or kids whose parents were teachers themselves, or naturally bilingual kids, or kids who just showed up being smart and special in average families. In Obie's family there were two; Obie, and his older sister Nathalie. We had all grown up together, the Vance kids, the Traiman kids, Dougie and Gary, and me. Obie Vance had always been different from the rest of us, darker, more secretive. We never quite understood Obie and the things he did. Ultimately, he was our leader, although none of us ever really tried the things he led us to, except the guys in the band. That's what Obie did, he played in the band, and it was that year, the year that things could have taken off for them, that Obie took that job at Trinity Doughnuts. You never do know what a person will pick as the thing to do.

Obie got his start at Trinity on the eleven-to-seven shift. He didn't wait counters or anything—it's not a twenty-four hour place. He was in the back, making doughnuts. The place was locked up at night, so it was just Obie and a guy named Matt and another guy named Kerry. Kerry was the one who was supposed to be in charge. He was Obie's age, but he had a kid and a wife. He lived in the trailer park near the taxidermist and the lot where everyone went every year to get their Christmas trees.

Obie liked Kerry. He was always asking him to come hear the band. "Yeah? When?" Kerry always asked, not really meaning *when,* raising his dough-covered hands and pantomiming handcuffs. He was stuck in his role as a husband and father for at least eighteen more years. He would be free again just before he turned forty. At the time he didn't seem to mind, or at least he didn't seem to have expected any different.

Trinity Doughnuts is located right on US1, close to the interstate exit. It isn't part of a shopping center or anything. Just out there all by itself, with the lights on all night. It was an easy target for theft, with the bonus that the thief could be zipping down the interstate in less than five minutes. It isn't very safe. That's what made the salary so high. The place had been cleaned out twice since Kerry had started working there.

Obie, Matt, and Kerry made doughnuts all night. They had a tape deck and a tiny black and white TV which didn't do them much good considering that during the hours they worked there was little or no broadcasting. It wasn't the kind of job that demanded peak performance every little minute; Obie spent his nights flapping around in the batter and sugar and those huge cloth funnels full of shiny lemon filling and creme for about eight hours, and had the place clean and neat by the time the morning people showed up. He would go home and sleep until four or five in the afternoon, then show up at Chris and Seth's at seven to practice. You could always tell when he'd been at Trinity. He never walked around with flour in his hair or anything, but he always smelled a little cakey, and usually had little red blisters splattered across his forearms, from the deep-fryers. At a quarter of eleven he'd leave for work again. Obie's schedule might've caused a few problems as far as arranging gigs and all went, but none arose. Gigs, I mean.

Obie started spending a lot more time with me after I told him he was a genius. On weekends he managed to get back on a daytime schedule, so we'd get together. I remember one Saturday night Obie invited me over to watch Peter Fonda in *The Trip*. He wanted to go look at harmonicas first, so he buzzed my house at about three and we went to Eleventh Street Music.

I flipped through some song anthologies while Obie spun the rotating harmonica display and asked the salesguy some questions. After a few minutes he chose his purchase, poking me to show it off, baring his teeth happily and holding out a curved, bow-shaped harmonica.

I didn't know anything about harmonicas. I figured Obie's pick was a good one. As much as I liked Obie, it was a chore sometimes hanging out with him. He seemed to pick such funny little boring details to get interested in.

On the way back we stopped at a 7-11 for some cheese corn and Cherry Coke. That was Obie's way of sticking it to his parents. Walking into their house with a sheet of acid tied to your head wouldn't have gotten to them. Cherry Coke got you a lecture, though. The Vances were macrobiotic. Obie just told them the snacks were for whoever he was bringing home at the time, as most of his friends weren't accustomed to eating seaweed. Obie was really an unconvincing liar, but his family liked him too much to mind. They didn't even care that he made doughnuts for a living, smart as he was. They thought it was important to let their kids do the things they wanted.

Obie had a TV and VCR in his room, along with a small, half-inflated life raft. "It's real comfortable," he said, pointing toward it as he plunked down the sodas and threw the bag of cheese corn on the bed. He dodged a huge, tattered, yarn God's Eye that was dangling from the light fixture.

"Nathalie made that at camp when she was like, eight," he told me, grinning incredulously. "Can you believe that?"

Obie's sister Nathalie was twenty-two then, and went to Vassar. It was hard to believe anybody we knew really went to Vassar, but postmarks don't lie. If she wasn't there, she was at least in the area. Doing whatever. Smart, like Obie.

Everybody thought that Obie could have pursued his music full time, and been very successful at it, too. Obie was a very good songwriter. The night after he had purchased the bowtie harmonica, he'd come to practice and whipped it out and given everyone a short demonstration of its powers. No one knew he could even play the harmonica. Obie could play an amazing number of instruments. In the Vances' living room was a little framed picture of Obie and me, taken when we were nine, going to Obie's violin recital. Obie looked very happy there, as usual.

He played the harmonica for a while that night, just making little things up, occasionally seeming to like certain bits better than others and wrestling guitars out of other people's hands and strumming to himself and frowning. That was how he wrote. Having the harmonica was a new thing, and at first it didn't sound right. It sounded kind of hick. In that spirit, Obie made up a song called "My Cousin Lives On A Sheep Farm," and then about ten minutes later changed it to "My Cousin Has a Prosthetic Arm." He seemed pretty happy with it, and he didn't write it down, because he never wrote them down.

"You know, you should start doing something with that stuff," Seth Traiman said.

"Nah," said Obie, who was picking his toes at the foot of the bed.

"Why not?"

"There's no *security* in it." Obie replied. "I'd have to have, like a union job to do something like that."

"Musicians union?" asked Chris Traiman.

"No, man. Union. Steelworkers. Solid labor. You know."

Everyone squinted with doubt. Obie continued. "Union jobs, you can be making all this money with benefits and all and then just take leave–I could go and see the country or become a miserable failure of a musician or whatever. . ." he gestured with a bottle of Orangina. Everyone was listening to him like they were in an E.F. Hutton commercial. ". . . then with the union and all, I could just start up again whenever I was ready. At like, an unbelievably high salary." He shook the soda. "I don't know. Glass making or something."

Chris and I were impressed. That was pretty good business acumen.

"That doesn't make any *sense,"* said Dougie Rutecki, who was wearing a shirt with a goddamn duck on it for whatever reason and it was secretly annoying the hell out of me.

Obie leaned in very close to him and tapped him on the forehead with the Orangina bottle.

"It's the only way," he said. "What, I'm gonna go make an ass of myself, just quit work and go play a washboard in the park or something? In a wheelchair?" He waved Dougie aside with a flourish of the bottle, then looked as though he were considering the idea briefly, exposing the dark chamber of his mouth in a vacuum cleaner grin. "Hey," he said, "Yeah."

We considered it, for a few minutes anyway, until we realized that not only did we not know where to get a wheelchair or a washboard, we had no nearby park. In no time Obie was again pushing for union employment.

"Steel plant, maybe," he said. He shrugged and picked up his guitar, closing the topic down for the time being. But it was those practical plans, those little insights into Obie's intellect, that helped to convince me that he was less of a jerk than a lot of folks. Obie was in no way your basic tortured artist. He was very practical.

"You know," I said to him later driving home, "You wouldn't end up a miserable failure of a musician. You wouldn't have to break your legs and play a washboard in a wheelchair."

"I'd probably fake the crippled part," he said seriously.

"No. Obie. You'd be great. It would just take some effort."

"I'm not up for effort," he said. "I've got a Lonesome Loser mentality."

"But you *shouldn't,*" I told him. "You'd be great."

"Nah," he said.

"Why not?" I asked.

"Because I'm a fuckin' Magical Sultan in addition to being a Lonesome Loser," he said, shaking his empty Orangina bottle. "Because I see the future. Because I couldn't. I just know."

Not even a month after he had begun, Obie's shift at Trinity Doughnuts switched from eleven-to-seven to seven-to-three. Obie wasn't too bugged by it. He didn't get to work with Kerry anymore, but he didn't have to work the counter, either. He was still making doughnuts. All by himself now. There was more on TV during the day, at least. It was all just fine by Obie. And even though he wasn't working the counter he wandered around behind it a lot, chumming it up with the people who did work there (Dave, Missy, and Missy) and occasionally speaking with the customers. Trinity Doughnuts pulled quite a few regulars. We often heard about them at practice: The Real Old Guy, Blond Guy With A Yarmulke, The Girl With All The Things In Her Hair, Toaster Head, Son Of Toasterhead, Anvilface. If anything, Obie was enjoying himself now more than ever, at work and with the band, and he had even persuaded Kerry to come down for a rehearsal one night.

Kerry brought with him his wife, Michelle, and their baby Kenzie, a generic-looking, dirty little kid gnawing and squeaking on the plastic nipple of a Donald Duck-shaped baby bottle filled with flat Pepsi. They'd barely started rehearsing when Michelle scooped Kenzie off the bed in a huff, claiming the noise would bust open the baby's eardrums and cause internal bleeding, and marched off to the car, dangling the keys on her MICHELLE keychain angrily.

"That's okay," said Obie. "Lately it's been getting kinda full in here."

We were surprised he'd noticed. Kerry either didn't notice or pretended he didn't. It was just as well by the rest of us though—it really was getting pretty crowded. Aside from Kerry and Gary and me, Dougie's girlfriend Liz was there and had her legs stretched out all over the place.

It happened gradually, as the news of a genius in the neighborhood is bound to spread gradually, and with some skepticism. But the bedroom that for years had mostly only held the band, Gary Dutka, and me, suddenly held more. No new faces, it seemed, but the body count rose anyway, like large drops of mercury being split into many smaller beads on the bathroom floor. First everyone in the band somehow managed to get a girlfriend; then they started bringing them all to practice. Kerry never came again, but was easily replaced by Dave, Missy, and Missy. Four girlfriends, three doughnut people, Gary, and me. Nine people plus four in the band.

Thirteen of us in Seth Traiman's bedroom, the door to which was kept open now for the sake of breathing; everyone very hot and invariably frustrated, Chris, Seth, and Dougie only minutes out of work and in their sweaty dress pants and shirts unbuttoned, V-neck undershirts showing, that prickly-cool smell of office photocopy-machine toner blending in with the warm fingerprint smell of the necks of their guitars. Obie always arrived last, in a t-shirt and shorts, his smile an earthquake on his face and with his everpresent bottle of Orangina. Everyone else drank beer, unbeknownst to Mr. and Mrs. Traiman. Obie was the only kid allowed to drink in front of his parents at home, and all he ever drank was that orange bilgewater.

Many nights he brought taped-up boxes of remnant doughnuts, ugly, sloppy things that were beyond retail but still edible, and usually insisted on making a major issue out of the dead skin on his feet for at least fifteen minutes before he was ready to play. It was his way of preparing himself for his craft. We kept the doughnuts out of the way.

The manager of the Red Roof Inn, Chris Traiman said, had offered them a spot to play Saturday nights. With pay. Half the door. "I don't know, man," said Obie, "with work and all, I need my time."

"Whadja join the band for," said Dougie Rutecki testily, "if you didn't wanna play out? What's the point of being in a band if you don't play out?"

"I didn't *join* the band, *man,*" said Obie. "I *started* it. You joined it."

"Still," said Dougie.

There wasn't much room for argument, because without Obie, there was no Screaming Mimes. Obie *was* the Screaming Mimes. Obie made up all the songs, which were usually considered brilliant and usually forgotten by Obie by the next day. Nothing was expected of the other members of the band but the ability to recognize and execute some simple chord progressions. They began to record rehearsals as a matter of routine so they would at least have some point of reference for what their repertoire was supposed to be, and soon there were tapes of Obie Vance and the Screaming Mimes being circulated all over the neighborhood. They sounded like they had been recorded through gelatin, with the guitarists wearing mittens and Obie carrying a mouthful of gravel. Everyone listened to them anyway. Kerry got hold of a practice tape and started playing it nights at Trinity; when Missy and Missy found it, it became the soundtrack of Trinity Doughnuts.

"What's that *shit* you're playing?" the guy they called Anvilface was reported to have said one afternoon over his Boston Creme, to which one of the Missys replied, in the true spirit of fandom, "You gotta listen to the words." Well, you also had to be able to *understand* the words. Not everybody understood them, but if you attended a few rehearsals, they came to you clearer, and then the tapes served as merely a memory trigger to the greatness that had been the previous night. That Obie. Man, people in the neighborhood loved those tapes. And while they kept his songs alive for his ever-growing audience, they didn't do a damn thing for Obie. He still never remembered what he sang. He would get requests; "Bastard at Yale" was very popular, as was "If I Marry Donald Sutherland," particularly with the Missys. But no matter what you asked for or how you asked it, the initial reaction would always be "Huh?" with a hurt, confused look like you'd see on a guy who'd mistakenly offered to pick up the tab for a table of ninety. Obie was never one for big crowds, and a big crowd was what we had, but knowing Obie we thought maybe he hadn't really noticed.

"Why are there so many of you?" Obie asked one night, nearly three weeks after all thirteen of us had been showing up for practice. We were surprised and did not answer. Obie looked at Dougie. "Hmm?"

"What?" said Dougie.

"I said, what are you all *doing* here? In this tiny little bedroom. Aren't you hot or anything?"

No one said a word. The girlfriends, even Obie's own, sat stiffly on the bed, looking like nothing but a pile of bare, tanned legs and ankle bracelets.

"Well?"

"I'm in the band," Dougie reminded Obie. Chris and Seth pointed themselves out and nodded, too.

Obie looked uncomfortable. "It's not like I was gonna ask anybody to *leave*. I was just *saying*. All the sudden there's quite a crowd in here of lately. Probably a major fire hazard or something."

Everyone just sort of shrugged and made little sorry birdnoises in the backs of their throats.

"Well, don't get all quiet on me now," Obie said apologetically. "You make me feel bad for saying anything. Jeez." He stood with his arms at his sides, his guitar rocking slightly across his stomach. Still, no one spoke up.

"This is your audience, man," said Dougie Rutecki, as in I-Told-You-So.

Obie began looking angry. "Well, I can't be bringing in doughnuts for this *audience* man."

Rimshot from Seth. Obie glared at him.

No one left. Obie didn't stomp out angrily or break down crying or anything like that. We weren't even sure of what it was he wanted us to do. The band just played and it wasn't very much fun. One long hour later Obie asked quietly, "Everybody get a doughnut?" We all nodded and Obie snapped his case shut and took off.

Obie didn't show up for the next practice session. "See?" said Dougie Rutecki. "He's getting cocky."

"What?" I said, angry now. "Obie's not cocky, man. Obie is just like he is."

"He never used to care about people coming to hear us," Seth said. "Next thing he'll be charging people."

"I don't think that's it at all," I said.

"Being one of the only people here not even in the *band,*" Dougie said, "maybe you need to pipe down about it." He had a jar of Goober Grape in his knapsack, and he was eating it with a plastic spoon.

"Pig," I said.

"You always were his biggest fan, you know," said Chris, in a sort of mean way.

"Who cares who's his fan? If he's uncomfortable with a room full of people listening to him sing, it's his decision," I said.

"But in my goddamn room," said Seth.

"You know Obie," I said. "He does what he likes."

"So let him go solo," said Dougie.

But going solo didn't just mean going without Chris and Seth and goddamn Dougie. It meant going without me. What would it make me, sitting alone with Obie in his bedroom, under Nathalie's ugly God's Eye, listening to him strum? Gary Dutka would never do it, never care to, probably never even be invited. I felt it the way the Missys must have felt it; Obie was a source of entertainment and adventure that was easy to get at. I was a hanger-on, a fan, who hadn't thought too much about the person involved. Who was supposed to have been my friend from as far back as kindergarten. I felt like a jerk, as much as I thought Seth and Doug and Chris were jerks. I didn't feel like a friend of Obie's.

There was no practice for a couple of weeks. Obie was too busy working. Finally, I went to Trinity to visit him.

On the door going in there was a large piece of blue posterboard, reading "IT'S A BOY!!!!" with squiggles and drawings of balloons on it. Inside Obie was sitting on a swivel stool as if he were a customer. The place was empty. The fluorescent overheads were clotted with dead bugs and made Obie's skin look weird and yellow.

He grinned at me and pushed his little paper cap forward on his big round head. "Hi," he said.

"See that sign?" he asked when I sat down next to him, pointing to the blue baby poster. "Know who that's for?"

I shook my head. "Nathalie," said Obie, eyes like headlights. "I'm telling you . . . Can you believe that?"

"Nope," I said. We never could believe anything Nathalie did.

Obie peered at me through a coffee stirrer, one eye squinted shut. "Obie and Nathalie Vance, never quite living up to anyone's expectations," he said.

"Hey man, you got a good job," I told him. A "good job" for anyone we knew was a job where you didn't have to listen to the easy-listening station all day. And it was more than most of us had. Seth and Chris and Dougie all worked in data processing for Chris and Seth's father's company. But Trinity Doughnuts still didn't seem like enough for Obie.

"The first thing she did when she came home was to take the kid with her to go visit her third grade teacher. Like he was an art project or something," Obie said. "But he's cute, I guess. No . . ." he thought for a minute. "He's ugly, actually. I don't know."

It was not hard for me to picture Obie with a tiny baby cradled in the crook of his bare, crossed leg, its head resting on his knee, with one of his calloused, sugary fingers in its shallow and toothless mouth. None of us could have done such a thing. That was what Obie would recognize as *quality* life, union job or gig at the Red Roof or no.

"You quitting the band?" I asked.

"The band is not fun," he replied. And I saw how it might not have been.

"You're still good," I said.

"Good enough for here," he said.

"You could cut a record, Obie," I said, getting excited for him again.

"*You* could cut a record," he said, messing with the spring of a napkin holder, working up to getting pissed off at me.

Talent and urge, I realized, didn't always have all that much to do with each other.

"See that," Chris Traiman said. "Nathalie back living with her parents with a goddamned baby, and Obie just working a damned doughnut counter, not even playing guitar or singing anymore. You see how people can turn out?"

"That guy Kerry, the same thing," said Gary Dutka. "He's a dad. He's a husband. He wasn't any of that before he started at Trinity. But once you got all that shit holding you down, how can you change? It'll happen to Obie, too, I'll bet."

"He had been getting on my nerves for so long," said Dougie Rutecki. "He had been getting on my nerves for so fucking long. I just didn't want to say anything."

"Obie's dad," said Seth Traiman, "he grew up in the Projects. They still got that Projects shit in them. That whole family. I'm not saying they're trash, man, but I can't believe how much better they used to seem to me."

"They always acted like they were," said Dougie.

"Fuckin' Trinity Doughnuts."

"That's like a *high school* job. Like an *underclassman* job."

"And he acts like it's something."

"Obie, man."

"I was always kinda jealous of him."

"You know," Chris Traiman said, "I been writing songs for this band for months. But no way was I ever gonna bring it up with Obie around. Fuck that. You wanna hear something? I call this 'Hepatitis Vaccine.'"

The Vances help to care for Zachary Dean, or Doobie, as they call him, Nathalie's baby, who is in fact downright ugly. Furry, in fact. Soft, black almost-feathers carry down from his forehead to the bridge of his nose. Obie cares for him as much as anybody; it was a surprise, to see him so serious about it. No one had thought he'd get so interested. And when he did, no one thought it would last. But he cares for Doobie as though the kid were his own.

I like to visit them, to sit and watch Nathalie squirming with Doobie in a corner of the couch, cooing and talking to him as though he were the best thing that ever happened, looking into his tiny crumpled face so hard for herself. It made me think about Nathalie the way I remembered her when we were little. She hasn't changed so much. Neither has Obie.

At home one night, I went up to our attic and dug up some old pictures of us together, Nathalie, Seth Traiman, and I, sitting against the railing of the Stegosaurus display at the Museum of Natural History. Nathalie's eyes burn a faded orange from the flash effect. I showed the picture to Obie, in training for the Manager's position at Trinity Dough-nuts. He has taken to walking around the neighborhood with his sister's baby in a pouch across his middle, the way he used to carry his guitar. He says Doobie's weight is similar. And he laughs, but Obie is not in the picture.

Prairie Schooner

∿∿∿

Immediate Needs and Possibilities: Publishing a Story in Prairie Schooner
Hilda Raz

Ellen Hunnicutt's manuscript in my mailbin was marked with the word CLIP, not an acronym but a souvenir of the disappearing paper clips we attached to envelopes from previous contributors. Three Hunnicutt stories had appeared in our pages. In an interview with *The New York Times* when she won the $7,5000 Drue Heinz prize for *In the Music Library*, a collection of stories, she named us as her first publisher. *Suite for Calliope*, her novel, had come into the office as a review book from Holt. The bins at *Prairie Schooner* are overflowing with manuscripts but I remembered the writer's credits and her loyalty and took the story "Tango" home to read.

Who is doing the reading, you might ask? What is her charge and the context for her reading? In *The New York Times Book Review*, Elizabeth Hardwick identified "the gifts necessary to an editor; that is evading, delaying, sliding, balancing friendship, courtesy and prudence against what are seen to be the immediate needs and possibilities of a periodical." This quote has been on my office door since my first day as editor here. As the fifth editor in sixty-eight years of continuous publication, and the second woman to edit *Prairie Schooner*, I inherited one of the magazine's charges: to publish the work of beginning writers. Mari Sandoz, Robert Heyden, Cyrus Colter, Eudora Welty, Cynthia Ozick, and Raymond Carver, for example, got started in our pages. So in this respect "Tango" had serous competition from beginning writers who are new to us. But I created a new charge for *Prairie Schooner* as well, one now possible to achieve: a balance of voices male and female, stories from many cultures, traditional and experimental fiction, translations, material for special issues, and writing that meets the needs of the multicultural classroom, which is largely ignored by anthologists and large publishers. "Tango," with its rich mix of narrative and formal invention, fed our hunger for innovative fiction.

Sometimes my own passions coincide with the needs and possibilities of the magazine. As I read, I identified with Hunnicutt's editor-protagonist Nora, laughed at her plight, and liked the form of her rescue. And I admire the feminist and multicultural tropes. Hunnicutt reminded me that her work is grounded in the notion of generation: "We work so hard for what we want. At the same time we're passing it on, we're giving it up," she said in a phone conversation.

"Tango" has the bold hilarity of pop-art ("As she pulled onto the expressway, she wondered if she might have dreamed all of her life up until now. Then she wished she had remarried. It seemed one of those important things she had simply forgotten to do, like locking a door or filling the car with gas"), parodies of the romance magazines young women of my generation were thought to read, and it has the feisty tone familiar to readers of one of my favorite writers, Elizabeth Jolley, whose work I read for the first time when *Prairie Schooner* published the Australian issue in 1988. I wasn't surprised to discover that Hunnicutt also loves Jolley's work. "Tango" first off made me laugh.

Nora (Ibsen's Nora? Nora Joyce?) is divorced, has a son in university. She has worked so long as the senior, only functioning editor for a small press specializing in books on Latin America she believes her own hype: she "never let herself imagine she was more than she actually was, someone who worked with minds more creative than her own. It let her talk to authors in a straight-forward way. There was never so much as a whisper of condescension in her voice." Nora knows the price of this ironic detachment is the loss of passionate resistance–to her son, her authors, her assistants, her boss, even to the incorrect etymologies of words she savors as they cross her desk. She has forgotten how to resist, to fight. And she also has surrendered the possibility of magic and inspiration in her life, closed off the routes to gestalt when old knowledge pops to the mind's surface to illuminate and redefine what's new. Nora knows her life can go on perfectly well without polarities. Her son is fine, she isn't needed to balance her assistant Amy's work, any more than hers needs to be balanced by her boss Charles. Nora's life by her preference is orderly, no longer polar. She is quite ready, as Hunnicutt said, to pass it on, give it up.

The details of her life–an array of young office assistants with outrageous costumes; Charles, the only man in the place; her son, whose engagement to a divorced woman with children promises unwanted foment; a car-phone-talking woman in traffic whose dog leaps madly in the back seat–Hunnicutt provides in a trenchant meld. When Amy comes to

Nora's desk wearing "the coat of a man's tuxedo over a silver satin dress," the story takes a necessary turn, like a suture in the heart. Nora in a magical flash remembers the correct answer to Amy's qustion and discovers she wants to change her life. No small chance that the answer comes from Africa, life's creche.

Hunnicutt's choice for the ironic final image in "Tango," one I remembered Susan Gubar discussing in her wonderful essay " 'The Blank Page' and the Issues of Female Creativity," caught my attention too. Nora finds a new way in our technological age to reach her son—she will write to him—but she complains to Charles that none of her letter paper is blank. Gubar says, "female authors exploit [the trope of the blank page] to expose how woman has been defined symbolically. . . as a tabula rasa, a lack, a negation, an absence," the blank pages upon which the pen writes, the "identification of women with blankness and passivity." But she also notes that in women's texts "blankness . . . is an act of defiance." As writer and editor I smile at the clever ways Hunnicutt addresses these important gender issues—Nora's attitude toward Amy, her straight talk to Charles, and her desire for "a sheet of paper in her desk that didn't have something printed on it." Hunnicutt's story mends the divisions in my life as a critic, teacher, writer, parent, and editor. She makes Nora's choice of writing a symbolic action for release (her son from her expectations) and connection (herself to disorder as well as delight, the messes and the pleasures of life).

On the radio I heard Brian Keenan, a hostage in Lebanon, quoted: "A man emerges back into life . . . There are many things a man can resist—pain, torture, loss of loved ones—but laughter ultimately he cannot resist." Comedy in the world of postmodern fiction isn't a story with a happy ending. It's what Ellen Hunnicut provides us in "Tango."

Tango

Ellen Hunnicutt

One morning Nora received a letter from her son at the university. He wrote that he was marrying Michelle, the woman with the two children. "Kim's the boy and Ashley's the girl," he explained. Then he wrote, "This is final, Mother. This is settled." First Nora wished the mail had come late, after she'd left for work. Now she'd have to sit all day at her desk with the words singing in her head. *The woman with the two children.* Already she was making it into a single word, a curl of sound that was too familiar and totally strange at the same time. There was something else she'd been about to think and now she could not remember what it was. Joseph was only a junior. He was tall and boyish, but always capable. Nora was proud of the way he could talk to anyone, that he never seemed ill at ease.

First he had wanted to go into social work. Then he'd decided it wasn't "hard edged" enough. "There's no firm body of knowledge," he said, "no real canon." He declared a major in economics. Through all of his quick intelligence, Nora felt she could see the pale outline of his fear. Now it seemed she had misread that fear, gotten it all wrong. Joseph lived on student aid and a part-time job. She was able to send him most of his tuition. His father, who had left them years ago, sent nothing. Without wishing to, Nora thought of pancakes and canned soup, how quickly she had learned what poor people ate; and the remarkable little boy who knew and didn't know, who told her pancakes made a party.

She read the letter again. This time she wondered if there was something radically wrong with a world where names no longer had recognizable gender. Kim's the boy and Ashley's the girl. Events might have causes beyond her control. She was thinking of things like stress or pollution or food additives.

Finally she dropped the letter onto the front seat of the car and gave the box she was carrying a little toss into the backseat, because she'd lingered too long and would now have to rush. But the lid of the box opened, the manuscript she'd brought home to read flew across the seat, pages curling and spilling everywhere. There were the winter boots she'd still not taken inside, although it was nearly May; her new umbrella along with the broken one, peeping out from the snowstorm of pages. Mad disorder.

As she pulled onto the expressway, she wondered if she might have dreamed all of her life up until now. Then she wished she had remarried. It seemed one of those important things she had simply forgotten to do, like locking a door or filling the car with gas.

She immediately found herself locked in behind a bus. A red sedan sat abreast of her, blocking access to the passing lane. The driver was a wild-looking young woman in some sort of metallic shirt, with her hair frizzed into a huge cloud about her head. Big hair, the girls in Nora's office called it. "Your hair is so big!" they told one another in admiration. A dog was jumping about in the back of the car, an Afghan or an Irish Wolfhound. Nora could see it was barking, trapped and desperate. She thought the girl should be talking to the dog, calming it. Instead, she was speaking into a car telephone. Nora could not imagine how the girl could talk to anyone with the dog barking.

The letter beside her had been written on pale ivory stationery that looked feminine. Joseph and Nora never wrote letters. They telephoned. She could imagine the woman, Michelle, holding out the sheet of paper, urging Joseph to take it. Write to your mother, she'd probably said. Don't phone and give her a chance to argue. Just state the facts. Nora had never met Michelle but felt certain she was the sort who said things like, Just state the facts.

She was two years older than Joseph, he had told his mother over the phone, and working as temporary help until she could find something better. The children went to daycare. When the woman found a good job, she'd be able to support all of them until Joseph graduated. When Joseph talked about the woman he said *consider* and *possibilities*. He said *options* and *the total picture*. Then Nora looked away from the phone, out of the window or off into the kitchen, as if there were many demands on her attention, even though Joseph couldn't see her. Only when he mentioned bringing Michelle home had she spoken out. "Under my roof you must respect my standards," she said, not unkindly. She meant Joseph couldn't sleep with the woman in Nora's house. It was what all of her friends told their grown children, the only workable way to cope. Then she told him, "I'm really pleased you're proceeding in a thoughtful manner." Keeping to a positive note.

She saw the dog had finally settled down. Panting, heated from his romp, he was sitting on the backseat looking out at traffic. His tongue lolled hugely from his mouth, rivers of saliva smeared the glass. Didn't the girl know enough to open a window part way for him? Nora saw now that he was actually a puppy, a very large puppy. The girl ignored him. Or was she saying into the telephone, "He'll be okay. God, a dog? Can I worry about him? I've got to get my own shit together." The girls in

Nora's office, with their big hair and their odd outfits, talked that way. One girl had come to work with men's long underwear showing beneath a leather miniskirt. Sometimes the girls wore men's suitcoats or work boots, combining them with chunky jewelry or bright belts.

When Joseph had first told Nora he might marry the woman, he said, "Sure I feel sorry for her, but that doesn't mean I don't love her." His voice had arched and Nora thought he sounded on the edge of panic. He said, "You're the one who told me it's too bad people don't get married anymore." Then he said, "You know how it is, Mother. After all, you got dumped too." Stung, Nora had drawn back from the phone to separate herself from the woman.

At last the red car shot ahead and she was able to move into the flow of traffic. She opened her own window a bit and the pages in the backseat began to flutter and blow about. It didn't much matter. The manuscript was weak and no one was going to publish it. That's what she'd have to tell Charles, her boss. She worked for a small press that specialized in books on Latin America. In her fourteen years on the job, she'd become an authority on Latin America. When she thought about it, the idea still amazed her.

At her exit from the expressway, where a sweeping curve of concrete plunged her into the snarl of city traffic, workmen were taking down an old building, smutty brick with traces of advertising signs still showing on its outer walls. The process had been going on for weeks. One day the broken wall had exposed a bathtub several floors above the ground, in a bathroom that had once been bright green. The near wall of the building carried a large advertisement for a shoe store that had gone out of business years ago. The picture and the words were coming down brick by brick, with the wall. This morning she saw that only a single large scruffy shoe remained. Still, the toe of the shoe looked jaunty, as if holding on, preserving the spirit of the entire picture.

Charles trapped her coming in the door ten minutes late, clutching the hastily assembled manuscript. "There you are!" he cried, as if he had been waiting hours for her. He was plump and soft, like an overripe eggplant, a man who did nothing but sit and read. "Well, what do you think of the manuscript?" He said it as if an answer was required that moment, as if publishing books was not a task that proceeded cautiously over weeks and months, even years sometimes. He was really telling her he'd caught her coming in late.

"I was locked in behind a bus, Charles!" she cried. "Between a bus and a huge dog!"

"A dog?"

"In a car! I've had a bad time and I wish you'd give me a moment to think. Can you do that, Charles?" She could not believe it was her own voice, shouting with such outrage.

Of course he thought she was ill. The expression his face assumed was not compassion, but a different kind of annoyance. "I suppose I can get someone else to review the manuscript," he said, put upon.

"There isn't anyone else, and you know it! Besides it's a terrible manuscript, and you know that, too." She was trying to get out of her coat without spilling the box again. When Joseph dropped out of school to marry the woman, there'd be no more tuition payments to make. Losing her job wouldn't matter. She marched past Charles with her head high, showing him that nothing mattered anymore. Then she remembered the box and had to turn back to put it into his hands. "I really don't know why you gave me this."

He followed her into her office. "Because we've already done two of this man's books and they were successful."

"Well, he's blown this one."

"Yes," said Charles, "he's blown it, but I had to be sure. You know I never trust a single opinion, even my own."

Finally, she felt remorse and wondered how much damage had been done. She really didn't want to lose her job, and have to go to work for temporary help while she looked for something better. "I'm sorry, Charles." She supposed Michelle also had a mother who wanted the best for her child. Or perhaps the mother had given up on the daughter and now worried only for the children, Kim and Ashley, seeing a chance to start over fresh with them.

"Thanks for reviewing the script," said Charles. "I'll call the author myself and tell him our decision." He always made Nora make the unpleasant calls. "What shall I say?"

"That a similar book has just come out. It's true enough." Then she sighed and took back the box. "No, I'll call him. Let him think incompetent underlings kept him from getting through to you. That will keep him going, and if he writes another book he'll come back to us, demanding to deal with you personally. The next one might be good."

"Thank you, Nora."

When Charles had gone, she honestly did not know if he had manipulated her. She found the number and picked up the phone. It rang with one of those queer deep purring sounds that sometimes came with long distance calls and always took her by surprise. To Nora it sounded rural and backward, and made her think of cottages on remote islands, although the author lived in a city. The summer Joseph was twelve, an acquaintance had lent her such a cottage. For two glorious weeks she and Joseph had fished every day, going out each morning in a weathered rowboat. The old boat belied the cost of the place. The following summer she had inquired about cottage rentals and been given a figure that was truly terrifying. Just that one summer, those two weeks.

When the man finally answered, she said, "I'm sorry I don't have better news," leaving Charles out of it, scrupulously citing the book that had just come out. It had taken her years to learn the civility of this business, never to say too much, and never ever to lie.

The author pretended to be elaborately unsurprised. "I thought I'd give you the first look," he said, as if his project was barely underway, as if nothing had really happened yet.

"And I'm grateful to have had that opportunity." Nora never let herself imagine she was more than she actually was, someone who worked with minds more creative than her own. It let her talk to authors in a straightforward way. There was never so much as a whisper of conde-scension in her voice.

"At least you're prompt with a reply," said the man, and at last he permitted himself a small, hostile chuckle.

"I do my best to be prompt," said Nora, making the issue courtesy, simply that, and passing up every opportunity he gave her to offer false praise for the manuscript. Then in the moment before she could decently hang up, she let him pretend there were any number of publishers eagerly awaiting his work–there were not, his subject was too specialized–and that Nora held no control at all over his life.

She put down the phone and checked the manuscript one last time to be sure the pages were in order, then called in one of the girls to wrap it for mailing.

"Book rate?" asked the girl, whose name was Amy. She was wearing the coat of a man's tuxedo over a silver satin dress. Her pinkish blonde hair had been teased into a small mountain.

"No, send it first class," said Nora. "He's a valued author." Amy was copy-editing a book on the history of Argentina and Nora had interrupted her. She carried a spelling dictionary in one hand. "Wait a moment," said Nora. "How do you like the book you're working on?"

"It's rather dry," said Amy, "but I enjoyed the part about the history of the tango. I like to dance. I've always wanted to learn the tango."

Now Nora discovered she could not stop talking. "The tango. Really! But I know so little about you. Tell me, do you have a dog?"

"Yes," said Amy, "a little poodle."

"And when you take your poodle in the car, what do you do? How do you handle it?" Distantly, she heard her own voice. It had climbed, turned bright and brittle.

"I don't have a car."

But Nora could not let her go. "Oh my, that must be inconvenient. Well, you're very young. You'll have things when you're older. Tell me, Amy, what do you hope for? What would you like to be doing five years from now? Ten?"

But she had frightened the girl. She saw the open, pleasant expression close and turn suspicious, heard the girl's breath catch in her throat. "I hope," said Amy in a flat, guarded voice, "to learn enough from people like you to become a valued employee."

Nora's odd fit passed as swiftly as it had come. She flushed, thinking how she must look to the girl—old, foolish, cruel. "I'm sorry," she said, "really sorry. I didn't mean to pry." On Nora's desk was a clever little ceramic jug filled with hard candies, a gift from one of her authors. He had labeled it, Magic, Take as Needed, but he'd used the wrong sort of paint and it had stayed tacky, even after months. She touched the "M" lightly with one finger, but of course it was sticky as ever. "I don't seem to be having a very good morning."

"It's all right," said Amy. Had she taken one step backward or did Nora imagine it? "That's okay." Amy produced a vague smile.

It looked provisional. Nora examined the girl for signs of injury. There was something dainty about her that went away if you kept on looking. The hem of the silver dress had been tacked up by hand, uneven stitches with a dull thread that didn't quite match the fabric, but she seemed intact.

She was turning to go. Then, as if to reassure Nora, she turned back. "This author wants to say 'tango' is from the Latin, *tangere,* to touch, but there isn't any real evidence for that." It was a question. "I always thought you could trust people." She meant authors, the solid square weight of words on the page. Nora remembered thinking the same at the beginning

"'Touch,'" said Nora, "would have a good bit of logic to it, wouldn't it? It's a very erotic dance. Do your best to get to the bottom of it."

"Of course!" said Amy.

But she spoke too quickly, too brightly. She had, after all, been wounded. One more thing, thought Nora, always one more thing.

She had no heart for work, but Charles had left a book proposal on her desk and she began to read. The author believed agricultural im-provements could solve every problem in Central America. A population with adequate protein would be energized, would opt for democratic government. The argument was naive, but the author was so good-hearted and optimistic Nora found herself drawn into it. Once she had imagined Joseph going to third world countries. He would take lagging economies in hand. His photograph would appear in the small, thoughtful journals, along with graphs and tables. The author of the manuscript meant to get lethargic people on their feet. He did not seem to know about the demonstrators who were already on their feet, fired with energy. After reading for most of an hour, she laid the manuscript aside.

Her house was small, but when Joseph married the woman she would probably have to take them all in, bed the children down in her little jewel of a den with the good Tiffany lamp, her single extravagance. Michelle would be pregnant the first year, to give Joseph his own child before he could tire of the other two. There would be no health insurance, no money for car repairs, for recreation. If she made it as bad as it could possibly be, she would at least get to the end of something. She would be able to pause and draw breath.

All that remained of the proposal was the final section, "Summary." She was putting it off because they always lived in hope, she and Charles. There were never enough good proposals, good manuscripts, good books. Sometimes what eluded an author for pages and pages could suddenly appear at the end, casting in relief all that had gone before, a thing pursued and finally captured.

But it did not happen. She gathered the pages together—the author had secured them with a paper clip, the kind Nora liked, double size, long and smooth without the irritating little grips—and began a memo to Charles. "I am truly engaged by the enthusiasm here." This tenderness was for the author, all of his goodwill, and for the way nearly everything human was bound to fail; but Charles would think she was trying to apologize for coming in late. "If you concur . . ." She'd been about to write, "I'll send a personal letter." A bit of hope to mitigate all that disappointment. But the word that slipped out was *tamgu*. To dance. African. Not Latin at all despite the superficial resemblance. She wrote the word on a scrap of paper and sat for a moment studying it, trying to imagine how it would look to someone seeing it for the first time, holding off the moment when she would feel the blow. In fourteen years, how many books had she done on Argentina? To think the ground could slide out from under her as easily as that.

Nora's doorway framed the common room across the hall. Whenever she looked up she saw the girls at their desks. On a shelf along the room's far wall were their newest books, slender volumes mostly. Beneath the dust jackets were quality bindings, lovely to hold in the hand. Charles placed them there to inspire, but they probably intimidated as well. When Nora hired the girls, she never made much of the books. Amy's desk was at the back. She was turned away from Nora copying something out of a book, sitting straight as a stick, still hot with resentment. Unless it was the awful coat with its too-wide shoulders, although they seemed to buy them large on purpose. Amy might have found the word already, Congolese or

Nigerian, no one was certain which. A drum dance with dim beginnings in black Africa, one of those ancient dances based on the beating of the heart. Amy had an instinct for the work to have caught the error in the first place. Sometimes that happened. The best people were always intuitive. It couldn't be explained to someone outside the business, that there were times when you knew what you did not know. The thrill of possibility could rise up unbidden, out of nothing it seemed, and inform you. In the next moment you forgot the feeling entirely and went back to thinking the world was a safe, logical place and you were going to live forever.

She laid the half-written memo aside and carried the book proposal back to Charles herself. She found him slumped in his chair not working at all, staring out of a window and nibbling one of the chocolate mints he loved. He let her do everything now. She worried about his blood pressure, those silent strokes she was always hearing about. She'd come to tell him that the proposal was disappointing, that Amy was working out better than expected, that the author on the phone had been angry but manageable; but what she said was, "Charles, do you think people are starting to write letters again?" And when he seemed not to understand, she explained. "Letters, Charles. I'll have to buy some stationery. I don't think I've had any in years." She knew without looking there wasn't a sheet of paper in her desk that didn't have something printed on it.

The Economy of Revelation

George Core

In the fall of 1992 *The Sewanee Review* celebrated its one hundred anniversary of continuous publication. No other literary quarterly in this country rivals this remarkable record of duration and achievement.

In connection with the centennial I edited a selection of stories from *The Sewanee Review*, most of which has been published during my nineteen years as editor. I found it impossible to include all the stories worthy of being anthologized and still have a single portable volume that would sell for a reasonable price. In the foreword I explained this painful circumstance and apologized for being unable to include fiction by such regular and valued contributors as Susan Engberg, George Garrett, and Gladys Swan. In that list should have appeared the name of Martha L. Hall, an established writer of short fiction as well as the long-time editor of fiction at the Louisiana State University Press.

I could easily edit another anthology of short fiction drawn from *The Sewanee Review*, including the authors just named and a good many more: J. W. Corrington, David Long, Kent Nelson, and Leslie Norris, to name but a few. In all likelihood it would rival or surpass the centennial anthology and its predecessor, *Craft and Vision* (1971), edited by Andrew Lytle.

The simple fact is that I have put more blood, sweat, toil, and tears into editing short fiction for *The Sewanee Review* than I have invested in the other forms of prose (criticism, book reviews, personal essays) or in poetry. That is the long and the short of it. I cannot fully account for this profound commitment, which exceeds the passion that my wife and I share for poetry and for the English theater. I do not write short fiction, and I seldom write about it. I am more inclined to write about criticism or autobiography and the personal essay than about fiction long or short. Nevertheless I have put more energy and thought into short fiction than any other department of the magazine, and I refer not only to the process of selection but the actual editing. The reason springs largely from my conviction that most readers, who are often invoked but rarely seen, are more drawn to fiction than to poetry or criticism.

The relevant statistics make me grit my teeth, but they yield a rough measure of that effort. I consider 125-150 stories for each one that sees print in *The Sewanee Review*. Some years, as in 1993, I have published as few as 4 or 5 stories; in other years, as many as 12 or 13.

In 1994 *The Sewanee Review* will include at least 9 stories. I think it valuable to publish stories in clusters that revolve around a common theme—for instance love or mortality or crime and punishment—so occasionally such a forum of short fiction appears in this magazine. Far more often, however, a given issue contains one story, and that story holds pride of place as the leading item in the magazine.

"Privacy" by Martha L. Hall appeared in the winter 1984 issue accompanied by stories written by Merrill Joan Gerber, William Hoffman, and Daniel Verdery under the collective heading "Married Life," an unvarnished title with considerably less poetry than "Love's Fell Hand" or "Sporting Sallies" or others I have coined or stolen—but one that does its work with absolute accuracy. The marriages in these four stories are in various stages of decay and collapse—one of them even before it gets underway; and it is deliciously ironic that the marriage of Miss Coralie and Mr. Buddy in "Privacy" is more stable than any of the others in the remaining stories, even though theirs is a marriage in name only—nothing more than a form of accommodation, one made possible by custom and habit and manners.

The reader must strain a little to see whatever romance must have led to this union, for World War II has passed, and Miss Coralie was courted by Mr. Buddy during World War I when Mr. Henry George was serving with the U.S. Expeditionary Force. Henry George performed heroically on battlefields of France while Buddy performed brilliantly on the football fields of the U.S. as a halfback for the University of Alabama. But, since his college heydey, Buddy has steadfastly avoided work and singlemindedly committed himself to cards and drink. Fortunately—or not—Miss Coralie's father left her with enough money to maintain their shabby gentility. Coralie works as hard at gardening, sewing, household repairs, ironing, and other aspects of domestic economy as Buddy does at avoiding work of any kind.

Buddy's life peaked while he was in college: he was born too late for war and too early for the National Football League, so he has nothing left but lesser forms of sport. Coralie, in contrast, is continuing her life—cooking and sewing, pursuing classical music, reading, traveling, and indulging herself in the advantages that privacy affords her. She tells all this to her insufferable sister, Ada Maude, who is outraged by Buddy but who apparently is the only person in town who actually dislikes him. Ada Maude never flags in sententiously reminding Coralie that she could have married Mr. Henry George Kell, the immensely rich hero, rather than Buddy, whose real name we never learn, yet who is perfectly named and nicknamed, for he hasn't grown up–the fate of most Buddys and Juniors, who have been so coddled by their families and friends that they have no way or reason to grow up.

Little does Ada Maude suspect that her sister and Henry George are lovers and have been for many years. Jane, our almost omniscient narrator, saves this revelation for the end of her story; but it is not a surprise ending of the kind O. Henry made famous: instead the ending proceeds naturally and inevitably from the action. We simply see an ordinary day unfold, and the "surprise" is the way that day ordinarily ends for Miss Coralie and Mr. Henry George.

The form of the story is one that few authors have mastered–the dramatic monologue. Except for some stories by Phillip Parotti, "Privacy" is the only dramatic monologue that I recall publishing. The speakers in most dramatic monologues take a greater part in the action than our Jane, who is the perfect observer but something more than a mere bystander, being the neighbor of both Coralie and her shiftless husband and of Mr. Henry George Kell. As a former student of Coralie's and the divorced wife of Ada Maude's nephew, in addition to being perfectly placed geographically, her vantage is unique. Without it there would be no story in a sense, which is to say that telling the story from the authorial standpoint would leave much to be desired, as would the roving point of view; and none of the other characters has the necessary distance to tell the whole story.

Jane can be seen as a younger version of Coralie, an independent woman who is intelligent, sophisticated, and content with her place in this southern town. She is also in some respects a mask of the author, whose experience includes a Mr. Buddy and a Miss Ada Maude but whose imagination created Miss Coralie and Mr. Henry George, characters far more important than the stereotypes of Buddy and Ada Maude, flat characters whom everyone in the South has met and typed.

Martha Hall says that "Privacy" is her most fully imagined story but that it could not have been written without her strong sense of the place in which the story is set. "The most compelling force for me," she has written, "was the setting, the narrator's house and yard, the geographic position in the small rather singular neighborhood." "I could not have invented 'Privacy,' " she explains, "without the sturdy sense of where the narrator was."

In "Privacy" the form of the story proceeds from the setting, just as its action unfolds from the temperaments of its characters, especially Miss Coralie, whose author says of her: "It is Miss Coralie I love. She is almost fearless. Her potential is so realized and so private. Because of her reserve she is hardly faking anything. She's cool and nice." Character, expressed and exposed as Henry James would say, drives the action and gives us the plot. It is not an accidental detail that our narrator is reading James when she witnesses the events she relates.

The little incident that makes this particular time special, the exact time to tell the story, is Mr. Buddy's lapse from perfect propriety when he urinates against the wall of the downtown post office on Sunday morning just as respectable folks are returning from church. The very next day Jane tells us what happened in consequence, giving us a little history of the characters in "Privacy," including herself, and Buddy's starring in the Rose Bowl to the death of his little dog.

In the comedy of manners, small incidents often generate action and reveal life's vicissitudes and ironies, its main streets and back alleys, the weather of its days and nights. Such is the effect of Buddy's failure of manners, his giving in to the force of nature and releasing his water in public. Poor Buddy, the hero of the Rose Bowl who has fallen from fame into lowlife but who, all the same, has a place in his community and whose wife still likes him and waits on him and makes his life not only possible but comfortable. Miss Coralie maintains her privacy and propriety even though Buddy abandons his.

The story ends at the perfect point. Martha Hall considered a continuation of it after Buddy dies, "leaving Miss Coralie and Mr. Henry George with the opportunity to marry." But she was right not to pursue that story and to stick with the "suspended ending," which seemed enough for her—and which in fact is exactly right. The conclusion, like everything else about "Privacy," including the title, is part and parcel of what she aptly calls "the economy of revelation," which results from the being deliberately stingy with fact. This is another of the story's virtues—its economy of means, an excellent instance of what James calls "the sublime economy of art" contrasting with the "splendid waste" of life.

Privacy
Martha L. Hall

Before I can press open my paperback, I hear Miss Ada Maude's Continental throb quietly into Miss Coralie's driveway, then sigh into silence, its baby-blue gloss barely visible through the dense foliage of Pride-of-Mobiles that separates us.

I settle back to read in my lawn chair, amid fig trees and shrubbery, the ripe-banana odor of fuscatas blending with the gentle spice of sweet olives in Miss Coralie's yard next door. The summer afternoon is made cooler by the sweep of the old Emerson oscillator that I have stationed on a fairly level pecan stump, relic of a historic windstorm. An extension cord drapes over a camellia from an outlet in the toolshed.

I watch the thick St. Augustine turf darken in the four-o'clock shadow of Mr. Henry George Kell's house, which rises three gingerbreaded stories tall at my back–Mr. Henry George, who fought alongside my father in the Battle of the Bulge, who wears an eyepatch over his wound, an empty eye socket or ruined eyeball, and who likes to play Handel's music in the early evenings, the Water Music flowing out the bay window of his library and over the ivied wall that gives us both privacy.

I know that Miss Coralie is in her swing on her side porch, because I can hear the gravelly whine of the chain as she gives herself the slightest push now and again. I am thinking, as I often do, that we have a special neighborhood, only three houses on a whole square, I on a corner, Mr. Henry George at my back, Miss Coralie and Mr. Buddy beside me, and the rest a playground, rather triangular, for children we never see and seldom hear. I was born here and have lived here for forty years, the last six alone, but not the least bit lonely. I read and I write; I am interested in the town, and I often have lunch or tea with Miss Coralie. I go to Mr. Henry George's at Christmastime.

As I hear the car doors open and shut, I am thinking that someone who didn't know would never guess that Miss Ada Maude and Miss Coralie are sisters. Miss Coralie is quiet, dark, slender, quick of movement, rather ageless, though I know she was eighteen when I was born. Miss Ada Maude is clabber-white and heavy, and certainly not quiet. Since her arthritis has gotten bad, she has a driver, Walter; and when she comes to see Miss Coralie, he sits in the car, or she tells him he can walk downtown for thirty minutes and get a coke out of the machine at the Gulf station. I have been caught at Miss Coralie's more than once when Miss Ada Maude comes for her Monday afternoons.

As Miss Ada Maude's foot comes down heavily, hollowly, on the first wood step, I am hearing her begin, in her choir contralto, on Mr. Buddy.

"Coralie, when are *you* going to get these porch steps painted? Buddy would let this place rot and fall down. Doesn't he ever do anything on this whole earth but drink beer at Bugga's and play cards every single night including Sundays down at the line? It's just as well Papa was spared seeing you living like this . . ."

I can barely hear Miss Coralie: "Afternoon, Sister. Pleasant weather for late June, isn't it? Just look at the crape myrtles." Miss Ada Maude is on the porch. "Take a rocker. I've just washed and ironed the covers."

I hear the wicker protest under Miss Ada Maude's weight, and I hear her heels come down on the porch floor, beginning a rhythm that will punctuate her afternoon's exhortations. I don't have to actually see these two to know how they look, seated amid nodding fronds of Boston and fishtail ferns, a background of gray clapboard wall, Miss Ada Maude in a flowered sheer, her blue hair in a tight perm, her white powder splotched with two rouge spots, twelve-millimeter faux pearl earbobs, three or four nondescript platinum filigree rings that match the little watch belted around her soft plump wrist. Miss Coralie is probably wearing Keds, slacks, and a plaid shirt. She is very likely to be mending one of the white oxford-cloth shirts that Mr. Buddy wears to town every day, or maybe working a neat monogram on the pocket.

"Now Coralie, I'm older than you are, and I've got eyes to see and ears to hear, which you seem to lack. There's something I am going to have to tell you. I had firmly made up my mind not to, but I decided it would be better for you to hear it from me than someone else." Miss Ada Maude pauses, clears her throat. Miss Coralie says nothing, and I can see her gently arched eyebrows lift slightly. I am thinking that I should leave. I settle back.

"Buddy pulled a stunt yesterday that has everybody in town talking. He is a laughingstock. And of course when this town laughs at him, they are laughing at you. And at me."

"Ada Maude . . . ?"

"He relieved himself against the post-office wall—right after noon when most of this town's respectable people were going home from church, including myself—your sister, the daughter, granddaughter, and widow of three of this town's most revered citizens. I had Olga and Neva Chichester in my car with me, taking them home from church, two absolutely perfect and patrician ladies—you cannot deny that—who don't even permit a TV set in their house, and just as we pulled up at the post office for Walter to pick up their mail for them, what do we behold but your husband turned around to this dark wet spot on the brick wall between the first two pittosporums, just, just . . ."

"Urinating," says Miss Coralie. And I am hoping she will tell me about this conversation later, in her own words knowing she can never dream I have sat here eavesdropping, needing to leave, not wanting to leave, and knowing that if I do, she and Miss Ada Maude might hear me, and Miss Ada Maude, who has not cared for me ever, but particularly not since I divorced her late husband's nephew six years ago, will find the most cutting way possible to let me know what she thinks of people lurking about in the shrubbery, listening.

"Drunk. At noon on Sunday. Either that or he's gone completely out of his mind."

Miss Coralie says, "Oh my, Ada Maude. And Chichesters with you."

"Oh my? Oh my? Is that all you have to say? What is the matter with you, Coralie?" Miss Ada Maude has stopped rocking. I can see her light-blue eyes bugging out behind her thick lenses. "Don't you realize we are humiliated? For thirty-five years you've sat here and let that . . . that reprobate spend practically every nickel Papa left you. He hasn't worked a lick at a stick since poor Papa's coffin was lowered into his grave. Just dolls himself up like a dandy twice a day and heads for Bugga's, hangs around that trashy cafe with the riffraff of this town till somebody gives him a ride down to Skinny's at night to play . . . play . . .

"Bourée."

"Well, whatever. And you are content to just sit here like a common person, wearing pants and working in your front yard like a field hand. No help in your house; never darkening the church door; a woman by herself in this house till all hours every night. Sometimes I . . ." Miss Ada Maude ran out of wind and couldn't finish.

Miss Coralie is saying, "Now, Sister, you exaggerate. I am not un-happy. I take my little trips in the spring and fall . . ."

"But always alone!" Miss Ada Maude is rocking again.

"I like working in my yard. You know that, Sister. I don't need a maid. And you know I like my privacy. Didn't you tell me you were bringing me a recipe?"

"What? Oh, yes." And I can hear her unsnapping her big handbag. "Purple-hull pea hull pea jelly."

"Purple-hull pea hull pea jelly?"

"Yes. Just a minute. I've got it here somewhere. It sounds wonderful. After you shell your peas, you boil the hulls till they are mush. Then you strain the mush through cheesecloth. That gives you your stock."

"Stock? Purple-hull pea hull stock? Ada Maude. What in the world does it taste like?"

"Well, purple-hull pea hulls, of course, but sweet. You add lots of sugar. And Certo. I found the recipe in a home demonstration pamphlet somebody had left sticking in *Southern Living* at the beauty parlor, and I just thought it sounded like something you'd like. I don't buy peas any more, myself, because they give me gas so bad. But all right. I can tell by your tone you don't want to try it." Miss Ada Maude's feelings are hurt, and for a few moments the only sounds are her heels. Then:

"An old man with college football trophies on his mantel like an eighteen-year-old. It was that trip to the Rose Bowl that did it. Ruined him. Pictures in papers all over the country. He never came back down to earth."

"Maybe he did, Ada Maude."

I am watching for Mr. Buddy to come walking home, up Wild Cherry Street. Wild Cherry runs into Connell, right toward the front of my house, so he's a familiar sight to me walking his route, four times a day usually, though I've known him to come in and leave again at midmorning and midafternoon. When Bugga's wife died and the cafe was closed with a wreath on the door, Mr. Buddy just walked back and forth all day for two days. I am remembering how sad it was to me to see him like a lost creature, sadder even than Bugga's wife's death—since she had been ill for years. For a moment I am seeing only Bugga's wife, over three hundred pounds, poor woman.

But now I see Mr. Buddy coming. The crape myrtles are in full bloom all the way down Wild Cherry, heavy ruffly watermelon-pink globes, still heavy from last night's shower, bending the long branches into roman arches over Mr. Buddy. Mr. Buddy is either tipsy or he is weaving to keep his head away from the bees. I watch Mr. Buddy, still nearly three blocks away, as he makes his way toward home and Miss Coralie and Miss Ada Maude.

Mr. Buddy is well over sixty, one of the handsomest men I have ever seen, elegant posture, tall, well groomed, his thick white hair parted and combed. Up close you can see a little mending here and there, a collar turned, but always a crisp white shirt, seersucker suit in the summertime, black-and-white oxfords, and, ever since I can remember, a straw katy, which he gets out on April first and puts away on September first. I can't imagine where he's gotten them these last years, when men here don't even wear panamas any more.

His straw katy is Mr. Buddy's chief means of communication on the street, though he is said to talk at the bourée table at night down at Skinny's just over the line in Louisiana. If he meets you on the street and he knows you pretty well—as well as he knows me, for instance—he reaches his smooth long-fingered hand up to barely lift the brim of his hat. No big gesture, just the politest little tip, and he says your name: "Jane," he will say to me, or "Miss Effie," or whoever it may be. He doesn't alter his pace, a long deliberate stride.

When he comes home, he walks in the side door—they haven't used the front door for years, since something caused the front porch to settle and the door to stick—and hangs his hat on the hall tree and says "Coralie," in really a very nice low tone of voice, and strides to the back stairs and up to his room where, as Miss Ada Maude says, he still has his trophies from an outstanding year at the University of Alabama. I happen to know that Miss Coralie sleeps downstairs in the little room on the other side of the house, where for years she gave me piano lessons. In those days she and Mr. Buddy used to talk.

Even now Miss Coralie takes Mr. Buddy a cup of coffee out on the latticed back gallery early every morning before he puts his tie on. She says "Have coffee, Buddy?" and he says pleasantly "Coralie," which seems to include Yes, thank you.

I am thinking, as I watch Mr. Buddy approach through the watermelon-pink archway like European royalty in an operetta, that he does drink a lot and that he has pulled some tricks over the years while under the influence. My wedding was probably the last social function he attended, fifteen years ago; and when Dr. Whitley solemnly requested that anyone who objected should speak now or forever hold his peace, Mr. Buddy hiccupped so loud you could hear it all over the church. An omen for both of us, maybe. And Mr. Buddy can properly be called trifling, and has been by plenty of others besides Miss Ada Maude, though she is the only person I know who really doesn't like him.

I am also remembering Mr. Buddy's little black rat terrier, Sport, whom he whistled into his car with him, a car he had bought just before Ford stopped manufacturing automobiles before World War II, a V–8 coupé, in which he did considerable damage to light poles, to the car itself, and to other people's cars. It gave up the ghost in the fifties, the same year that Sport, old and deaf, was hit by a delivery truck in front of their house. And I remember how Miss Coralie and I, a child, ran to the little dog while he was still jerking, his eyes glazing, and how she had him taken away so Mr. Buddy wouldn't have to see him like that. She told him that Sport was dead when he walked home for lunch from Bugga's, after I had gone home feeling terrible.

I am watching Mr. Buddy walking home, lifting his knees high in his way, swinging his arms easily, his head erect. I am waiting for him to catch sight of Miss Ada Maude's baby-blue Continental.

He is alert.

Ah, he sees it. Without interrupting his gait, he makes a U–turn on the walk and heads back to town. He has a problem, now. It is nearly five, and he must get home, have a bite of supper, bathe, dress, and be ready for his ride to Skinny's when the cardplayers head south.

Miss Ada Maude and Miss Coralie cannot see him, though Miss Coralie must surely have an eye out for him. Miss Ada Maude is saying "I know you don't like for me to bring this up, but I can't help thinking of how different your life might have been if you'd married Henry George. How he loved you! You could have had everything. Everything, Coralie, if Buddy, the great football star, hadn't shown up while Henry George was gone, offering his life for his country on foreign fields.

"Ada Maude, for pity's sake. Can't we forego the ancient history, just this once?"

"Oh, I don't care." There is abandon in Miss Ada Maude's voice. "It's true. Buddy swept you off your feet when you were too young to know what you were doing. And there sits that rich Henry George over there with only one eye, carrying the torch for you to this day." I clap my hand over my mouth at this jumble of images, and I am seeing Miss Ada Maude's upper arm flap its sagging muscle as she waves a hand high over my head toward the shingled tower on Mr. Henry George's mansion.

"Don't be ridiculous, Ada Maude," Miss Coralie is saying. "I never heard of anything so absurd." She is getting weary, thinking she needs to be warming up Mr. Buddy's supper.

"Why are you so loyal to a man who doesn't even talk to you? Just tell me how you feel toward one who is so completely irresponsible, who spends your money, dwells among the lowlife of the town of your birth– he wasn't even born here and who staggers around smelling like a brewery morning, noon, and night. Do you even know when he comes in at night? How do you even know he is playing cards? Just answer me."

"I'll answer nothing, Ada Maude. You know very well that I am fond of Buddy. He does not stagger. He has his faults . . . He . . . we get along as well as . . .

"Get along? Get along? Is living your whole life under the same roof with a man who . . . who . . ."

"Just once. Just once. Pees on the courthouse wall?" says Miss Coralie angrily.

"Post-office," Miss Ada Maude hisses.

Miss Coralie is going on: "Whether you can understand or not, Sister, I am not an unhappy woman. Think of how many interests I have: I have my music; I cook; I sew; I garden; I read; I'm handy with just about any small tool." I am fearing that Miss Ada Maude is going to be reminded that the last gift Mr. Buddy gave Miss Coralie years ago was a small shovel called a lady's spade that he won on a punchboard. "Did you notice I've attached that loose gutter at the corner of the porch? You mentioned it last week."

"You! Up on a stepladder. Oh, Coralie, you are hopeless. Why do I worry so about you? Why don't I give up?"

"Why don't you, Sister?" Miss Coralie's voice is sounding hopeful, friendly.

Now I see Mr. Buddy coming back up Wild Cherry, faster this time. He can see Miss Ada Maude's car, but on he comes, and I realize he has no choice but to run the gauntlet if he is to play bourée tonight. On he comes, his bearing commanding, courageous. At the corner of Connell, named for his father-in-law, he must stop for a car that passes deliberately, and tip his hat. Miss Ada Maude and Miss Coralie are surely seeing him now, Miss Ada Maude bristling, Miss Coralie feeling sorry for him. Up the driveway he walks, past the Continental. His feet are on the steps, and he stamps them as he reaches the high porch to shake off grit from the street.

"Well, Buddy, are we to have the pleasure of your company? Bugga's Café must have closed its doors for the day." I hold my breath. Perhaps her sarcasm will break the great reserve. But of course it does not.

"Ada Maude," he says nicely. "Coralie." He is removing his straw katy.

"Evening, Buddy," says Miss Coralie. The screened door shuts quietly, and the sounds of Mr. Buddy's footsteps fade quickly inside the house.

Miss Ada Maude's feet hit the porch floor with her full 160 pounds, and she is standing. "He's just too much, Coralie, that man. And you are a fool. You are my sister, and I love you. But you have sacrificed your youth to him, and you've martyred yourself for nothing so far as I can see. You could have spent your whole adult life in the finest house in Sweet Bay with a cultured gentleman, who would be doting on you to this good day. With all due respect you *are* a fool."

"You could be right about that, Ada Maude. If it makes you feel any better, sometimes I feel like one."

From the porch Miss Ada Maude calls: "Wake up, Walter." And to Miss Coralie she says: "Just look at that mouth hanging open." Now I hear Walter opening the Continental's door, where Miss Ada Maude is pausing. "You'll never hear another word of any of this from me again, Coralie. Never. Never. Never. And I mean it this time." Her heels thump down seven wood steps.

"See you next Monday," Miss Coralie says, as Walter backs the car into Connell.

I need to go into my own house, begin preparing my own supper. I pick up my abandoned James reader. Here is my chance to move unobserved, conceal my eavesdropping. But I cannot. I must stay to see Mr. Buddy on his way, back downtown. I am wondering why I should care what they are doing; why I should sit here listening to my neighbors. Later I will believe that I stayed because I anticipated something–some change in Mr. Buddy's usual departure for Skinny's perhaps.

Mr. Buddy comes back out onto the porch, and I hear him strike a match on the sole of his wing-tipped shoe. Miss Coralie has broken all records tonight. He will get back in time. She, too, is on the porch, and I hear the swing chains crunch as she says "Have a nice evening, Buddy."

"Coralie," he says, his tone mellow. I watch him cross Connell and walk down Wild Cherry, tall, straight, dodging the crape myrtle blossoms till he is out of sight.

I sigh and am about to get up when I hear Miss Coralie coming down her steps, quickly, lightly, like a girl. She is humming. She walks toward the back of her place, not more than ten feet from where I sit, my tailbone numb. In the gathering dusk I imagine her slim form, legs swinging in her slacks–her "pants"–her dark hair pulled away from her tanned oval face, her eyes peaceable under her dark graceful eyebrows.

I hear a metallic latch lift, a gate swing, not silently, but not in the rust of neglect. The latch falls. Voices. A man's:

"Sweetheart. You're late. Did Buddy's ride go down late tonight?"

"No, he was delayed. I'm sure they waited for him at Bugga's. They've never left without him. Ada Maude was here so late that poor Buddy couldn't get on in to eat and freshen up."

"Oh. Ada Maude," Mr. Henry George sighs. "It is Monday, isn't it. Why does Ada Maude give Buddy such a hard time after all these years." These were not questions.

Miss Coralie says, "Buddy really got himself into it yesterday.

"I heard," says Mr. Henry George.

"Already?"

"I went to the barber shop this afternoon."

"Oh. Of course."

"Try not to be upset, Corrie."

"Well, I hate it. Can you imagine a fastidious man like Buddy doing such a thing?"

"He didn't know what he was doing, honey."

"I guess not." Miss Coralie is sounding consoled.

Then they are quiet. Or they do not speak. I can hear them sighing, murmuring, whispering softly. They are embracing. Kissing. I am no longer a mere eavesdropper. I am moving down to voyeur, hoping they do not hear me as I drag the heavy chair back up to the patio behind my house. I go back to unplug my fan.

"I have fillets. Do you want to do them inside or out, darling? Makes no difference to me. I haven't seen any mosquitoes out here." Mr. Henry George sounds so casual.

"Oh . . . let's cook inside tonight." Miss Coralie is walking across Mr. Henry George's patio. I know that they are arm-in-arm as they go into his kitchen, where I imagine two thick dark red and perfect fillets lying on a cuttingboard. Lettuce is washed, crisping in the refrigerator. Potatoes are oiled by Mr. Henry George's own hands, lovingly, in anticipation.

Lovers. Miss Coralie and Mr. Henry George.

In my own kitchen I am scrounging for some supper, pondering, undecided, staring at the leftovers on the cold shelves of the refrigerator. I decide to have a bowl of ice cream. I eat it at my kitchen counter. It is sweet, rich. Delicious. I roll my eyes as a sweet glob slides down my throat, and I wonder, and smile as though I am not alone but have someone there to smile back at me. The Water Music changes to the Royal Fireworks, flowing out Mr. Henry George's library window and over the ivied wall that gives me and Mr. Henry George our privacy.

Shenandoah

~~~~

Just Visiting
Dabney Stuart

Selecting one story as a center for the six years I have been the editor here is more difficult than the daily routine that culminates each quarter in an issue of *Shenandoah*. I read between 2,500 and 3,000 stories a year (that's a ten-month "year," since I don't read unsolicited manuscripts in the summer) and print less than one percent of them. For this anthology my field is narrowed to about 90 stories, leaving the percentage slightly higher, but the group I begin with is 100% competitive. That's the rub. Though I have come inevitably to think some of the pieces I've printed are better than others, they are all rendered equal again by the circumstances of a new selection.

Though I think it accurate to say I don't look for a particular kind of story for *Shenandoah*, I am reasonably alert for certain qualities in the fiction I read. My predisposition is toward warmth, good nature, hopefulness, curiosity, and a general illusion that, though the story focuses the particular incarnation its author makes of theme and character, life is complicated and interwoven, involving people whose vulnerability and unpredictable forms of growth are to be nourished and honored. The fictions which embody this illusion most complexly, and with the most affecting resonance and probity, form the field from which *Shenandoah's* contents eventually emerge. Each story, of course, is an occasion in which its author comments on all fiction, and is about itself and the choices from which it rises. I tend, however, to prefer those pieces in which such theory is so deftly woven into the fabric of the fiction itself that it becomes an unobtrusive part of the carpet. It may seem paradoxical, therefore, to say that I care most about literature that cares beyond itself.

I am also especially responsive to prose which establishes similarly subtle associative connections as it builds its story (Lisa Sandlin's use of the participle "wheeling," for instance, in the next-to-last paragraph of "Fish"), pervasively reticulate so that if twitched in one spot it shimmers lightly at other removes. Clarity is central, too, an aspect of art I have grown to equate with mystery. I am among the apparently always small company of readers which values economy and patience, and who believes pace and rhythm as indispensable to good fiction as they are to good poetry.

Humor is important to me as well, not jokes and witticisms and anecdotes, but the leaven of vision such as is kneaded into Sherwood Anderson's "The Egg," or Fred Chappell's "Mankind Journeys Through a Forest of Symbols," or Flannery O'Connor's "The Displaced Person." Humor, in short, that spreads into a story from a comedic vision that threads light into seriousness, so that, in Robert Frost's words, "the work is play for mortal stakes." Supreme instances of this are Dante's *Divine Comedy* and Cervantes' *Don Quixote.* One doesn't have to be an editor slogging through the quagmire of manuscripts in the office to know how rare this kind of writing is, in any age.

"Just Visiting," the phrase printed on a T-shirt Tommy wears, suggests much of all this to me, in the context Sandlin creates for it.

Rachel and Dalton are, of course, the visitors in Tommy's apartment, so the phrase on Tommy's shirt resides in the pattern of reversals of place and expectation within the two (or three?) families in the story; it also connects more immediately with Rachel's "hostessy" feeling, confusing further her being unwillingly cast again as Tommy's caregiver. The story's composition suggests that none of the human characters are at home, or, in Tommy and Rachel's cases, ever have been; perhaps there are no families at all, only one hodge-podge of shifting and unfixable relationships merging, scattering, and reemerging into different conjunctions. In this sense the human figures are all visitors in the various groupings that occur. (Our, and his, one connection with Dalton's father is a postcard, a traveller's gesture.) Tommy's travel book extends "just visiting" to an international dimension. The characters are visitors in the still larger sense, too, of being temporary inhabitants of the planet which they share with other species, one of which, the dolphins, may be the true hosts of the story.

Visitors are usually tentative (the stereotypical brashness of tourists is probably a defense), transitory, and vulnerable. I don't mean to turn this brief essay into a detailed commentary, but in this regard note the precision and spareness with which Sandlin accomplishes her entry into the precarious world of her fiction. Three of the four characters whose energies drive the story appear in the first two-and-one-sixth paragraphs, along with focused suggestions about their relationships one to the other, the theme of dependence, the blurring of clear roles, and, most poignantly, of Rachel's problem with control and self-betrayal. The images of the New Mexico wind, her sweatshirt, and especially the hairs on her arms, indicate that her defenses against the forces exerted on her are indeed "puny." The third sentence of the story suggests, too, the extreme, but complementary, opposite of the planetary aspect of "just visiting":

> Rachel would like to move into herself and feel at home there, finally.

Grateful myself to be visiting this *nonce* forum, I want to add that I undertook the editorship of *Shenandoah* believing that a literary journal exists to serve its writers, not its editor. That continues to be my primary and guiding concern. In that light, and considering again the difficulty of selection that I remarked at the outset, I'd like to acknowledge some of the other writers to whom *Shenandoah* is indebted: Tony Ardizzone, Richard Burgin, Frederick Busch, Kelly Cherry, Alyson Hagy, William Hoffman, David Jauss, Greg Johnson, Joseph Maiolo, Heather Ross Miller, Kent Nelson, Janet Peery, Richard Russo, Marjorie Sandor, Floyd Skloot, and Steve Yarbrough. I apologize for omitting the group of other contributors whom space doesn't permit me to list. Thank you all.

Speaking to the Fish

Lisa Sandlin

For some time now, Rachel has been trying to trust herself. Her goal seems so simple: determine what is right, and do it. Rachel would like to move into herself and feel at home there, finally. But she is not very good at this, having just betrayed herself again.

Rachel is packing the car. She has on her yellow sweatshirt, but it is washed out of shape and its defenses are puny. Pitiless, the New Mexico wind shoots down both sleeves. The hairs on her arms are rising. Rachel doesn't want to make this trip, but she has let her mother persuade her.

"He wants to see you, Rachel. I'll pay for your tickets. And a car from the airport. Please go and see your brother." Her mother's voice had been strained. Rachel could see her. The tears were waiting there just below the rims of her reddened eyes, waiting to pop out of their tiny holes. "The doctors say it's not as bad as it seems. His voice would come back if he'd go to the therapy. You make him go. Your dad, he said he was going to tell Tommy he was acting like a whimp. Can you understand somebody that mean? In all my life I'll never understand somebody that mean."

"'Wimp,' Mother," Rachel said. She had learned long ago not to take sides, for fear of her words rebounding as fresh ammunition. At some forgotten point, she'd hardened, banished all attachment to her mother's distress. But when she was little she thought she might die watching her mother cry. Mouths stretched like baby birds, she and Tommy cried too; they trailed their mother in forlorn circles, frantically patting with their small hands whichever part of her was reachable.

Rachel wrote Tommy when she heard about the accident. She had no plans to visit. For one thing, she and her brother are not close. For another, she's got enough problems with her son Dalton since her ex-husband moved away with no definite forwarding address.

"You know," her mother continued, "it might take Dalton's mind off . . . things . . . to get out and go somewhere." Before Rachel could reflect on the honesty of this suggestion, her mother interrupted herself.

"Rachel."

Her voice had been eager then, and soft as it could get with all the strain in it. Rachel tightened her stomach muscles.

"Remember when you were kids? Remember how he followed you around?" Now the tears were tracking down her face, riding piggyback in twos and threes. Rachel could see them. "Poor Tommy, if the moon had cracked into pieces he would have brought it to you to fix. Oh, Rachel."

This is not how Rachel remembers it. The last time she and Tommy actually touched, when they were teenagers, he tried to choke her, backing her into the louvered doors of their mother's closet. The doors gave, they fell, and they sat there on a jumble of shoes punching each other and spitting out names.

But here she is, packing the car.

Rachel squints against the sunshine. Leaves are falling wholesale from the October trees. Dried creatures, they skitter crazily across her feet in crispy mass, looking for a place to sleep. She draws her yellow sleeves over crabbed fingers and clumsily checks the mailbox. In it is a surprise . . . a postcard to Dalton from his father.

Studying the pastel sketch of a saguaro cactus, Rachel feels a shimmering wave of relief at her son's not having been totally abandoned. This surge of good will is for fate, God, the skeletal moon meandering off the far edge of the sky. It even extends to Dalton's father.

But the next surprise is that she bites the postcard so hard that her teeth cut little stitch marks in the glossy paper. The comfort she receives from this is the tiniest of somethings; Rachel holds onto it. She leans against the cold tin mailbox and dredges it. Her hair flies about her head. Leaves crash into her. Though her mind is racing, when Rachel comes to the sad conclusion, it is really not unwelcome at all: there is nothing she can do to fix this situation for Dalton. As she could never ever seem to fix anything for his father.

"I'm so tired of fixing," Rachel tells the fading moon. "Sick to death of it." She will go and visit her brother, she will do that much. She will sit and eat and talk pleasantly and that is all she will do.

The gate bangs. When Dalton appears, he is whistling his two-note version of Andy Griffith's eternal theme song, which trails off as he takes the card. Chunks of blond hair fan in the sharp wind, showing off Rachel's amateur haircut. Dalton's face flushes delicately. His lips purse into a button. With considerable effort, he folds the card into precise quadrants and pushes it down in his pocket; he does not read it. Another surprise, but then Dalton often does the very thing she would not expect.

They leave the airport in a dull-red, Rabbit rent-a-car. As always, Houston is warm and wet. A lazy mist rolls across the amber-lit streets like movie smoke; Rachel creeps along trying to recall the freeway system. Huddled into the door, Dalton nods off, and Rachel checks to see that the lock button is indeed down. It's difficult, but she forces herself not to look again.

When they find Tommy's driveway, Rachel slips a hand onto Dalton's shoulder and whispers his name in his ear. At eight, he's too big to carry far. Dalton ambles to the door on his own, laughing a little under his breath, 90-percent asleep.

Tommy is burrowed into a wheelchair. The black-and-white movie he's watching has a strobe effect in his darkened living room. Lit up in the crazy light, Tommy gives them a Halloween grin. He's a big handsome guy, 28 years old, with a homemade comforter tucked around his knees; he's eating divinity off a saucer.

Disconcerted by the wheelchair, Rachel smiles back. Tommy's cheeks seem puffy. Other than that he looks about the same: striking face with hard and perfect angles—something like James Dean, but without the aura—a little hopeless around the mouth, missing something. His arm muscles look great, but his feet . . . arranged on the chair's footrest, his bare feet have an air of involuntary surrender about them, like skinned animals.

Tommy lifts a fat pad off his knees, a big yellow tablet, block-prints a greeting in capital letters, and peels it off: *HOWDY STRANGERS*.

Weaving, Dalton rubs his eyes, then slumps into a worn velour bean-bag. When Tommy offers the saucer, Dalton pushes himself up again. He scoops a candy without even bothering to select it, and stands there shy, biting the inside of his cheek. Then, ignoring the divinity ball, he dips his head to Tommy's shoulder and slides his arm around his neck, patting the wheelchair on the back. "Hi, Uncle Tommy," he says. He takes his candy and heads back to the beanbag.

Tommy looks surprised. Rachel certainly is. Dalton's only seen him three or four times in his life. Since the divorce, she's gone out with one guy; Dalton has not taken to him. When the man speaks to him, Dalton looks as if a terribly strong light is shining in his face. He never answers.

Curled up now, Dalton gives the divinity test licks. Rachel bends down and lightly taps her brother's cheek. She can tell he's glad to see her, but he pulls back reflexively, stretching his neck in an odd way. He forces a cough that has a creaky ring to it.

"So when'd you get the chair? I thought you could walk."

Tommy nods toward Dalton and fixes his hand high in the air, to indicate how he's grown.

"No kidding. He eats like a wolf."

Tommy writes something and holds it out to her, but it's hard to decipher in the flickery light. Rachel searches for a wall switch.

"Don't."

At least that's what she thinks he's said. It shocks her, that shrieky voice, but she doesn't want to let on. Dalton's jumped a little, and dropped the divinity on the carpet. When Rachel looks at Tommy, he doesn't meet her eyes. He clears his throat, and sits there biting a knuckle, a droplet of spit running down one finger. Then he ducks his head and rubs his throat, strokes it absentmindedly like a pet.

She tries not to follow that hand. When Tommy was six or seven, their parents got into a fight over a light bulb they were changing in Tommy's room. In the midst of the bitter argument, the ladder slipped, squeezing their mother's fingers in the metal braces. She screamed at their father to come down, but he took his time, one heavy step after another. "Rachel!" their mother screamed, "Rachel, make him get down!" With Tommy behind her, Rachel stood there, arms out, opening and closing her mouth.

Next morning, Tommy hid in the garage when their mother tried to make him go to school, sliding under the car into the oil spots. When Rachel got home, her mother was twisting her hands so hard her puffed fingers gave a crack. "Oh, if Dad finds him here, it'll drag the whole thing up again," she said. "He was sorry after, he was, and we'd forgotten all about it, hadn't we, Rachel? Oh, tell Tommy what his father did isn't his fault," she begged. It was almost five o'clock. Rachel had gotten down on her hands and knees to look for her little brother. It happened in Tommy's room, and Rachel hadn't made her father get off the ladder. What did she mean, it wasn't their fault?

"Don't worry," Rachel says brightly now, "your voice will come back. Mother said that with the speech therapy it's only a matter of time." His knee flinches when she touches it and she draws abruptly away.

Dalton's staring at Tommy openmouthed; Rachel's not close enough to elbow him. Tommy clears his throat two or three more times, doodling on the tablet. Under the comforter, his knees shift around.

"Wow, Uncle Tommy. You sound like sonar. I bet you could talk to fish."

Jesus. Rachel pulls on her hair. The admiration in Dalton's tone is clear; still, what a thing to say.

Thank goodness, Tommy likes it. He laughs, but it's awful; he doesn't let out any sound. In the TV light, he looks like a mime, like a ventriloquist's dummy with the bottom half of himself covered up to hide the fact that there is no bottom half.

Chair is for convenience, he writes. *Get tired and stumble a lot. Company sent it. You know everything's paid for? Even my mortgage?*

"So you're not going to sue?"

"What for? I'm set. Don't put out a dime for the duration.

Dalton's sitting up at attention. Rachel knows he's dying to get Tommy to talk again, but she refuses to give him the chance. "Look, all we know is what Mother said. What happened exactly? Are you any better?"

Tommy prints fast, so fast she can tell he's done a lot of it. Rachel angles the note toward the television.

Working with a new pesticide. Me and Aron Sampson. I'd been there a month, Aron longer. Wore thick gloves. Not thick enough. Hoarse all the time, joked about it, said our voices were changing. One day Aron fell down, had a fit. I was ready to quit then, but it was too late.

"Let me see, too," Dalton begs. Rachel passes the note to him, but he's stopped by "pesticide." His eyelids flutter briefly.

"Look, you're not cooped up here all the time, are you?" Rachel cannot seem to lose the hostessy tone. "What about going somewhere? Dalton loves the movies."

At the mention of his name, Dalton rallies. His small back, which had just begun to relax into the beanbag, jerks upright. "Want to hear about one?" he asks Tommy.

Tommy settles his clasped hands and tilts his head invitingly. Rachel loves him for this. For a split second, she sees herself at seven, waiting for the school bus, and Tommy pattering down the driveway in a diaper, his fat pink arms and legs and belly and keening face as perfect as they come.

Encouraged, Dalton approaches his uncle recounting in rapid, scrambled order the plot of a movie he and Rachel have recently seen. Dalton had been especially taken with the character of a Spanish swordfighter bent on revenge.

"Here's how he went," he tells Tommy. Dalton is rolling his eyes, standing bowlegged on the outsides of his feet, embarrassed but enjoying himself.

"He said it a lot of times. He said, 'Hello. My name is Montoya. You killed my father. Prepare to die.'" Just as he finishes the speech, Dalton remembers the sword and thrusts his arm at Tommy's chest. There is a Ta Da! flourish to Dalton's gesture, but he says nothing more. Tommy grins. As Dalton shuffles over to his spot, he glances back once, smiling.

The tablet jiggles as Tommy begins another note; his hands aren't all that steady. Rachel notices this, even though she is still affected by her son's shy backward glance. She stares out into the room at the pale shapes of furniture.

Don't get out much.

"Maybe we could take you a few places."

He shrugs like it's not all that important to him. It's hard to tell in the jerky light, but he seems nervous. He peels off another note.

Wish I was back on the rig. Guys out there missing a finger or two, but that's all. I don't know if I'm better or not.

"You miss the rigs? Hey, oil'll make a comeback. I bet you money."

Tommy went everywhere when he bossed the offshore drilling rigs. One Christmas Rachel got 500 rupiahs folded in a card, pale magenta bills pretty enough to tack on the wall; on another, a forearm's worth of fake malachite bracelets. Then the bottom dropped out of oil and Tommy's job evaporated. He took what he could get—Ibex Chemical, R&D, Pesticide Division.

Sure, Tommy writes. *What do you call a petroleum engineer?* He holds up the tablet like a cue card and Rachel mumbles the familiar punchline at the same time, *Hey, Waiter;* underneath that Tommy's written *HAHAHA.*

There is a little snort from Dalton, and he's gone, his cheek pressed flat against the beige velour. That's it, anyway: Rachel is tired from traveling; she gathers her boy from the moundy chair.

"Where do we sleep?" she asks.

Dalton drapes over her shoulder; she can hardly carry him. Tommy points in a direction, combining it with a goodnight salute. Then he turns toward the television, drags up the comforter, and scooches deeper into the wheelchair. Hands full with Dalton, Rachel might have kissed the air in his general direction, but that is the kind of casual gesture that has never passed between them. She and Tommy were obliged to be always alert. But Rachel could swear that as they go by, her brother reaches out to brush Dalton's hair with the lightest touch.

In the morning, Tommy smiles at Rachel when she enters the kitchen, but Dalton doesn't even look up from his drawing pad. It's a nice kitchen: microwave, gleaming no-wax floor, etched glass over the sink, gloss on the cabinets. Over the microwave is a pop-art clock: a gigantic wristwatch, caution yellow. It actually ticks.

Tommy has on a black T-shirt that reads *Just Visiting,* and his damp hair is combed straight back, furrowed from the comb. Beyond that, he's not so glamorous. There's a trace of the rash Rachel's mother told her about, and one eye is clotted with a gruesome blood explosion. On the table near him beside some kind of wire contraption lies a pair of Wayfarer sunglasses.

Dalton's drawing fins. There are lights in his eyes. "Mom." He waves Rachel closer, letting her in on the joke. He says, "Mom, guess what. Uncle Tommy can talk to fish. Did you know that? He can talk to porpoises and sharks and whales. Did you know that my uncle can do that?"

Tommy shrugs, meaning *pretty stupid,* but he's kind of blushing. Rachel is vaguely discomfited by Dalton's excitement, but she tells herself that the attention is good for him. Still, it's odd, seeing him hang onto Tommy like this. Tommy looks up, his bloodshot eyes confused and pleased. He scribbles something and holds out his tablet in Rachel's direction. When she takes it, he lets go and grabs Dalton's hands, pretending to gnaw on them. Dalton shrieks with delight.

None of my X-rated X-girlfriends want kids, she reads. *I always wanted one.*

Tommy keeps playing with Dalton. He doesn't look at Rachel when she sets the pad back on his lap, but his face flames uniformly until the rash is blended into a suntan effect. He's handsome again. A ratchet turn in Rachel's chest releases a little pressure; she feels expansive.

"So let's go out to AquaWorld this afternoon," she says. "Or to a movie or somewhere."

"AquaWorld!" Dalton hollers.

Tommy doesn't say anything. He writes on the tablet and lets Dalton see it, then pushes it toward Rachel.

Probably closed. Have to call.

"Tomorrow would be okay," Dalton ventures, shooting a glance at his mother and then Tommy. "If your eye doesn't hurt."

Rachel shakes out cereal into bowls. When she sets them on the table, Tommy's got his sunglasses on and he and Dalton are bent over the wire thing, fiddling.

"This is a puzzle Uncle Tommy got when he worked on the oil rigs," Dalton informs her. "You have to get the loose wire out of the rest of it. There's a trick, and Uncle Tommy beat everybody. He won four hundred dollars." Dalton's on his knees crowding Tommy's hands. Tommy wiggles the loose wire around a framework of more twisted wire, pulling at each corner, searching for exits.

"I tried it but it wouldn't come," Dalton says. He frowns at the cereal. "We already ate, Mom."

Rachel spoons her cereal. Their father loved puzzles. He would set up the card table and dump out a puzzle, quickly picking through the squiggle-cut bits of cardboard. Searching out Rachel and Tommy, he would shyly clink the change in his pockets while inviting them to help. He was so careful to temper enthusiasm or irritation, biting his lip to impress on them that he could be a gentle opponent, that the three of them sat around the table like stiff-faced actors. Rachel learned to understand these sessions as awkward apologies. "Tom," their father would call softly, "Gimme a piece here, Tom, Tom, the piper's son."

"Stick it in that corner, " Dalton urges. His hands are crushed together into one still fist.

After bobbling the wire puzzle, Tommy pauses to get a firmer grasp on it. Rachel can hear him exhaling. She starts to notice that he's not so calm about this. His shoulders are folded in, the tendons in his forearms straining. Become important, the wire puzzle shivers with Tommy's handling. He drops the wire piece, flexes his trembling fingers, and picks it up again. A furrow of hair parts and flaps onto his forehead. The thing can't weigh an ounce, it'll break. Above the black-faced microwave, the enormous toy watch ticks like a bomb.

"It's just a puzzle, guys," Rachel murmurs. Her chest has tightened again. Her mother used to say that, say, "It's just a game," as the tears rolled down her face and she dragged the bat behind her like a tail. She had been an All-State athlete in high school and at every dreadful family picnic, their father burned them by her, taunting her with "Okay, champ, try this one on for size, champ!" Their mother never got to hit the ball, never touched first base. Rachel hated to play catcher, but someone had to.

Tommy's hands squeeze and the puzzle shoots off the table and bounces under it. Rachel scrapes back her chair, but Dalton's got the thing already, snatching it from the floor, the wire in the middle still dangling, attached.

They're all quiet. Standing apart, Dalton pinches the puzzle between his fingers. His mouth is prim with tension.

"Hello. My name is Dalton," Dalton says. "You killed my father. Prepare to die." He wrenches the puzzle around until it's out of shape and the hanging wire pops out, tinkling to the no-wax floor.

"Hey, you broke it, Dalton, that's no way—"

But round-shouldered Tommy throws up a fist, rolls over to Dalton and hoists his small sword arm in the air. Tommy seems to be laughing. His mouth is open and the flat belly of his black T-shirt shakes.

Flushed with pleasure, Dalton bumps Tommy out the back door, down a new-looking plywood ramp. Head down, toes digging in, Dalton shoves the chair with all his might over the patchy grass. Tommy supplements with an occasional spin until they come to rest beside a spindly mimosa staked with twine. When Rachel sees they are settled, she bypasses the dishwasher to fill the sink with soapy water. The hot water runs until her face is beaded and the etched glass is steamed a matte white. Curious hootings float from the mimosa, muted notes that ascend in scale as though thrown out from a creature rising through deep water to reach the salty air.

Without Dalton to focus on, Rachel and Tommy stare at the late news and try not to look around. A tequila bottle sits on the coffee table between them like a boundary marker. They've drunk a whole pitcher of limeade Margaritas, and when Rachel prods her closed eyes, they creak. But the long evening of television has given her the opportunity to consult herself. She has decided that she and Tommy have nothing to say. He walked enough during the day for her to see he can. He'll be all right eventually. Tomorrow, after AquaWorld, she and Dalton can ride the red Rabbit back to the airport, and she will be glad. Why did Tommy really want them to come?

When Rachel stands up, her highball glass hits the table somewhat before she expected it to. To finish off the visit, to have done with it—isn't that why she says it?—she asks him, "So, you going to speech therapy soon?"

Tommy sits bolt upright, so suddenly that the wheelchair travels forward an inch. His accusing face startles Rachel. She's not judging anybody; she doesn't have the room for it. But he must think she is. Holding up a finger, Tommy wheels over to a bookcase stacked with magazines. He brings back a photo album and shoves it into her hands. Confused, Rachel sits down.

The first picture is of a dark man in a burnoose. With the black eyebrows and suntan, the arched nose, the man could easily be Arabic, but self-conscious eyes betray him. Tommy in dress-up. He takes a swig from the half-empty tequila bottle on the coffee table and hands her a note.

Riyahd, American compound.

"It's your travel book?"

He nods and she turns the heavy pages. There's Tommy in a field of tulips, serious, legs apart and hands folded like a high-school coach. Tommy trying on a Walkman in a crowded alley market, his Banlon chest surrounded by oriental profiles. Waving at her to skip forward, he sits up in the chair expectantly, already jotting on the tablet.

Rachel finds a whole series of shots—native men with painted faces and . . . spears? She looks up at Tommy.

"Where's this?"

New Guinea. Tribes came out to bless the rig. Got in a fight. One guy hit another with a two-by-four. Had to call the local police. Real tense. When the police got there, they listened, then they took the guy that hit the first guy and they busted him over the head with the same two-by-four. Everybody was happy.

Tommy lifts the bottle. Past tasting now, he glugs it. Uncertainly, Rachel peers down again.

Tommy is slouching in the chair. Hazy-eyed behind the thick black lashes, he flicks his hand impatiently, motioning at her to turn the page.

Here he is on rocky ground before a stand of gnarled trees, and a fuzzy horse, no, a donkey, yoked to a kind of mill. An old man in a dusty black suit and cap hovers smiling at Tommy's shoulder. His face is so creased it looks like cookie dough bashed with knife blades. But his toothless smile is sweet. Tommy passes Rachel the bottle and she tilts it.

"Where's this?"

Tommy works slowly over the tablet. For once, he seems to enjoy forming the letters, swirling the commas, twisting the felt tip to make the dot of a period. Rachel drinks a teeny swallow, rolling the stuff around in her mouth while he's writing. Then she trades him the bottle for the note.

Sicily. Had an apartment upstairs from these people, the Scicatellis. Whole place to myself: They were crowded in like sardines. Used to invite me down to eat. Never went. Embarrassed about the language barrier. Had some Berlitz cassettes, but when I was with them, never seemed to hear the same words. They kept on asking. Waved their hands around and talked like I was deaf: Smiled all the time. Guess I did, too. Si. No. Prego. Non parlo Italiano, midispiace. Grazie mille, signor and signora. Buona sera, amici.

The Italian words are the ones written in fine script, labored over, and they strike Rachel's ears clearly, as though Tommy had pronounced them. Now she thinks she knows what he is getting at; she thinks she under-stands: Tommy's voice was injured long before the accident. How you are isn't my fault, she wants to tell him. She is only the safest one near him, like she was always the safest one.

Tommy's feelings are in his eyes, shining. And if she said to him, "It wasn't so easy, was it, our growing up? They were supposed to be the parents." That is what he wants to talk about, isn't it? That is the issue here. Rachel knows he can't make a further effort; she knows she can't make a graceful one.

Avoiding Tommy, she stares down at Mr. Scicatelli. Mr. Scicatelli smiles back at her like a grandfather. He makes a blessing. *Avanti, bambina,* he urges, kindly. He touches her forehead with a kiss. Rachel tries to duck, but the kiss lands on her anyway–it would find her anywhere. Rachel shuts her eyes so she cannot see her brother's sad, shining ones. Her mother appears with a diffident, childlike smile. She has just had a photograph enlarged, a flattering snap of herself in sunglasses, on a hillside. She is pleased with the photo. Citing silly vanity, Rachel's father plucks it from her and tears it up.

This is hard for Rachel. Her eyes are still closed. "We only knew what we saw," she says to her brother. "We couldn't see into their hearts. Who knows what was there?"

Tommy makes no move to write. They sit in silence.

Rachel has never said any of this before; she has barely thought it. It hurts to say it. "It's hard, isn't it, learning how to be, when no one ever showed us a way we wanted to be?" she says. Her voice squeaks embarrassingly.

Still he sits, blinking.

Mortified by her brother's lack of response, Rachel closes the album, smoothing its cover, and sets it with both hands on the coffee table. "You want to come to AquaWorld with us, fine. You don't, you don't have to."

His foot zooms out and kicks her ankle, a little kick. She remembers lying on the closet floor, throwing punches, what a relief it was.

Tommy looks up at her, sincere and soggy, as though the fine bones in his face have collapsed. He's in a state, writing furiously, big sloppy letters. The felt tip caroms off the pad. Tommy shakes his head clumsily and tries again.

When he gives her the note, Rachel sees that she has misunderstood everything.

What if we go to AquaWorld, he writes. *I sit there blipping out sounds. Nothing happens. I set myself up to be a total washout for Dalton. Like his father. Or these snouts ease out of the water and talk back to me. I couldn't understand them. How would I know I wouldn't say something rude and hurt their feelings? Or say nonsense words: germ whiskey nerves stupid broke nuthouse? They'd sink*

*down without talking back again. Who's that dry idjit up there with wheels
talking like a crazy fish?*

It is all Rachel can do not to give Tommy a tremendous kick in return.
She's hurt herself for nothing. And as for AquaWorld, it's just a simple
excursion; Dalton doesn't want him to prove anything. But Rachel is too
upset to say any of this. She leans into her brother's face and she shouts:
"Oh, Tommy, you know? You know? You know?"

Tommy refuses to know the very first thing: that he doesn't know, that
before you begin to find your own way, you have to admit that the old
way won't serve. Tommy only wants the old one. Rachel sees it now. He
wants her to do it again, and she despairs for both of them because the
people she fixes don't stay fixed. She hates this, but she stoops down to
him. She touches his clenched hands. "Tommy, Tommy, remember when
you hid under the car and wouldn't come out?"

His forehead wrinkles a second, then he nods.

Rachel talks right into Tommy's face, like he is deaf, like he has to
read her lips.

"Stay here if you want to. Stay here in this wheelchair till you feel like
getting out. Everything's paid for, right? Take your time, no matter what
anybody says. It's all right."

She puts a hand to her cheek. It feels like a rubber ball with the air let
out. Rachel sees it all again: the gritty garage floor, the small luminous
face under the car like a white balloon, misplaced, with desperate eyes.

But Tommy smiles, remembering. It's what she told him, talking fast
on her stomach on the concrete floor of the garage before their father
could get home. Where did she come up with those preposterous words
that she wished with all her heart were true? How did she imagine them?
Rachel told him she'd already talked to their parents and they'd said,
"Oh, we didn't understand before. We'll be nice to each other now, we
promise. Thank you, Rachel, it's okay that Tommy's under the car. Tell
him hello, will you?" He was six, or seven. She doesn't even know if he
believed her then, but he crawled out, oily, teary, hopeful. He only
wanted to know that hiding was always a possibility. He only wanted to
know that one person thought he was all right. It was that simple.

COME ON DOWN, Tommy writes. Rachel's hair swings forward as he
hugs her. When she rises, Tommy stands up, too, catching the low back of
the wheelchair. He assembles himself, pushing back his wide shoulders,
locking his knees. He strides off to bed, bracing himself with such force
that his arms don't swing.

Rachel sinks into the beanbag and holds her throbbing head. Two
images have just collided in her mind: her twelve-year-old self, face

smudged from the garage floor, frantically setting out the card table and 1000 pieces of the Eiffel Tower, engineering her father's apology. And Dalton, his clear eyes hooded, fixing once and for all the murderous wire puzzle.

The October afternoon is spread over by a sharp blue sky. It is AquaWorld's closing performance. Dalton loves every minute of the smirky tail-walking dolphins, the leaping whales. Hungover, Rachel and Tommy exchange grimaces at the sappy recorded music. Tommy has on his Wayfarers and a jammed down baseball cap. He slouches in the wheelchair, occasionally nibbling some of Dalton's popcorn and ignoring Dalton's nudges. Early in the show, Rachel caught him smiling at Dalton's bright face, but as the afternoon fades, he strokes his neck. He rolls his program into a baton and aimlessly beats his knee with it.

After the show, they keep their places, waiting for the crowd to thin. Rachel's idea is to linger poolside so that Dalton can watch the beautiful fish flash beneath the water. Not for long. Just long enough to put her arm around him and around Tommy, try to make a friendly moment of it. Their flight is at seven.

Rachel stations Tommy at the top of the exit ramp until she can talk to the guard. He's way up in the bleachers, so she hikes up and asks him outright if they can stay a few minutes to watch the animals swim. "Ten minutes, no problem," the guard says, glancing at Tommy's wheelchair. Dalton's voice pierces the air. Rachel shades her eyes to find him.

"I wanna see them now! I want you to tell them something for me!" Dalton's holding the popcorn and the chair with one hand, jumping all around, tickling the top of Tommy's cap, but Tommy isn't laughing. He bats at Dalton's hand and Dalton, not even thinking, lets go of the chair.

"Dalton, don't!"

But he's off, popcorn bouncing from the box, yelling, "C'mon, Uncle Tommy!"

Poised at the top of the ramp, the chair begins to roll backward. People are already gone. There's no one to stop it, and Rachel's too far away. She takes three steps at a jump, thinking that if she can't get there, surely Tommy will reach down with his stout arms and stop it himself. But he's rolling backward, picking up speed, shocked blank.

He lunges, and the wheelchair spills him out and skids, empty, to a stop. Rachel can hear him curse, his voice cracking, splintering from soprano to bass to mushy tenor. Tommy gets up; all on his own he actually makes it to his feet. But he doesn't join Dalton. He turns his back to the arena and heads for the parking lot. No hesitation, no hitch breaks Tommy's hustling gait. He doesn't look back.

Openmouthed at his nimble retreat, Rachel still doesn't call out. Look at him, just look–he's really covering ground, her brother, stepping fast and high, elbows jerking like Walter Brennan. No, she's going to trust Tommy to fix this situation himself. And trust herself to let him do it. The decision produces such a heady feeling; it seizes her like a sudden, hot embrace. Rachel is dizzied by the strange and amazing ease of letting go. As the afternoon lowers around her, she grasps a steel rail. She's free enough to rise; she could float right off into the strong blue sky, lighter and lighter and lighter.

She almost doesn't notice the oddest sound coming from beside the pool, the purest, most incomprehensible fluting cry, like geese beseeching the sky for one lost member. As the sound registers, Rachel looks down, giddy. God, he's believed it all, believed it was true.

Mouth a perfect O, eyes fervently closed, pale-haired Dalton is speaking to the fish.

His earnest face is stricken as he turns, expectantly, from the glassy water to see the overturned chair and his uncle a flailing, far-gone figure on the dusky pavement. Dalton drops the popcorn. It showers down into the water as he bounds for the ramp. "Don't go, please wait with me!" he cries. With the ramp's running start Dalton is almost flying, his heels high in the air, head back and arms wheeling.

He never sees the gray face that surfaces then, breaking from the pool with a whoosh! and a fine misty spray that hangs in the last sunlight like the smallest and most costly of jewels.

~~~~~

Look for Everything in the Sweeping and It Is There

Elizabeth Mills

When I arrived at the *Southwest Review* almost ten years ago, an inordinate number of hunting and fishing stories clogged our mail—an association with the old southwest, perhaps? Four or five years of persistent efforts—handwritten notes suggesting they try a trade magazine—and frequent fan letters to people whose work we admire resulted in a prodigious pool of talent from which to choose. Halfway through my tenure the *O. Henry* prize collection, *New Stories from the South*, and *The Best American Short Stories* also began to feature short stories that had appeared in our pages.

There is much good fiction writing available to a magazine in search of high literary quality, and there are too few places for a writer to send it, despite the proliferation of literary magazines in the last several years. We generally have room to publish only fifteen to twenty works of fiction during the year, depending on length. When asked what we are looking for we invariably say, what is good; and what is good is hard to define, though I know when I have it in hand.

This is how it works: the mail arrives and often I scan the envelopes for interesting and familiar names. The mail is then opened and date stamped, and submissions are entered in a log and placed in bins by category: nonfiction, poems, and fiction. Willard Spiegelman handles the nonfiction and poetry, I read the fiction and pass along to him the ones I want to publish, with my recommendations. Fortunately, he usually concurs. On a daily basis I sift through the fiction submissions and reject a good portion of them based on reading the first page, first paragraph, or

sometimes even the first line. For the first couple of years I read everything to the end, but now I do not apologize for putting something down;
it is up to the writer to make the reader want to continue. What impels me
to stop reading and eliminate a submission from further consideration
based on a cursory reading is most often bad writing–ungrammatical
phrasing, incorrect punctuation, obvious religious, pornographic, or sentimental writing–the writing of someone who does not read magazines like
the *Southwest Review.* Sloppiness in manuscript preparation always seems
to indicate sloppiness at a higher level.

A second screening of submissions eliminates anecdotal bits and writing that follows a televisionary, rather than literary, muse; this includes
raw autobiographical material, "feel-good" writing that is jokey or ma-
nipulative and tries to elicit a specific emotional response. A lot of these
submissions take plot as their main interest, and the writing in them is flat,
unexciting, and has little psychological depth. Of themselves, situations
are not interesting; it is how people handle them. For some time, for instance, I looked for a short story about care for an aging parent that we
could publish–and finally found it, in Jeanne Schinto's "Speaking on Condition of Anonymity" (spring 1991). What set this story apart are the clarity of the author's voice, the beautiful writing, warmth, and humor. Realizing that she needs to take her mother along if she wants to go to a
Halloween party, a woman dresses her mother, who is suffering from
Alzheimer's, in a chef's costume. As you might imagine, the situation
spawns lovely misunderstandings and misperceptions that allow the
reader to see an intelligent, deeply affecting relationship between mother
and daughter that does not sink into the bathetic, that spares the reader
pages of tedium on the subject of nursing homes, for instance, and intra-
venous tubes. Another example is James Gill's excellent "Cemetrization"
(winter 1993), on the subject of medically supervised suicide. Gill's writing is engaging and beautiful, touching the reader by its wit and intelligence.

With every horrific new disease there is a new genre of writing. We
have cancer stories, and AIDS stories. In selecting fiction for the *Southwest
Review,* I am not interested in writing that emphasizes the physical horrors
that mark these diseases; intelligent writing that manifests what is essentially human in any situation–whether traditional or experimental in
form, and especially humorous writing that understates its message, so difficult to achieve–I prize above all else.

Many well-written submissions are returned because their subjects are
not of interest to me–hunting and fishing stories, for example (I lie: there
is a hunting story I once published)–or because they are unfocused, they
need further development, I think there is more to come out in them, or

they are too small. Since the fiction we publish is anywhere from nine to fifty pages in manuscript, length is not so much an issue as design.

The language and subject must be powerful and compelling. Sometimes I'll set something compelling aside for a day or a week to see if it retains its hold on my imagination. But when I find something whose fire is unequivocal, I thrill to the certain knowledge that the work is splendid and that I want it for the *Southwest Review*. This is an intuitive rather than rational process; like a person of quality crossing one's path, a voice inside me says stop, pay attention, and I trust that voice.

There is a recklessness in my decision to publish that probably stems from not having to objectify the process for another person. But part of what supports me is the inherent risk, the anxiety that I might pass over something truly splendid. In ten years I have turned down the works of people who have gone on to become celebrated and some who were already celebrated; even seeing them in beautifully typeset form, I know I could not have published them.

When Jill Koenigsdorf's story "The Way That I Sweep" came in over the transom it immediately distinguished itself from many others. Her unusual opening lines swept me into her world, which I haven't left yet, six months later. "You can tell a lot about a person by the way they sweep," she writes. "I know. I've owned a flower stand right on the street for ten years now, and people, strangers sometimes, are just compelled to take the broom right from my hands at closing time and offer to help. People like to sweep." Her whimsical address of mortal quirkiness and the promise of spiritual attentiveness in everyday activities like sweeping, swimming, and shelling peas touched my heart, struck lightning in my own experience—and while this is not a requisite for publication in the *Southwest Review*, this is why I have chosen to write about and reprint it here.

Jill Koenigsdorf has style, she has a beautiful command of the English language, and she is observant of many things, like the way Europeans carry their flowers upside down. This is an intelligent story: the grammar is impeccable, the language is powerful, and everything in the story contributes to her theme. Not one word is discarded or hangs loose as a question; the story has focus. The plot is simple: girl meets boy, girl gives up boy. But we have all the complexity of her character's personality expressed in subtle terms. One of the first things she tells us is that one of her dearest wishes is to find someone with whom she can share a creamy bar of French soap; yet, when this person appears, she is not willing to risk the life she has to stay with him. She loves him, but she is someone who does not take risks, and Jake's invitation is only implicit. The story's strength is in Jill Koenigsdorf's ability to let the reader feel that balance between two worlds: a life one loves, peopled with interesting friends, flowers, and good food; and her life with Jake, which graces her existence in other ways.

Just as I was working on this essay about sweeping a remarkable quotation about sweeping came to me in the mail, in a copy of the Swedenborgian journal *Chrysalis* sent by a friend. The epigraph that appears on the title page of the summer 1993 issue took my breath away; the issue is devoted to the theme of work, the quote is from philosopher Wilson Van Dusen:

> There is a world of difference between simply sweeping the floor so it is clean, sweeping as an effort to improve things, or sweeping as a devotional speaking to the highest one can conceive of. If I am sweeping just to remove the dirt from the floor, that is all that will be accomplished. The very process of sweeping when used as a means of reaching out will reveal the response I am seeking. I would also emphasize that the amount found is in direct relation to the seeking. Seek little, find little. Look for everything in the sweeping and, by golly, it is there.

One of the reasons I had to publish "The Way That I Sweep" may be that Jill Koenigsdorf writes about the kinds of activities I perform daily–swimming, shelling peas, snipping the ends off green beans, and culling good fiction from the mails. But it is her essential wisdom and the beauty of her achievement in this story that have claimed an ascendant place in my imagination.

The Way that I Sweep
Jill Koenigsdorf

You can tell a lot about a person by the way they sweep. I know. I've owned a flower stand right on the street for ten years now, and people, strangers sometimes, are just compelled to take the broom right from my hands at closing time and offer to help. People like to sweep. It's a job where you can see the results of your efforts immediately and that's gratifying. I hate to generalize, but about flowers and sweeping, it's pretty clear cut. Italians and Spanish people buy their flowers full blown, voluptuous, at their peak that very day. Americans and French, they buy them showing some color, but still a bit unripe. Germans and Scandinavians buy all their flowers green and tight and that may be smart because they'll last longer, but for my money, a bud is less seductive than a flower. The common bond for Europeans, however, is that they always carry their wrapped flowers away upside down, away from their bodies.

My friend Abe is a lawyer and sweeps pretty much how you'd expect. Pursed lips, furrowed brow, going over and over the same spot so no stray shred of tobacco or gum wrapper remains, squashing the straw of the broom into the pavement like a punishment. Afterwards, the street in front of my shop is devoid of debris and Abe has sweat on his forehead and needs some congratulations. Lauren's a travel agent and she sweeps like she's waltzing with the broom. Sometimes, the straw doesn't even make contact with the ground, and the stems and bottle caps are just barely disturbed by the breeze she leaves in the wake of her swooping arcs. She talks to me the entire time about Bora Bora or Costa Rica. I tell every person who helps that they're the best sweeper. But Jake, he really is.

I didn't meet Jake at the stand, but at another place that had been my own well-kept secret for three months. When we met up there, in the hills, Jake had just returned from a major journey. He had followed through on his plan to drive an empty flat-bed truck across the Deep South via the Ozarks and en route, to spend his life savings, about four thousand dollars, on every piece of cane furniture he could strap on board. Then, as he tells it, he came back to California, laden like some purposeful marsupial, saw the spot where he wanted his shop, and spotted me at the same time, right next door. I, as it turned out, would end up lending him the first month's rent money for his shop, the shop that he would name, of course, "Raising Cane." The plan was to quadruple the prices he had paid for the furniture, stick around only long enough to make a bundle, then buy land in and move to Sitka, Alaska. Looking back, I see that there was never any doubt in his mind that he would make all of this happen. I always meet people who are able to make longshots pay off and harebrained schemes sound irresistible. Plus: he swept as if he wanted the ground to rise up under his feet and follow him somewhere. I could have learned something from this. The ground and me—we should have been more willing to be charmed.

Jake is the one who presented me with my two best brooms, the only things in this life I would trust enough to call indestructible. The handles were sassafras bark which, like good leather, just gets prettier the more your sweat and dirt work into it. It never splinters. And because whittling is the pride of the Ozarks, an art form as revered as banjo or mouth harp, each handle had some bearded Druid-type character carved into the top. These brooms reminded me of my earliest relationships with trees, because for many years, I saw wise, old faces emerging from the tree bark, faces that spoke to me. I took pleasure in forests and still tend to pat trees when I'm on a hike, like one would a dog. Jake says the Indians thank a tree before they chop it down for firewood. But now, everyone around here sees trees, especially Eucalyptus, as villains because of the fire.

The fire brought Jake, as well as the secret swimming hole, well, more accurately, swimming pool, into my life, so I have a hard time appreciating the immensity of the tragedy. It's only been a year now since the hills burned, but the T.V. execs have already made a movie about it, grabby as they tend to be for a good disaster. I watched it last night, my rocking chair and eyesight dangerously close to the glowing box. To its credit, the show did have documentary footage woven into the standard T.V. melodrama. I cringed at the way the fire took on a life of its own, like some ravenous, mindless, chimera. Panic, however, is a state I'm already intimate with, and don't need the sight of flames to induce. My parents explained it as my having an overactive imagination. I'm watching T.V. again, like I was before I met Jake, because well, he's already gone.

Before I met him I was, admittedly, blue, or more accurately, depressed. People think: "Jesus, Lucy, you spend the whole day elbow deep in Narcissus and Enchantment Lilies, you own your own business, no one's in a bad mood when they're buying flowers, WHAT have you got to be sad about?" And it's true, I enjoy my work. I dream at night of the different arrangements I will make. I will switch on the light to write down some bouquet idea involving French Heather or Butterfly Miniature Carnations, and a particular breed of Peruvian Lily called Rosario, which I will have to comb the Flower Market for at two in the morning, simply because it has the same shade of burgundy in its freckles as the minis have in their throats.

The flowers in my bouquets must spend their entire life in the vase in a state of giddy reunion, the colors complimenting and sashaying, as if having been deprived of one another's company for far too long. My customers expect exquisite compositions from me. They rely on me to think of putting butter-colored double-headed freesia alongside plum-hued Parrot Tulips, knowing that somehow I alone will have detected that faint fuchsia blush in both breeds that it takes breath of Heaven to bring out. They come to my place for that, but Jake thinks it's more for general cheerfulness and a sympathetic ear. He says we're all starved for some sense of community, lacking church or barn dances or whatever people used to have.

Yet swathed as I am, day in, day out, in so much sensuality, fragrance, color, and the miracle of people spontaneously purchasing single long-stem red roses and carrying them off whistling and serene, I often sweep with my lips pursed, muttering and choking the broomstick. I often go home, pour some hot water over a Cup-'O-Noodles, and eat them alone, reading the morning paper at nine o'clock at night. I hunch over, chew loudly, and sigh frequently, just to underline my sad condition. If one is going to be maudlin, one might as well wallow.

The day Jake appeared in my life, I had started my day off badly, contemplating an organic banana for which I had paid almost a dollar, thinking how it didn't taste any better than a regular banana and how typical that was of my life, having such high expectations of everything and being so disappointed. Then I was despairing about how long it takes me lately to go through a nice bar of fatty, sweetly scented soap. I will gladly pay five dollars for creamy bars of soap from France if they will ultimately be used to soap someone's back or stomach. We could then grope damply down my candlelit hallway to fall, enmeshed, into clean sheets. Stranger things have been known to happen. But this possibility was not on the horizon and it was raining, yet again. I was wearing so many layers, because I work in the elements, that I could barely bend my arms. All that day at work, I was grouchy and worried that I was wasting the prime years of my life. I was ready for just about anything, as long as it was new. I am an impatient person, overly fond of drama. Lately, I found myself unable to focus on the bright side, which troubled me, as all my friends kept insisting that I had the ideal life. I badly needed to swim.

There are only two things that calm my pacing, jackal-like brain: shelling peas and swimming. I like nothing more than sitting on my kitchen floor, wearing a full skirt, no bra, some soft, old, robin's egg-blue tank top, with the pads of my seasoned feet pressed together, humming and shelling peas, popping the occasional raw one into my happy mouth. Of course fresh pea season is brief, and swimming is something I can now do every day.

The day I was gloomy about the larger significance of the organic banana, I wheeled Key Lime out of the cellar. I name my bikes and my cars, one of the two traits I have apparently inherited from my mother, although Jake says it's because I live in a cartoon. She had a red Falcon named Judy, and a Blue Malibu named Rob Roy, and so on. She also refused to proclaim a paper towel officially dead for days. Hence, her kitchen and, horrifyingly, my own, is strewn, hither and thither, with wadded up paper towels; towels that are plucked, used, left to dry out, reused, and, only when disintegrating, are thrown away. Sort of like the progression of most relationships, I have discovered. But Jake would have called that cynicism, a trait he had very little tolerance for.

I named Jake's truck "Otto," short for "automatic," because it had a fluke where Jake could be driving along at sixty miles per hour, turn to me in the front seat, pull the keys out of the ignition, say: "Here, catch!" and the truck would keep running. He over-threw one day and almost tossed them out the window, which gave me this oddly thrilling feeling that we would be forced to drive around for eternity, unable to slow down or stop moving forward. I had forgotten about the concept of brakes, or running out of fuel. I was surprised how much I enjoyed that brief sensation of being captive aboard a machine locked on automatic pilot.

I mounted Key Lime as if on a mission, and headed up into the hills for a ride in the rain. I wanted to see if the house I had once lived in was still standing. Everything up there was so charred and scorched I almost expected hissing noises when this rain made contact with the remains. Only two weeks had gone by since the fire, but the hills were already deserted. The area seemed jinxed now, and people avoided it like contagion. Oglers with cameras, actually pushing baby carriages and walking their dogs, had come the days immediately following, but they were shamed away, forced to show some respect for the loss. Now, I could barely recognize my old street, since all foundations looked pretty much the same and street signs were a thing of the past. Blackened trees clawed for the cool sky, wailing with the same agony.

A few blocks down, I encountered a perspiring man, mumbling to himself and sifting through the rubble. He was very excited to see me, motioned for me to come down, and began describing all the renovations he and his wife had just completed before the fire. He actually gave me a tour of the levelled plot of dirt, making grand gestures with his arms and saying: "Here is where the living room was. Oh and there? We had knocked out a wall and put in a bar and a spiral staircase. To your right was the display case where my wife kept her collection of Victorian lace fans." He was ruined by this disaster, lopsided as a broken toy.

I finally recognized my former home, many days later, by the swimming pool only. Five of us had lived there, skinny dipping every morning in the summer, or diving in despite the chill after hours of dancing at our infamous Halloween parties. The pool was right outside my bedroom window, and many nights I had been awakened by raccoons chasing each other and chortling in the water. It had been a good house. Camaraderie and never fewer than ten people at the dinner table. And now, there was only the pool, perfectly clean and intact, crystal blue and inviting. There were no ashes marring the surface, no debris cluttering the bottom.

Oddly, the pool was being kept up, although no one lived anywhere in the vicinity to swim in it. I had heard that certain people actually survived the fire by jumping into their swimming pools and coming up for air under a plastic tarp. This pool would make everything better. This pool was a place for survivors. It was almost dark and no one was around anyway, so I took off all my clothes and plunged in.

I enjoy swimming most at dusk. I kick and splash very hard to make tunnels of bubbles ahead of myself. Then, the pool lights come on, and I can see them hovering in front of me and I can swim through them so they fizz and skitter across my skin. Putting my head into or thrusting my hand into this funnel of effervescence I have created always makes me laugh. Even in this ghost town pool, the lights came on promptly at twilight. Clearly, the owners moved away and forgot to tell the maintenance people to stop upkeep. I swam the last twenty laps in the dark, shook off like a dog, then whistled and shivered back down the hill, trying to use the brakes as little as possible as some good-luck dare. There's nothing so renewing as a swim and a secret. I was not aware that this was the second time Jake had noticed me, nor that he had been watching me all that evening.

He was pretty good about letting me keep my secret pleasure, limiting his own swims to well before dusk. One evening, deep into the heady, lavender-starred, Magnolia-drunk portion of spring, when all the eucalyptus acorns are wearing their pink hula skirts and no one has much on their minds beyond a milkshake and a stroll, Jake wanted me to discover him. I had been looking forward to the swim all day and when I heard a distinct splashing as I approached "my" pool, I felt hugely disappointed, as if it marked the end of my exclusive haven. Then I felt territorial, willing to confront this trespasser and tell him I had first dibs. I dismounted and tiptoed into the bushes above the pool, the same bushes where Jake had positioned himself like a spy for weeks to watch me. The sight of him carving up that azure water was a marvel. It would have been a crime to stop him.

Watching him, I had a wonderful memory involving a tumbler, the machine that transforms drab, commonplace rocks into glossy, polished substances you want to touch. My best friend's older brother had such a machine in his cellar and once a week, when he had collected the proper stones and was ready to begin the process, I would peddle down to his house, position myself on the ping-pong table, and watch. He would spread the gray pebbles on a piece of burlap in front of me and explain to me the bounties hidden within. They all looked basically the same, except for the occasional tell-tale sparkle or blush or vein of color. The sheet of black velvet was reserved for the next day, when the finished stones would be spilled out upon it like some gorgeous harvest. The stones had names that made my mouth water: "Moonstone," "Heliotrope," "Aquamarine," "Jasper." I wasn't sure what the tumbler did overnight to induce such a glorious transformation, but I was convinced it had something to do with water and movement. I have always believed in this powerful magic, and watching the way Jake inhabited the pool, I knew he did as well.

I was just thinking how his body had the ropey muscles that come from actual labor or activity, not pumping iron, when Jake hollered up: "It's O.K. to come down, you know." I froze, didn't make a peep. After he had been catching his breath on the side for awhile, he said, with his back still turned: "We can share this place."

"How did you know I was up here?" I shouted, trying to regain my composure.

"Oh, I've been letting you have it all to yourself for awhile now. But tonight . . . it didn't seem fair that you got all the moonlight."

"Oh I see! So how long have you been spying on me?"

"Just get in; I promise I won't look . . . although I've seen it all before . . ."

The water was perfect, the temperature of tears, and just as soft. We swam smooth laps with some invisible line dividing the pool into private halves. We both focused on the swimming to distract from the giddy reality of two naked strangers on private property together in the dark. I could feel a fleeting warmth wash over me when he passed alongside and I swam through his wake. Our initial getting acquainted took place up to our necks, away from the lights, in these silken waters.

"When I first saw this pool, this perfect blue square in the middle of all this wasteland, I thought it was a mirage," Jake said. "Then when I saw you in it, I was even more uncertain. I couldn't believe it, because I'd seen you before at your stand and had wanted to ask you a favor, but really, even just talking with you would have been fine. So I came back every day to watch you swim, just to make sure I could keep these coincidences happening, that my eyes would continue to play tricks on me."

"Well, are they now?"

"Hard to say; the light's failing and I am badly in need of nourishment . . . let's find food and shelter."

"That's what I like," I said. "A man with big assumptions."

Jake told me right off that he wanted to go to Sitka, Alaska, because it was considered the "Paris of Alaska" and he had no desire to live in Europe. He wanted to see moose, lightning bugs the size of Christmas ornaments, and Aurora Borealis all in one evening. He liked the idea of earning all of these sights by doing what he called "snow penance." I told him I had always had a fantasy of riding through the snow in the back of a horse-drawn sleigh, cozied up against someone I was about to build an Indian fire for.

"That's what I like," he laughed. "A woman with big assumptions . . . So what's an Indian fire?"

"You send as many people as you can, in our case the two of us, off to search for wood. Each person is given an assignment as to the size twigs they are to bring back. Then, everyone congregates, and you have assorted piles, from pinky-size kindling all the way up to forearm-size wood. And you build the fire in this graduated way. It's a small, efficient fire with lovely blue flames and it starts very easily and you have to draw in close to it to appreciate the way all those finger-size sticks burn."

"I want you to teach me more things," Jake said. "I want you to show me how to swim like you do, like an otter."

Foresight has never been my strong suit, so I did not hesitate to spend every minute for the next three months getting closer and closer to someone who was moving far away. We spent many hours in the water. I stood behind Jake, my arms pressed against the length of his like Siamese eels and taught him to keep his fingers together when he reached out to do the crawl so that he would push more water aside and swim faster. "Swim like there's a strong line that runs from the base of your spine out the top of your head and someone at the other end of the pool is pulling you. Then, you'll just glide through that water." He taught me to do somersault turns on each end to save time, to keep perpetually moving forward. They made me dizzy but I gave them a try.

One month before Jake left for Sitka, we were in the barren echo-chamber of what was left of Raising Cane, gulping, sighing, and shifting back and forth on our feet too often. He had, in these months, sold all the furniture and I volunteered like a lunatic to rent the space for him so he could hit the road north as soon as possible. I pictured myself paying rent on the empty place myself, in no hurry to get rid of this souvenir, mooning about inside. I would be like the survivor in couples who often leave the room their dear departed had inhabited exactly as it was when they were alive, because that way, it might stay wonderfully haunted. Jake fanned me with the "For Rent" sign in a sweet way, but his gestures were laden now, abbreviated, contained versions of the all-out wailing and clutching that wanted to happen. I finally kicked one of the hoop-back chairs someone had left for Jake to fix, but never came back for. Every time we discussed the separation, I broke something close at hand, ranted and raved, while he watched me directly, never bowing his head. He knew this flurry was easier for me than crying. After work, I swept so fiercely that stems and clods of dirt went flying all the way out under the wheels of oncoming cars. Drivers glared as if I were aiming.

"It doesn't make sense," I said. "Why leave when your business is doing so well and we're teaching each other new things and you don't even have the land up there yet!"

"That's what you like about me," he said. "My senselessness."

"Don't you have any feelings? How can you joke about this?"

"Listen, we both knew I was leaving from the first day. Besides, I'm not forbidding you to join me."

"Yeah, but you're not inviting me either."

"Hey," said Jake, forcing me to meet his eyes. "You follow your heart."

"I can't just give up my life, the stand, everything for your dream. I'm too old . . ."

He stopped me: "That's why I'm not asking you to."

The night before Jake left, the moon was the color of an old man's toenail and we sat together by the pool feeling sick-hearted, eating Cracker Jacks and drinking Campari and sodas. I wanted to send him off excited about the venture, with my best wishes, but I was feeling miserly and scared. I told Jake I knew as of this moment that the world was divided into two types of people: those who needed things from the outside, and those who generated them from within. He took this in, felt the compliment, then tried to lighten things up:

"Really," he said. "And here all this time I thought it was people who sang along with the radio, and people who didn't."

"People who take baths, and people who shower."

"People who like late night and people who like early morning."

"Hey Lucy? Which kind are you?"

"Which? Well I'm . . . I'm . . . Oh Jake, please don't go."

It's not raining so much here anymore, and at night there's some flowering tree that blooms outside my window far more intoxicating than any blossoms I sell. People seem to be in a better mood. It's still winter in Alaska and Jake writes that he has bought a husky. He says he is working on assembling enough of them for a dog sled. I know he is saying this for my benefit, a statement of promise, but I am here now, trying to rent out Raising Cane, scribbling down this new combo I pictured of lapis-colored anemones clashing brazenly with orange ranunculas. Frequently, I feel the way you feel when you look at a pair of wool mittens on a hot July day. Not disoriented exactly, but wrong. Jake says we were drawn to each other like ants to a pie tin. I go up to the pool at dusk still, but there is construction everywhere and I am too selfish to take comfort in this as some sign that life goes on. Right before I closed today, I noticed a bead of water balanced on the head of a droopy Bleeding Heart. It filled me with suspense waiting to see if it would cling or fall off. Everything seems symbolic. I'm looking for clues. And every day, I sweep a little less assuredly. I sweep like I want the ground to teach me something. I sweep like I'm willing to learn.

∾∾∾

For "The Whole Story"
George Garrett

Editing almost continuously since the 1940s, I have never thought of my-self as an editor. I have always imagined that I am a writer first and an editor only for the time being. A professional writer and an amateur edi-tor. That attitude makes some differences. One difference is that I tend to believe that the writer knows what he or she is doing and is therefore re-sponsible for what he or she has done. A lot of editors I know like to think that the writer is specially gifted and mostly unconscious; that it's hit or miss; that the writer doesn't know when work is good or bad and needs the editor to tell him or her what the score is; that some writers are just luckier than others. On the other hand, I have always tended to believe that the writer has overcome doubts and arrived at the judgment that the submitted work is (for the time being) as good as it's going to be; that it is worthy. Most of the time I assume that the writer has honorably taken his or her best shot.

The principal occupation of editors is to *reject things*. Somewhere along the line hundreds of stories (thousands in the case of the big quarterlies and the few commercial magazines that still publish fiction) are funnelled down to a precious few. So all of us spend the overwhelming part of out time looking for good reasons to reject things. We editors are *rejectors* by trade who, from time to time, accept something for publication. Second thing to realize is this–that context is urgently important. If there is an art of editing, it lies in putting together a good and interesting magazine, issue by issue. The duty of the fiction editor is to serve the magazine and its overall editor, putting together the best possible conjunction of subordi-nate parts. With each rejection the context changes. ("I have rejected bet-ter stories than this.") With every acceptance the context changes even more. If I have already accepted, say, a good first-person story set in the city and involving adultery and murder, I am unlikely to take another one like it even though the other one may be of superior quality. With each decision the context of the forthcoming magazine changes. Soon we are sending back stories of the highest quality for reasons simply of form or content. Writers write stories and editors organize issues of a magazine, an art form a little like collage. And, finally, individual issues of a magazine relate to each other over a period of time. Your cowboy story two issues ago.

One thing more. A lot of editors don't and won't admit the things I have just asserted. They feel it necessary to pretend that quality is at the heart of their primary action—acceptance or rejection. Nobody is going to write you and say: "Hey, this is a wonderful little story, but I already accepted one that, like yours, takes place on the nudist beach of Greek island. Yours is funnier and better, really; but I am already committed to the other one. (Besides the other one is by a reliably well-known person and, as far as I am concerned, you are pretty much a nobody at this stage.) Sorry. You are just unlucky this time." NO. They are going to tell you that the story doesn't quite "work" for them. Maybe they will even make a few suggestions for improving your story. Don't, repeat *do not*, revise it according to their suggestions and send it back unless they specifically invite you to do so. You will be wasting your time. Chances are that their advice is worthless anyway (you know the story better than they can or do). A letter of this kind, though, may indicate that you should try them with other things.

For *The Texas Review* I am looking for *variety* in form and content. I am interested in representing the diverse kinds of fiction around and about these days. That means that I am deliberately seeking the unfashionable as well as the usual tropes and tricks of contemporary fiction. We have nothing against the usual "names" or against the literary establishment. But we don't seek out the known and we do not consider ourselves as distant servants of the establishment. Quite the contrary. We like to think of ourselves as critics of the establishment. What this means is that, probably, something innovative or original, outside of establishment guidelines, gets more attention from us, as does something "old-fashioned" in the sense that it does not adhere to the latest conventions. We seem to like variety in setting. Over the past few years we have published a good many stories with international, often Third World settings. We like variety in subject, setting, technique. We want to be open-minded which means we are not always going to be politically correct.

Finally, we are looking to introduce new names and talents. We try to have one or more "discovery" stories in each issue, stories by previously unpublished writers. It is our version of the old "Atlantic First" stories. We want to continue to reserve a place for the new writer, young or old.

What do I look for as defining "quality"? Not perfection. Every story is made up of choices, some of them arbitrary or whimsical. In a good story, though, you don't feel these choices and compromises. In a good story you are hooked, first to last. A good story can be seriously flawed in a technical sense, yet still work like a charm. So one of the things I look for in any story is "authority," the confident sense, while the illusion lasts, that this is the only way to tell this tale. The writer knows better and so does the reader, but the reader is involved enough to believe in the tale and its telling. One thing that brings the reader into the story is the surface, the details of perception that aestheticians call the *sensuous affective experience*. It is in that way that all art speaks to us. Without it there is not story, whether the story is fantasy or "realism." I am also looking for suspense, for an urge to follow the story to its appropriate end. This is a matter of skill–of avoiding repetition and complex layers of exposition, of holding back and making the reader desire to know more, to turn the page . . . It is also a matter of caring. Whatever its form, its subject and treatment, the story and the people and events in it must matter enough so that it is worth a reader's energy and time. Hand-in-glove with caring is artistic integrity which means that the reader is not cheated, that the story by the end delivers what it promises.

Since all of it is done with words, I look from the beginning to end for a language that is fresh and alive and yet always appropriate to the subject, even though it may well go against the grain of that subject.

How do we go about judging at *The Texas Review*? Because I am older and busier now than ever I don't get to see everything. The editor, Paul Ruffin, reads everything that comes in. From these he selects a dozen or two and sends them to me, without additional instruction or advice other than the implicit understanding that these are the "best" of the bunch, that any one of these stories is probably eligible. From this batch I must select five or six; actually, I rank the stories in my order of preference, add a few notes for each and return them, knowing that only five or six will make it into the magazine. This leads to another criterion–length. Like every other editor I know of, I am always hoping to get as much space, as much representation of my particular constituency, fiction, as I possibly can. A long story, anything over about 15 pages of typescript, is always at a distinct disadvantage. More stories by more writers can be published if the stories are shorter, 10 to 15 pages. Therefore a longer story has to be obviously worth two or more of the shorter ones, that is about twice as "good." Of course, because I am always skeptical of rules, I tend to break this one when I can; but, even so, longer stories are subjected to more exacting judgment.

Now for the story of a specific story. I have chosen "Dad is Here," by Hilary Masters, which first appeared in *The Texas Review*, Volume XII, Numbers 1 & 2 (a double issue) for Spring/Summer 1991. For that issue we had, between us, chosen five stories out of the final short list of 12 or 15. Hilary Masters' story, unsolicited, was in the same batch. Just what I needed for the issue any number of ways. Although I had not expected to find a Masters story and was surprised when I opened the envelope, I was familiar with his work and an admirer of the novels in *The Hudson Valley Trilogy*. I had been much moved by his autobiographical book, *Last Stands: Notes from Memory*, which is mostly about his maternal grandfather, a veteran of the Indian Wars, and his father. I had seen stories by Masters in the magazines. His presence in the issue could give us something we did not otherwise have this time—star quality. One work by a well-known and well-regarded writer could be helpful to the other stories. These things affect each other.

Precisely *because* I already had a highly favorable impression of Masters and his work and because a story by him would be something of a "catch" for this issue, to be an honest editor I would have to counteract both feelings. That is, I would have to be all the more demanding of this particular story than I might have if it had come in anonymously or from a perfect stranger.

And there is another factor. If it had been a story by, say, Ann Beattie, I would have known that it had already been rejected by *The New Yorker* and probably other magazines. Similarly, I had to assume that Masters had submitted the story to some of the major magazines and quarterlies.

That it was submitted to us proved to me that he believed in it. Even in the face of rejection. No artist with integrity sends out a story or a poem he or she does not believe in. It's always possible that the writer is wrong, but not as often as you might think.

I didn't have to get far into "Dad is Here" to realize it was a story that met my criteria for quality. It had suspense—who is talking to whom and what's this all about—and the surprise that the first-person narrator is a woman. It has, from the beginning, the details that bring a story to life: that "dirty-boy talk that went along with clapping erasers together in the 6th grade outside of Horace Mann in Blue Springs"; the physicality of the father's image in the third paragraph. We are plunged into the story, then led along. And the exposition is graceful, adroitly in place. As the story develops we are in the time outside of time that is the essence of any first-person story, a special kind of first-person because it is addressed to a specific listener, an offstage character. We soon discover that we are *eavesdrop-*

ping in this story. And the voice of the speaker-narrator is wonderfully wide-ranging and evocative. At times cooly analytical and self-conscious: "All this shocks me a little, mixing all these things up together, but not the language or the activities. Just the mix of them." Other times pushing to the edges of the lyric poem ("Oh, he would push me so high that I leave my breath there in the leaves. You push me high like that sometimes, but I know better to trust your opinion about plumbing."). It is funny and sad, complex and accessible, condensed and demanding. Finally, it is artistically and thematically *true*. I say, yes, that's it, that's how it has to be. It has pure authority.

And I think the way it should be, too, for the most professional of the writers on board to be represented by a story that only a very skilled and experienced writer would conceive of and could execute.

I am thinking that I have no idea why other editors turned this one down (if they did); but I know I lucked out for this issue and for the magazine I work for.

Dad Is Here
Hilary Masters

Dad is here, I say, and then you answer something like Oh, I'm happy you are having this time together though just a minute before you were saying you had this problem you hoped I could take care of, thinking your words were daring, dirty-boy talk that went along with clapping erasers together in the 6th grade outside of Horace Mann in Blue Springs—Hey, Emily, we got problems with our homework. Give us a hand with it?

"What's that, Dad?"

He is saying that he has to use the last four numbers of his social security number as a code to get into this new apartment complex he's moved to from Blue Springs. He is sitting at the kitchen table, playing solitaire, and I can see his neck has got thin, the cords pull out and up into his skull like cables pulling the rest of him up, holding the rest of him up by his ears it seems like because they have got much larger.

"It's a damn nuisance," he says and lays down a black seven neatly on top of a red eight.

"What's that, Dad?"

"Memorizing those damn numbers. You have to punch them into this panel by the mail boxes and then run across the foyer to the door to grab it while it's still buzzing."

"I guess it must be for your security, though," I say.

"I never had to remember my social security number before," he says. "Never." He gets an ace free.

You'll have to get that cleaned off, Momma would say. I'm serving dinner in ten minutes. Hold your horses, he'd say. I almost got this worked out. Why don't you give me a hand and I'll get done faster.

So, you all talk like that no matter what age whether it's playing cards or whatever. Just last week, this director of consumer relations leans across the crudité and says he would like to pin the subject down, open it up and see what it is made of and so I pass him the olives that have all these toothpicks sticking up in the air and he looks at them for a second and then says, no thanks.

Sometimes I must remind myself that I am a woman with a boy-child who is almost half your age, like tonight, when I heard your voice on the phone, saying those dumb shit things, and I'm going along with it—I reach up to my hair and expect to find rollers—and then I turn around and there's Dad with his cards all laid out and stuck on the fridge door is that card Billy gave me—Happy Birthday to Mom, the Apple of My Eye.

Your eyes have a way of rolling up sometimes so you look like Our Savior on the cross, I mean those statues I used to pray to, look up to from my knees and catch just a glimmer of whites as He bore His blessed agony. "I didn't know feminists went in for this sort of thing," you said the other afternoon and then I saw your eyes slip back into your skull though I expect your agony was not all that unbearable. All this shocks me a little, mixing all these things up together, but not the language or the various activities. Just the mix of them.

"Playing those drums noon and night," Dad is saying. "They must be students from Africa who have rented the apartments below me. I've spoken to the people in the front office about it. But they're a whole new crew down there—bunch of young girls who don't care about anything but fixing up their faces and going out to lunch. Meanwhile, its Boom-la, Boom-la, Boom-LA–BOOM." The four of hearts cracks down and a whole run is precipitated. He might win this game.

"Did you talk to the students about the noise, Dad?"

"That does no good. They won't listen to me."

Is that true about ears getting bigger as you get older? Dad's ears seem to stick out a lot more than I remember. I think of one fall afternoon, tramping through the woods back of our house, trying to keep up with him, wanting to snuggle into his broad red and black plaid back against the autumn chill and his shoulders large, and his neck just right and his ears neat-tucked into his Minnesota Viking cap. He walked so fast.

You told me the ears keep growing. Too bad for you, you said, that all the other parts stop and I laughed so you wouldn't be embarrassed by the silly-ass purity of your remark—your humor is sometimes like black socks, if you know what I mean—nor give you any idea that I might have been offended. All these names you give things, all the parts have to be called something—it's a nomenclature I find gratuitous—but the names don't bother me. They bother you, I think. You say them sometimes just to bother yourself. The language is almost enough for you which brings me back to the ears business. I was laughing, even threw a pillow at you if I remember rightly, so as to keep you busy while I had time for my real thoughts. If the ears get larger we should hear better, we should be able to listen to each other. Better.

"It's terrible," Dad says. "You can't hear yourself think."

"I get the feeling," I say, "that you don't like where you're living." And that stops him. He has to think about that for a while. He pats the cards, pats them straight.

Let me get back to being shocked. It's not what you think. You might think I am having trouble keeping my different selves apart—the old naming of the parts again. But why is it you have to separate everything; I guess putting a tag on something is to claim it? But to identify is not to understand anything. One is subjective, comes from the imagination of the beholder and the second is a given—the basic rose, you might say.

Last week I glanced in the mirror on the way to the bathroom and I saw Billy's Mom, the Apple of His Eye, and just then you said my ass looked like a peach. I am an orchard, is that it—a one tree orchard and all of you perched on different limbs, enjoying different fruit, but one tree? You understand? I don't think you do. Listen to this.

Tuesday, I had gone to bed early to work on some reports and the door opens and here comes Billy to climb under the covers and lie against me, all barely five feet of him from toe to hip to shoulder lined up against me. So, I shift from vice-president of the credit bureau to Mom and then I think of Billy's father—because that's why the boy's in bed with me, he's lonesome for his father and I'm only a substitute—then the phone rings and I know it's you. Remember, you were calling from a bar in Germantown? Want to come out and play, you were saying, like you had just discovered sand boxes, and you were cute, right enough, and I admit to a little burn even with Billy lying close beside me and these market analyses in my lap.

"There, Dad," I say. I am reaching over his shoulder and point to the nine of hearts.

"I see it," he says. "I was just looking for a better play." But he hadn't seen it and he has no better play and his voice had that edge to it that Momma used to laugh at and turn back to the kitchen after she had wondered out loud if it wasn't a good idea to call the plumbers about the leak instead of him trying to patch it himself so as to save his good clothes for Sunday. And I would agree with his labeling of her, with the sound in his voice right then that said she didn't know what she was talking about—oh, I wish we could run things backwards like a movie, so Momma would come backwards out of the kitchen, turn around just after Dad had snapped at her so I can say,—look here, Momma, he can't even spot the nine of hearts, can't see that card exposed right here under his nose. But the reason I said nothing then is the same reason I put up with your dumb shit talk—I was waiting right then for him to come out and push me in that swing he had rigged up in a big oak in the side yard. Oh, he would push me so high that I'd leave my breath up there in the leaves. You push me high like that sometimes, but I know better to trust your opinion about plumbing. Do you follow me? I have picked up on a few points.

So, we've made some gains, maybe—but it's still swing time; and I'm the tree. That story you told me the other night about that girl changing into a tree to escape Apollo, was it? You like those corny plots, old time gods chasing girls into trees and you recite them to me as if they prove something about us—you almost get teary with the telling of it. How romantic, how wonderfully sad it was that the gods felt sorry for the girl and changed her into this tree so as to escape Apollo and it was a laurel tree—that's right, a laurel tree—so all the heroes got to wear her leaves around their heads ever after. But why did she have to become a tree at all? Why didn't Apollo leave her alone in the first place? Why didn't the gods change him into something—say, a rock or a stump?

Dad is here to help me move my furniture. The new suite arrived on Friday. He doesn't so much move as be a pivot. Billy's away with his wilderness group and don't be hurt that I didn't call you to give me a hand—I thought of it, believe me—but Dad needs some activity, some rolling up the sleeves to look things over.—What do you call that? he said yesterday. That's a lamp, I said. But before that, he went on. Well, I guess it was one of those Russian samovars, I replied. To make tea in. And he steps back to squint at it.

It's the most he can do these days—that stepping back for a second, incredulous look—to evaluate my way of doing things. He took the divorce harder than I or even Billy have. When I divorced David, I deprived Dad of a companion in disbelief, a fellowship in shirt sleeves —the two of them turning to each other and saying, Just what in hell is she up to now? United Chums and I'm something from the Third World to shake their heads over. What's the offer? Sovereignty? Is that it? My own flag and certain trade rights?

"Boom-la!" Dad says. He's just uncovered the King of Hearts that he's needed for several hands. Now he shifts the Queen of Clubs over and that uncovers the Ace of Diamonds, the last bullet.

"You're going to win it, Dad." I'm losing you—tell me the truth. I can smell it on you like rain coming. You're telling me right now about your week's schedule, you're telling me about this problem you have—but all by telephone. You used to appear on my doorstep with your problem, like the paper boy—in fact, you bear some resemblance to the paper boy or maybe I think of you bringing me the bad news along with the good. I'm always saying or doing things that shock you and I guess that's my appeal because you feel free to do and say what you had always wanted to say back in the sixth grade, and it tickles you that I know all those words, and that it's okay to say them to someone who looks like me: a Mom and a vice-president.

But it's the words beyond those I want to use and that bothers all of you; that would make it all come out right, card for card. Maybe I don't like where I'm living either, and I have a whole bunch of numbers to memorize just to get through doors that ought to be open to me around the clock—but that's the way you like to do things for my security, you say, but is it for mine or yours? Just to walk through the same door, even together, is not the limit of my aspiration. But, I prefer it to being given my own door on the other side. Sovereignty is no guarantee of equality.

"It's not the same thing," I tell Dad. I just caught him shuffling the last of his playing cards. "You have to play them as they come out."

He needs one card to clear the board, win the game, and it's the ten of hearts—he can see it in the pack and he's started to shuffle the cards to get it to come up on top. I've ruined it for him, handed back to him the rules of solitaire he taught me, and I can see he's a little angry to be caught out.

"Damn it, look at that," he says. He's gone through the same set of cards several times, and the red ten stays in the same place—one card from the top, one card away from freeing up the rest of them.

"I'm sorry, Dad," I say as you're saying these things to me across the wire that stretches taut from the wall when I lean across his shoulder.

Tenderloin black and blue. A bottle of 1978 Bordeaux. And this problem of yours that is getting bigger by the minute. Yes, I am tempted. But I'm tantalized by something else, which is what I've been trying to say to you all along

"Do it again, Dad. Try a new game." He's been grimly obeying the rule I have reminded him of. The ten of hearts just stays where it is in the pack, to be seen but never played out. It never gets clear between us either even though we keep turning it over and over and you think these highs you push me to are the solution—that I like them so much somehow puts us on the same level or I'll go along with the rest. Like I'm on your side.

But as the lady said, *I find this frenzy insufficient reason/For conversation when next we meet.* Can you imagine Edna St. Vincent Millay being changed into a tree? Not on your tin-type or me either. But all the time, I see something that's never played out if we go by the rules. I keep seeing it just under the top card—always there teasing me to turn the same ones over, time and again, which is why I'm more than willing to play with you because I hope one of these games will come out right sometime; that red ten will come free—will set us both free.

But not tonight. And I don't know when either. Maybe, never. You don't like to hear that. You say you love me but that scares me a little. But a lady can change her mind. That's one of those rules the United Chums have passed for the benefit of us in the Third World to make us feel equal. It comes with our sovereignty—we're allowed to change our minds. It's expected of us. Like some of the other natives being slow in the sun.

"Those are the rules you taught me, Dad," I say. He mumbles something under his breath but slowly scoops all the cards up, starts to shuffle the whole deck together. He was only about nine or ten cards from winning. I'm hanging up now. Enjoy your steak and the St. Emilion. I'm getting out the other deck of cards and we'll see how we do doubled up. Maybe it will come out right. Thanks for calling.

Getting It Right

Wendy Lesser

I first saw "Picture Perfect" as a manuscript turned in to a Creative Writing class. It was not my class (I rarely teach, and never Creative Writing), but that of Leonard Michaels, who has been a consulting editor to *The Threepenny Review* since its first or second year. Lenny has spotted some of my best discoveries for me: it was he, for instance, who found Natalie Kusz and Sigrid Nunez, both of whom went on to win General Electric/ Younger Writer Awards for their work in *Threepenny*. Sometimes I don't like the work Lenny unearths for me, but more often I do, and I always read it with care, because I trust his sensibility. His sensibility as a reader consists in large part of admiring even those writers who do not share his sensibility as an author. This is valuable, to him as a teacher and to me as an editor.

Leigh Anne Jones, I was told, had never been published before. She did not know that I was looking at this story for *The Threepenny Review*; she had not, for that matter, heard of *The Threepenny Review*. But I could explain all this after I read the story.

I knew by the second paragraph that this was the work of a talented writer. I think the specific sentence that clued me in was: "Herculeans took strangely empty flash photos of the flaws in their lives, to show the insurance company or the manufacturer or the small-claims court: a dented fender, a pitched windowsill, a cracked driveway." It was not only the idea of taking pictures of "flaws in their lives" that appealed to me, but the cadence of the sentence–the way the three parts of the sentence themselves fell into triplets (Herculeans/photos/flaws, insurance companies/ manufacturer/court, fender/windowsill/driveway). This, I could tell, was a fiction writer with a poet's ear–just what I'm always looking for.

I didn't decide to accept the story, though, until I had read it all the way through. Talented young writers are often talented at ruining their own stories; even people with excellent ears introduce sentimental plot lines or silly final remarks. But in this case the story just kept getting more interesting and stronger as it went along. When I got to the end, I had one minor complaint–a final sentence that was in the first draft but is no longer there. (I think she had Laurie picking up a bridal magazine and settling down for a good read, or some such thing.) But I don't feel hesitant about asking authors to cut final sentences. You'd be surprised how many really good writers add on something false: even Paul Bowles did it once and, when I queried him, agreed that he had only added it after the rest of the story was written and that it indeed deserved to be cut. So I almost assume that a certain percentage of the stories I accept will need to have their final sentences cut. (Either that, or their opening paragraphs, which are sometimes in the nature of authorial throat-clearing.) But, aside from that, "Picture Perfect" seemed to me perfect. I asked Lenny Michaels for Leigh Anne's phone number so I could call her with the good news.

You would think that would be the end of it: Younger Writer hears from Benevolent Editor; Younger Writer expresses thrills and gratitude; Benevolent Editor publishes story. But no. Leigh Anne Jones knew her worth. Or perhaps doubted it. When I called her to tell her that her teacher had passed the story along to me, and that I was graciously deigning to publish it in my magazine, she sounded hesitant. Not negative, not rejecting, not even suspicious–just hesitant. It wasn't that she wanted more money for the story, or that she wanted to send it to a fancier place. I, rushing in where angels fear to tread, suggested that if she didn't feel right giving the story to this unknown (to her) quarterly, maybe she should send it first to *The New Yorker*. I believe my interior monologue went something like, "Let her get a little taste of rejection first. *Then* she'll be grateful, the wretch." But Leigh Anne Jones declined that, too. (I was beginning to feel I was dealing with Bartleby the Scrivener.) It turned out that she simply felt the story wasn't yet ready for publication.

"I've been working on it since I turned it in to Professor Michaels," she eventually said. "Do you want to see the new draft? I could send it to you when it's finished."

"Fine," I practically snapped. "Send it to me when it's ready." *So let her stew*, I thought.

But I was the one who did the stewing. Weeks passed, and I still didn't have a new draft of the story. I complained to Lenny; he told her that she really should get a copy to me; she promised she would. Nothing.

Then, finally, a second draft arrived. It wasn't very different from the first: it was about the same length, it followed roughly the same sequence of events, it had all the same characters. It even had the last line cut, as I had recommended. But it wasn't the story I had accepted. Throughout the story, in sentence after sentence, Leigh Ann Jones had smoothed out her own quirks. She had tried to make everything seem more continuous, less jerky, more cause-and-effect, less happenstance. She had introduced a lot of "because" and "meanwhile" clauses. And in doing so, she had ruined her story. Or, let us say, she had ruined the story *I* wanted for *The Threepenny Review.*

I called her up to plead with her.

"But *why* is the first version better?" she asked.

I tried to explain that the first version, for me, echoed Laurie's way of thinking, and that one of the things that made the story work was Laurie's peculiarly disconnected relation to the idea of cause-and-effect. To introduce linear logic into the narrative voice, therefore, violated the character of Laurie, made it less her story. It also made it sound a lot more like other people's stories—well written still, but much less quirky and original. I invoked Flannery O'Connor, Eudora Welty, Leonard Michaels himself, in the effort to get Leigh Anne to appreciate the virtues of quirky narration.

"All right," she finally agreed. "But send me back my original version so I can see what it is you want to publish."

"I'll make a copy today; you'll have it tomorrow," I said. (At the time Leigh Anne lived in Oakland, just a few miles from my office.)

"No, send me the original," she said.

At this *I* became quirky and insistent. "No," I said. "I want to hold onto the original, so I can compare it with what you send back. I want to make sure I'm getting the same story I accepted." We were like battling parents in a custody fight, each treasuring the object of our shared desire, each insisting on our rights.

"But I don't like the idea of your having a story I'm not sure I like."

"I promise you," I said, "I won't publish it without your permission. You have the final say. But just let me hold onto the original."

"All right," she finally, grudgingly, conceded.

Again, weeks passed, this time mounting into months. Sometime during this period Leigh Anne graduated from Berkeley and received a fellowship to the Iowa Writers Workshop. She relocated to Iowa City. Still no story appeared, nor any letter or phone call permitting me to publish it.

"When are you going to bring out Leigh Anne's story?" Lenny asked me one day.

"As soon as she tells me I can," I answered irately.

Lenny got on the phone. Two days later, the story arrived–the original version, the one I wanted. But with it came another note of hesitation. The cover letter read:

> Here is my permission to publish the story "Photo Girl," also known as "Picture Perfect," in whatever form you choose, so long as any changes, omissions, or additions you make are faithful to my overall intentions.

> I hope Lenny told you that I submitted it to my workshop here and everyone hated it. No one said anything positive. The teacher called the character "a stick figure, a cartoon . . . totally psychologically impenetrable." I want to publish the story now, not so much to "show them" as to achieve some sort of equilibrium and closure. It might be a dumb thing for me to do, under the circumstances, but I really can't see why you would agree to publish it if it isn't *any* good.

In a P.S., Leigh Anne added: "The guy who taught the workshop especially hated the 'hula dancer' bit, which I had taken out once before and put back in because you liked it. He said it feminized Marty in such a way that no woman could be attracted to Marty."

I won't bother to quote you the "hula dancer" bit–you'll recognize it yourself when you read the story. And I hope that when you do, you'll see that it's a wonderful piece of description, capturing not just the character of Marty himself but also Laurie's perceptions of him. As to whether "no woman" could be attracted to a man who made that particular gesture: Aside from wondering what nationwide (or perhaps international) survey this teacher had performed to come up with this conclusion, I'd want to point out just how tenuous Laurie's attraction to Marty is. And I'd want to suggest that part of what makes Laurie a complicated, interesting character (not a "stick figure" or a "cartoon") is her capacity to notice and characterize a rather offputting detail like that, and *still* want to view Marty as a potential figure in a romance.

But don't get me started on what's wrong with writing schools, and how they try to train all the originality and quirkiness and true literary ability out of their otherwise talented students. Suffice to say that when I eventually published the story, Leigh Anne Jones got letters from agents and editors across the country. So I was right. But I would have been right about this story even if subsequent events had not vindicated me. And so would Leigh Anne have been: her first take, however weird, was the right one, and she only needed to learn to trust herself. *That's* the point.

Picture Perfect

Leigh Anne Jones

Laurie worked at the Picture-Perfect One-Hour Photo Lab and Mini Portrait Studio in Hercules, California, and she could tell a lot about a person after only two or three rolls of film. Hercules took its name from the old dynamite factory that once graced its low hills, but at twenty-three Laurie was older than the town. Interstate 80 laced the neck of the place, and in the pink of early morning the townspeople parceled out to nearby oil refineries and offices in San Francisco. A commuter's drive to the city could take more than an hour. It was a bedroom community with a long hall.

The people of Hercules tended not to do very much out of the ordinary, or if they did, they didn't take pictures of it. Or if they did, they didn't have their film processed at Picture-Perfect. Laurie saw mostly new babies, vacations, weddings, proms, graduations, and birthday parties, with an occasional baseball game, car show, stag party or deer-hunting expedition thrown in for variety. Herculeans took strangely empty flash photos of the flaws in their lives, to show the insurance company or the manufacturer or the small-claims court: a dented fender, a pitched windowsill, a cracked driveway. The local police and highway patrol supplied more gruesome images from accident scenes. Only once in a great while were there pictures so out-of-the-ordinary that Laurie's imagination was forced to create a context.

There were business customers, too, who had accounts with the store: real estate appraisers who took pictures of property; a baker who took pictures of her cakes; a corrupt building contractor who took pictures of half-framed tract houses and bragged to Laurie about cheating on his income tax. One of these business accounts was held by Marty Gallo, who worked for the state as a demolitions expert. He brought in pictures of bombs and guns and firecracker caches he'd confiscated. He knew all about Molotov cocktails. When Laurie started working at Picture-Perfect, her boss Marlene had warned her that Marty was so gruff he was almost rude, and that he never made eye contact. But Laurie had not found this to be the case at all.

Marty almost always came in on Thursday afternoons and occasionally on Tuesdays, but lately he had been coming in most any day of the week except Sunday, when Picture-Perfect was closed. Today was a Tuesday and sure enough, around four o'clock Laurie saw a late-model white sedan pull into the parking lot. Down the counter, out the window, Laurie watched the driver exit the vehicle, noticing, as the car door opened, the seal of the state of California affixed thereto. Marty's thick shoulders rose above the horizon as he strode toward the store. Halfway there he hooked his hands over his belt and tucked his shirttails in with the backs of his thumbs. He spread his hands out to his hips, fanning his fingers over the lip of his slacks like a hula dancer, then hiked the pants up gently. It was a subtle gesture common in self-made men.

Bells rang when he pushed the Picture-Perfect door open against the nap of the steel-blue carpet. He started to smile even before his eyes met Laurie's. He did not place any film canisters on the counter, nor bid her fetch his finished order with a clipped delivery of his surname. Instead he said, "I hoped you would be here."

Laurie worked nine to six every day except Thursday and Sunday, when the store was closed.

"Here I am," she said.

They made small talk. "Do you live in Hercules?" Marty asked her.

"No, I live in Pinole."

"Pin-hole? You live in *Pin-hole?"* he said, teasing her.

Laurie smiled patiently. It was an old joke.

Marty cleared his throat. "Well, I was thinking. Every few months we blow up a building, for practice, like a barn or something. We have food, beer, and stuff. It's usually pretty fun."

"It sounds like fun."

"Well, that's what I was thinking. I was wondering if maybe you'd want to come the next time we do it."

"That would be great," Laurie said. She tried to make her eyes sparkle.

"Good, good." Marty was grinning. "Well, I'll just have to let you know then. I'll just let you know when it is then, the next time we have one."

"Great."

Laurie felt hyper as she snapped on a synthetic white glove and extracted a yard-long curl of brown film from the processor. First she thought about Marty and then she thought about love. Laurie thought about love all the time. She wanted to be in love. She had read *Romeo and Juliet* but that wasn't her idea of an ideal love at all. People going around killing themselves. Why didn't Juliet just leave? Besides, you don't really know who you're going to love forever when you're fourteen, anyway.

Maybe that was an Italian ideal of love, *Romeo and Juliet,* but it didn't seem like an American ideal of love. In America, for people to go around killing themselves, there usually needs to be a third person involved. It has to be a case of cheating or unrequited love.

If Laurie went out with Marty, they might fall in love. Maybe Marty would be able to make a magic leap into the realm of specialness that Laurie knew existed. But even if that happened, especially if that happened, there would come a day when he would demand satisfaction.

How could Laurie ever tell Marty that she was a virgin? It was all very complicated. She wasn't religious or anything. Of course, there was also AIDS and herpes and VD, and all that business about when you sleep with someone, you're sleeping with everyone else that person had ever slept with. Laurie didn't think she could trust anyone enough to tell her the truth about all the people they had slept with. Any man who had been in the military, for example, had probably slept with a prostitute–though he wouldn't admit it. So in that sense, she was afraid. Besides, even without sleeping with anyone, Laurie felt particularly susceptible to sex diseases.

Plus she wanted the first time to be memorable, nothing she would regret later. But each of the men she had gone out with had disturbed or embarrassed her somehow. She didn't know how to meet a nice guy. Laurie's boss Marlene's husband was an umpire for an adult softball league, and once Marlene had invited Laurie to a game when there would be a picnic afterward. Laurie might have met some men there, but what on earth would she say to them? "No, I'm not on one of the teams, I just work for Len Osborne's wife at the photo store in the Town and Country Shopping Center." Oh, that would go over great, wouldn't it? In other words, I have no business being here. I'm just on the prowl. They'd think I was some kind of praying mantis.

Although she felt funny about being a virgin, in the sense that no one else seemed to be–not that she discussed it with anyone, of course–Laurie didn't feel bad about it. She had read articles in magazines about other women's sex lives, both celebrities and regular people, and some of their experiences were so horrible and pathetic. At least I don't have something like that to be ashamed of, Laurie figured. The worst part was probably knowing that the older she got, the more nervous she would be the first time, wondering if the man knew, and not wanting him to think there was something wrong with her because she had never done it before now.

Now with Marty, if they did sleep together, she knew she wouldn't tell him she was a virgin, but he would probably figure it out since she wouldn't know what she was doing. But if somehow they could get past that difficulty, then everything might work out. They would probably get married, and she could have a small, tasteful wedding.

As Laurie unlocked the front door of her apartment, the telephone was ringing. She slammed the door and dropped her bag on the floor and ran across the room. Laurie stopped in front of the little telephone table and listened. The dull green rotary phone whirred mildly. She had not actually answered her telephone in three years. After four rings the answering machine dutifully picked up. "This is seven four one, one five one seven," Laurie's voice murmured. She included her phone number in the outgoing message as a courtesy to those who misdialed. "At the tone, please leave a message of no more than one minute in length." Laurie concentrated, closed her eyes, held her breath, and cocked her ear toward the machine. She kept the speaker volume turned down low, so the neighbors couldn't hear her messages through the thin walls. But after the beep came a sonorous dial tone; the caller had hung up. Was it someone she knew? Or just a wrong number? Laurie couldn't think who it might be.

But Laurie didn't let the disappointment set her back. Instead, she changed into her Tasmanian Devil sleepshirt and a pair of purple leggings, nuked dinner, turned on the TV, and grabbed her comforter off the bed. Her comforter was printed in a pattern called "mille fleur" and it showed bouquets of bright flowers against a champagne-colored background. Laurie had studied French in high school, so she knew what *mille fleur* meant. She had a Smurfs comforter, too, but she would probably have to get rid of it if she and Marty got married. She knelt beside her bed and pulled out two armfuls of bridal magazines from underneath it, then carried them, thick and glossy, over to the loveseat. With the TV dial in reach, her yankee pot roast steaming on the coffee table, Laurie burrowed into a warm space between the cirrus folds of her comforter and the welcoming paunch of the loveseat. She arranged her bridal magazines in careful ramparts around her and settled in to an evening.

When she came to a dress she liked, she carefully pulled the page from the magazine. With just the right amount of pressure, it wouldn't tear. She filled out a bridal questionnaire, too. She wasn't sure if her entertaining style was formal or casual, since she'd never invited anyone over to her apartment. She guessed casual. In the backs of the magazines she found postcards to fill out and send away for catalogues from manufacturers of household goods and the inevitable china, crystal and silver.

She filled out a handful of them and popped them in the mail drop outside, in bare feet.

Around eight o'clock Laurie heard her neighbor Rob's key turn in his door. She jumped up and moved over to the wall, next to her kitchen window. This was a little ritual for her, and pretty soon she began to hear voices.

First came Monique, Rob's new (and soon-to-be-old, Laurie decided) girlfriend. She wanted to know why Rob hadn't returned her last message, and she wondered if maybe his machine hadn't recorded it for some reason, so she was leaving another message, just in case. "Don't beg, Monique," Laurie thought. Laurie felt sorry for Monique. She seemed like a nice enough girl– just naive and too insecure for being as attractive as she undoubtedly was. She'd probably been a late bloomer. Laurie felt certain she was a petite blond, unlike Rob's last girlfriend, Desiree. Laurie had called her the Catwoman, and thought she must be quite tall and have dark hair, a deep tan with dark freckles, and very long fingernails. She had a husky voice that made Laurie think she had been a cheerleader in high school, and she seemed like the kind of woman who wore tube tops and cuffed tennis shorts with high heels. She still left messages now and again, and unlike most of his girlfriends, *she* had broken up with him. On the machine, no less! That was a good one.

The next caller didn't identify himself, just said hurriedly, "You got anything? Call me." That was a drug connection. Laurie knew Rob wasn't a dealer, exactly, but he procured for friends in a pinch. The last call was Rob's mother, who identified herself half the time as "Dorothy," the rest of the time as "Mom." This had been a little confusing to Laurie at first. Dorothy explained that the cops had come around looking for Dan, Rob's brother, but she didn't know why. Dan was nothing but trouble, as far as Laurie could see. The last time Dan had left a message had been to ask for a $300 loan–not that Laurie thought he'd ever pay it back. Rob might cross the border of legality now and again, but at least he had a job as a salesman at Circuit City– and wore a suit to work every day.

Laurie knew that listening to Rob's messages should be ethically troubling to her, but it wasn't. She really couldn't see how there was any harm in it. After all, she couldn't help but hear the messages, they came right through the wall. She didn't want to do anything with the information, like blackmail Rob or something. It was just something she did for fun. Rob hardly recognized her enough to say hello in the hall, and that was fine by Laurie.

Someone knocked at the door and Laurie stood perfectly still. It was a simple knock, three raps. Nothing threatening in that, really, but she couldn't quite bring herself to answer. She certainly wasn't expecting anyone. Whoever it was, if she opened the door there was sure to be an awkward conversation. Someone wanting to borrow something, to use the phone; a travelling salesman, a child selling candy, someone to help her register to vote. She didn't want to see any of those people. She was sure that, no matter who it might be, no one truly *needed* to talk to her. She thought about shouting "Go away," but she didn't want to seem eccentric. She tiptoed to the door as quietly as she could and peered through the peephole. A handsome man she didn't recognize stood before her, waiting, then swiftly bent over for no apparent reason. It struck Laurie as suspicious. Was he pressing his ear against the door, trying to hear if she was inside? She couldn't see that far down, through the peephole. Maybe he was picking the lock. Laurie's heart beat faster and she wondered what she ought to do. She put her hand around the doorknob, to make sure it stayed locked. Suddenly, she felt a wispy pressure on her foot and half screamed as she jumped sideways, bumping against the door. Frantically, she pressed her eye against the peephole, only to find the circle darkened by the man's own eye. She jerked her head away from the door in fear, then heard footsteps as he walked away. She slumped against the door and panted, her hand still gripped around the doorknob. Down at her feet, she saw an envelope resting lightly over her toes. It was a notice from the new building manager, listing his name and phone number, and mentioning that the driveway would be repaved the following week.

That night Laurie dreamed that she and Marty were lying on her bed, with their clothes on, and Marty was lying perpendicular to Laurie, with his head on her stomach. The funny thing is he held her foot in his big hand, and he was stroking the arch of her foot with his forefinger. It was a delicious feeling, very natural and not scary at all. In the dream, the roof of Laurie's apartment was a skylight, and together Laurie and Marty stared up at the night sky. "Look," Marty said, pointing to a constellation, "there's Marilyn." Because in the dream there was an actual constellation of stars called Marilyn Monroe, and if you traced over the stars it looked like Marilyn in her halter dress standing over the blower grate. And Laurie felt exhilarated, like the goddess of love had given them her blessing.

The next day at work Laurie hoped against hope that Marty would show up, but he didn't. It was stupid to expect him to come again so soon, Laurie knew. How much photo work could one person have? Linda Wendell did come, with her two annoying children. She had an eight-year-old daughter named Brianne who talked with a baby lisp. The kid kept her tongue stuck in the front of her mouth, flaccid against her lower lip, so that every word she spoke had to limp across the awkward threshold, aspirated and soggy. She always had a sticky film of red and brown at the corners of her mouth, sometimes with a faint down of lint over it.

Dangling like a coat hanger, her stringy arms tangled around her mother's dimpled elbow, Brianne would roll her spine until her chest slumped against the display case, her narrow butt angled out, knees locked like a flamingo, and roll her head around until the base of her skull rested on her back. Staring up at her mother with big, dull cow eyes, her mouth slack and her tongue hanging out, she began to bleat.

"Mommy, thath a litthle kidth camera ri-there," she said thickly, disengaging one thin arm to point a drooping finger.

"Yes, Brianne," her mother said, not looking.

"Can. . . nigh. . . av. . . vit?" Brianne whined, using her mother's arm as a brace from which to sway side to side. Behind Brianne, her brother Trent, insolent and thirteen, lounged unnecessarily against the photocopy machine as if it were a pool table.

Laurie's eyes narrowed with ill will.

"Not right now," Linda said, digging around in her leather sling purse for her roll of film. Finally, she thrust it on the counter, and continued to dig in her purse for a few moments more, mysteriously, before giving up. Laurie picked up the film, and just before she stuck it in the envelope noticed a fingerprint on the canister etched in chocolate. She thrust it into the bag with distaste and when she looked up, she saw Trent sitting on top of the photocopy machine.

"Please don't sit there. That's a very expensive machine," Laurie said, forcing a courtesy that pained her. Linda Wendell didn't even turn around to look. She was staring at a flier posted over Laurie's head.

"How much is your portrait package?"

"Twenty-nine ninety-five," Laurie reported, knowing that it was printed on the flier in two-inch type. "One eight-by-ten, two five-by-sevens, eight wallet-size." Marlene always said she lost money on the deal, but it brought in new business.

"Oh, that's great. I'll have to come in with these guys when I get some of this weight off. I haven't always been this big. You should have seen me two years ago. You'd never recognize me if you'd known me then." More than just fat, Linda had fuzzy, overbleached hair and dark patches around her eyes and mouth, like tea stains.

Laurie smiled and nodded. Working the counter, she sometimes imagined herself as one of those dogs with bobbing heads people prop up in the back window of their car.

When Linda and her entourage left, Laurie moved quickly to process the roll. Laurie didn't like Linda, but she liked to look at her pictures.

Without any effort whatsoever, Linda had become a reasonably rich woman, because her husband had something to do with computers that was very lucrative. He had built some kind of thing, or knew how to fix some kind of thing, and had these big contracts or something, Laurie couldn't remember exactly. But in the manner of Americans everywhere who worship the source of their wealth, they had a huge computer keyboard painted at the bottom of their swimming pool. Their large house was filled with reproduction 1950s memorabilia, and they threw lavish pool parties at which Linda, with her frizzed hair and ill-fitting loungewear, never looked completely at ease.

This roll was especially interesting because there was an attractive, darkhaired woman in a turquoise jumpsuit who turned up in four different shots talking to Linda's husband Dale, including one in which she was sitting on the same lawn chair as Dale. It wasn't difficult to figure out what was going on. But maybe not. After all, Dale wasn't such a prize himself, and Laurie believed in the sanctity of marriage. But no—the definitive shot reared its ugly head. There sat the dark-haired woman on Dale's lap, of all places, both of them laughing, and though it was hard to make out, it seemed to Laurie that the dark-haired woman had Dale's left nipple clenched between her thumb and index finger. Laurie tried to imagine the sort of poolside banter that could lead to such a pose, but failed. Linda was also in the picture, but only a small figure at the far end of the pool, holding a towel out toward a dripping and shivering Brianne.

There was another picture of Brianne with her hair curled, standing in the doorway of the bathroom, and you could tell it was a total pigsty behind her. There were towels all over the floor, and the counter around the sink was totally covered with health and beauty products, including a shrink-wrapped set of three boxes of Miss Clairol that Linda had probably bought at Price Club. Laurie couldn't figure out why, with all her money, Linda insisted on bleaching her own hair. Laurie figured Linda had started in high school and just didn't know enough to have it done at a salon.

After Linda's roll Laurie did two rolls of the Maldonado family at Disneyland, then a stag party. The stag party pictures would have been much more interesting if the photographer had managed to stay sober. Instead the pictures were rather impressionistic, and included one blurred close-up of a single breast.

Just before closing, Marlene, Laurie's boss, stopped by unexpectedly, as usual. She sat in the back room smoking her narrow women's cigarettes and while Laurie shut down the machines she talked about her life. Marlene thought she treated Laurie like a daughter. She talked about the business, her marriage, her early years. Sometimes she took out her frustrations on Laurie in bitchiness. But Laurie didn't complain. If she had stopped to notice, Marlene would have maintained that her bitching didn't bother Laurie, that Laurie took it all in stride. That Laurie understood. Because whenever Marlene was mean to Laurie, Laurie didn't say a word. She just took it out in merchandise.

If Marlene said something snide, Laurie would take a small item, like a lens cleaning cloth or a dust blower. Rudeness called for a roll of film or two, which went promptly into the vegetable bin in the refrigerator at home, waiting for the day when Laurie could afford to buy a good camera. When Marlene made Laurie's life miserable, it was a leather photo album, for which Laurie secured a steady supply of individual replacement pages in bitter little increments.

Laurie didn't feel bad about taking the stuff because Marlene got lots of products off-price from Mexico somehow, just before or after they were due to expire, and in this way she ripped off the customers. The one-hour photos and portraits were top quality, but the rest of the stock was real iffy. Laurie didn't like selling the stuff. She felt embarrassed when people returned the dead batteries, and tried to replace them with a fresher vintage. The film seemed to print okay, though, and no one seemed to mind that the box said "pelicula."

After work Laurie tried to recreate the happy expectation of the night before, but it didn't work. She was overcome by worries about her impending marriage. All she could think of were the reasons why it wouldn't work. The first time they had sex would be a nightmare. It was unimaginable. Marty would storm off in a fury. He would laugh at her. He would have hair on his back and it would make her sick to her stomach. He wouldn't want to have sex with her because he would think no one else had ever wanted to before, which wasn't true, but how to explain? Who would believe that she had wanted to wait, so that everything would be perfect? Only she had waited so long, she had waited too long. It could never be perfect now.

And that was the least of their problems. She had gotten used to living alone, she had her own routine, and she liked it. Not to mention her bad temper. And what if, deep down, he thought that women weren't as good as men? Or what if he were one of those violent types, and you never knew it at first but by the time you figure it out you're so far in you can't get out?

One out of every three men, Laurie had read. What if he drank too much on Saturday nights and smelled like vomit on Sunday mornings? And all that wasn't counting the diseases. That wasn't even taking the diseases into account.

That night Laurie woke to hear noises coming from Rob's apartment. It sounded like he was moving furniture. Then sometime after 1:00 A.M. Rob's phone rang and Laurie waited, with still expectation, only to feel something like terror when the machine clicked on and she could barely hear it. She couldn't really make out the words at all; Rob had actually moved his answering machine. Laurie couldn't go back to sleep after that.

A few days later Marty came to the store with a lily for Laurie.

"You know who you remind me of?" Marty asked her. She shrugged. "There's this picture of a beautiful girl I saw at the mall. It's a famous painting. I wrote it down." He flipped open his wallet and with thick fingers pulled out a slip of lined paper and showed it to her. *"Broken Pitcher," by Adolphe Bouguereau,* it read. They were alone in the store, and they spoke easily about work, his truck, her idea about taking classes at community college. In a low voice, he said, "You have beautiful hair. Did anyone ever tell you that?" It made Laurie uncomfortable, but his voice felt warm. She didn't like her hair ever since she had gotten a spiral perm. She thought the spiral made her hair look like Top Ramen. But before she could answer, he stretched his arm across the span of the counter to where she stood and brushed his fingertips along her hair gently, once.

All of the muscles in Laurie's face locked rigid. She pushed with her fingertips hard against the glass top of the display case, rocking backward, away from Marty, until her shoulder blades pressed against the film display. "Thank you," she said automatically, without moving her lips, staring just past him. She knew it was irrational, but she felt violated. A single phrase reverberated wildly in her head: Don't touch me. Don't touch me. Don't touch me.

He made no move to leave—he didn't even seem to be aware of his transgression. Laurie felt feverish and panicky. She wished simultaneously that he would sense how upset she was, that he would get it, and that he wouldn't notice at all, because she didn't want to embarrass him. She desperately tried to think of a way to get rid of him. Finally she said, "I have to print a roll now. You should probably go."

"Okay," Marty said. "I'll see you later."

Laurie smiled and nodded with strange energy until he left. She made sure he was out of the parking lot, then shut down the machines and started to cry. He had ruined everything. They had been going along fine until now. God! It could have been so perfect. So perfect.

After work, Laurie stopped at Hilltop Mall. She went to the poster shop and found the Bouguereau print in the fine arts bin. She bought it.

At home, in the mail, a long, slim box waited for her. It was addressed

"To the New Bride." The return address was "Butler Cutlery." Inside was a Free Gift, a serrated bread knife. She turned it over in the palm of her hand.

In the kitchen she sat down at the table for a while. She heard Rob next door come in and she stood up automatically and moved to the wall. But the dim voices only reminded her that he had moved the answering machine. Her eyes filled with tears. She moved over to the wall and pressed her ear against it, but she just heard a loud vibration, from the refrigerator, she supposed. She moved along the wall to where the voices were loudest. She tried listening through a glass held against the wall but it didn't work. Now the tears began to spill.

The messages ended and after a time, long enough for him to shower, shave and change clothes, Rob left. She heard his deadbolt, substantial, slide into its cavity.

Laurie walked from the wall to the kitchen table and back again. She looked at the opened box on the table, torn flaps of corrugated cardboard, and the serrated bread knife she had received in the mail. She picked it up and ran her forefinger across the blade, to judge its sharpness. Then she turned and thrust the blade over her shoulder into the wall. The knife stabbed right in through the soft sheetrock, and she sawed it down jaggedly, in a more or less straight line. The knife went in easier than it pulled out, and she had to step to the side to keep from hitting herself in the eye with her fist as she jerked it back. After sawing down about nine or ten inches, she pulled the knife out and punched it back in at a ninety-degree angle. She continued this way until she had carved a box. She tapped the loosened square of sheetrock with the blunt handle of the knife until it tipped, and she tugged it out by its corner. With her bare hands she pulled out big puffs of fiberglass insulation, like pink tulle, and stuffed it all into a garage bag. Through the hole she could see studs and the back of Rob's own sheetrock wall.

Laurie felt a sudden nervousness, staring at the big gaping hole in her kitchen wall. She wondered how she would explain it to the new building manager if he ever came inside her apartment. She washed her hands twice and remembered the Bouguereau print. She unrolled it over the hole and tacked its four corners up. When she stepped back, the hole was invisible. She sat down again and pressed her wet palms to her forehead.

Rob's phone rang then. Laurie heard the beep and then the message began. "Rob, it's Monique," the voice said. Laurie could hear it perfectly. She sighed with relief and satisfaction. The print looked good, it looked like her. It was about time for something new in the apartment, a change.

The Making of the Pulitzer Prize
Staige D. Blackford

One hot summer day in 1990 between the publication of my spring issue and the preparation of my fall issue, I was making my weekly journey through the pile of unsolicited manuscripts. My usual practice is to go through the unsolicited stories and sort out those that seem to have some merit and then send them on to volunteer outside readers of whom I have four, all fiction writers themselves, and all unpaid. That's one nice thing about having the Hoynes Fellowship Program at the University of Virginia, and it is also nice that so many writers have chosen to live in Charlottesville.

On this particular day, and in this particular case, however, I came across a story from a writer in Louisiana of whom I had never heard. The story gripped me from the opening paragraph which began with the very simple sentence, "I like the way fairy tales start in America," and "Fairy Tale" was the title of the story itself. It was a tale about a Saigon hooker who winds up working as a stripper on Bourbon Street in New Orleans. The character of the stripper, Miss Noi, was enchanting, and her story was as unusual as it was captivating. I didn't bother to send it to any outside readers, and I scheduled it right away for publication in my autumn 1990 issue. Every now and then a story comes along that you know has got it. You don't know exactly why. It is a matter of instinct I guess. I just knew "Fairy Tale" was an extraordinary story.

As it turned out, I was right. In November 1990 shortly after "Fairy Tale" was published, my Advisory Board met to make its annual selection of the best published short story and best published poem to appear in the journal during the past calendar year for selection as the winner of the Emily Clark Balch Prize, a prize the *VQR* has been giving since the mid 1950's. In those years it has acquired quite a bit of prestige. Sometimes the Board deliberates for hours before making a choice, but in the case of "Fairy Tale," it deliberated for about five minutes before naming Robert Olen Butler's story winner of the 1990 Balch Prize. "Fairy Tale" later appeared in a collection of stories assembled by Mr. Butler and published by Henry Holt called *A Good Scent From a Strange Mountain.* That collection became the first short story collection to win a Pulitzer Prize since the collected stories of John Cheever, Mr. Butler receiving the Pulitzer in the spring of 1993. On April 10, 1993, I received a letter from Bob Butler, and it read:

> "Dear Staige, it was a very great pleasure speaking with you yesterday. I look forward to meeting you someday. Without you and the *VQR* I don't think *A Good Scent from a Strange Mountain* would have been as successful a creation as it is. Only a very few of the stories were written when you accepted "Fairy Tale." That was a risky story and I have come to realize that I hung at that moment in the balance between restraint and freedom in the writing of the rest of the book. For you and the *VQR* . . . to accept that story with such enthusiasm freed me utterly for the rest of the work I had to do. My deep and abiding thanks to you."

It's that kind of letter that makes this kind of job worthwhile.

Fairy Tale
Robert Olen Butler

I like the way fairy tales start in America. When I learn English for real, I buy books for children and I read, "Once upon a time." I recognize this word "upon" from some GI who buys me Saigon teas and spends some time with me and he is a cowboy from the great state of Texas. He tells me he gets up on the back of a bull and he rides it. I tell him he is joking with Miss Noi (that's my Vietnam name), but he says no, he really gets up on a bull. I make him explain that "up on" so I know I am hearing right. I want to know for true so I can tell this story to all my friends so that they understand, no lie, what this man who stays with me can do. After that, a few years later, I come to America and I read some fairy tales to help me learn more English and I see this word and I ask a man in the place I work on Bourbon Street in New Orleans if this is the same. Up on and upon. He is a nice man who comes late in the evening to clean up after the men who see the show. He says this is a good question and he thinks about it and he says that yes, they are the same. I think this is very nice, how you get up on the back of time and ride and you don't know where it will go or how it will try to throw you off.

Once upon a time I was a dumb Saigon bargirl. If you want to know how dumb some Vietnam bargirl can be, I can give you one example. A man brought me to America in 1974. He says he loves me and I say I love that man. When I meet him in Saigon, he works in the embassy of America. He can bring me to this country even before he marries me. He says that he wants to marry me and maybe I think that this idea scares me one little bit. But I say, what the hell. I love him. Then boom. I'm in America and this man is different from in Vietnam, and I guess he thinks I am different too. How dumb is a Saigon bargirl is this. I hear him talk to a big crowd of important people in Vietnam, businessman, politician, big people like that. I am there too and I wear my best ao dai, red like an apple and my quan, my silk trousers, are white. He speaks in English to these Vietnam people because they are big, so they know English. Also my boyfriend does not speak Vietnam. But at the end of his speech he says something in my language and it is very important to me.

You must understand one thing about the Vietnam language. We use tones to make our words. The sound you say is important but just as important is what your voice does, if it goes up or down or stays the same or it curls around or it comes from your throat, very tight. These all change the meaning of the word, sometimes very much, and if you say one tone and I hear a certain word, there is no reason for me to think that you mean some other tone and some other word. It was not until everything is too late and I am in America that I realize something is wrong in what I am hearing that day. Even after this man is gone and I am in New Orleans, I have to sit down and try all different tones to know what he wanted to say to those people in Saigon.

He wanted to say in my language, "May Vietnam live for ten thousand years!" What he said, very clear, was, "The sunburnt duck is lying down." Now if I think this man says that Vietnam should live for ten thousand years, I think he is a certain kind of man. But when he says that a sunburnt duck is lying down—boom, my heart melts. We have many tales in Vietnam, some about ducks. I never hear this tale that he is telling us about, but it sounds like it is very good. I should ask him that night what this tale is, but we make love and we talk about me going to America and I think I understand anyway. The duck is not burned up, destroyed. He is only sunburnt. Vietnam women don't like the sun. It makes their skin dark, like the peasants. I understand. And the duck is not crushed on the ground. He is just lying down and he can get up when he wants to. I love that man for telling the Vietnam people this true thing. So I come to America and when I come here I do not know I will be in more bars. I come thinking I still love that man and I will be a housewife with a toaster machine and a vacuum cleaner. Then when I think I don't love him anymore I try one last time and I ask him in the dark night to tell me about the sunburnt duck, what is that story. He thinks I am one crazy Vietnam girl and he says things that can burn Miss Noi more than the sun.

So boom, I am gone from that man. There is no more South Vietnam and he gives me all the right papers so I can be American and he can look like a good man. This is all happening in Atlanta. Then I hear about New Orleans. I am a Catholic girl and I am a bargirl, and this city sounds for me like I can be both those things. I am 25 years old and my titties are small, especially in America, but I am still number one girl. I can shake it baby, and soon I am a dancer in a bar on Bourbon Street and everybody likes me to stay a Vietnam girl. Maybe some men have nice memories of Vietnam girls.

I have nice memories. In Saigon I work in a bar they call Blossoms. I am one blossom. Around the corner I have a little apartment. You have to walk into the alley and then you go up the stairs three floors and I have a place there where all the shouting and the crying and sometimes the gunfire in the street sounds very far away. I do not mix with the other girls. They do bad things. Take drugs, steal from the men. One girl lives next to me in Saigon and she does bad things. Soon people begin to come in a black car. She goes. She likes that, but I do not talk to her. One day she goes in the black car and does not come back. She leaves everything in her place. Even her Buddha shrine to her parents. Very bad. I live alone in Saigon. I have a double bed with a very nice sheet. Two pillows. A cedar closet with my clothes, which are very nice. Three ao dais, one apple red, one blue like you see in the eyes of some American man, one black like my hair. I have a glass cabinet with pictures. My father. Some two or three American men who like me very special. My mother. My son.

Yes, I have a son. One American give me that son, but my boy is living in Vietnam with my mother. My mother says I cannot bring up a child with my life. I say to her that my son should have the best. If Miss

Noi is not best for my son, then my son should be someplace different. When the man brings me to America, he does not want a son either, and my mother does not talk to me very much anyway except to say my son is Vietnam boy, not American boy. At least my mother is my blood, though sometimes she is unhappy about that, I think. I do not think they are happy in Vietnam now, but who can say? You have a mother and then you have a son and then boom, you do not have either a mother or a son, though they are alive somewhere, so I do not have to pray for their souls. I do not have to be unhappy.

I pray in my little room in Saigon. I am a Catholic girl and I have a large statue of Mary in my room. That statue is Mary the mother of God, not Mary Magdalen who was a bargirl one time too. My statue of Mary the mother of God is very beautiful. She is wearing a blue robe and her bare feet are sticking out of the bottom. Her feet are beautiful like the feet of a Vietnam girl, and I pray to Mary and I paint her toenails and I talk to her. She faces the door and does not see my bed.

I sleep with men in Saigon. This is true. But I sleep with only one at a time. I do not take drugs with any man. I do not steal from any man. I give some man love when he is alone and frightened and he wants something soft to be close to him. I take money for this loving, but I do not ask them to take me to restaurants or to movie shows or to buy me jewelry or any gifts. If a girl does not take money but makes him take her to a restaurant and a movie show and buy her jewelry and then gives him loving, is this different? I would not take a man to my room and love him if I did not want to do that. The others could buy me Saigon tea in the Blossoms bar. The men would water the blossoms with Saigon tea. I talk with them and they put their arm around me and play music on the jukebox, but I do not take them to my room unless I would like them to be there. Then they would give me money, but I ask for nothing else. Only when they love me very much I ask them to get me something. In the place where the GI eats, they have something I cannot get in Saigon. This thing is an apple. I only ask for apples. I buy mangoes and papayas and pineapples and other sweet things to eat in the market, but in South Vietnam, an apple is a special thing. I hold an apple and it fills my hand and it is very smooth and very hard and it is red like my favorite ao dai. So red. I bite it and it is very sweet, like sweet water, like a stream of water from a mountain, and it is not stringy like a pineapple, and it is not mushy like a mango or papaya.

In New Orleans I buy many apples. I eat them in America whenever I want to. But is that memory not better? A GI who loves me brings me an apple and I put it on the table where Mary sits and after that man is sleeping and the room is dark, I walk across the floor and I am naked and the air feels cool on me and I take that apple and go to the window and I watch the dark roofs of Saigon and the moon rising and I eat my apple.

In New Orleans, there are apples in the stores and I buy them and I eat too many. The taste is still good but it is not special anymore. I am sometimes very tired. I take off my clothes on the stage of the club. I am not a blossom in New Orleans. I am a voodoo girl. The manager of the club gives me a necklace of bones to wear and the faces of the men are raised to me and I am naked. Many eyes see me. Many men want to touch Miss Noi, and I sleep with men in New Orleans. I still do not take them to my bed if I am not ready to like them. When they get up in the morning I always make sure they shave right. Many of the men miss a place at the back of their jaw or under their bottom lip. I make sure they have a clean shirt. I am ready to wash their shirt if they want me to. But they pay me money and they go, and they do not let me clean their shirt. Sometimes they go before the night is done. These are the men who have wives. I can see the place on their fingers where the sun has tanned around the ring which they took off to come to the bar. Their finger is dark skinned, but the band of flesh is white and they look naked there, even more naked than I must look to them on the stage. Their ring is in some pocket. I worry about their rings. What if the ring is to fall out on my floor and is kicked under the bed? What do they say to their wife when she sees their naked hand?

How does a life change? You meet some man who says he will take you away across the sea and he will marry you. A blossom and even a voodoo girl gets many men who talk about love and some of them talk about marriage. You are very careful about that. Many girls on Bourbon Street tell stories and laugh very hard about the men who say they want to marry them. I do not tell the story about the embassy man and the sunburnt duck. They would not understand. I dance naked on the stage and one night the announcer makes a big deal about Miss Noi being Vietnam girl. Sometimes he does this, sometimes Miss Noi is just some voodoo girl. But this night he sees some men in the audience with jackets on that says they were in Vietnam, so he says I am from Saigon and I am ready to please.

After I dance and put on my clothes and go and sit at the bar, these men in the jackets do not come near me. But one other man comes and stands beside me and he calls me "Miss." He says, "Miss, may I sit down?" If you want to sit next to a bargirl and hope that she will think you are an okay man, this is a good way to start, with "May I sit down, Miss." I look at this man and he is a tall man with a long neck so that he seems to stretch up as high as he can to see over a fence. His skin is dark, like he's been in the sun too long, and he is wearing a plaid shirt and blue jeans and his hands are rough, but there is no white band where a ring has been taken off. I look at his face and his eyes are black, but very small. His nose is long. Vietnam noses are not long and though I know many Americans in my life and some French too, I still lean back just a little when there is a long nose, because it seems to be pointing at me.

This man is not number one for looking at him, but he calls me "Miss" and he stands with his eyes looking down and then he peeks at me and then he lowers his eyes again as he waits for me to say if he can sit down. So I say yes. He seems like a nice man.

"You are very beautiful, Miss Noi," this man says.

This is 1981 and Miss Noi is 30 years old and I am glad to hear some man say it this way. I am not sexy bitch, wiggle it baby, oh boy oh boy it's hot, it feels good. These are okay things, too, for Miss Noi. These men give me money and they love me. But this man says I am beautiful and I say, "Thank you. You buy me a drink, okay?" I say this to all the men who sit next to me at the bar. This is what I am supposed to do. But I want this man to buy me a drink because he thinks I am beautiful. So he buys me a drink and I say he must buy one too and he buys a Dr. Pepper, even though it is the same price as a drink of liquor. My drink is supposed to be liquor but it is mostly water, like Saigon tea. They make it the same in New Orleans, the New Orleans tea.

We sip our drinks and he does not have many words to say. He sips and looks at me and sips and I have many words I use on men. You from this town? You in New Orleans for long? You like Bourbon Street? You listen to jazz music? What is your work? But I do not use these words. I tell you I am sometimes very tired. This man's long nose dips down toward his Dr. Pepper like he's going to drink through it, but it stops and then he lifts his chin a little and sips at his straw. His face seems very strange-looking and his hair is black but a little greasy and I just let him be quiet if he wants and I am quiet too. Then he says, "It was nice to see you dance."

"You come often and see me dance and buy me drinks, okay?"

"You look different," he says.

"Miss Noi is a Vietnam girl. You never see that before."

"I have seen it," this man says. "I was in Vietnam."

I have many men say they were in my country and they always sound a little funny, like they have a nasty secret or a sickness that you should be careful not to catch. And sometimes they just call it "Nam" saying that word with broken glass in their voice or saying it through their noses and their noses wrinkle up like the word smells when it comes out. But this man says the name of my country quiet and I don't always understand what American voices do, but he sounds sad to me. I say to him, "You didn't like being there? It makes you sad?"

He lifts his face and looks at me and he says, "I was very happy there. Weren't you?"

Well, this is something for me to think about. I could just answer this man, who is only one more man who saw me dance naked. I could just say yes or no and I could talk about reasons why. I am good at bargirl bullshit when I want to talk like that. But this man's eyes look at mine and I look away and sip my drink.

What do I know about men, after all? I can't tell anything anymore. I take men to my bed and I save my money and there have been very many men, I guess. It's like eating too many apples. You take a bite now and you can make yourself remember that apples are sweet but it is like the apple in your mouth is not even there. You eat too many apples and all you can do is remember them. So this man who comes with his strange face and sounds sad when he talks about Vietnam because he was so happy there–I don't know what to make of him and so I take him to my room and he is very happy about that.

He tells me his name is Fontenot. He lives far away from New Orleans. He owns a little boat and he works fixing car engines. He was in Saigon one year working on car engines and he loved that city very much. I ask him why but he can't really explain. This is all of our talk, every bit of it, except before he makes love to me he says he is sorry he can never get his hands clean. He shows me how the grease from the car engines gets around his fingernails and he can't get them clean. I tell him not to worry and he makes love to me and when he gets off me and lies down, he turns his head and I think that is because he does not want me to see that he is crying. I want to ask if he is very sad again, but I don't say anything. His face is away from me and he wants it like that and so I say nothing. Those are all the words of that night. In the morning I go into the bathroom and he is in the tub and I kneel beside him and take his hands and I have a cuticle file and I clean the grease away. He kisses my hands when he leaves.

What do I know about men anymore? That is not much to say about Mr. Fontenot. He came to see Miss Noi on a Saturday night and left on Sunday morning. Then the next Saturday night I was naked on the stage and I saw his face at the foot of the runway, looking up with his long nose pointed at my special part and I felt a strange thing. My face got warm and I turned my back to him and danced away. After I finished my dance, I got dressed and came out to the bar, but he was not there. I asked the guy behind the bar, "Did you see that tall man with the thin neck and the long nose that I had a drink with last week?"

This guy says, "The one who looks like a goddam goose?"

I don't like this guy behind the bar. I never even learn his name. So I say, "Go to hell, you," and I go outside and there is Mr. Fontenot waiting on the sidewalk. I go to him and I take his arm and we go around the corner and down the block and he says, "I couldn't hang around in there, Miss Noi. It makes me uncomfortable to talk to you in there."

I say, "I know, honey. I know." I see all types of men, though I realize I don't understand any of them deep down. But I know some men feel nervous in a bar. They come there to meet me but then they tell themselves that I really don't belong there, it's not worthy of me. And if I take this type of man to my room, they give me money quiet, folding the bills and putting them under a vase or somewhere, like it's not really happening. I know that kind of man. They can be very sweet sometimes.

We go up to my apartment again. It is a small place, like Saigon. I am comfortable there. Outside my window is a phony balcony. It looks like a balcony but it is only a foot wide, just a grill on the window. But it is nice. It looks like lace, though it is made of iron. I close the shade and turn to Mr. Fontenot and he is sitting on my bed. I go and sit next to him.

"I've been thinking about you," he says.

"You drive all the way back to New Orleans just to see Miss Noi again?"

"Of course," he says. His voice is gentle, but there's also something in it that says I should know this already. This is plenty strange to me, because I know nothing about Mr. Fontenot, really. A few words. He's a quiet man. I know nothing more about him than any man.

Then he says, "Look," and he shows me his hands. I don't understand. "I got one of those things you used on me last week." I look closer and I see that his hands are clean.

This makes me feel one more strange thing, a little sinking inside me. I say, "See? You have no need for Miss Noi anymore."

He takes me serious. He puts his arm around my shoulders and he is right to do this. "Don't say that, Miss Noi."

So then we make love. When we are finished, he turns his face away from me again and I reach over and turn it back. There are no tears, but he is looking very serious. I say, "Tell me one thing you like in Saigon."

Mr. Fontenot wiggles his shoulders and looks away. "Everything," he says.

"Why should I not think you are a crazy man? Everybody knows Americans go to Vietnam and they want to go home quick and forget everything. When they think they like Vietnam while they are there, they come home and they know it was all just a dream."

Mr. Fontenot looks at me one more time. "I'm not crazy. I liked everything there."

"'Everything' means same as 'nothing'. I do not understand that. One thing. Just think about you on a street in Saigon and you tell me one thing."

"Okay," he says and then he says it again louder, "Okay," like I just push him some more, though I say nothing. It is louder but not angry. He sounds like a little boy. He wrinkles his brow and his little black eyes close. He stays like this for too long.

I ask, "So?"

"I can't think."

"You are on a street. Just one moment for me."

"Okay," he says. "A street. It's hot in Saigon, like Louisiana. I like it hot. I walk around. There's lots of people rushing around, all of them pretty as a nutria."

"Pretty as what?"

"It's a little animal that has a pretty coat. It's good."

"Tell me more."

"Okay," he says. "Here's something. It's hot and I'm sweating and I'm walking through your markets in the open air and when I get back to my quarters, my sweat smells like the fruit and the vegetables in your markets."

I look at Mr. Fontenot and his eyes are on me and he's very serious. I do not understand a word he's saying now, but I know he's not saying any bullshit, that's for sure. He sweats and smells like fruit in Saigon. I want to talk to him now, but what am I to say to this? So I just start in about fruit. I tell him the markets have many good fruits, which I like very much. Mangoes, mangosteens, jackfruit, durians, papaya. I ask him and he says he has not eaten any of these. I still want to say words, to keep this going, so I tell him, "One fruit we do not have in South Vietnam is apples. I loved apples in Saigon when GI bring me apples from their mess hall. I never have apples till the GIs give them to me."

As soon as I say this, Mr. Fontenot's brow wrinkles again and I feel like there's a little animal, maybe a nutria, trying to claw his way out from inside Miss Noi. I have made this man think about all the GIs that I sleep with in Saigon. He knows now what kind of girl he is talking to. This time I turn my face away from him to hide tears. Then we stop talking and we sleep and in the morning he goes and I do not come to help him bathe because he learns from Miss Noi already how to clean his hands.

Is this a sad story or a happy story for Miss Noi? The next Saturday Mr. Fontenot does not come and see me dance naked. I sit at the bar with my clothes on and I am upon a time and I wonder if I'm going to fall off now. Then boom. I go out of that place and Mr. Fontenot is standing on the sidewalk. He is wearing a suit with a tie and his neck reaches up high out of his white shirt and I can bet his hands are clean and he moves to me and one of his hands comes out from behind his back and he gives me an apple and he says he wants to marry Miss Noi.

Once upon a time there was a duck with a long neck and a long beak like all ducks and he lives in a place all alone and he does not know how to build a nest or preen his own feathers. Because of this, the sun shines down and burns him, makes his feathers turn dark and makes him very sad. When he lies down to sleep, you think that he is dead, he is so sad and still. Then one day he flies to another part of the land and he finds a little animal with a nice coat and though that animal is different from him, a nutria, still he lies down beside her. He seems to be all burnt up and dead. But the nutria does not think so and she licks his feathers and makes him well. Then he takes her with him to live in Thibodaux, Louisiana, where he fixes cars and she has a nice little house and she is a housewife with a toaster machine and they go fishing together in his little boat and she never eats an apple unless he thinks to give it to her. Though this may not be very often, they taste very good to her.

Editors

Marianne Abel works as freelance editor and writer from her farm in rural Cedar Falls, Iowa. She has edited the award-winning *Iowa Woman* since 1990 and a collection of short fiction by women with stories set in Iowa, *Farm Wives and Other Stories*. She has also published her own essays, feature articles, and interviews in many national publications.

Allan Aycock teaches writing at the City College of New York. He has been managing editor at *Fiction* since 1990. His essays have appeared in the *American Book Review* and *Another Chicago Magazine*.

Staige D. Blackford is a native of Virginia who attended the University of Virginia, Queens College and Oxford University as a Rhodes Scholar. His early ventures in the publishing business were with Time, Inc. and Grolier Encyclopedia, followed by a brief stint as an editor at LSU Press. In 1962, he moved to Atlanta where he worked for the Southern Regional Council. He then became a political reporter for the Norfolk *Virginia Pilot* and later press secretary and speech writer for Gov. Linwood Holton of Virginia. In 1974, he returned to his alma mater, first as an assistant to the president and for the last twenty years, as editor of *The Virginia Quarterly Review*.

Jim Clark is the director of the M.F.A. Writing Program at the University of North Carolina at Greensboro and editor of *The Greensboro Review*. A former snake hunter, community organizer and newspaper editor, he is now finishing a collection of short stories, *Quiet Village*, set in Miami, Florida.

George Core, who has edited *The Sewanee Review* since 1973, is a frequent contributor to literary magazines. His most recent book is *The Critics Who Made Us*, a collection of essays.

294 The Whole Story

Cara Diaconoff is a student in the M.F.A. program in creative writing at Indiana University where she serves as associate editor of the *Indiana Review*. She was the 1991-92 recipient of an Ernest Hemingway fellowship in fiction at Indiana.

Robert S. Fogarty has been editor of *The Antioch Review* since 1977. In another life, he is a social historian and has published seven books on American utopias; the latest, *Special Love/Special Sex*, in 1994. His essays have appeared in *The Nation* and *The Missouri Review*. He has been a visiting Fellow at All Souls College, Oxford and the New York Institute for the Humanities.

George Garrett has served as an editor of eighteen magazines. He was co-founder and poetry editor of *The Transatlantic Review* and he is now the fiction editor of *The Texas Review*. He is also the author of twenty-seven books and editor or co-editor of nineteen others.

David Hamilton has been editor of *The Iowa Review* since 1979. A professor of English at the University of Iowa, he teaches medieval English and modern American literature and non-fiction writing. His own essays have appeared in a variety of magazines including the *North Dakota Quarterly, The Gettysburg Review*, and *The Missouri Review*.

Devon Jersild is associate editor of the *New England Review* and co-edited *The Unfeigned Word: Fifteen Years of New England Review*. She has published fiction in *The Kenyon Review* and *The North American Review*. One of her stories was selected for inclusion in an *O. Henry Prize Collection*. Her book reviews appear in newspapers such as the *Los Angeles Times Book Review, Chicago Tribune, The New York Times Book Review* and *USA Today*. She lives in Weybridge, Vermont with her husband and two sons.

Wendy Lesser is the editor of *The Threepenny Review*, which she founded in 1980. She is also the author of three books of non-fiction: *The Life Below the Ground, His Other Half: Men Looking at Women Through Art* and *Pictures at an Execution*. Recently, she edited *Hiding in Plain Sight*, a selection of essays from the first fifty issues of the review.

Stanley Lindberg is a professor of English at the University of Georgia and since 1977 he has been the editor of *The Georgia Review*. He has received editing awards from the American Society for Magazine Editors, the National Endowment for the Arts and the Coordinating Council of

Literary Magazines. Cofounder of *The Ohio Review,* where he was an editor from 1970 to 1977, he is the author of *The Annotated McGuffey, Van Nostrand's Plain English Handbook* and *The Legacy of Erskine Caldwell.* He is the coauthor, with L. Ray Paterson, of *The Nature of Copyright: A Law of Users' Rights* and serves as the literary advisor to the Cultural Olympiad for the 1996 Olympic Games in Atlanta.

Beverly McFarland has been a member of the *CALYX* editorial collective for five years. A half-time *CALYX* staff member, she is editorial coordinator and managing editor of the literary program. She has extensive literary and technical experience and has taught in public schools.

Elizabeth Mills is senior editor and director of development of the *Southwest Review* and she was chair of the literature panel of the Texas Commission on the Arts in 1993 and 1994. She has worked as a publicity director for Wesleyan University Press, a professor at the University of Iowa, an archivist at Sterling Library at Yale, and a freelance editor of books and museum catalogs.

Mark Mirsky is the editor of *Fiction* and a professor of English at the City College of New York. He has published eight books, including four novels. Among his most recent are *The Absent Shakespeare, The Red Adam* and the anthology, *Rabbinic Fantasies.*

Sonia Raiziss is widely recognized for her translations of Eugenio Montale. She received a Guggenheim fellowship for her own poetry. In addition to writing two books of poetry, *Through a Glass Darkly* and *Bucks County Blues,* and two books of criticism, *The Metaphysical Passion* and *La poésie américaine "moderniste,"* she edited *Chelsea* for thirty-five years. She died in 1994 at the age of eighty-five.

Hilda Raz is the editor of *Prairie Schooner* and an associate professor of English at the University of Nebraska. Her poems, essays and reviews have appeared in the *Denver Quarterly, The Kenyon Review, The North American Review, Women's Review of Books* as well as *The Bread Loaf Anthology of Contemporary Nature Poetry* and *American Nature Writers.* She has published two collections of poetry, *What Is Good* and *Bone Dish.*

Micki Reaman has been a member of the *CALYX* editorial collective for two years. She oversees the Lila Wallace-Readers's Digest Publishers Marketing grant program and is coeditorial coordinator. Her background includes a variety of experience as a scientific technician with fisheries, a bookseller, writing tutor, and *CALYX* intern.

Warren Slesinger is the founding editor and publisher of The Bench Press. He has spent most of his time in the publishing business as a salesman, marketing manager and editor while writing and teaching on a part-time basis. His poems have appeared in *The American Poetry Review, The Antioch Review, The Georgia Review, The Iowa Review, The North American Review,* and *Northwest Review* but he has not written a single word of fiction. He is the senior editor at the University of South Carolina Press.

Ronald Spatz is executive editor of the *Alaska Quarterly Review* and direc- tor of the M.F.A. writing program at the University of Alaska. His fiction has appeared in magazines and anthologies, and he has been recognized by awards from the National Endowment for the Arts and the Alaska State Council on the Arts. His short films have been selected for film festivals, shown at schools and colleges, and recognized with several awards. His most recent film, *For the Love of Ben,* was broadcast nationally on public television.

Robert Stewart is managing editor of *New Letters.* His own books include *Letters from the Living* (poems and an essay on travel and myth) and *Plumb- ers* (poems), among others. He teaches editing and magazine writing in the professional writing program at the University of Missouri in Kansas City.

Peter Stitt is the founding editor of *The Gettysburg Review* which first appeared in 1988. He was the inaugural winner of the biannual PEN/ Nora Magid Award for editors of literary magazines in 1993. A poet as well as an essayist, he has published *The World's Hieroglyphic Beauty: Five American Poets* and is presently writing a biography of James Wright and coediting with Garrison Keillor *The Oxford Book of American Humor.*

Dabney Stuart is the author of eleven volumes of poetry, criticism and fiction. His most recent is *Light Years: New and Selected Poems.* As the S. Blount Professor of English at Washington and Lee University, he has held two NEA fellowships and a Guggenheim fellowship in poetry. He has edited *Shenandoah* since 1988.

Amber Vogel, formerly the editor of *The Black Warrior Review,* currently edits *The Carolina Quarterly.* With the assistance of an NEA grant, she edited a collection of contemporary literary anecdotes. She has published *The Minor Official,* a book of poetry.

Hannah Wilson is the fiction editor of the *Northwest Review* and teaches at the University of Oregon. She has published fiction and poetry in *Calyx* and other magazines and two anthologies, *The Wedding Cake in the Middle of the Road* and *The Times of Our Lives*. She has written texts and taught English in Istanbul and Ibadan as well as the United States.

Robley Wilson has edited *The North American Review* since 1968. He is a professor of English at the University of Northern Iowa which owns and publishes the magazine. He is also a fiction writer and poet. His most recent books are *Terrible Kisses*, a collection of short stories, *The Victim's Daughter*, a novel and *A Pleasure Tree*, a collection of poems.

Authors

Beth Bosworth teaches English at Saint Ann's School in Brooklyn, NY. She is a student in the Graduate Writing Program at New York University. In addition to *CALYX* which published her story, "Sheets," her stories have appeared in *Hanging Loose* and elsewhere. She is the mother of two sons.

Robert Olen Butler served with the U.S. Army in Vietnam as a linguist. He has published six novels and a volume of short fiction, *A Good Scent from a Strange Mountain,* which won the Pulitzer Prize in 1993. His stories have appeared in several magazines including *The Virginia Quarterly Review* which published "Fairy Tale," *The Sewanee Review,* and *New England Review.* They have been anthologized in the 1991 and 1992 editions of *The Best American Short Stories* and the 1991, 1992, and 1993 editions of *New Stories from the South.* He is presently a professor of English at McNeese State University.

Emile Capouya studied at Columbia University after service in the merchant marine, and at Oriel College, Oxford. He also served with the U.S. Army in Korea. An editor at several publishing houses and the literary editor of *The Nation,* he now heads his own publishing house, New Amsterdam Books. He has published one collection of stories, *In the Sparrow Hills.* Most of these stories, including "In the Sparrow Hills," appeared first in *The Antioch Review.*

Mary Clark's poetry has appeared in *The Iowa Review, Ploughshares, Black Warrior Review* and elsewhere. "The Red-Headed Man" which appeared in *Fiction* is her first published story. Another story is forthcoming in the *New England Review.* She lives in the Boston area.

Amber Dorko received a Pennsylvania Council on the Arts Fellowship for 1993. A regular contributor to the *Northwest Review*, where "Trinity Doughnuts" appeared, she has also published in the *Alaska Quarterly Review*. She is completing a collection of short stories and lives in Philadelphia.

Louis Gallo's non-fiction and poetry have appeared in *The Missouri Review*, *Poet & Critic*, *Mississippi Review*, *Modern Fiction Studies* and elsewhere. In addition to *The Greensboro Review*, which published "Bodies Set in Motion," his recent short stories have appeared in *Louisiana Literature*, the *Black River Review* and other magazines. He is presently a professor of English at Radford University.

Martha L. Hall worked for many years at the Louisiana State University Press as managing editor and fiction editor. Her stories have appeared in *Shenandoah*, the *Southern Review*, and *The Virginia Quarterly Review* in addition to *The Sewanee Review* which published "Privacy." Her collections of stories include *Music Lesson* and *The Green Apple Triumph*.

Mary Hood, a native of coastal Georgia, lives and writes in the foothills of the Blue Ridge. Her short stories and essays have appeared in *The North American Review*, *Kenyon Review*, *The Gettysburg Review* and *The Georgia Review* which published "Manly Conclusions." She has published two collections of short fiction, *How Far She Went* and *And Venus Is Blue*, and a novel, *Familiar Heat*.

Ellen Hunnicutt's stories have appeared in *The North American Review*, *Michigan Quarterly Review*, *Mississippi Review* and *Prairie Schooner* which published "Tango." She has also published a novel, *Suite for Calliope*, and a collection of stories, *In the Music Library,* which won the *Drue Heinz Literature Prize*. She teachers in the writing program at the University of Wisconsin-Milwaukee.

Leigh Anne Jones wrote "Picture Perfect" while she was an undergraduate at the University of California in Berkeley. It was her first published story when it appeared in *The Threepenny Review*. She is now in the M.F.A. program at the University of Iowa.

Thomas E. Kennedy is on the faculty of the *Ploughshares*/Emerson College International Writing Seminar in the Netherlands and has been a visiting lecturer at numerous universities in the United States and Europe. In addition to *New Letters* which published "What Does God Care About

Your Dignity, Victor Travesti?" his stories have appeared in *The Virginia Quarterly Review*, *The Gettysburg Review* and other magazines. Two of his stories were selected for *The Pushcart Prize* and for *Prize Stories: The O. Henry Prize* collections. An except from his newest novel, *The Book of Angels*, appeared in the *Southwest Review*. In recent years, he had made his home in Denmark where he lives with his wife and two children.

Jill Koenigsdorf was awarded a scholarship to the Napa Writers' Conference in 1992. In addition to the *Southwest Review* which published "The Way That I Sweep," her work has appeared in *Zyzzyva*, *Quarry West*, and elsewhere. She lives in the San Francisco Bay area and is preparing a collection of her stories.

Norman Lavers who published "The Translator" in *The North American Review* teaches creative writing at Arkansas State University. A graduate of the Iowa Writers' Workshop, he has twice held fellowships from the National Endowment for the Arts. Two of his stories have been included in *The Pushcart Prize* and *Prize Stories: The O. Henry Prize* collections.

Deborah Larsen won a Wallace Stegner Fellowship for graduate study at Stanford University and a Discovery/*The Nation* Award for her poetry. "Father Pat Springer" which appeared in *The Gettysburg Review* is her first published story. Primarily a poet, she has published a book of poems, *Stitching Porcelain: Through China with Matteo Ricci*, and she was just appointed to the M.S. Boyer Chair in Poetry at Gettysburg College.

Hilary Masters is the director of the creative writing program at Carnegie-Mellon University. Since the 1960s he has published five novels, two collections of stories, *Hammertown Tales* and *Success*, and a non-fiction book about himself and several generations of his family, *Last Stands: Notes from Memory*. His essays, articles and stories appear in numerous magazines including *The Texas Review* which published "Dad Is Here." Like his friend, Wright Morris, he is a professional photographer whose work has been widely exhibited.

Elizabeth McBride writes poetry, fiction, and art criticism. In addition to *Chelsea* which published "Final Exam: History of Art 321," her work has appeared in *The Georgia Review* and *The Ohio Review*. She is a columnist for *ArtScene Magazine*.

Robert Morgan grew up in the Blue Ridge Mountains, the setting of "A Fading Light" which appeared in *The Carolina Quarterly*. Since 1971, he has taught at Cornell University where he is now Kappa Alpha Professor of English. He has published several books of poetry, most recently *Sigodlin* and *Green River: New and Selected Poems*. He has also published two books of short stories, *The Blue Valleys* and *The Mountains Won't Remember Us*, and a novel, *The Hinterlands*.

W.B. Pescosolido teaches at Emerson College. A graduate of Harvard College, he has worked as a farm laborer, a gasoline trader, and a cataloger of rare books. "Mother," which appeared in the *Indiana Review*, is his first published story.

Eileen Pollack is the author of a collection of short fiction called *The Rabbi in the Attic* and a children's book about AIDS called *Whisper, Whisper Jesse*. A graduate of Yale and the Iowa Writers' Workshop, she has received a Michener Fellowship, a Pushcart Prize, a literature grant from the NEA and the Cohen Award for best fiction of the year in *Ploughshares*. In addition to the *New England Review* which published "A Sense of Aesthetics," her work has appeared in the *Prairie Schooner, Literary Review* and other magazines. She lives in the Boston area and is currently at work on a novel.

Norman Sage lives near Solon, Iowa. For several years he worked with the Printing Department of the University of Iowa, for which he designed both books and journals. He also owns and operates his own small press which has published numerous broadsides, chapbooks and books. "Seven Blackberries" is from a set of five stories published in *The Iowa Review*.

Lisa Sandlin is a Texan who has spent much of her life in New Mexico and now teaches at Southern Methodist University. In addition to *Shenandoah* which published "Speaking to the Fish," her work has appeared in the *Mississippi Review* and elsewhere. Her first book, *The Famous Thing about Death*, was published in 1992 and she received an NEA Literary Fellowship in 1994.

Lloyd Shaw teaches at Prince George's Community College. After he published "The Disillusioned" in *The Carolina Quarterly*, he gradually became more interested in poetry than fiction. Over the years, he has published three short stories and a dozen poems in literary magazines but he writes little of either today.

Cory Wade teaches at Santa Clara University. In addition to the *Alaska Quarterly Review* which published "The Woman Who Slept with a Tortoise," her work has appeared in *The Georgia Review, The Carolina Quarterly,* and *Western Humanities Review.*

Pamela Walker grew up in Iowa and graduated from the Iowa Writers' Workshop but has lived for the past twenty years with her husband and two children in the Bronx. In addition to *Iowa Woman* which published "Good Shabbos," her work has appeared in the *Hawaii Review* and elsewhere. She has published a novel, *Twyla.*